THE

ANALYTICAL HISTORY OF INDIA

THE

ANALYTICAL HISTORY OF INDIA,

FROM THE EARLIEST TIMES TO THE ABOLITION OF THE HONOURABLE EAST INDIA COMPANY IN 1858.

ROBERT SEWELL

GYAN

Published by

GYAN

Gyan Publishing House
5, Ansari Road
Daryaganj, New Delhi-110002
Phone: 011-47034999, 9811692060
E-mail: books@gyanbooks.com

Distribution Network
gyanbooks.com
India, USA, Canada, UK, Australia

ISBN: 978-93-6433-262-0 (PB)
First Published, 1870

2nd Impression 2024

Printed at: Gyan Press, Delhi.

THE ANALYTICAL HISTORY OF INDIA
Author: ROBERT SEWELL

THE

ANALYTICAL HISTORY OF INDIA,

FROM THE EARLIEST TIMES TO THE ABOLITION OF THE HONOURABLE EAST INDIA COMPANY IN 1858.

ROBERT SEWELL,

Madras Civil Service.

LONDON:

Wm. H. ALLEN & CO., 13, WATERLOO PLACE,

PALL MALL, S.W.

1870.

PREFACE.

THE object of the Author in compiling the following Analytical Sketch of Indian History, has been to supply a want felt by most students of the more voluminous standard works of Mill, Elphinstone, Thornton, and Marshman, for a condensed outline in one small volume, which should serve at once to recall the memory and guide the eye.

At the same time he has attempted to render it interesting to the general reader, by preserving a medium between a bare analysis and a complete history; so that, without consulting the eminent authorities mentioned above, the mind may readily grasp the principal outlines of the early condition of India, and the rise and progress of the East India Company.

The division of the work is fourfold:—(1) Embracing a period dating from the earliest days to the establishment of the Moguls at Delhi, in A.D. 1526; (2) The Mogul Empire of India (1526—1761); (3) The rise and consolidation of the English power in India, being the period between the years 1600 and 1827 A.D.; (4) The interval between 1827 and 1858 A.D.; from the full establishment of the authority of the East India Company to its final extinction, and the absorption of the Government of the country by the Imperial authorities of Great Britain.

For the more full comprehension of these facts, the Author has provided, in addition to a Table of Contents and a Chronological Index, an Index to the geographical position of the places to which reference is made in the text, bearing the latitudes and longitudes as given in Thornton's "Gazetteer of India." This will be found not only to aid the student who is but partially acquainted with the map of India, but also, by means of occasional accents, to guide him in the ordinary pronunciation of the names.

A List of the principal authorities consulted in the compilation of this work will be found on the next page.

The Author is desirous of acknowledging his obligations in dealing with the history of the Company's legal administration, to Mr. Standish Grove Grady, of the Temple, Recorder of Gravesend, whose lectures he had the privilege of attending.

BONCHURCH,
October, 1869.

LIST OF AUTHORITIES CONSULTED IN THE COMPILATION OF THIS WORK.

Elphinstone's "History of India." 2 vols. 1841. *Murray.*

Mill's "History of British India." 9 vols.

Thornton's "History of British India." Third Edition, in one volume. 1862. *Wm. H. Allen & Co.*

Trotter's "History of the British Empire in India." Sequel to Thornton's History. 2. vols. 1866. *Wm. H. Allen & Co.*

Marshman's "History of India." 3 vols. 1867. *Longmans.*

Thornton's "Gazetteer of India." 4 vols. 1854. *Wm. H. Allen & Co.*

Kaye's "War in Afghanistan." 3 vols. 1857. *Bentley.*

"Analysis of the Constitution of the East India Company," by Auber. 1826. *Allen & Co.*

Grady's "Hindu Law of Inheritance." 1868. *Wildy & Sons.*

Ferrier's "History of the Afghans." Translated by Jesse. 1858. *Murray.*

"Autobiography of the Emperor Baber." Translated by Leyden & Erskine, 1826.

"Vindication of the Character and Administration of Sir Thomas Rumbold," by his Daughter. 1869. *Longmans.*

ANALYTICAL HISTORY OF INDIA.

TABLE OF CONTENTS AND CHRONOLOGICAL INDEX.

PART I.

FROM THE EARLIEST TIMES TO THE ESTABLISHMENT OF THE HOUSE OF TEIMUR IN INDIA.

PART II.

THE MOGUL EMPIRE IN INDIA, 1526—1761.

PAGE

Section III.—*Reign of Akber* (1556—1605.)

Section IV.—*A Sketch of Akber's Policy and System of Government.*

Section V.—*Reign of Jehangir* (1605—1627.)

PAGE

Section VI.—*Reign of Shah Jehan* (1627—1658.)

Section VII.—*Reign of Aurangzebe, and Rise of the Mahrattas* (1658—1707.)

PAGE

Section VIII.—*Successors of Aurangzebe to the Great Battle of Panipat, and the Extinction of the Mogul Sovereignty*, 1707—1761.

PART III.

THE ENGLISH IN INDIA TO THE DOWNFALL OF THE MAHRATTAS IN 1823.

Section I.—*History of the East India Company.*

Section IV.—*Events in Bengal*, 1755—1773. *Career of Lord Clive.*

Section V.—*Affairs in Madras and Bombay* (1761—1773). *War with Hyder.*

PART IV.

Section I.—*Lord Amherst's Administration*, 1823—1828.

Section II.—*Lord William Bentinck's Administration*, 1828—1835.

Section III.—*Sir Charles Metcalfe Provisionary Governor-General*, 1835—1836.

Section IV.—*Lord Auckland's Administration*, 1836—1842.

CONTENTS OF PART I.

ANALYTICAL HISTORY OF INDIA.

PART I

THE EARLIEST TIMES TO THE ESTABLISHMENT OF THE HOUSE OF TEIMUR IN INDIA.

(DATE—EARLIEST DAYS TO 1526 A.D.)

(I.)—*Earliest Notices of India.*

Early Legendary History.—Every history of India must commence with some notice of the work called "The Institutes of Menu," for it is in that work that the earliest mention of Hindostan is found; and it is itself the oldest authentic production in writing that can be discovered, except the fragmentary religious poems called "The Vedas."

The age of "The Vedas" is a disputed point. The most satisfactory opinion is that held by Mr. Colebrooke, who fixes them in the fourteenth century before Christ. "Menu's Code" is a work founded on "The Vedas," and is supposed by Elphinstone to have been written about B.C. 900, though Sir William Jones, the translator, places it about B.C. 1280.

In "The Institutes of Menu" (Book II. v. 17, &c.), the tract of land between the Sersooty and Caggar rivers is declared to be the ancient holy country; this is a tract 100 miles N.W. of Delhi, including the lands about Amballa; the next in holiness being the country about the Jumna and the Ganges, including North Behar. The legends say that ninety-five generations of princes, called the kings of the "Solar Race" reigned in Oude, while forty-eight kings of the "Lunar Race" are named as kings of the country about the Jumna; and then we come to the more celebrated hero, *Rama*, king of Oude, who conquered the Lunar kings, and assumed universal monarchy.

Rama's deeds are celebrated in the great poem called "The Ramayana." His name is believed to be authentic, and his date is fixed roughly at about 1400 B.C. The poem makes him conqueror of the Deckan, and of Ceylon, where he is said to have destroyed great tribes of apes and bears, typical, probably, of the savage races existing there at that period.

The next historical poem in order of date is the "Mahabharata," the Iliad of Hindu literature. It describes the wars of two branches of the reigning family of Hastinapuram, the Pandians, and the Curuvans, for the sovereignty of that state. *Chrishna*, a hero who, like Rama, was deified, fought for the Pandians. He came off victorious, but the Pandians were overwhelmed with their own losses. Chrishna was king of Guzerat, and fell in the contest. The Pandian kingdom was transferred to Delhi, and thus we obtain the first mention of that illustrious city.

(II.)—*Invasions of India according to Classical Authors.*

Semiramis, 2034 B.C.—The earliest invasion that is mentioned is that of the somewhat legendary Semiramis, widow of Ninus, whom Diodorus Siculus declares to have crossed the Indus from Balkh, with an army numbering some millions; and to have been signally defeated and put to flight by an Indian prince named Strabrobates, in the year 2034 B.C.

Rameses the Second, 981 B.C.—Diodorus Siculus also records a great march of "Sesostris," or Rameses the Second, king of Egypt, through the heart of Hindostan, which he subjugated; and then returned to his own country, after exacting tribute in the year 981 B.C. Arrian denies both these stories.

Cyrus.—In 557 B.C. the frontier of Persia, then under Cyrus, son of Cambyses the First, extended to the borders of Hindostan; but this prince is believed never to have crossed the Indus.

Darius, B.C. 521.—Cyrus was succeeded by his son, Cambyses the Second, and after the death of the latter the throne was seized by a Magian, named Gomates. He did not long enjoy his dignity, for a conspiracy was raised against him: he was overthrown, and Darius, son of Hystaspes, was placed on the throne. This monarch extended the dominions of Persia considerably, and levied a heavy tribute on the Afghans.

Alexander.—Nearly two centuries later, namely, in the year B.C. 334, we find Darius Codomanus, successor of Arses, on the throne of Persia; while Alexander, a youth of twenty years of age, has succeeded to the monarchy of his father, Philip of Macedon, and is planning a universal extension of his dominions. In the spring of that year Alexander invaded the territories of Persia, and defeated Darius, first at the Granicus, in Bithynia; then at the decisive battle of Issus, in Cilicia (B C. 333); and, after a two years' campaign, wherein Tyre, Jerusalem, and Egypt were subdued, he finally defeated the Persian king in B.C. 331, at the battle of Arbela, near the mountains of Kurdestan. Darius was soon afterwards murdered by one of his officers, Bessus, satrap of Balkh; and Alexander laid waste the satrapy to avenge the death of his noble enemy.

In 327 B.C. Alexander marched towards India. With considerable difficulty he reduced Afghanistan, and then crossed the Indus into a territory called Taxila. With the chief of this country he made an alliance, the Hindu being anxious to secure the co-operation of the invaders against the great Rajah, Porus, or Puru, reigning in Canouj, and enjoying the monarchy over all Hindostan. In 326 Alexander advanced, and was resolutely opposed by Porus on the eastern bank of the Jhelum, or Hydaspes river. The Hindus were defeated in a pitched battle; but Alexander finding his army unwilling to advance further into India, retraced his steps, took his whole force on board a vast number of galleys, and sailed down the Hydaspes to the Indus. After severe fighting at several places on the route, he reached the mouth of the Indus in safety, and divided his army into two parts, one division under Nearchus, having orders to sail up the Persian Gulf, while Alexander himself went by land. This was the last invasion of India before that of the Mahommedans.

(III.)—*The various Ancient States of Hindostan and the Deckan.*

The history of these states is gathered from several sources, partly from "Menu's Code," partly from the mention of them in the "Ramayana," and "Mahabharata," and partly from the Greek writers, Arrian, Herodotus, Strabo, and others who describe the expeditions of Alexander and Darius. The ingenious researches of Mr. Prinsep into the Pali rock-inscriptions have also been of great service to historians.

There seem to have been six principal states in Hindostan, namely, Hastinapuram, Mattra, Panchala, Benares, Magada, and Bengal; and ten lesser ones, Malwa, Guzerat, Canouj, elhi, Ajmir, Mewar, Jesulmir, Jeypore, Sinde, and Cashmir.

In the Deckan there were ten—Pandya, Chola, Chera, Kerala, Carnata, the Chalukyas of Calinga, Andra, and Orissa.

The Ancient States of Hindostan.—We will consider these at somewhat greater length. First the kingdoms of Hindostan—

Hastinapuram has been mentioned as that petty state concerning which the terrible internecine war of the "Mahabharata" took place. Nothing more is known about it that can be definitely stated.

Mattra was an ancient religious city, which, at the time of Mahmud of Ghazni, who conquered the state in 1017 A.D., was filled with temples and shrines. It was the birthplace of the great Chrishna.

Panchala is only known by its name. Menu places it in the region by the Ganges called "Brahmaverta."

Benares was a kingdom of far greater power than either of those previously mentioned. The kings all bore the patronymic of "*Pala.*" It fell to the king of Canouj about the end of the 11th century, A.D., and greatly increased his power.

Magada.—The Buddhist kings of this state had extensive authority. They belonged for many years to the warrior, or *Cshetriya*[1] caste, till a *Sudra*,[2] named Chandragupta murdered the king, and assumed the sovereignty. He was reigning when Seleucus, the great general of Alexander, invaded India. Chandragupta (called *Sandracottus* by the Greeks) opposed him, apparently with success, for the treaty that was made was very much in favour of the Hindus. Arrian also mentions King Asoca, the third in descent from Chandragupta, calling his subjects the *Prasii.* The family of the "Maurya" kings reigned over Magada for ten generations, and were succeeded by three Sudra dynasties, which came to an end with one Andra in A.D. 436. After this the history becomes too confused to be detailed.

Bengal.—The "Mahabharata" mentions a king of this country as allied to Magada. It was evidently a great kingdom, for some of the newly decyphered rock-inscriptions state that supreme authority over the whole of India was enjoyed by its monarchs. The exaggeration of this assertion is shown from the coeval existence of several other monarchies, such as Canouj and Delhi; but the fact of the inscription seems to point to a more extended authority than can be traced in the history of the other kingdoms. The

[1] The *Cshetriya*, or warrior caste is, next to the Brahmins, the most honourable of the four classes into which the Hindus were divided by Menu.

[2] The *Sudra* caste is the lowest of the four.

dynasty which had most influence was, like that of Benares, termed "Pala." We gather much information, though of questionable accuracy, concerning the kings of Bengal, from the work known as the "Ayeni Akberi," wherein the names of five dynasties are given, ending in that of "Pala." The kingdom of Bengal was destroyed by the Mahommedans about A.D. 1203, during the reign of a king of the sixth, or "Sena" dynasty.

Malwa.—It is from the name of one of the kings of this small and unimportant state that historians are enabled to fix accurately the first reliable date in Indian history. It is that of the celebrated *Vikramaditya*, "the Haroun-al-Raschid of Hindu tales," (as Elphinstone calls him) who reigned at Ujein in the year 58 B C. The Hindu calendar always bears the date of the æra of Vikramaditya to this day.[1] Another celebrated name is found in this little kingdom, that of the Raja Bhoja, whose memory is cherished as one of the greatest heroes of early Indian history, and who died in 1070 A D. The monarchy was extinguished by the Mahommedans in 1231 A.D.

Guzerat was established, according to legend, by Chrishna; but the earliest known fact is, that in the 2nd century of the present æra there was a race of kings established at Ballabi, terminating in 579 A.D. with Nourshirwan. The kings were Rajputs, who with characteristic gallantry conquered Mewar from the monarchs of Malwa, who had captured that state. In 724 A.D, the "Chaura" dynasty of Guzerat succeeded in establishing their kingdom at Pattan, and became the greatest power in India The last "Chaura" king died in 931 A.D., and was succeeded by the renowned Salonka, who conquered the whole of Malwa. His descendants, bearing the same name, reigned in succession till the destruction of the kingdom by the Mahommedans in 1297 A D.

Canouj is named as one of the wealthiest states in Hindostan. Its riches, when Mahmud of Ghazni seized the city in 1017 A D., are mentioned as of fabulous amount. On account of the great beauty of its temples and palaces Mahmud refrained from inflicting any injury; but his followers sacked the city, and destroyed the monarchy in 1193 A.D. The reigning sovereign, Sivaji, then fled to Jodhpore, in Marwar, where he established a Rajput state, now one of the wealthiest in India.

[1] The present year, 1869, is, according to Hindu calendars, the year 1927 of the era of Vikramaditya, and the year 4971 of the Kaliyug; the Mahommedan year of the Hijra being 1286, and the Fasli year 1279.

Delhi was in early times very unimportant. It fell to Visal, king of Ajmir, in 1050 A.D.

Ajmir was equally unimportant. This State, with its dependent, Delhi, was overthrown by the Mussulmans in 1192 A.D.

Mewar, *Jesulmir*, and *Jeypore*, are still existing, the Mewar family being the oldest in India.

Sinde was an independent sovereignty in the time of Alexander (*i.e.*) B.C. 325. It was afterwards divided, and again reunited. The Mahommedans invaded its territories in 711 A.D., but were beaten back by the Rajput leader at the head of the Samera tribe. It finally fell to the Mahommedans in 1205 A.D., when Shahab-u-din Ghori, the greatest conqueror of the age, subjugated the country.

Cashmir has a history so confused, and so unconnected with Indian events that it is useless to enter into it. It is mentioned in the year 1400 B.C. (according to Elphinstone), and fell to Mahmud of Ghazni in 1015 A.D.

The Ancient Kingdoms of the Deckan.—The History of the Deckan Kingdoms[1] is neither so old nor so interesting as that of the kingdoms of Hindostan. The Hindus, when they colonized that country, after the great invasion of Rama, with which the history opens. found there many civilized nations of Tamulians, speaking the Tamil language, and others in the Telinga country, whose vernacular was Telugu.

The most ancient kingdoms were the Tamil.

[1] The languages of the Deckan are five in number. Their distribution is as follows :—

Tamil is spoken in the "Dravira," country *i.e.* the extreme south, bounded by a line passing through Pulicat, Bangalore, and so along the ghauts to Coimbatore, and Calicut.

Canarese, a dialect of Telugu, in North and South Canara, a district enclosed by a line drawn from Goa to Malabar, and bounded by the western coast.

Telugu is spoken in Mysore and the countries to the north. A line drawn from Pulicat to Bangalore, thence along the ghauts to Goa, then in an E.N.E. direction to Cicacole in the northern Circars would enclose this country.

Mahratta, written in the Devanagari alphabet has the following limits. Northern, the Sutpura mountains ; southern, the Telugu country, called Telingana ; Eastern the River Warda ; western, the hills.

Urya, a rough dialect spoken in Orissa.

The space left between Orissa and the Mahratta country is inhabited by Khonds, who talk a sort of rough jargon.

Pandya was founded by a shepherd king of that name, about the 5th century B.C. The extent of country under the Pandians was small, their capital city being the ancient town of Madura, and the territory embracing the present districts of Madura and Tinnevelly. It remained independent till as recently as 1736 A.D, when it was conquered by the Nabob of Arcot.

Chola.—The proper limits of this sovereignty are the lands in which the Tamil language is spoken; but they were probably at one time wider. The capital city was Congeveram. In 1678 a Mahratta chieftain Vencaji, supplanted the monarch, and became the first of the present Rajahs of Tanjore.

Chera was a little state including Travancore, Coimbatore, and part of Malabar.

Kerala was colonized by Brahmans from Hindostan, and governed by an aristocracy of that caste. It included Malabar and Canara. By degrees the country became split up into factions and went to pieces, Malabar going into the possession of the "Zamorins," or Rajahs of Calicut, while Canara was seized by the Rajahs of Vijayanagar.

Carnata was probably at one time united, but the earliest accounts divide it between the Pandya and Chera princes. It had one great and powerful family, the "Belala" Rajahs, who were overthrown by the Mahommedans in 1310 A.D.

The *Yadavas* are mentioned; but their locality is very obscure, and nothing is known of them.

The *Chalukyas of Carnata* were a Rajput family living at Calian, to the west of Bidr.

The *Chalukyas of Calinga.*—Another branch of the same family ruling over a tract in East Telingana, which extended along the coast up to the borders of Orissa. The kingdom was subverted by the Rajahs of Cuttack.

Andra.—The capital city was named Warangal, situated about 80 miles N.E. of Hyderabad.[1] Several dynasties, of whom the "Ganapati" Rajahs attained to great eminence, succeeded one another over this territory. They reigned for four centuries, and were overthrown by the Mahommedans in 1332 A.D.

Orissa.—The first notice we have of this Raj is from the "Mahabharata," which speaks of it in rather confused terms. The earliest authentic date is the expulsion of the invading

[1] The four ruined gates of the Temple of Siva are all that remain to attest the grandeur of this once important city.

"Yavanas," in 473 A.D., by the ruling family. Thirty-five "Hesari" rajahs followed one another, till in the year 1131 A.D., this dynasty was overthrown by that of Ganga Vansa. This last family remained on the throne till 1550 A.D., when the Mahomedans seized the country.

Tagara and Plithana.—There are two cities mentioned by the Greek author of "Periplus" as being of great importance and size, as trading marts on the coast. They are called "Tagara" and "Plithana." The site of these has never been discovered, but it is supposed to be somewhere near the Godaveri river.

(IV.)—*Mahomet, and the Conquests of his Followers in India.*

The real history of India commences, not with the incursions of the Greeks and Macedonians under Alexander, whose permanent influence was very slight, if indeed any existed at all; but with the invasions of the Arabs, the followers of the great Mahomet, who succeeded in subverting nearly all of the ancient kingdoms of India from the Himalayas to Cape Comorin.

Life of Mahomet.—It is well known that Mahomet was born at Mecca, in year 570 A.D., of poor, but respectable and highly educated parents. At the age of 25 he married a wealthy widow, and raised himself to independence. Being naturally of a thoughtful turn of mind, he became discontented with the idolatrous worship of the Arabs, their want of any real religious feeling, and their laxity of morals. Up to the age of 40 he lived a life of retirement and study, searching especially into the Hebrew scriptures, in the acquirement of which he was assisted by a cousin of his wife. By this time he had worked himself into the belief that he was an inspired prophet, destined to spread the doctrine of the unity of the Godhead; and three years later he commenced preaching. For ten years Mahomet endured every form of insult and ignominy, and in the year 620 A.D. the chief men of Mecca determined to put him to death. He fled to Medina and raised the standard of religious war. This is the date from which Mahommedans have calculated ever since. It is called the year of the "Hegira" or "Hijra" (*Anglicé* flight). Mahomet was surrounded at once by enthusiastic followers, and proclaimed the fanatic doctrine of "Death to unbelievers!" He died in 630 A.D., and with his last breath enjoined on those around him that their duty was to conquer in order to convert. During his own life time Mahomet succeeded in establishing his temporal and religious sovereignty only over the Arabian Peninsula.

Conquests of his Followers.—In 632 A.D., the Arabs, headed by their Caliph Abou Bekr, invaded Syria; and in the same year attacked Persia, which in six years was utterly crushed, and her king driven beyond the Oxus. About the same time Egypt was conquered by Amrou, one of the caliph's lieutenants.

In 650 A.D., the King of Persia made a desperate effort to regain his lost position; but was beaten and lost his life in the fight. The Arabs thus had the whole country up to the Oxus at their feet.

Between Persia and India there now remained a large district containing the three great divisions of Cabul to the north, and Beloochistan to the South, separated by the wild country of Afghanistan; its northern boundary being the mountains of Ghor, the southern the Indian Ocean.

In 664 A.D. took place the first expedition of the Mussulmans into this country; they advanced as far as Cabul, and are said to have made 12,000 converts; but were beaten in a mountainous defile, and laid down their arms. Hearing this, the Arab governor of Sistan advanced to the rescue, and was partially successful. At that time there was a Mussulman governor at Bosrah, at the head of the Persian Gulf, named Hejaj. He sent out in the year 690 A.D. his celebrated general, Abdurehman,[1] who completed the conquest of Cabul. The death of this general, in open revolt against Hejaj, in 705 A.D., seemed to have no effect in checking the ambition of his followers, who soon established themselves also in Afghanistan.

First Arab Entry into India, A.D. 664.—The first Mahommedan entry into India took place in 664 A.D. (year 44 of the Hijra).

In that year Mohalib, a clever officer, penetrated into Multan, but brought back an unfavourable report.

[1] The sequel of the story of this man's life is curious. Elphinstone says that Hejaj was of a "furious and sanguinary disposition," and hated Abdurehman so bitterly that "he never looked upon him without feeling a violent inclination to cut his throat. These kindly sentiments led to so violent a censure that Abdurehman, stung by the unmerited reproaches of his chief, and perhaps apprehending more serious effects from his hatred, immediately made an alliance with his late enemy the Prince of Cabul, and assembling a numerous army, appeared in open rebellion not only against the governor but the calif." He advanced and actually conquered Bosrah itself, but was deserted by his allies, and to avoid being betrayed to Hejaj, put an end to his own life after six years of revolt.

Sinde Taken, A.D. 711.—No further steps were taken till 711 A.D., when a pretext was seized, and Sinde conquered. It happened thus;—The Rajah Dahir was then ruling over Sinde, near which country, but beyond the limits of his authority, was a sea-port town, called Dewal [1] An Arab ship was seized there, and Dahir was called on for restitution. He pleaded that Dewal was out of his jurisdiction, but, disdaining further parley, Mohammed Casim, nephew to Hejaj, sailed from Bosrah, and seized the offending town. The Arab force then sailed up the Indus and stormed Hydrabad and Sehwan. Sailing still northwards they came to the capital city, Alor,[2] which was also stormed. The Hindus fought with desperate courage. Dahir fell, sword in hand, in the midst of Arab cavalry, while his widow and children, rather than be captured, sacrificed themselves in the flames of the burning palace.

Brahmanabad[3] was taken without difficulty, but, at Ashcandra, the Hindus made a desperate stand in vain.

Finally, the whole of Sinde was reduced.

Mohammed Casim, though only twenty-one years of age, behaved with the greatest moderation He was murdered by the Caliph Walid, out of jealousy, in 714,[4] the effect of which rash act was the downfall of Mohammedanism in Sinde. Thirty years later not an Arab remained behind.

Conversion of the Persians and Hindus.—Elphinstone re-

[1] Captain M'Murdo thinks that Dewal must have been somewhere near Kurrachee, the present sea-port of Sinde. The exact site is unknown.—(Journal of the Royal Asiatic Society, vol. i. p. 29.)

[2] Alor, or Aror, was situated on the left back of the great river in Lat. N. 27° 40′, Lon. E. 69° 2′. The ruins still remain.

[3] Brahmanabad is supposed to be somewhere near Tattah, on the right bank of the Indus, just above the Delta.

[4] The story of the murder of poor Mohammed Casim is attended with some romantic details. It is said, that the Raja Dahir had a very beautiful daughter, who was sent by the conqueror as a present to the caliph, Walid. The girl on arriving at his court declared that the present was an insult to the dignity of the caliph, since Mohammed had himself dishonoured her before he sent her away. Walid, enraged, ordered Mohammed's head to be struck off and sent to him. His orders were obeyed; when the princess exultingly declared that she was now amply revenged for the death of her father; for that her tale was false, and Casim innocent. Walid had deep cause to regret his hastiness. He had cut off in early youth the life of one who bid fair to become one of the finest generals that India has seen!

marks, that the Persians were far more rapidly converted to Mahommedanism than the Hindus, and he gives the following reasons in explanation. Religion in Persia was not much encouraged, the priests being of the lowest and most degraded class; hence there was no powerful political incentive amongst the people to cleave to their own doctrines. In India, on the contrary, the Brahmin priesthood was the most powerful political agent in the Commonwealth. Again, the doctrines of the Persians were such as to render a conscientious trust in them, a somewhat troublesome and restless quality; since they inculcated the belief in two equally matched powers of good and evil, always struggling with equal chance of success for the mastery. Each man had to wrestle with the Evil Being, because the good was too weak to help him. Hence, when the Arabs came preaching a One Omnipotent All-good God, it was like a triumph of the Good Principle to the sincere Persian, and the number of converts was immense. To the Hindu, on the contrary, the new faith was a subversion of a deep-rooted ancient theological system, supported by the highest class in the land as their peculiar prerogative; and the substitution of one which in their eyes had no higher recommendation.[1]

(V.)—*Mussulman Dynasties in Khorassan.*

It was in the year A.D. 713 that the Arabs became established in Transoxiana. They crossed the Oxus in 670, and, somewhat later, took Bokhara and Samarcand from the Turks (or "Turkmans"), who had governed the land for many centuries. A great quarrel arose at this time between two relations of the Prophet Mahomet for the office of the Caliphate over this newly acquired territory. The disputants were of the families of Fatima, sister of Mahomet, and Abbas, his uncle.

Haroun al Raschid.—The family of Abbas gained the ascendancy at last, and the 5th Caliph of that race was the celebrated *Haroun al Raschid*, who died in 806 A.D.

[1] It will be remembered that in the days of which we are speaking the faith of the Hindus was in a far purer state than is the case at the present time. They believed more generally in the One Omnipotent Being, of whom the Triad, and the Deified Heroes, were merely incarnations Afterwards these were considered as separate deities.

"Taherite" Dynasty of Khorassan.—Haroun-al-Raschid was on a journey into Transoxiana to quell a rebellion that had broken out there when he died; and his son, Mahmud, after having re-established the Arab dominion in Khorassan, returned as Governor of that country, and shortly afterwards became Caliph of Bagdad, in the room of his father. But his minister, Tahir, revolted, and established himself as an independent sovereign in Khorassan in 820. Tahir's descendants reigned in Khorassan for fifty years, but were deposed by the family of the "*Sofarides.*"

"Sofaride" Dynasty.—The Sofarides remained possessors of the regal power for forty years, namely, from 872 to 913, when Yacub, the last, was defeated by the house of "*Samani.*"

"Samani" Dynasty.—The *Samanis* founded a dynasty, which ruled till the year 999. But it was not an undisturbed possession. Several members of the same family, who owned independent territory in Transoxiana, crossed the Oxus to the Persian side, and, by dint of hard fighting, succeeded in seizing a large territory there. But the house of Buya (often called "The Deilemites"), who were then in possession of the Caliphate of Bagdad, overthrew these invaders, and drove them back into Khorassan, where they remained.

Alptegin of Ghazni—In the reign of Abdulmelek, fifth king of the house of Samani, a Turki slave, named Alptegin, who had entered the royal service as court-tumbler and jester, rose, post after post, to such great favour and eminence, that in 961 A.D. he was made governor of the town of Khorassan. His patron died soon after, and Alptegin incurred the displeasure of the new king; so that, in fear for his life, he fled with a chosen body of followers to Ghazni, where he established himself as governor.

Sebektegin of Ghazni.—One of Alptegin's slaves succeeded him, in the same manner as he himself had risen in the Court at Khorassan. This Sebektegin, as he was named, was the father of the great Mahmud. Ghazni was only 200 miles from the Hindu frontier, and Jeipal, Rajah of Lahore, becoming anxious on account of the presence of this Mahommedan government so close to his territories led an army against Ghazni. A compromise was effected; but the Hindu neglected to fulfil his share of the agreement, and Sebektegin invaded India, passing through the mountains of Soliman. Jeipal made a confederacy with the Rajahs of Delhi, Ajmir, Canouj, and Calinjer, and advanced with an immense army numbering several hundred thousand men. This host Sebektegin defeated. He soon afterwards retired, leaving a Mahommedan officer, Governor of Peshawur, in the Punjaub.

Noh of Khorassan.—Meanwhile, a Tartar revolt attended with success, had taken place against the Samani king, Noh, the seventh of his family, and the insurgents drove him to the Persian side of the Oxus. Sebektegin came to his assistance, and drove off the rebels, when the king, out of gratitude, made Sebektegin's son, Mahmud, Governor of Khorassan.

(VI.)—*Mahmud of Ghazni and his Invasions of India.*

Mahmud being absent at Sebektegin's death, his younger brother, Ismael, seized the throne of Ghazni; but Mahmud attacked, defeated, and imprisoned him.

Counterfeiting humility, he then sent an embassy to the Samani king, Mansur, craving to be acknowledged as Governor of Ghazni. Mansur refused; and Mahmud at once threw off the mask, hoisting his standard and declaring himself independent king of Ghazni. Mansur was shortly afterwards dethroned, and Mahmud assumed the title of "Sultan," A.D. 999.

At this time one of Mansur's chieftains, by name Elik Khan, taking advantage of the fall of the Samanis, seized on Bokhara, and all the Mussulman territories in Transoxiana.

In the year 1000 A.D. Mahmud planned an extension of his kingdom eastwards. In order to this he made peace with Elik Khan, and married his daughter.

Three and a half centuries had now passed since the Mahommedans first attacked Persia.

Mahmud's 1st Indian Invasion. Lahore.—Mahmud commenced by leading a large army through the Soliman mountains, and attacking Jeipal, the Rajah of Lahore, near Peshawur. Thence he marched beyond the Sutlej River to Batinda, which he took; and leaving Anang Pal, Jeipal's son, as Rajah, returned in triumph to Ghazni in 1001 A.D.

2nd. Bhatia.—Anang Pal performed his share of the treaty of peace with strict honesty; but one of the parties, the Rajah of Bhatia, refused to pay tribute. Therefore, in 1003, Mahmud went against him and defeated him.

3rd. Multan.—The Afghan chief of Multan, by name Abul Futteh Lodi, revolted in 1005, and Mahmud took this opportunity of giving him a lesson. He defeated him, and levied a contribution.

Meanwhile, Elik Khan, taking advantage of Mahmud's absence, crossed the Oxus and attacked Khorassan with a large Tartar army. The Sultan went in hot haste from Ghazni to Khorassan, taking with him a number of elephants which he brought from India. These animals so frightened the Tartars, who had never seen them before, that an easy victory was obtained, and Elik Khan was driven again into Bokhara.

4th. Punjaub. Temple of Nagarcot.—In the year 1008, Anang Pal of Batinda made an extensive combination of Indian chieftains to restrain the encroachments of Mahmud, and by their aid he got together an immense army from Ujein, Gwalior, Calinjer, Canouj, Delhi, and Ajmir. The Sultan was alarmed at the numbers and enthusiasm of the Hindus, whose religious fanaticism was aroused against himself and his followers. He made an attack as a feint, which was repulsed, and the whole army of the enemy then advanced. Mahmud had well-nigh given up hope, when he perceived that the elephant on which Anang Pal was mounted had fled, terror-stricken, from the field, and that the Hindus, discouraged, had broken their ranks. He then gained an easy victory, and the pursuit was characterized by terrible carnage. The Sultan at once pushed on and sacked Nagarcot, a city filled with rich temples and jewels, returning to Ghazni laden with riches of a fabulous amount.[1]

In 1010 the kingdom of Ghor, inhabited by Afghans,[2] was conquered.

5th. Multan.—In the winter of the same year, Mahmud seized some frivolous pretext to invade Multan a second time. He took Abul Futteh Lodi prisoner, and brought him to Ghazni.

6th. Tanesar.—In 1011 he captured a rich temple at Tanesar on the Jumna, retiring before the somewhat dilatory princes could assemble their armies.

7th and 8th. Cashmir.—In 1013 and 1014 the Sultan made two slight predatory and reconnoitring incursions into Cashmir.

Elik Khan had died in 1013, and the Sultan, immediately on his return from Cashmir, determined to gain Bokhara, He

[1] Ferishta mentions the spoil taken as consisting of 700,000 golden dinars, 700 mauns of plate, 200 mauns of pure gold in bars, 2000 mauns of bar silver, and 20 mauns of jewels collected since the time of the Raja Bhima, the legendary hero of Malwa. A maun weighs 80 lbs.

[2] The descendants of these same Ghorians afterwards overthrew the family of Mahmud of Ghazni.

seized an opportunity in 1016, and took Bokhara and Samarcand, completing the conquest of the whole of Transoxiana in the following year.

9th. Canouj and Mattra.—In the winter of 1017, Mahmud made a grand expedition solely with the desire for conquest; marched through Peshawur to Cashmir; and thence to the Jumna, which having crossed, he advanced to Canouj. This ancient city submitted without a contest, though it was of amazing wealth and beauty. Its size was great, and the buildings of such elegance that the Sultan spared them and passed on to Mattra, which he razed to the ground, the temples only being left standing. After sacking Mahawan and Munj, he returned home in triumph.

10th, 11th. Canouj, Lahore.—After this Mahmud rested five years, and at the end of that time he made two campaigns to the relief of the Rajah of Canouj, who had been expelled from his city. In one of these, Lahore was absolutely reduced.

12th.—Guzerat and Somnath.—Two years later, namely in 1024, the Sultan made his last great expedition. He marched from Ghazni to Multan, and thence across the burning desert of Sinde to Guzerat, reaching that country safely and quite unexpectedly. He took the capital city Anhalwara almost without a struggle, ravaging on his way the territories of the Raja of Ajmir. Then he bent his energies to the capture of the rich temple of Somnath. It was gallantly defended at all points, the Rajput garrison fighting desperately for their idol. On the third day, just when the Mussulmans were losing heart, Mahmud himself led a forlorn hope; and was followed with such energy that the fort was stormed at once. He saw in the temple an idol which the priests in vain implored him to spare; but Mahmud, true to his faith, broke open the image and found it filled with diamonds and other jewels of amazing richness and beauty;[1]—so that the treasure taken on this occasion exceeded that of all his former expeditions.[2]

[1] Thornton says that this story is a myth;—that the idol was solid and contained no jewels. He does not state his authorities.—(History of British India, p. 3.)

[2] The history of the "Gates of Somnath" is interesting. The massive gates of the great temple were carved very beautifully in sandal-wood, and were of such elegance and costliness that Mahmud took them with him to Ghazni where they remained till his death. His son and successor, Masaud, made them part of the beautiful tomb erected in honour of his renowned sire; and here they were left till eight centuries later when Lord Ellen-

Mahmud then retired to Anhalwara, where he rested a year. His march homewards was disastrous. The sufferings of the army in the Desert were excessive; the fatigue of the long march through the hot sands, the intense thirst, and intolerable diseases, thinned the ranks of the Mahomedans by many thousands.

In the year 1027 the Turki tribe of the *Seljuks*, of whom we hear more in the later history, revolted, and were crushed by the Sultan.

The next year saw the whole of Persia under his rule, by the conquest of Persian Irak from the Deilemites.

Death of Mahmud.—But in the very height of his glory Mahmud died (April 29th, 1030) of a disease supposed to have been contracted in the desert.

State of his Court.—Sultan Mahmud seems to have encouraged the arts and sciences very largely. The great epic poet, Ferdousi, flourished in his reign, and lived at court. It is related that once, being offended by the Sultan, he wrote a bitter satire on the mean birth and miserable avarice of the great conqueror.

Architecture was much studied at this period, and Mahmud built a palace of marble and granite so beautiful that from all countries round came people to see it; and his nobles, following his example, made of Ghazni a magnificent city.

There were various tribes constituting the population of the kingdom. The army was for the most part composed of the conquered *Turks*, who were considered slaves to the Persians, and were formed into regiments of "*Mameluk*" (or slave) guards. The shepherds were principally *Tartars*. They were sociable and good-natured, but destitute of any religion. The nobles and the bulk of the higher population were *Arabs*; in general proud, jealous, and unprincipled. With them lay all powers of justice and religion. The civil government was mostly carried on by *Persians* who combined the euergy of the Arabs with the suppleness and acuteness of the Hindus. They were lively, refined, and agreeable.

borough, after the Afghan war, wishing to humble his enemies, carried off the gates into India again, with a great procession, intending to replace them in their ancient dignity in Guzerat. But they never travelled further than Agra, where they were consigned to a degrading oblivion in a room in the fort.

VII.—*Subsequent Kings of Ghazni and Ghor.*

Mahmud left three sons, Mohammed, Masaud, and Abul Raschid. He preferred the eldest, and on his death, appointed him successor.

But Masaud, who was a brave and impetuous fellow, and a great favourite with the soldiers, seized Mohammed the same year (1030 A.D.) blinded him, threw him into prison, and took possession of the throne.

Sultan Masaud the First, 1030. *Rise of the "Seljuks."*—At this period the Turki tribe of the Seljuks had become very powerful on the other side of the Oxus. Some of them crossed the river and became independent, but Masaud put down their revolt and drove them back to their own country.

In 1034, the Sultan was forced to enter India to quell some disturbances at Lahore, and on his return he went in person against the Seljuks; but though brave he was inexperienced as a general, and after frittering away five years in marching and countermarching, he was utterly defeated at Zendecan, near Merv, and fled into India.

The consequence of this defeat was that his officers mutinied, and declared the throne vacant. They placed on the throne Mohammed's son, Ahmed, who caused the unfortunate Masaud to be pursued, captured, and put to death. This took place in 1041.

Sultan Ahmed, 1041.—Ahmed's reign was of short duration, for the murdered Sultan's son, Modud, who was in Balkh, set out in haste with a small army, met Ahmed at Laghman, de feated him, and put him and all his family to death.

He then proclaimed himself Sultan.

Sultan Modud, 1041—1050.—The Seljuks in Transoxiana chose themselves a leader, one Toghral Beg, and went to seek conquests in all directions. Their force was thus scattered, and Modud was enabled to conquer Transoxiana.

Meanwhile he lost many Indian possessions, for the King of Delhi rose, and recovered from the Mahomedans Tanesar, Nagarcot, and all the territory beyond the Sutlej except Lahore, which was saved by means little short of miraculous; for at the last gasp the defenders made a desperate sortie; some panic seized the Hindus, and they fled, though they far outnumbered the garrison.[1]

In 1046, Modud, who had all his reign been operating against the Seljuks, was implored by the Rajah of Ghor to aid him against that dreaded tribe. He consented, but, possessed with a wild desire for annexation, he murdered his ally and seized Ghor.[2]

He died at Ghazni in 1050 A.D.

Sultan Abul Hassan, 1050—1051.—Modud's younger brother Abul Hassan succeeded. The whole country revolted, and nothing was left him but Ghazni itself. His general, Ali Ben Rabia, went to India and made many conquests on his own account. All the west was in arms in favour of the Sultan's uncle, Abul Raschid, youngest son of Sultan Mahmud. He advanced against Ghazni and deposed the enfeebled monarch.

Sultan Abul Raschid, 1051—1052.—Ali Ben Rabia returned to his duty and all looked prosperous; but Abul Raschid built too much on his hopes. He was besieged in Ghazni by a rebel chief named Togral; the fort was stormed, and the Sultan with nine royal princes was murdered. But Togral himself was put to death by the infuriated populace, and his tribe driven off. The Mussulmans searched the kingdom for some prince of the house of Sebektegin to succeed Abul Raschid; and finding one Farokshad imprisoned in a fort, they released him, and set him on the throne.

Sultan Farokshad, 1052—1058.—Farokshad had reason to be grateful to Providence for his good fortune. He reigned peacefully and happily for six years, at the end of which period he died naturally,—(an uncommon event amongst Eastern potentates.)

Sultan Ibrahim, 1058—1089.—He was succeeded by his brother, Ibrahim, a very religious man and a sincere Mussulman. The reign was so uneventful that historians are uncertain as to the year of his death; but the probable date is 1089 A.D. Many anecdotes are narrated of his love of the fine arts.

Sultan Masaud II. 1089—1114.—Masaud the Second, Ibrahim's son, proved somewhat more energetic, for he carried

[1] These panics have often been the cause of the defeat of immense armies of Hindus by handfuls of men. Compare the battle of Assaye, and the gallant action of Knox at Patna in 1760.

[2] Mahomedan writers uphold all these violent measures, declaring them to have been done in sincere desire for the spread of their faith.

the Mahomedan arms beyond the Ganges. Dying in 1114, he was succeeded by his son, Arslan.

Sultan Arslan, 1114—1118.—Arslan seized and imprisoned all his brothers, with the exception of Behram, who escaped and fled to the Seljuks for refuge. They took up his cause, marched against Arslan and defeated him. He fled, and thus Behram gained the throne in 1118.

Sultan Behram, 1118—1152.—Behram reigned quietly for some years and might have continued at peace, had he not unfortunately interfered with Ghor, and put one of the princes to death. Seif-u-din, brother of the murdered man, marched at once against Behram, captured Ghazni, and drove the monarch into the mountains. Behram returned, defeated, and seized Seif-u-din, and, a second time blinded by his anger, cruelly tortured his prisoner to death; the consequence of which was that Ala-u-din, another brother, in bitter hate, came with an army of Ghorians, utterly destroyed Ghazni, razed it to the ground, and broke down all the fine buildings of Mahmud and his chiefs.[1] Behram fled to Lahore; and the Ghaznevite dynasty was at at an end.

The royal family of Ghazni ruled at Lahore for thirty years more, and then became extinct.

So ended the grandeur of Mahmud's dynasty, 183 years after the great Sultan had proclaimed himself independent sovereign.

House of Ghor, at Ghazni.

We now come to the House of Ghor, which established itself on the ruins of that of Sebektegin.

Ala-u-din, when he had conquered Ghazni, proclaimed himself king of that place, and assumed regal authority in 1152 A.D.

Ala-u-din, 1152—1156.—It happened that the Sultan Behram, when he fled from his brother Arslan to the Seljuks, had promised to pay the latter tribe a sort of black-mail if they put him on the throne; and he had performed his promise regularly up to the time of his expulsion When Ala-u-din proclaimed himself King of Ghazni, the Seljuks, aiming at conquest, affected to consider him also liable to this tribute. Sanjar, their chief, therefore haughtily demanded payment. Ala-u-din refused; and Sanjar, leading an army against him took him prisoner. The

[1] It is related that Ala-u-din spared only three buildings in Ghazni; these were the tombs of Mahmud, Masaud I., and Ibrahim, on account of the valour of the two former, and the sanctity of the last.

royal captive made himself so agreeable to his captor, that Sanjar released him; and he was thus re-instated in the sovereignty of Ghazni.

Next year the Tartar tribe of the "*Euzes*" overran the territories of both Sanjar and Ala-u-din. The latter of whom died in 1156 A.D.

Seif-u-din, 1156—1157.—His son, Seif-u-din, succeeded, and might have proved a good monarch but for his early death. He quarrelled with one of the nobles, and, unable to restrain his wrath within due bounds, murdered his opponent. In just anger the deceased man's brother killed the king.

Gheias-u-din, 1157—1202.—There were two nephews of Ala-u-din living, Gheias-u-din, and Shahab-u-din, brothers. Gheias succeeded to the throne, but being of a peaceful disposition, he made Shahab commander of the armies, and associate with himself. The two brothers worked well together, and conquered Khorassan from the Seljuks. In 1176, Shahab-u-din went to India, and destroyed the last hopes of the Ghaznevites at Lahore, by defeating Khusru II., who was the last representative of the House of Mahmud. He took Sinde in 1181, and in 1186 put Khusru into prison. Then he turned his attention to the powerful Rajput principalities in Hindostan. He was beaten in an attack on Delhi by the great Pritwi Rajah, who then ruled over Delhi and Ajmir, and was driven back to Ghazni.

In 1193, Shahab again invaded India for the purpose of revenging himself on Pritwi Rajah. He met that prince, and having by clever strategy succeeded in defeating him, at once put the Hindu to death in cold blood, and retired, leaving Kutb-u-din, an ennobled slave, Governor of Ajmir.

This officer captured Delhi, and remained there as governor; but afterwards declaring himself independent, became the first Mahomedan King of Delhi.

Shahab took Canouj and Benares in 1194 A.D., driving the Rajah of the former city with his family to Marwar, where they established a principality now in alliance with England.[1]

Gheias was all this time remaining quietly at Ghazni, while Shahab, bent on conquest, annexed Gwalior. Kutb-u-din in India ravaged Guzerat, Oude, North Behar, and Bengal.

Shahab came to the throne in 1202 by the death of his brother Gheias.

[1] The head of the state is now called the "Maharajah of Jodhpore," taking his name from the capital city of Marwar.

Shahab-u-din, 1202—1206.—His first act was to attempt the conquest of Kharism in Transoxiana, but he was beaten and forced to fly for his life. Reports of his death carried to Ghazni caused great confusion, but Shahab succeeded in restoring peace; and at once fitted out a second expedition against Kharism. While on the march in 1206, some Gakkars (a robber-tribe) murdered him when separated from his escort. He was succeeded by his nephew, Mahmud.

Mahmud, 1206.—This prince was not strong enough to save the kingdom from internal dissensions, and on the death of his uncle, it fell to pieces: the various portions going to Shahab's favourite slaves whom he had advanced.

Division of the Sultanate.—Kutb-u-din seized Delhi, and the Indian possessions. Eldoz, a slave, took Ghazni, but was turned out by the King of Kharism, and driven to seek refuge in India; while Nasir-u-din, another slave, made himself master of Multan and Sinde.

We must now shift the scene of the story from ruined and desolate Ghazni, to Delhi in the infancy of its greatness. It had, previously to this, been the capital of a kingdom, though a small and insignificant one, for twelve centuries. Now it was seized by a Mahomedan slave, and soon was to become the capital city of perhaps the finest empire in the world.

(VIII.)—*The Slave Kings of Delhi.*

Kutb-u-din lived only four years after his proclamation of independence at Delhi. He was succeeded by his son Aram in 1210, who in turn was next year deposed by his powerful brother-in-law Shams-u-din Altamsh, with whom begins the real history of the dynasty.

Shams-u-din Altamsh, 1211—1236.—Shams-u-din Altamsh received the usurper Eldoz, with kindness, after his ejection from Ghazni, by the King of Kharism.

First Irruption of Moguls under Chengiz Khan, 1217.—We now come to an event which is of very great importance in the History of India, namely, the first irruption of the Moguls from Tartary. In the year 1217 an enormous army of Moguls under their Prince Chengiz Khan, burst upon Kharism and laid it waste. The King, Jelal, defended himself bravely, and fought to the banks of the Indus across which he was driven. None of the princes dared give him a refuge for fear of the Moguls, so he collected a band of Gakkars and plundered far and wide.

Chengiz Khan then threw an army into Nasir-u-din's territory of Multan and Sinde, which caused great damage; and on its retirement across the Indus, Shams-u-din, taking treacherous advantage of the impoverished condition of the country, seized the opportunity to invade, conquer, and annex it.

He reduced Behar and Malwa in 1225, and by the year 1232, all Hindostan-proper acknowledged him as king. He died four years later, in the zenith of his power.

Rukn-u-din, 1236.—Rukn-u-din, son of Shams-u-din, succeeded; but being a weak and foolish prince, his sister, the clever Sultana Rezia, seized the throne and deposed him the same year.

Sultana Rezia, 1236—1239.—This princess was possessed of great talents, and by her clever intrigues so undermined all combinations against her that she was left in undisturbed possession of the kingdom. She, however, offended the nobles by her undisguised partiality for an Abyssinian slave at the court; and Altunia, chief of Batinda, revolted. Rezia was taken prisoner, but afterwards fell in love with her captor and married him; and he then led an army to Delhi; but the nobles defeated him, and put the Sultana to death.

Moizz-u-din Behram, 1239—1241.—Her brother, Moizz-u-din Behram was placed on the throne, who, being a terrible despot, was soon murdered.

Ala-u-din Masaud, 1241—1246.—Rukn-u-din's son, Ala-u-din Masaud, succeeded. He proved very licentious and very foolish, and, after a reign of five years, was in his turn assassinated

Nasir-u-din Mahmud, 1246—1266.—A grandson of Shams-u-din Altamsh, son of Moizz-u-din Behram, was invested with the regal authority. His name was Nasir-u-din Mahmud, and, contrary to the example of predecessors, he led a virtuous and frugal life. A slave named Gheias.u-din Bulbun, was made vizier, and proved an able and energetic minister. Bulbun united the frontier into a powerful confederacy to repel the attacks of the Moguls, and defeated many of the smaller Hindu states. Soon the king became jealous of his vizier's rising power, and removed him from office; but his conduct had the undesired effect of creating various parties at court; and Nasir, seeing less danger in possessing his friendship than his enmity, reinstated him in office. He had no cause to regret his conduct, for in 1253

Gheias bravely repelled another Mogul attack on the Punjaub. The king died in 1266, and was long and deservedly regretted.

Gheias-u-din Bulbun, 1266—1286.—On Nasir's death, without issue, his minister, Gheias-u-din Bulbun, succeeded to the throne. His was a curious reign. At the outset all was quiet, and Gheias devoted himself to the improvement of his subjects. But he set to work in a very peculiar way. Being himself a strict ascetic, and believing, as is common with all narrow-minded persons, that whatever he did must not only be right, but must also conduce to the welfare of those around him, he made numberless laws for the private conduct of his subjects, in matters of eating, drinking, and dressing—laws so absurd and so intricate that all classes were annoyed and harassed by them. He was, moreover, excessively strict in justice, and punished with unnecessary severity all detected infringements of his rules.[1] Notwithstanding this, his court was filled with the most celebrated characters of the time—princes, poets, sculptors, and men of genius,—a circumstance due partly to the fear of the Moguls, partly to the fact that his was the only Mahomedan court in India.

An insurrection in Bengal called him into active service in 1279; and during his absence, Togral, the Governor of Delhi, revolted and assumed the sovereignty of that city. Gheias returned, defeated him, and put the rebel and 100,000 prisoners to death. (He had previously beheaded his own commanding officer for being beaten in one fight.)

The king died of a broken heart in 1286, in consequence of the death of his son and heir apparent.

Kei Kobad, 1286—1288.—Gheias's second son, Bakarra Khan, had a son, Kei Kobad, who now succeeded to the sovereignty. The eldest son, Mohammed, had also left a son named Kei Khusru, who was appointed Governor of Multan, and acquiesced in the arrangement. Bakarra Khan was also alive, but did not oppose his son's elevation. Kobad gave himself up to intemperance in every way, and had the misfortune to be burdened with an ambitious and hostile minister, one Nizam-u-din, who plotted with Kei Khusru; but afterwards murdered that prince. To alienate the Moguls from Kobad's cause, the vizier persuaded the king to have all the Moguls at his court treacherously murdered at a banquet. Bakarra Khan implored his son

[1] It is said that he interdicted the use of strong liquors, even to a moderate extent; and frequently ordered the public flogging of Governors of Provinces if anything went wrong under their jurisdiction.

to dismiss this evil adviser. The king refused to do so for some months, but finally, in 1287, he poisoned the vizier. This threw the whole country and court into confusion.

The chief party at Delhi at this period was the ancient Ghaznevite family of the "*Khiljies;*" and these now dethroned Kei Kobad, put him to death, and raised their own leader, Jelal-u-din Khilji to the throne.

The dynasty he founded, though of short duration, was an important one.

(IX.)—*The House of Khilji*, 1288—1321.

Jelal-u-din Khilji, 1288—1295.—Jelal began his reign cautiously and discreetly, by a show of great clemency and mildness, perhaps counterfeited as an antidote to the ferocity of Gheias-u-din Bulbun and his successor. He pardoned a rebel chief, nephew of Gheias-u-din, and on quelling an incursion of the Moguls, set free all the prisoners. In 1293, three thousand Moguls joined him, and were established at Delhi.

Soon, his nephew, Ala-u-din, being made Governor of Oude, planning an invasion of the Deckan; and, marching through Elichpore to Deogiri (now called Doulatabad), found the Hindu Rajah there in profound peace. He behaved with great cruelty, plundering the city and treasures, and pillaging the surrounding country. The Rajah came to terms, and Ala-u-din then retired to Malwa.

He at once marched on Delhi against his uncle the king; but removed any suspicions that might arise by proclaiming that he was only coming to receive the thanks of his sovereign on the occasion of the victory. While the king was actually embracing his nephew, in joy at his safe return, the base prince stabbed him to the heart.

Ala-u-din Khilji, 1295 - 1317.—Ala-u-din possessed one of the most ferocious and sanguinary dispositions on record. After the murder of his uncle, he put to death that monarch's sons and widow. A rising took place, which he quelled by a wholesale massacre of the wives and children of the rebels. In 1297 he took Guzerat. Soon afterwards, a Mogul army advanced on Delhi, which was crowded with fugitives and unprepared for defence. Ala-u-din therefore marched out, fought a furious battle, and drove back the invading army.

Next year the king was on a hunting expedition, when his

nephew, Prince Soliman, finding Ala-u-din separated from his followers, attacked, wounded him, and left him for dead. The Prince then flew to Delhi and claimed the throne; but Ala-u-din recovered, and showed himself to the army, which came to him *en masse*. Soliman and two other nephews were beheaded.

The people rose in fury on all sides, but the king quelled the rebellions by terrible displays of cruelty.

In 1303 he took Chitore in Mewar, one of the most celebrated hill forts in India, from a rebellious Rajput; and drove back another incursion of Moguls. The next year the Moguls made three separate attempts to force an entrance into Hindostan, but were each time repulsed. This was their last effort for many years.[1]

In 1306 the Sultan found it necessary to make an expedition into the Deckan, for the Rajah of Deogiri refused to pay the tribute imposed on him by Jelal-u-din, and Ala-u-din despatched a large army under the command of an eunuch, Malik Cafur, who had been a slave, to bring him to submission. The Rajah was conquered and carried to Delhi, where he spent the remainder of his life.

A romantic anecdote connected with this expedition, is told of the beautiful Princess Dewal Devi.[2]

[1] Ferishta says that on these occasions all the Mogul prisoners brought into camp were put to death in cold blood.

[2] When Alp Khan, by Ala-u-din's orders, had captured Guzerat, in 1297, the fugitive Rajah of that country took refuge in the fortress of Baglana He had a daughter there with him, of exquisite beauty and goodness, the Princess Dewal Devi. Ala-u-din, hearing the rumour of her graceful qualities, sent to Alp Khan ordering him to seize the girl and send her to Delhi to adorn his harem. But the unhappy father, sooner than submit to this, determined to give her in marriage to one who had for years been desperately in love with her, but had been hitherto considered as not of sufficiently high rank; this was the eldest son of the Rajah of Deogiri. Overjoyed at the intelligence, the young prince came with an escort, carried her off, and proceeded on his way to his capital. But by this time (1306) the country was overrun by the armies of Malik Cafur, and a body of marauding soldiers attacked and defeated the escort, and bore off the Princess to camp. Cafur sent her to Delhi. Here she remained for some time, and Khizr Khan, the king's eldest son, a man of a far more prepossessing character than his father, succeeded in gaining her affection and her hand. (There is a long and beautiful poem in Persian, containing the story of their love.) Thus they remained till the barbarous Mobarik blinded Dewal Devi's husband; and shortly afterwards Khusru Khan, the quondam slave, carried her off to his own house. On his death, Gheias-u-din Toghlak, who acceded to the throne, took her under his protection, and treated her with great gentleness and kindness till her death.

Malik Cafur returned in 1309, and was again sent into the south; this time to Telingana, where he was victorious, capturing the strong fort of Warangal. Next year he conquered Carnata, and the whole of the eastern coast down to Cape Comorin, returning to Delhi laden with treasures. This was the first Mahomedan invasion of the Tamil country.[1]

Ala-u-din's ferocity now again displayed itself in his slaughter of all the 15,000 Moguls at Delhi. Cafur soon afterwards began intriguing for the succession, and the country was in great disorder; for the people were furious at the king's atrocities and tyranny. Ala-u-din's death was but a continuation of the deeds of his life. It was caused by a fit of apoplexy, after a violent outburst of rage, in 1316.[2]

Malik Cafur made an attempt to seize the throne, but was murdered, and the king's third son, Mobarik Khilji, succeeded.

Mobarik Khilji, 1317—1320.—Mobarik Khilji commenced his reign in the style of his excellent father, of happy memory. He blinded his three brothers, and murdered the two powerful officers who had placed him on the throne. Then he disbanded the entire army, and thus fancied he had removed all opposition. Next he made a slave, by name Khusru Khan, his vizier—a worthy minister to such a king,—and, flattering himself that all things requisite were now accomplished, gave himself up to the most degrading debaucheries. Khusru conquered Malabar in 1319, and, returning next year, slew the king, and freed the country from the Khiljies, by murdering all the survivors of that house.

Khusru then seized the throne, transferred Dewal Devi, nearly dying of grief and despair, to his own seraglio, and prepared to govern the kingdom. But providentially his hopes were frustrated by the arrival before Delhi of a large army from the Punjaub, under the command of Gheias-u-din Toghlak, Governor of that province. Delhi was sacked, Khusru murdered, and the ex-Governor became king, and founder of the house of Toghlak, which ruled over Delhi for a hundred years.

[1] Malik Cafur built a mosque at Cape Comorin to commemorate the extent of his conquests.

[2] Elphinstone gives an interesting account of this man's character and tyranny.—(Vol. ii. p. 50).

(X).—*House of Toghlak* (1321—1414).

Gheias-u-din Toghlak the First, 1321—1325.—Gheias-u-din Toghlak was the son of a slave of Gheias-u-din Bulbun, the vizier and successor of Nasir-u-din Mahmud. His reign, though short, was remarkable for the extreme moderation and gentleness with which he ruled. It was a great and blessed change from the wild atrocities of his predecessors. In 1324 he went on an expedition to Bengal, leaving his son, Juna Khan, in the government. On his return, in 1325, Juna prepared a state reception for his father, and caused a wooden pavilion to be erected, which fell, and killed Gheias.

Mohammed Toghlak, 1325—1351.—Juna Khan succeeded, under the title of "Mohammed Toghlak." He was the most accomplished prince of the age, being gifted with superb talents; but, unhappily, he wasted them on schemes of such stupendous greatness that success was an impossibility, and he often suffered himself to be led by his momentary fancies into deeds which his own better nature would scorn to approve. His first action showed some political skill, for he bought off the Moguls, and conciliated them so far that in his reign the country was undisturbed by their incursions. He then reduced the Deckan to submission.

Now began his wild schemes of universal empire. He beggared himself by collecting an army for the conquest of Persia, so vast that his treasury could not find pay for the troops.[1] Next he turned his attention to a reduction of China under his rule, and sent 100,000 men to find a passage through the Himalayas. They perished, almost to a man, in the jungles of the "Terai."

Finding his treasury empty, he made the most ruinous exactions on the people, and taxed them so heavily, that the poor fled to the forests. From the manner in which he revenged himself it is difficult to suppose that he could have been in his right senses. He caused a cordon of troops to be drawn round the forests, and then had the fugitives slaughtered in a grand battue, in which he took part, as at a hunting party, riding the men down like game! The natural consequence of this conduct, half barbarous, half insane, was a total failure of crops, and a terrible famine.

[1] Ferishta says that this "army of Persia" numbered as many as 370,000 horse, and that the infantry and camp-followers were innumerable.

Rebellions broke out in all directions. Those in Malwa and the Punjaub were easily suppressed; but another in Bengal, in 1340, was completely successful. The Coromandel coast, (*i.e*, the eastern coast of India, from the River Kistna to Cape Comorin) revolted, and became free. The Afghans were ravaging the Punjaub. Carnata and Telingana successfully revolted, and Guzerat rebelled. To crown the Sultan's misfortunes, the famine was at its height. The king went to quell the rising in Guzerat, and his manner of treating it was characteristic. He ravaged the whole province, as if it had been an enemy's country, though it was his own territory! and then hurried about the country, trying to suppress each rebellion in turn, till, from his over-anxiety of mind and restless activity of body, he died of fever at Tattah, in Sinde. This happened in 1351.[1] Elphinstone makes the terse remark:—"There is in general so little scruple about getting rid of a bad king in the east, that it is seldom such extensive mischief is brought about by the misgovernment of one man."

Firuz Toghlak, 1351—1388.—His nephew, Firuz Toghlak, succeeded. After a vain attempt to recover Bengal, he recognised the independence of that province and the Deckan. His was an unimportant reign, of slight rebellions and slight wars; and when in the year 1385 he became too old to govern, he appointed a vizier; and, in 1386, made his son, Nasir-u-din, king in his place. But the ex-king's nephews drove Nasir from the capital, and declared Firuz to have abdicated in favour of his grandson, Gheias-u-din. The aged monarch died next year at the age of ninety.

Gheias-u-din Toghlak the Second, 1388—1389.—Gheias-u-din, immediately on his accession, was foolish enough to quarrel with the cousins who had elevated him to the throne, and was soon afterwards deposed by them. He forgot that he had at no time a shadow of right to hold the throne, and soon discovered that

[1] Amongst other curious fancies, Mohammed once determined to remove his capital from Delhi to Deogiri. He re-named the latter city "Doulatabad;" caused a magnificent and impregnable fort to be cut out of the solid rock, and then ordered the whole of the inhabitants of Delhi one fine day instantly to march for the new capital. "After this he twice permitted them to return to Delhi, and twice compelled them, on pain of death, to leave it. One of these movements took place during the famine, and caused a prodigious loss of life. The plan entirely failed in the end."—(Elphinstone, vol. ii. p. 65).

usurpers ought to pursue a line of conduct towards the nobles surrounding them, very different from that of those princes who succeed as of right.

Abubekr Toghlak, 1389—1390.—His brother, Abubekr, was made king in his stead. But no sooner was he comfortably settled than Nasir, his uncle, came down on Delhi, with a large army, and made him prisoner.

Nasir-u-din Toghlak, 1390—1394.—Thus Nasir at last got his rights, and reigned quietly for four years, when he died. His eldest son, Humayun, succeeded, but died, after forty-five days' enjoyment of the pleasures of monarchy, and Mahmud Toghlak, his brother, stepped into his place.

Mahmud Toghlak, 1394—1414.—The reign of this prince was disastrous. It was a long succession of revolts, factions, and wars. Malwa, Guzerat, and Candeish, at once threw off all submission. Delhi itself was a constant scene of fights and disturbances between the parties into which it was divided. But soon all internal dissensions were forgotten in the presence of a common enemy; for the Moguls, under the terrible Tamerlane (or "Teimur the Tartar"),[1] swarmed like locusts over the north, and, uniting their armies, marched in one great host against Delhi.

Tamerlane's first Invasion, 1398.—The proper name of their leader was the Ameer Teimur. He had overrun Persia, Transoxiana, Tartary, and Siberia, and now (1398) bent his attention to India. Tamerlane entered *viâ* Cabul, while his grandson, Pir Mahommed, attacked Multan. The two armies joined on the Sutlej, and advanced on Delhi, ravaging the country on their way.

Mahmud Toghlak fled to Guzerat, while Delhi was sacked and burned, and the inhabitants ruthlessly massacred. The Moguls next took Meerut, and retired (1399) by Cabul into Transoxiana, laden with spoil. Mahmud returned to Delhi, and died there in 1414, leaving a governor, Khizr Khan, who assumed the

[1] Of the two early leaders of the great Mogul expeditions, Chengiz Khan and Teimur, the former was by far the most violent and unscrupulous. But, perhaps, he was not such an enemy to mankind as Teimur, whose character was at once sanguinary and perfidious. The latter was a wily politician at the same time that his inclinations led him to deeds of atrocity and violence, a mixture of qualities exceedingly dangerous to those around him.

I may here notice that "Teimur the *Tartar*" is a misnomer. He was not a Tartar, but a Mogul.

sovereignty, under the title of "*The Seiad,*"[1] or lineal descendant of the Prophet.

Delhi was governed by the Seiads for forty-six years.

(XI.)—*Government of the Seiads* (1414—1450).

Seiad Khizr Khan, 1414—1421.—At the accession of this governor nothing remained to Delhi but the city and a small territory around, all the rest of the acquisitions of Ala-u din Khilji having been lost. Khizr Khan affected to consider himself merely a deputy acting for Tamerlane, but in reality was a petty independent monarch. His only important act was a levy of tribute on Rohilcund and Gwalior.

Seiad Mobarik, 1421—1436.—He was succeeded in 1421 by his son Mobarik, who reigned quietly for some years. There was a good deal of disturbance in the Punjaub, but nothing to influence the little state of the Seiads. Mobarik was murdered by his vizier in 1436.

Seiad Mohammed, 1436 — 1444. — His son, Mohammed, claimed the crown, and was acnowledged. The only event of interest was an invasion of the Delhi country by the king of Malwa. The Seiad beat him back by calling in the aid of Behlol Khan Lodi, governor of the Punjaub. On Mohammed's death, in 1444, he was succeeded by his son, Ala-u-din.

Seiad Ala-u-din, 1444—1450.—Ala-u-din removed his capital to Budayun, beyond the Ganges, though for what reason does not appear. The effect was instantaneous. The energetic Behlol Lodi seized Delhi; and his family ruled the country for more than seventy years, when they were superseded by the Moguls.

(XII.)—*House of Lodi.*

Behlol Lodi, 1450—1488.—Behlol Lodi seized the throne of Delhi in 1450, and as his own territory had previously been that of the Punjaub, his accession re-united that country to Delhi. In 1452 the Rajah of Jounpore laid siege to Delhi, and a war ensued which lasted 26 years, ending in the total defeat of the Rajah and the annexation of his country by the king of Delhi. Behlol made several other conquests, and at his death the kingdom was much extended, comprising the land from the Jumna to

[1] "*Seiad.*" This is the same word as the more generally known "Seid," or "Sidi." "Mot arabe qui veut dire seigneur, le même que celui de *cid*, est un titre d'honneur que prennent tous ceux qui prétendent descendre de Mahomet. Il est aussi porté par tous les Ismaéliens."—(Bouillet, under head "Seid.")

the Himalayas, eastwards to Benares, and westwards as far as Bundelcund. He died in 1488, and was succeeded by his son, Secunder.

Secunder Lodi, 1488—1506.—Secunder Lodi's only action of note was the re-annexation of Behar. He was a very able and peaceful sovereign, and on his death, in 1506, a change for the worse came over Delhi.

Ibrahim Lodi, 1506—1526.—His son, Ibrahim, came to the throne in 1506, and reigned 20 years. He was a proud and tyrannical prince; and, following in the footsteps of his ferocious predecessors, Gheias-u-din, and Ala-u-din, murdered all the chiefs at court in order to preclude the possibility of any opposition to his rule. He was about to do the same kindness to the governor of the Punjaub, when that officer, in fear for his life, called in the aid of a power that at once revolutionized India, overthrew every Hindu state, and in a few years established a universal empire over the whole territory now ruled by the English. These were the Moguls, who, under the great *Baber*, sixth in descent from Tamerlane, invaded India in 1524.

Baber's Invasion of India. 1524.—Baber unhesitatingly accepted the offer of the governor of the Punjaub, and advanced with a large army. He seized the governor, threw him into prison, and took Lahore, where Ala-u-din, a brother of the king of Delhi, who was covetous of the sovereignty of Ibrahim, joined him, and at the head of a Mogul army was sent to conquer the capital. But Ibrahim utterly defeated him.

1*st Battle of Panipat*, 1526.—Baber then came down in person, and the two armies met at Panipat, a battle ground which has twice seen the destinies of India changed, and dynasties overthrown which once seemed invincible.

Ibrahim's force was defeated with immense slaughter, and himself, with 40,000 Hindus, were left dead on the field.

So Baber took possession of Delhi and Agra.

(XIII.)—*States of India at the time of Baber.*

On the break-up of the kingdom of Mohammed Toghlak, in 1351, various new states were formed; and by the year 1398 all India was free, except a few miles round Delhi.

Bahmani Kings of the Deckan.—The "*Bahmani*" kingdoms of the Deckan are amongst the best known. They were founded by a poor man, named *Gangu Bahmani*, who rose to eminence and independence at Culbarga. In 1421 the Bahmani king drove the Telingana king from Warangal; and later, took Rajamandri, Masulipatam, and Congeveram. Many internal commotions ensued soon afterwards, created by the religious sects of the "*Shias*" and "*Sunnis.*" The Sunnis under Eusof Adil went to Bijapore, and established a kingdom there, calling their leader King *Adil Shah.*

Bijapore—Ahmednuggur.—The dynasty lasted from 1489 to 1579. It was in this little kingdom that the Mahrattas rose; and, issuing with his disciples from thence, a celebrated Brahman founded the kingdom of Ahmednuggur.

Golconda—Berar—Beder.—Three other small states at Golconda, Berar, and Beder, arose in much the same manner, and lasted till towârds the end of the 16th century.

Guzerat.—The state of Guzerat was founded by Mozaffer Shah, a Rajput, and a fine soldier, who was appointed governor of that country by Firuz Toghlak. In later years his successors annexed Malwa after hard fighting. The kingdom lasted from 1396—1561.

Malwa.—Malwa became independent at the same time as Guzerat, and was ruled by a Ghorian family till, in 1531, Bahadur Shah, of Guzerat, permanently annexed Malwa.

Candeish.—Candeish became an independent state in 1399, and was re-annexed to Delhi by Akber, in 1599.

Rajput States.—There were also several Rajput states, in central India generally formed of the wild mountain tribes, magnificent soldiers, and highly honourable. The principal of these were *Chitore*, *Marwar*, (or *Jodhpore*), *Bikanir*, *Jesulmir*, and *Jeypore.*

Such was the condition of India when the Moguls came down under Tamerlane, and commenced their conquest of the whole country.

XIV.—*The Tartars, Moguls, and Turks.—The Early Days of Baber.*

It will not, I think, be considered out of place to give here a slight sketch of the history of those wandering tribes of Asia, the Tartars, Moguls and Turks, who have exercised such a powerful influence on the history of the world, establishing the largest empire that has ever existed. This is the more necessary, as there have ever been many misconceptions concerning the origin of these tribes; and the names that have been given by geographers to the countries and peoples of Asia tend still more to create confusion in the mind. I shall make this digression as short and as clear as I can.

In very early days there were three great races in Asia,—*Turks*, living in the region about Bokhara, and westwards to the Caspian; *Tartars*, inhabiting part of Russia and Siberia, their principal tribes being at Astrachan and Kazan, and overspreading the entire country north of the Turki tribes; and *Moguls*, or *Mongols*, occupying Mongolia, Thibet, and Mandchouri.

They were all shepherd tribes, but differed much in qualities and habits. The Moguls were the most spirited and energetic; the Tartars, next to them in these physical qualities; and the Turkis last. The latter seem to have been born to make splendid servants, but never to rule.

The Moguls were of the Turanian race, and professed the religion of Lama; they were nomadic, and dwellers in tents. There were western Moguls, or "Kalmucks," and eastern Moguls, divided into many tribes or "*oulouss*." These "*oulouss*" or clans frequently united under some one leader by a sort of mutual alliance.

In 1164 A.D. Chengiz Khan was born. He was a chief of an unimportant clan in the west who paid tribute to the Khitan Tartars; but having ambitious schemes in his mind, he united many "oulouss," became their leader, and invaded the Tartar country. The less active Tartars were no match for the Moguls, and speedily a vast portion of that people were vanquished. Chengiz Khan made them join his armies, and soon the Tartars in his host far outnumbered their commanders.[1]

With this immense force, Chengiz Khan overran the country of East Mongolia, and northern China, and then Transoxiana and Khorassan. Finally he conquered the Turki country, namely Bokhara, Kharism, and Persia, and afterwards turned his attention towards India, which he invaded.

His empire at that time extended from the Caspian Sea to Pekin—northwards to the Sea, and southwards to the Indian Ocean and the Himalayas, including for its western boundary Astrachan and Kazan—perhaps the largest territory ever acknowledging the supremacy of one man.

On Chengiz Khan's death his empire was divided into four,—

[1] This explains why the Hindu historians called the whole army "Tartars."

Kaptchak, Iran, Djaggathai, and Mongolia with China. The three first were governed by Khans; the ruler of the last, as being the original dominant country, was called Supreme or Great Khan. Hence it is that the emperors of China have ever had so high an opinion of their own power and greatness; for they feel that theirs is the kingdom which gave birth to the vast empire of the Moguls.

A century later Tamerlane was born at Kech, in Djaggathai. His father was Prince of Kech, and on the death of Toghlak-Timour, Khan of Djaggathai, Tamerlane seized the Khanate and soon afterwards began his conquests. In 1398, having previously overrun and subdued very nearly the whole of Chengiz Khan's great kingdom, he invaded India, as narrated on a previous page, uprooted the kingdom of Delhi, and left there a Mogul Mussulman as governor. Next he ravaged Syria and Bagdad, conquered the aristocratic Ottoman Turks on the Caspian, reduced Asia Minor, and in 1404 marched to China, but died on the route. His empire broke up, and the pieces were seized by his sons and grandsons—Pir Mahommed, second son of Tamerlane's eldest son, obtaining the largest share.

Sixth in descent from Tamerlane, came Baber, whose father was King of Ferghana.

Opinions are much divided concerning the origin of the *Turks*. I believe the most rational theory to be that which I have suggested—that they were a separate tribe inhabiting the country of Bokhara and westwards. Their principal families were the "Ottomans," the "Seljuks," and the "Usbeks;" and from them came the great dynasty of Ghazni. The Ottomans went westwards in the 14th century and established their power in Phrygia, from which they were never driven. The Seljuks were principally found in Persia, Syria, and Iconium. The Uzbeks arose in 1305. They were Turks of Kaptchak, and took their name from their Khan, who was born in that year. They were very powerful in Baber's time.

The Turks have been confounded with the Tartars, and the Tartars with the Moguls so frequently, that this short account of their separate histories appeared requisite before considering the Mogul Empire of India.

Baber was son of Omer-Sheik-Mirza, King of Ferghana, and was lineally descended from the Mogul Tamerlane. His life is in itself a very interesting one; and the more so as he is the only Mogul monarch who has left us his personal narrative. This autobiography is supposed to have been dictated by the Emperor to his scribe, and copied in the Djaggathai Turki (or Tartar) language. It was translated in full by Leyden and Erskine.

Here is Baber's own account of his father's death, and his accession to the monarchy.—"At this very crisis," (when the kingdom was being disturbed by civil war) "a singular incident occurred. It has been already mentioned that the fort of Akhsi is situated on a steep precipice, on the very edge of which some of its buildings are erected. On Monday, the 4th of the month Ramazan, of the year that has been mentioned (A.H. 899) Omer Sheik-Mirza was precipitated from the top of the steep with his pigeons and pigeon-house, and took his flight into another world." So that "in the month Ramazan, in the year 899, and in the twelfth year of my age, I became King of Ferghana." The year of our Lord is 1493.

Baber conquered Bokhara and Samarcand in 1498, but, while absent from Ferghana, lost that by a rebellion, 1498. He heard this disastrous news while at Samarcand, and at once hastened to his capital; but while yet on the route, messengers overtook him from Samarcand, saying, that his uncle had returned and re captured that country; so that he was left without any territory at all. He regained Ferghana next year, but was again driven out and forced to fly to the mountains in the East.

Here a trusty servant brought him word that the Uzbecs had left Samarcand, and Baber at once dashed down and took the city. He suffered a close siege for six months, but was then starved out, and forced to surrender the place.[1]

[1] "The ancients have said that to maintain a fortress, a head, two hands and two feet are necessary. The head is a captain, the two hands are two friendly forces that must advance from opposite sides, the two feet are water and stores of provision within the fort. I looked for aid and assistance from the princes, my neighbours, but each of them had his attention fixed on some other object." . . . . . "the soldiers and inhabitants at last began to lose all hope, went off by ones and twos, escaped from the city, and deserted. I also moved my head-quarters." . . . . . "I now despaired of assistance or relief from any quarter." . . . . . "In these circumstances Sheibani Khan proposed terms. Had I had the slightest hope of relief, or had any stores remained within the place, never would I have listened to him. Compelled, however, by necessity, a sort of capitulation was agreed upon, and about midnight I left the place accompanied by my mother the Khanum." Baber was received kindly by the Governor of Dizak, and rapturously describes the pleasures of eating fresh fruit and good food after his terrible sufferings.—(Baber's Autobiography.)

In 1501 Baber regained Ferghana, and was a third time driven out; when, in despair, leaving his kingdom, he went to Hindu Cush, accompanied by only two or three faithful attendants. He was then twenty-five years of age.

At this point, in the middle of a sentence of despair, the narrative breaks off suddenly, Baber's spirit seemed nearly crushed; but he soon regained his equanimity on experiencing a favourable reception by the Governor of Balkh; and three years later, mustering a small army, he took Cabul, and established himself as ruler in that province, where he remained six years.

In 1510, the Uzbek King of Samarcand died, and Baber attempted to retake that country, but failed. He then collected large armies, and bent his attention to India. It was in 1526 that the Governor of the Punjaub, anxious to be protected from the violence of Ibrahim Lodi, of Delhi, invited Baber to aid him in an attack on that city and Agra. The Mogul readily consented, and came with an immense army to India. The result has been narrated above.[1]

[1] Page 33.

CONTENTS OF PART II.

PART II.

THE MOGUL EMPIRE IN INDIA.

(1526—1761).

(I.)—*Reign of Baber*, 1526—1530.

WHEN Baber had captured Delhi he made great rejoicings there, and at once assumed sovereignty; but soon, as might have been expected, he discovered that many intrigues had been set on foot against him, and that owing to the excessive heat of the weather that year, disaffection had spread among his troops to such an extent that they were anxious to return to Cabul. Baber therefore organized a grand review, and made a proclamation that such of his soldiers as wished to retire might do so, but that for himself he intended to remain and rule in India. The plan was successful, for the bulk of the army was ashamed to desert its great leader.

His eldest son, Humayun, was made commander-in-chief, and in four months had reduced all the country held by Ibrahim Lodi.

Next year (1527) Sanga, King of Mewar, a Rajput prince, who had brought Ajmir and Malwa under his rule, and was recognised as feudatory leader by Marwar and Jeypore, brought a large army from all these states against Delhi. He took Biana, a small station near Agra, and beat a detachment of Baber's force.

Battle of Sikri. ("*The Indian Hastings.*")—Then ensued the famous battle of Sikri, which has been called the "*Indian Hastings.*" It well deserves the title, for there is a strong resemblance in the situation of the parties. On one side was an army of the finest soldiers in India, fighting for their fatherland and their freedom. On the other a resolute body of Moguls, invaders, who had for centuries been the great conquering nation of the world. Each side looked forward with undisguised anxiety to the result. Baber himself renounced all habits of drinking and dissipation, and, vowing many reforms if he gained the victory, devoted himself for ever to the service of his Maker. On the day of the battle, recovering all his wonted energy, he made a fiery speech to animate his soldiers. His example roused all the courage of his troops, and the Moguls gained a great victory; Sanga fled and many other leaders were slain.[1] This established his power in India.

The next six months were spent in quieting and settling the country, and Baber then bent his energies to extending his dominions

Chanderi, belonging to a Rajput prince, was taken with great loss, the garrison, fighting desperately, being killed to a man. (1528.)

The same year Humayun was beaten by the Afghans of Oude, Baber marched from Chanderi to his assistance, and after signally defeating the enemy, returned to Delhi. Sanga soon afterwards surrendered the fine fortress of Rintambore.

During these latter years Baber was slowly losing health, and after his expedition to Oude, he gave himself up to peace and rest at Delhi.

But in 1529, hearing that Mahmud Lodi had seized on Behar, the emperor marched an army against that prince and having defeated him, annexed his territories. He then defeated the King of Bengal who held north Behar, at the fords of the Gogra River; and finished the campaign by decimating a tribe of half-wild Afghans who had seized Lahore.

Death of Baber.—On his return to Delhi, Baber heard that his eldest son, Humayun, had been seized with an illness and was at the point of death; and the anxiety of this, coupled with his own indisposition, threw the emperor into a violent fever, of which he died, December 26th, 1530. He was buried in great splendour in Cabul, on a spot that he had chosen.[2]

His Character.—This great conqueror's character is very clearly displayed by his writings. He was gifted with great

[1] In Baber's later battles he used both gunpowder and arrows. He speaks of his mortars and matchlockmen, and of his bowmen. He himself was a fine shot with bow and arrow.

[2] Burnes gives a graceful sketch of this place:—"He had directed his body to be interred in this place, to him the choicest in his wide dominions. . . . . . A running and clear stream yet waters the fragrant flowers of the cemetery, which is the holiday resort of the people of Cabul. In the front

talents, and was at once a poet,[1] scholar, and musician. He was manly, bold, and prudent; but on occasionally very violent, and when in these fits could be guilty of any amount of cruelty. Baber was immensely fond of wine, and describes with great candour, and some pride, the numerous occasions on which he became intoxicated. Perhaps the most prominent quality that he possessed was the wonderful buoyancy of spirits,[2] which preserved him from despondency, even when all around seemed dark and threatening. He was, moreover, thoroughly conscientious in religious matters;[3] and it is a pleasure to be able to record that towards the close of his life, he deliberately repented of his sins, and, ordering all his drinking vessels to be destroyed, vowed never more to touch intoxicating liquors. He steadily kept his vow.

of the grave is a small but chaste mosque of white marble. . . . . There is a noble prospect from the hill that overlooks Baber's tomb."—(Burnes's Travels, vol. i. p. 141.)

[1] Baber often quotes his own impromptu quatrains, and on August 30, 1526, his diary records: "On this occasion I composed the verses. . . . . in five hundred and four measures, and collected them in a book."

[2] On one occasion, when King of Ferghana, Baber was besieged for six months in Samarcand, where every form of starvation and misery was for months nobly endured by the unfortunate prince, whose spirits never for one instant deserted him. After a time all his officers fled to the enemy; the garrison was decimated by sickness; no succours were at hand; provisions of every kind had utterly failed; and Baber was compelled to save the lives of himself and the residue of his men by voluntarily submitting without terms. The enemy turned him out of the city like a dog in the middle of the night; and he was left a houseless wanderer in the mazes of the canals, without army, without kingdom, and followed only by two or three faithful friends. All this suffering, this miserable termination to his best endeavours, was surely sufficient to break the spirit of the proudest! But see the emperor's own account of his first performance when daylight the next morning came to shew the fugitives the road they should take. "*On the way I had a race with Kamber Ali and Kastin Beg!* My horse got the lead. As I turned round on my seat to see how far I had left them behind, my saddle-girth being slack, the saddle turned round, and I came to the ground right on my head. Although I immediately sprang up and remounted, yet I did not recover the full possession of my faculties till the evening." Their supper that day consisted of a steak cut out of a dead horse that had been so starved, it could no longer move one foot before the other!

[3] The following anecdote conveys a lesson to all. "It was wonderfully cold and the wind of Haderwish had here lost none of its violence and blew keen. So excessive was the cold that in the course of two or three days we lost two or three persons from its severity. I required to bathe

(II)—*First and Second reign of Humayun, with the intermediate Government of the House of Sur*, 1530—1556.

Baber left four sons, Humayun, Camran, Hindal, and Mirza Askeri.

Humayun succeeded him. Camran had been made Governor of Cabul, of which he declared himself independent sovereign on his father's death. Hindal was Governor of Sambal; and Mirza Askeri, an intrepid soldier, of Mewat.

Humayun Emperor.—Humayun having recovered his illness, succeeded without opposition in 1530.

His first act was to quell a rebellion in Jounpore; and he was soon involved in a general war with Guzerat; for Bahadur Shah, king of that country, took the opportunity of Baber's death to declare war against the Moguls. He fought Humayun for five years, at the end of which time the army of Guzerat was destroyed. The emperor then took Champanir, a very steep hill fort to which Bahadur had fled, himself gallantly leading the forlorn hope, and directing the assault. Here Humayun captured his foe; but, treating him with great cordiality, disarmed his suspicions, and prevailed on him to disclose the place where he kept all his treasures.

Campaigns against Shir Shah.—This show of mutual goodwill did not last long; for next year, the emperor being actively engaged against Shir Khan, who was operating against Bengal, Bahadur Shah retook Guzerat, and attacked Malwa (1537.)

> *Shir Shah.*—Shir Khan, afterwards called Shir Shah (by which name he is better known), was a descendant of the Ghorian kings of Delhi. Being ill-treated by his father, he left his family and enlisted as a private soldier in the ranks of the Rajah of Jounpore. But, disgusted with this degraded position, Shir Khan returned to his own home, where he remained till the overthrow of the Lodis in 1526. In 1527 he joined Baber's army

on account of my religious purifications, and went down for that purpose to a rivulet, which was frozen on the banks, but not in the middle, from the rapidity of the current. I plunged myself into the water and dived sixteen times. The extreme chilliness of the water quite penetrated me. Next morning I passed the river of Khojend on the ice."

as an officer, in which position he so distinguished himself that the emperor entrusted him with a command in Behar. In 1529 Mahmud Lodi took Behar, and Shir Khan, fearful of Baber's displeasure, joined the Lodi. On Mahmud's death he made himself master of Behar, and when, in 1532, Humayun was in Guzerat, Shir Khan advanced into Bengal. Humayun, therefore, led an army against him in 1537.

The keystone of Shir Khan's position was the strong hill fortress of Chunar in Bengal, where he made his stand. This fort commanded the passage of the river, up which the emperor wished to carry his guns and commissariat stores; and it was therefore necessary first to capture the place. Chunar yielded, after six months' siege, and Shir Khan moved his property and family to Rohtas till the rainy season, which had then set in, should be over. Meanwhile Humayun put his troops into cantonments, never dreaming that Shir Khan would move during the rains. But, contrary to his expectation, that prince was very active, seizing Benares, Chunar, and Canouj before the emperor again took the field.

When the emperor prepared to open the campaign in the winter, finding his army very much reduced by disease and desertion, he decided to retreat to Agra. But Shir Khan heard of this movement and advanced by forced marches to cut off his retreat. He came up with Humayun while in camp one day on the Ganges, and at once attacked him. The Imperial army was thoroughly worsted, and Humayun, in flight, narrowly escaped an ignominious death by drowning. This was in 1539.

Shir Khan then seized Bengal, while the emperor repaired his losses.

Continued Defeats.—In 1540, Humayun took the initiative, and opened the campaign by marching on Canouj. He was again defeated and again nearly drowned in the Ganges while in flight. He then went to Agra, and finally evacuated both that city and Delhi, removing the court and his family and treasures to Lahore.

The Emperor's Flight, and Birth of Akber.—Shir Khan pursued the emperor to Lahore, and Humayun in terror fled towards Sinde, where at least he thought to find safety. Unhappily he was again doomed to disappointment. After one or two fruitless sieges he fled to Jodhpore, but the Rajah refused to admit him, and the emperor was driven out like a vagabond into the Deserts of

Jesulmir. The little band of wanderers suffered much from privation, illness, and desertion in these sandy wastes. Besides the frightful thirst from want of water, and the diseases that broke out, they experienced also all the horrors of war; for their remorseless foes constantly assailed their encampments and carried off everything they could lay their hands on. Sharing the distress of their lord, were some of the females of his court, one of whom, Hamida, a dancing girl of great beauty in his harem,[1] and to whom he was much attached, gave birth to a son just at the period when their fortunes seemed at the lowest ebb (on Oct. 14th, 1542.)

They called this boy "*Akber*," and little thought that it was he who was destined to raise the Indian Empire to its greatest height of prosperity!

Soon after this the wanderers reached Omerkote, and were hospitably received. They had been then wandering helpless outcasts in the sandy wastes for a year and a half.

In 1542, Humayun made another attempt to reduce Sinde, which failed; and he was permitted to retire to Candahar, where he found the province in the possession of his brother, Mirza-Askeri. This prince refused to help him and Humayun again fled—this time to Herat, in Persia.

Meanwhile Shir Khan had seized the throne of Delhi, and altered his title from "*Khan*" to "*Shah*"

Shir Shah at Delhi, 1540—1545.—In 1540, Shir Shah took possession of all Humayun's dominions; and afterwards reduced several other places, namely, Malwa, in 1541, Raisin, in 1542, and Marwar in 1544. He was besieging Chitore in 1545, when a chance shot from one of the batteries of the city put an end to his strange career.

Selim Shah Sur, 1545—1553.—His younger son, Jelal Khan, was made Shah of Delhi under the title of Selim Shah Sur. The eldest son, Adil, attempted to gain his rightful sovereignty, but was defeated, and fled. Selim reigned very peacefully and well, and died in 1553, leaving many fine public works to testify to his able government.

Mohammed Shah Sur Adil, 1553—1554—On his death Adil at once came and seized the crown, murdering his young nephew, the late king's son. Adil was an iguorant prince, and entirely

[1] I believe it to be a disputed point whether or not the emperor was married to Hamida.

given up to amusements; and soon a rebellion ensued, headed by one of his own family, Ibrahim Sur, who drove him from his kingdom and seized Delhi and Agra. The Punjaub, Bengal, and Malwa then threw off all subjection.

Humayun's Second Reign, 1555—1556.—Hearing of these disturbances, Humayun gathered an army and came from Cabul to claim his throne.

He had been well received in Persia; but was treated as a captive, and forced into degrading acts of humiliation, the Shah Tahmasp compelling him to join the "*Safavi*" religion.[1] In 1545, however, Tahmasp assisted the exiled monarch by sending him to India with 14,000 horse. Humayun entered Afghanistan and took Candahar from Mirza Askeri; having the forbearance to resent the advice of his officers when they advised that his brother should be put to death. He then took Cabul, where Hindal, Baber's third son, joined him. And in 1548 Camran, who had rebelled and been forgiven, joined his standard. Thus, by Humayun's nobility and gentleness of character a reconciliation was brought about between the brothers, and all four were now re-united, bent on attaining one object—the glory of their family. One, however, Camran, was unworthy of the alliance, and again revolted. He was subdued in 1551, but was again troublesome; and when made prisoner in 1553 Humayun was, much against his will, compelled to throw him into prison and put out his eyes.

In January, 1555, Humayun set out from Cabul to regain his throne; he invaded the Punjaub; took Lahore, Delhi, and Agra without difficulty; and was at last restored to all his original grandeur in July of the same year.

Death of Humayun.—He enjoyed this dominion only six months, being killed by an accidental fall on some smooth marble, which caused concussion of the brain (January, 1556).

[1] The "*Safavi*" or "*Sophi*" kings were descended from a family of sainted dervishes, of the "Shia" sect, who attained sovereignty, and established a scheme of religion, which was called after their name. This became the religion of Persia, to which the inhabitants were as fully devoted as the most bigoted adherents of the "Shia" or "Sunni" doctrines.

(III.)—*Reign of Akber* (1556—1605).

When Humayun died, young prince Akber, aged thirteen, was with his father's minister, Behram Khan, in the Punjaub, and was at once brought down to Delhi.

Behram Khan.—At first, as was natural, Behram Khan was the actual governor, and he carried out the duties of his high office with energy and faithfulness; but while he was engaged in settling the affairs of home government at Delhi, Mirza Soliman, king of Badakshan, took Cabul; and at the same time Hemu, minister of Shah Adil, raised a rebellion.

2nd Battle of Panipat, 1556.—Hemu took Agra, and was advancing on Lahore, when Behram went out to meet him. The armies met at Panipat, where was fought the second battle of that name. It ended in the defeat of Hemu, and his death by the hand of Behram himself. Thus the hopes of the family of Shir Khan were for ever destroyed.

On his return to Delhi, Behram permitted his pride to overwhelm all other considerations. He behaved in the most overweening and despotic manner, alienating all the nobles that were once well-disposed to Akber; and even went so far as to authorize the cold-blooded murder of many who presumed to differ from him. This course of conduct being especially pursued towards those personal friends of the young monarch's, whom Behram supposed to be ingratiating themselves in the Imperial favour, a constant irritation and annoyance was kept up in Akber's mind; so that, being a bold young fellow, he threw off the shackles in the year 1560, and himself assumed the reins of government.

Death of Behram—Behram went to Nagore; and when Akber publicly dismissed him from office, he revolted, and the emperor had to send an army against him. Behram was defeated, but pardoned. The ex-vizier, soon, however, paid the penalty for his crimes: for a brother of one of the murdered nobles assassinated him in revenge.

Conquests of Akber.—Akber was now sole ruler, at the age of eighteen, his territory consisting of the country about Delhi and Agra, with the Punjaub. But his mind was bent on conquest, and all his energies were directed to the attainment of this object

Ajmir, Gwalior, and Lucknow were taken almost immediately.

while Malwa was recaptured from its rebellious governor, Abdullah Khan, in 1561, and the Khan banished.

This ruler being an Uzbek, the consequence of his banishment was a rizing of that tribe in 1564, which was of some importance. Akber went against them in person in 1567, and, by a very brave attack, defeated them.

The previous year (1566) Prince Hakim, Akber's brother, had seized on Cabul, of which country he for a long time remained master.

The Rajput States.—Akber now (1568) found leisure to mature his schemes against the nations and states around him; and the same year he commenced operations against the Rajputs. He besieged Chitore, which manfully held out during a long siege, and might ultimately have baffled his utmost endeavours, had not the emperor, with his own hand, by a lucky accident, shot the Rajput chief through the head with an arrow, as he was standing on the battlements. On seeing their leader's fall, the garrison devoted themselves to death with their wives and children; and after the latter had been slain, the men, rushing out against the Moguls, were almost annihilated. The survivors retired on Oodipore, where their royal family formed a new state, and where they have been ever since.

After this success the emperor, considering his power better consolidated by diplomacy than by war, married two Rajput queens, in order to form a peaceable connection with Jeypore and Marwar.

He took Rintambore, and Calinjer, in 1570, and thus added two more Rajput states to his rule.

Affairs in Guzerat.—In 1572 affairs in Guzerat became so disturbed, that the governor there, Etimad Khan, implored Akber to come and quiet the country by placing it under imperial government. The disputants belonged to three parties, the most violent of which consisted of the *Mirzas*, descendants of Tamerlane, and therefore connections of the emperor, who had revolted at Sambal, in 1566, and, being defeated, had fled to Guzerat. Akber went to Guzerat in person, received the sovereignty of that state, and then marched against the Mirzas, whom he defeated (1573). He then returned to Agra, but was recalled to quell another Mirza rising; and, reaching Guzerat by forced marches, he finally crushed them, leaving the province in tranquillity.

Bengal.—Disturbances in Bengal next claimed his attention, for the prince, Daud by name, who had been paying steady tribute since Akber's accession, now threw off his allegiance, and declared for himself. The emperor invaded Bengal in 1575, overran that province, and drove the prince into Orissa. On Akber's retiring, Daud advanced and regained his territory, but was defeated in a pitched battle and killed.

Behar.—Behar, which had been governed by the family of Shir Khan since 1530, was then re-annexed; and thus was swept away the last trace of Ghorian ascendancy in Hindostan.

But soon a rebellion broke out amongst the imperial troops in Bengal and Behar, which was not satisfactorily quelled for three years; and owing to this disturbance, the Afghans, driven out of Behar, were enabled to seize and hold the province of Orissa for some time. They were finally crushed by one of the emperor's officers in 1592.

In 1582, Prince Hakim left Cabul and invaded the Punjaub. Akber went against him, and not only drove him from the Punjaub, but seized Cabul. He behaved as usual with great moderation, and pardoning Hakim, left him to rule as lieutenant-governor of the province for the emperor of Delhi.

Settlement of the Empire.—No other disturbance occurred till that in Cabul three years later; and meanwhile Akber was busily at work, settling the kingdom and maturing his plans of home government. He behaved with great judgment, and collected about him the wisest and clearest heads to be his assistants in the grand work. The result was one of the finest systems of administration ever known in the East. (A sketch of this will be given at the close of the present section).

Cashmir.—The affair in Cabul of 1585 arose from a threatened invasion of Uzbeks into that province. But Akber quieted these fears by a great display of force; and on his return decided to attack Cashmir. He failed in 1586, but succeeded in conquering and annexing that country the next year.

Disastrous War in the North-west.—Now ensued a disastrous campaign against the Afghans of Peshawur and the north-western districts. The country was held by the powerful Afghan tribe of the "*Euzofzeis.*" They belonged to the fanatical religious sect called the "*Roushenias,*" and became so troublesome to Cabul that Akber sent two divisions against them in 1587, one commanded by Rajah Bir Bal, and the other by Zein Khan. The force under the former lost its way amongst the mountains, and was nearly destroyed by the Afghans in impenetrable gorges: Zein Khan, therefore, marched to the rescue, and the two divisions joined company. But afterwards, unwisely separating a second time, both armies were attacked in one night. Bir Bal was trying to force a difficult defile, when the Afghans rushed down on him from the mountains round, and a terrible slaughter followed, the Rajah and all the chief officers being killed. At the same time, Zein Khan's division was attacked in the plain with the same result, and the whole imperial army fled towards Attok. Akber immediately sent another force, which drove the Afghans back to their mountains; but this was the only success he ever attained over these fine soldiers.

Sinde.—In 1591, the Emperor took advantage of some internal quarrels to invade Sinde, and, without much difficulty, he induced the chief to give up that province. (It is said that in this war he used Portuguese soldiers from Goa.)

Candahar.—In 1594 he recovered Candahar from the Persians, who had retaken it on the death of Humayun.

Thus, by 1594, the whole of the north of India was under the dominion of the Moguls.

Wars in the Deckan.—Akber now turned his attention to the Deckan, and determined to take advantage of the confusion then existing at Ahmednuggur to conquer that state.

Chand Sultana.—He sent two armies into the Deckan under Prince Morad, his second son, and Mirza Khan. They met at Ahmednuggur, and found the city in the hands of Chand Sultana, a bold and energetic princess, one of the most distinguished women of India, who behaved with the greatest bravery on this occasion. Hearing of the advance of the imperial troops, she succeeded, by clever intrigue, in effecting an extensive combination of Indian princes against the Moguls. Soon the combined armies of the emperor arrived at Ahmednuggur, and invested the place; but Chand Sultana held out the siege with such indomitable courage, that the Moguls, after assaulting the city for many months, were forced to come to terms, and Akber was allowed to annex Berar (1596).

Next year hostilities broke out afresh, and the emperor was reinforced by the submission of the Raja of Candeish, who joined his armies. An action, fought by Morad on the Godaveri river, proved indecisive, and Akber felt that his own presence was necessary to ensure success. He therefore took the field in person, and joined his army on the Nerbudda. Prince Danial, his youngest son, was sent forward to invest Ahmednuggur a second time, and when Akber joined him, the garrison became so disheartened that they foully murdered the gallant Sultana, and abandoned the city to the Moguls. This was in 1600.

Revolt of Selim.—Akber was recalled to Hindostan by the revolt of his eldest son, Selim, who had taken advantage of the emperor's absence to seize Oude and Behar. He was forgiven, and in order to content him, was given Bengal and Orissa. But the prince was of a very violent character, and was guilty of such frightful cruelties that his father, deeply grieved at his troublesome conduct, had to take decided steps against him. Selim felt it necessary to confess himself in the wrong, and come to Agra.

He, however, behaved disgracefully to all around him, and was particularly bitter against his eldest son, whom he fancied to be in league with the emperor to cut him off from the succession.

Death of Akber.—The emperor's sons, Morad and Danial, both died at this time somewhat suddenly; and the grief caused by this, coupled with Selim's outrageous behaviour, so afflicted Akber that he was seized with a terrible illness and died in the year 1605, at the age of sixty-three.

In person, Akber was strong and handsome, and of graceful and captivating manners. He was very abstemious, and fond of exercise of all kinds. In character, prudent, enterprising, bold, and gifted with great talents.

(IV.)—*A Sketch of Akber's Policy and System of Government.*

Religion.—In religious matters Akber was tolerant and impartial. He was in early life firm to the faith of his fathers, but afterwards allowed to himself as well as others greater liberty of conscience. His principal religious and literary advisers were Feizi, and Abul Fazl, the former of whom is well-known as the learned and diligent translator of several of the old Sanscrit poems, including the "Ramayana" and the "Mahabharata." Akber brought a Christian priest from Goa, a Roman Catholic Portuguese, and caused Feizi to translate the Evangelists. There were numerous learned men about the court, and the emperor encouraged public religious disputes between men of all religions. He was slightly inclined to Christianity, being struck with the beauty and purity of the faith.

Reforms.—In his dealings with the Hindus he was indulgent; but insisted always on the abolition of certain of the more prominent abuses, such as "*suttee*," or the burning of widows on their husband's funeral pyre, and others. He abolished the "*jezia*" or capitation tax, which every Hindu had been compelled to pay to the Mussulman Government; and he ordered that henceforth, in war, prisoners should never be enslaved.

Revenue System.—His revenue system was a great success. Shortly, the scheme was as follows.

In collection of revenue from cultivators there are three necessary preliminaries:—

1. To get a correct measurement of the land.
2. To ascertain the produce of each separate "*bigah*," and hence the amount it ought to pay to the government.
3. To settle the equivalent of this amount in money.

To obtain the first, Akber established an uniform standard of measurement, and had a regular survey system set on foot.

For the second,—He divided the land into three different classes, according to their varying degrees of fertility. Then, for each bigah, the average yield of its class was taken, and the king's share was made at one-third of this amount in kind.

For the third,—Regular statements of prices over all the country for nineteen years were taken, and the average was the amount demanded in coin.

He took care at the same time to guard against the abuse of power by petty officials.

The result of this system was to decrease the amount of revenue actually derived, but at the same time to lessen the expenses of collection; and hence the same net revenue was obtained in a manner pleasing to the people, and calculated to afford them a grateful conviction of settlement and security. At the same time Akber abolished the custom of farming the revenues, which had given rise to so much cruelty and extortion.

The author and completer of this fine system was the celebrated Rajah Toder Mull, the finance minister.

Division of the Empire.—The empire was divided into fifteen provinces, the chief officer in each being called the "Viceroy."

Justice.—Justice was administered by a "*Mir Adel*," or Lord Chief Justice, and by a "*Cazi*;" the latter representing the law, and stating the case after full trial; the former, representing the will of the sovereign, hearing the conclusion and passing sentence. Akber also reformed the code of punishments, founding them partly on Mahomedan custom, and partly on the laws of Menu.

The Army.—The pay system in the army had fallen into great confusion, and Akber stopped the abuses by paying the troops regularly from the treasury, and keeping lists of all the soldiers enrolled in each regiment.

The Court.—He kept his household and court in great splendour, and as became an emperor of such dignity. And with the desire to beautify his city, he filled Delhi with magnificent monuments and public buildings. The city must at this period have been one of the largest and handsomest in the world. It is said to have measured 30 miles in circumference.

In fine, Akber lived with all tho splendour of an Asiatic prince, but personally was simple, methodical, and of frugal habits.

(V.)—*Reign of Jehangir*, 1605—1627.

Prince Selim, the only surviving son of the deceased emperor, succeeded him, under the lofty title of "*Jehangir*," or "conqueror of the world."

At his accession Hindostan was quiet, but in the Deckan there were disturbances, and the war with Oodipore was proceeding. Jehangir commenced wisely, by confirming all his father's chief officers in their posts, and making some useful reforms; restoring the Mahomedan faith as the established church, and declaring his intention to maintain the law as heretofore.

Rebellion and Defeat of Prince Khusru.—His son, Prince Khusru, with whom he had so violently quarrelled, went off to Delhi and Lahore (the emperor being at Agra), and raised the standard of revolt. He was pursued, defeated, and imprisoned; and the emperor barbarously caused 700 of his followers to be impaled on spikes, and his son to be then paraded between these ghastly rows. The horrible sight nearly killed the unfortunate prince

Malik Amber.—In 1610 Jehangir sent out two armies, one to the Deckan, another to Oodipore. The first was destined for the defeat of Malik Amber, the able and resolute minister of the young king of Ahmednuggur, who had removed the site of his government to Aurangabad, and now seized the ancient capital, defeating the Mogul garrison which had been left there by Akber. The army of the Deckan commanded by Prince Parviz, being joined by another Mogul army from Guzerat under Abdullah Khan, advanced against Malik Amber; but that clever general, knowing his weakness in the field, so wore out the Moguls by constant harassing without coming to an engagement, and by cutting off their supplies, that it was nearly seven years before he could be defeated; and even then it was the desertion of his allies, not an open fight, which ruined him. The cause of this defection was the arrival of Prince Khurram, known as "*Shah Jehan*," the king's third son, to take command of the armies, and, since he was notoriously a good general, his enemies became disheartened.

In 1611 Jehangir married Nur Jehan, whose power over him became immense.

Nur Jehan.—Her history is a very curious one. She was the daughter of an emigrant from Persia; and was born at Candahar, at a time when, from various misfortunes, her father's fortunes seemed at the lowest ebb. He had not the smallest means at his command, and sold his daughter to a caravan. A wealthy merchant in this party educated and took care of her, at the same time treating kindly her miserable parents. They were placed in some small government office, and rose to power. Nur Jehan was excessively beautiful, and as her mother had free access to the harem the girl was observed by Prince Selim, who fell in love with her. She was then forced to marry a Persian of good family, and sent to Bengal. Selim wrote to the Viceroy of that province to obtain for him the wife of this officer, and the Viceroy, demanding this gift, was instantly murdered by the incensed husband. The attendants stabbed the murderer to the heart, and carried Nur Jehan to Delhi. She for a long time repelled Selim's advances, but when he became emperor she publicly married him. Henceforth her will was law.

Reduction of Oodipore and Marwar.—In 1612 Khurran, whom we shall hereafter term Shah Jéhan, conquered Oodipore, and reduced Marwar.

Sir Thomas Roe at Delhi.—In 1615, an Englishman appeared for the first time at the court of Delhi,—Sir Thomas Roe, who went on an embassy from James the First concerning the then embryo "East India Company." Two of the emperor's nephews embraced Christianity in 1618.

Jehangir now nominated Shah Jehan as his successor, excluding his eldest son, Khusru, in prison, and his second, Parviz, as incompetent. He made Shah Jehan Viceroy of Guzerat, and sent him against Malik Amber, who had again risen in arms.

Khusru died, 1621, in prison.

Shah Jehan Banished.—In that year Nur Jehan, finding Shah Jehan a somewhat unmanageable step-son, persuaded Jehangir to send him to Candahar, in order that he might be absent from Delhi, while she secured the succession to the throne for her favourite son, Prince Parviz. Shah Jehan had reached Mandu, on the Vindhya mountains, before he perceived the reason for his dismissal. He hesitated to leave India, and sent to Delhi, refusing to proceed unless some security was afforded to him. Jehangir, persuaded that he was rebellious, removed him from his command in Candahar, and ordered him to the Deckan; sending Mohabat Khan, a general in great favour with Nur Jehan, to see these commands carried out. The prince then advanced in a hostile attitude to Agra, but altering his mind, crossed the Nerbudda to Burhampore. Thence he marched to Masulipatam, and, in 1624, took Bengal and Behar. He was attacked and defeated by Mohabat Khan, and fled for aid to Malik Amber, who joyfully received him, But failing in some sieges, and worn out by his exertions and his defeats, Shah Jehan sent to the emperor offering submission, which, being accepted, he returned to Delhi.

Mohabat Khan's Rebellion.—Soon afterwards Mohabat Khan came in for a share of Nur Jehan's kind attentions, he, in some way unknown, having offended her. He was summoned back to court from the Deckan, and, on arriving, was so coldly received by the emperor that in high dudgeon he retired, Jehangir was on the point of undertaking a journey to Cabul, and he forced the general to accompany him; but behaved towards him with such harshness that Mohabat, in a frenzy of rage, seized an opportunity one day when all the imperial troops had crossed the Hydaspes and the emperor remained behind, to seize the sacred person of the "conqueror of the world," and carry him off captive to his own camp. Nur Jehan at once crossed the river and attacked Mohabat, but was defeated with heavy loss; after which, finding it impossible to effect anything by force, and confident of her own powers of intrigue, the empress made an appearance of submission, and joined her husband in his captivity.

Mohabat carried the royal captives about with him in camp for some time, treating them with distinction; while Nur Jehan succeeded in getting a large body of adherents around her, by making them enlist one by one in Mohabat's army. Then, at a grand review that was held, Jehangir by her instructions cantered away from the staff that surrounded the general, and, approaching a body of troops composed entirely of his own followers, was at once surrounded and rescued by them (1627).

Mohabat was forgiven, and sent against Shah Jehan; but fraternized with the latter as soon as they met.

Death of Jehangir.—The same year Jehangir died on a journey to Lahore, October 28, 1627.

(VI.)—*Reign of Shah Jehan*, 1627—1658.

Asof Khan had been left governor of Delhi, and hearing of the emperor's death he at once sent for Shah Jehan, who arrived accompanied by Mohabat Khan soon after. He was crowned with immense pomp at Agra,[1] and Nur Jehan, much to her annoyance, was compelled to retire into private life.

Revolt of Khan Jehan Lodi.—An affair of some importance now occurred which kept the emperor engaged for three years. One of Prince Parviz's generals, Khan Jehan Lodi, revolted and joined the armies of Malik Amber's son; that chieftain being dead. He was promised forgiveness and on those terms returned to Delhi. But becoming distrustful of the emperor, he fled to the Chambal River, and there engaged the royal troops; but was defeated, and crossing the river, fled through Bundelcund to Ahmednuggur. Here he remained till 1629.

In that year Shah Jehan took the field against the rebel in person, and went to the Deckan. At Burhampore he found his enemy, and drove him to Ahmednuggur. Advancing, he fought him step by step, the Lodi retreating in good order, as far as Bijapore. At this place Khan Jehan hoped to be safe under the protection of his good friend Mohammed Adil Shah. But the latter, seeing a fine large fighting army coming up behind, refused the chief admission; so he fled to Malwa, and there, while trying to force his way into Bundelcund, was defeated and slain.

The emperor marched in triumph to revenge his losses on Ahmednuggur; and next year, while the royal armies were investing Ahmednuggur, Fatteh Shah, the treacherous minister of the king of that city, murdered his master, and gave up the place to Shah Jehan.

Unsuccessful attempts against Bijapore.—The emperor then marched on Bijapore, which was invested closely; Asof Khan directing the siege. But with such energy and perseverance was the defence carried on that the Mogul armies, worn out with their long toil, left the city uncaptured.

Shah Jehan returned to Delhi, leaving Mohabat Khan commanding in the Deckan. This general was notably unsuccessful,

[1] It is said that the magnificent ceremonials held on this occasion cost as much as £1,600,000 in English money.

and in 1634 was recalled, after having in vain besieged Bijapore. Next year the emperor in person took command of the besieging forces, but with equal want of success; and in 1636 he made peace with the king, giving him the territories of Ahmednuggur, which state was thus for ever extinguished as an independent sovereignty. Bijapore had held out against a constant siege for six years; and at the end, its king, Mohammed Adil Shah, could boast that he had foiled the endeavours of the whole army of the Moguls.

Balkh taken.—In 1637, Shah Jehan went on an expedition to Cabul; and gave Ali Merdan Khan, (governor of the new Mogul province of Candahar, which had been taken in 1594 from the Persians by Akber), and his own son Morad, the command of an army to operate against Balkh. They were completely successful and annexed that province in 1646.

Balkh was entrusted to the government of Aurangzebe, the emperor's third son. He was besieged therein by the Uzbeks in 1647, was defeated, and obliged to fly with great loss and with much difficulty into India.

And retaken.—Then the Persians under Shah Abbas took advantage of this to invade and retake Candahar (1648). Aurangzebe was sent to recover this province, but the enemy cut off his supplies and he had to retire to Cabul. In 1652, another attempt to recover Candahar failed; and in 1653, Dara Sheko, the king's eldest son, failed also in a final attack. The Moguls then retired, and Candahar became once more Persian.

This was followed by two years of tranquillity, at the end of which the Mogul armies were again in the Deckan, owing to the application of Mir Jumla, vizier at Golconda, who had been threatened with death by his master, the Rajah Abdullah Khan. The emperor seized this excuse with readiness, and Aurangzebe took possession of Hyderabad, and besieged Golconda, when Abdullah Khan came to terms with much humility, promising to pay £1,000,000 sterling annually as a tribute.

Shah Jehan's illness.—Aurangzebe was hastily recalled to Delhi, by hearing that Shah Jehan was excessively ill, and for the next year and a half the country was harassed by a civil war, ending in the deposition of the emperor.

Intrigues for the succession.—Shah Jehan had four sons,—Dara Sheko, Shuja, Aurangzebe, and Morad. Dara, now Viceroy, was a bold, frank, and high-spirited prince: Shuja, Governor of Bengal, voluptuous and impulsive; Aurangzebe, calculating and cold; while Morad, the youngest, Governor of Guzerat, was brave and generous, but not gifted with great powers of mind.

Aurangzebe aimed at the sovereignty, and as he perceived religion to be the great motive power of the empire, he applied himself to gain popularity by assuming the character of champion of Islam.

Rebellion of the princes.—During his illness the emperor entrusted the affairs of the government to his eldest son, Dara. Thereupon Shuja rebelled and marched to Behar; and Morad who was in Guzerat raised his standard and laid siege to Surat. Aurangzebe behaved with great caution. He left Dara Sheko and Shuja to weaken themselves by fighting, while with his army he marched to join Morad; declaring that though he was about to retire from the world into religious life, he would first help his young brother to gain the throne.

Shuja was defeated by Dara Sheko, and the Viceroy then attacked the combined armies of Aurangzebe and Morad. The allies beat the Imperialists; and Aurangzebe quieted any fears in his brother's mind by giving the latter all the praise, and assuming himself a humble position at his feet.

Next year, against the express wish of his father, Dara Sheko, took the field again. The armies met at Samaghur, near Agra, where a sanguinary battle was fought; in which, owing to the daring intrepidity of Morad, who, causing his elephant's feet to be chained so that it could not retreat, sustained without giving way innumerable terrific charges from the royal troops, the battle was won by the rebels. Dara Sheko fled to his father at Agra, and Aurangzebe advancing to the capital, placed the emperor and the heir apparent in prison in a secure spot within the palace. He then treacherously seized Morad and threw him into confinement in Selimghur, a fort on the river opposite Delhi, afterwards removing him in chains to the fortress of Gwalior. Aurangzebe thus remained master of the field, and at once proclaimed himself emperor, in the place of Shah Jehan, deposed. (1658.)

(Shah Jehan was the emperor who built the magnificent "*Taj Mahal*,"[1] at Agra. It was erected in memory of Mumtaz Mahal, his queen.)

[1] "'*Taj Mahal*,' is a corruption of Mumtaz Mahal, the name of Shah Jehan's queen, whose sepulchre it forms. It stands on a marble terrace over the Jumna, is flanked at a moderate distance by two mosques, and is surrounded by extensive gardens. The building itself on the outside is of

(VII.) *Reign of Aurangzebe and Rise of the Mahrattas* (1658—1707.)

Aurangzebe took the title of "Alamgir," but is more generally known by his own name.

Dara Sheko managed to escape, and fled to Lahore, where Soliman his son tried to join him, but was intercepted and kept prisoner at Sirinagar, the capital of Cashmir. Dara then fled to Sinde, while Shuja advanced on Delhi. Aurangzebe went to meet the latter, fought him at Cajwa, and defeated him in spite of the desertion during the battle of a body of imperial troops under the Rajah Jeswant Singh, who, on the defeat of Shuja, fled to Jodhpore.

Defeat and Death of Dara Sheko.—Soon Dara appeared again in the field, and was defeated at Ajmir. Then he fled successively to Ahmedabad, Cutch, Candahar, and Jun, in Sinde. At the latter place he was received with great warmth, and was rejoicing at his relief from the intense sufferings he had undergone, when the treacherous inhabitants came upon him, bound him hand and foot, and sent him to Delhi. Immediately on his arrival, Aurangzebe, against the wishes of the whole people, put him to death. The emperor behaved with cold brutality on this occasion, and the inhabitants of Delhi became riotous in favour of the real heir, but were suppressed by force.

Flight of Shuja.—In 1660 Prince Mohammed Sultan, son of Aurangzebe, and Mir Jumla, the late minister of Golconda, who had been advanced to high military command in the royal armies, went against Shuja, in Bengal. The commanders quarrelled with one another,[1] but the expedition was successful; for Shuja fled to Aracan, and was never again heard of.

white marble with a high cupola and four minarets. In the centre of the inside is a lofty hall of a circular form under a dome, in the middle of which is the tomb enclosed within an open screen of elaborate tracery, formed of marble and mosaics. The walls are of white marble with borders of a running pattern of flowers in mosaic. . . . . . The materials are lapis lazuli, jasper, heliotrope, or blood stone, a sort of golden stone (not well understood) with calcedony, and other agates, cornelians, jade, and various stones of the same description. . . . . . The mosaics of the Taj are said, with great probability, to be the work of Italians."—(Elphinstone.)

[1] Mohammed Sultan had revolted from Mir Jumla, and again returned to duty. For this breach of loyalty Aurangzebe kept his daring and ambitious son in prison for many years, till he was relieved by death.

Murder of Morad.—The same year the Rajah of Sirinagar, to propitiate Aurangzebe, sent Soliman, Dara Sheko's son, prisoner to Agra. Soliman *died* (?) soon after, somewhat suddenly, in prison, and at the same time Morad was murdered in cold blood.[1] Aurangzebe was thus left entire master of the situation. His father was in prison; the heir and his son both dead; and of his brothers, one dead, the other a fugitive.

The same year Mir Jumla, who had been made Vizier, died at Dacca, while on an expedition to Assam; and in his stead Mohammed Amir, his eldest son, was made minister.

We now come to the rise of that power which had most influence on the after history of the Hindu States of the Deckan, the *Mahrattas.*[2]

Rise of the Mahrattas.—One of the officers of Malik Amber, by name Maloji Bosla, had a son, Shahji, who married a daughter of Jadu Rao, an officer in high command. The issue of this marriage was a son, Sevaji, who from constant contact with the rude soldiers of his father's "*jagir,*"[3] acquired a love for wildness and robbery, which he early practised in company with his adherents. Sevaji commenced operations on a grander scale, by seizing a hill-fort belonging to his father, and thence ravaging the country round. Then he seized his father's own territory, and managed by stratagems of various kinds, but without bloodshed, to capture many other forts. Soon he began an open rebellion by seizing a convoy of royal treasure; and his lieutenant took prisoner the governor of the Concans, and occupied all his country, with its capital, Calian. Sevaji, after this success, thought himself justified in making overtures to Shah Jehan, and he was received not unfavourably. Afterwards he seized

[1] When Soliman was brought before the emperor, the latter professed great compassion for his nephew, and promised him kind treatment in his imprisonment; but as three of the young princes all died very shortly afterwards, and Morad was deliberately executed, it is believed Soliman was poisoned.

[2] The proper limits of the Mahratta country are defined by Elphinstone to be from the Sutpura mountains on the north, to Goa on the south; bounded by the Indian Ocean on the west, and a line drawn through Goa, Beder, Chanda on the River Warda, Nagpore, and the River Nerbudda.

[3] A "jagir," or "jaghire" was a tract of land given by the sovereign to an individual as a reward for distinguished merit.

the South Concan, and went on extending his authority till, in 1655, Aurangzebe was sent down by Shah Jehan to humble the pride of the Mahratta. Sevaji intrigued and cajoled till he was forgiven; and immediately on the departure of the imperial force, renewed his attacks on Bijapore. Afzul Khan, governor of Bijapore, was foolish enough to consent to a private interview with Sevaji, unattended, at which the Mahratta brutally murdered him with his own hand, and then defeated the panic-stricken army of the Khan. In 1660 an army was sent against the now numerous bands of Sevaji's followers, but in vain; and next year the new governor of Bijapore led a force to the Mahratta country. He defeated Sevaji, and in 1662 made a favourable peace with him, leaving the rebel secured in a jagir in the Concans.

Hostile Attitude of the Mahrattas.—It was now the year 1662, and Sevaji, discontented with the quiet possession of his own jagir, began ravaging the Mogul territory. Aurangzebe sent against him one of his generals, Shaista Khan, who marched from Aurangabad to Poonah, which he captured. Here he remained in winter quarters, and during his residence there, Sevaji in person came by night, and nearly succeeded in murdering the Khan, but he escaped. After the rains Shaista Khan went to Aurangabad, and at once Sevaji plundered Surat.

Sevaji Assumes the Title of Rajah.—In 1664, Shahji, who had acquired large territories in the East, died, and thus Sevaji became possessed of Tanjore and Madras in right of his father, as well as the Concans, which he himself had conquered.

After this he assumed the title of "Rajah of the Mahrattas" and plundered the country far and wide.

The Mahratta "Chout."—This so enraged the Emperor that an army was despatched in two divisions against him in 1665. Sevaji submitted, and a treaty was made by which he was given another jagir, consisting of twelve out of the thirty-two forts he had captured, with their territory. In addition, he was granted a sort of black-mail to be levied on all the Mogul land in the Deckan. It was called the "*chout;*" and was afterwards the Mahratta pretext for quarrelling with the nations surrounding them and encroaching on their territory.

Sevaji then went as a guest to Delhi, but was so coldly received that he returned to the Deckan in indignation (1666).

Death of Shah Jehan, 1666.—The same year the unfortunate Shah Jehan died in prison, where he had been pining for eight years, leaving Aurangzebe emperor in his own right.

Sevaji recognized as Rajah.—In 1667, Sevaji, by clever intrigues, succeeded in procuring a very favourable treaty with the emperor, having his title of "Rajah" recognized. He then overawed Bijapore and Golconda, and levied tribute on these countries.

By this time the new Rajah found his kingdom somewhat in disorder, and spent two years in arranging and settling it. The result showed great talent, and this being followed up by advantageous treaties with the Rajputs and other nations round, consolidated his power very effectually. It may therefore be taken that the Mahrattas actually became a nation, governed by an independent sovereign, in the year 1669.

Mahratta War.—War broke out again in 1670, commenced by a deliberate breach of the peace on the part of the indignant emperor. Sevaji was the first to commence operations by seizing Poonah, and plundering Surat and Candeish, while Moazzim, the emperor's son, remained inactive at Aurangabad. Mohabat Khan was sent from head-quarters, and engaged Sevaji in the field; but as he was terribly beaten, the emperor thought it better to recall the armies and suspend hostilities.

Decline of Aurangzebe's Influence.—Aurangzebe's power and influence began to wane at this period, for all parties were irritated with him. He had showed himself unequal to cope with the Mahrattas, and this incensed his soldiers, hitherto so uniformly victorious. He behaved with great hostility to the Hindus, reviving the "jezia," and persecuting them on all sides; and thus succeeded in creating disaffection amongst the greater part of his subjects. And to complete his difficulties he alienated to a man the finest soldiers in his army, the Rajputs, by his conduct to the widow and children of their great chief, the Rajah Jeswant Singh, who died in 1678.

Durga Das, the Rajah's son, plotted with Aurangzebe's son, Prince Akber, and marched against Delhi with 70,000 Rajputs. The combination was broken up by intrigue and defection, and the army disbanded before any action had been fought; Akber and Durga Das taking refuge with the Mahrattas under Sambaji, son of Sevaji.

In Mewar and Jodhpore the war was still carried on, both sides engaging in desultory and ineffectual combats, till a treaty was made in 1681.

Mahratta Successes.—Meantime, the Mahrattas, under Sevaji, had overrun the whole of the Deckan, seizing the Concans (1673), ravaging the Mogul provinces of Berar and Candeish (1674), capturing successively Kurnoul, Cuddapah,[1] Jinji, and Vellore (1677), Mysore and Tanjore (1678), and in 1680 making a dash at Bijapore, and cutting off the supplies of the Mogul army. On this expedition Sevaji died, and Sambaji, his son, took command of the Mahratta forces.

Sambaji becomes Rajah.—Sambaji was a cruel and debauched prince, and in character so different from the dashing and gallant Sevaji, that his power at once declined; and had the Moguls been commanded by a really good general, it is probable that the Mahratta power might never have survived the blow it sustained in the death of its founder.

In 1683, Sambaji defeated Prince Moazzim, who had been sent into the Concans; and the Mahrattas ravaged the country in the rear of the Mogul army, and burned the city of Burhampore.

Disturbed State of the Deckan.—Then the opposing forces parted company, Moazzim plundering Hyderabad, and making a treaty with the King of Golconda; while the Mahrattas, marching northwards, plundered Baroch. Afterwards Aurangzebe, heading another Mogul army, destroyed the city and Raj of Bijapore; and then treacherously broke the peace with Golconda and captured that city.

For some reason unknown, Aurangzebe now began to be afraid of his own sons. He was conscience-stricken at his own conduct to his father; and lived in such a continual state of agitation and fear that the peace of his life was destroyed, and he regarded everyone with suspicion and distrust. In 1687 this fear grew into a sort of madness, and, without the slightest provocation, he threw his eldest son, Moazzim, into prison, where he remained for seven years.

Continued Misfortunes.—From this period dates the fall of the Mogul empire; for the whole of Deckan was in a state of confusion, the native states were broken up, and the country covered with bodies of wild and undisciplined marauders, against whom no regular troops could act; the Mahrattas were a great power, and the tribes of the North, the Rajputs and Sikhs, were permanently alienated. A train of misfortunes ensued.

Death of Sambaji.—At first there was a gleam of hope, for

[1] In this year, 1677, he passed close to Madras, and the Englishmen in the factories there were thrown into the greatest terror by the presence of these dangerous warriors. (May, 1677. Madras Records.)

one day a Mogul officer named Tokarrab Khan, Governor of Colapore, near the Ghauts, hearing that Sambaji was on a hunting expedition near, and unguarded, managed to seize his person and send him prisoner to Aurangzebe, who at once had him beheaded (1689).

Sahoo Succeeds.—Sambaji's infant son Saho (or Sahoo), succeeded, and the regent was the bold and prudent Rajah Ram.

In 1692 the Regent re-organised the Mahratta predatory bands, and placing the chieftains Santaji and Danaji in command, sent them against the Mogul armies. They defeated the Imperial troops in a number of small engagements, and were universally successful for a period of five years, three of which were occupied by the siege of Jinji.

Siege of Jinji.—Jinji was occupied by the Mahrattas; and in 1694 Aurangzebe sent his general, Zulfikar Khan, to besiege that fort. Zulfikar Khan applied for reinforcements, but was refused, and Prince Cambaksh was sent to take superior command. This so incensed the general, that he resolved to spin out the siege in order to vex the emperor. He held constant communications with the Mahrattas; and thus three years passed in an ineffectual and weak attempt on the part of Cambaksh to take the place.

In 1697, Santaji came and succeeded in raising the siege, while the disaffection of the Mogul commander increased. But in 1698 Aurangzebe was so peremptory that Zulfikar Khan felt he must either take Jinji or be disgraced. He therefore permitted the Mahratta leader to escape, and then stormed the fort with the greatest ease.

Dissensions then began to arise amongst the Mahrattas, and Danaji brought matters to a crisis by murdering Santaji with his own hand.

Open hostilities soon commenced again; Rajah Ram taking the field, in person, at the head of a large army, and Aurangzebe himself leading the Moguls. The emperor, in 1700, took Sattara, and by 1704 had taken a great many Mahratta fortresses. Rajah Ram died the same year.

The emperor had now reached the age of 86; and though possessed of a fine constitution, he was worn down by mental anxieties, and constant fear and distrust of those around him, and the last four years of his life were, it is said, passed very miserably.

Decay of the Empire.—The whole government of the country was disorganized at this period. The Mahrattas began to recover their forts and multiply in number. A terrible famine exhausted the provisions for the troops, and drained the treasury. The soldiers became mutinous for want of pay; and as the Mahrattas were pressing him hard, the emperor was at his wit's end. He retreated to Ahmednuggur in great confusion and distress, and fell ill.

Death of the Emperor.—At his last agony he refused to let any of his sons approach his bed-side; and so died, with no hand near to comfort him, on Feb. 21st, 1707, at the age of 89.

His Character.—Aurangzebe was gifted with great talents, which he displayed in various ways. He was a poet in his way; and a wit, when he was in good spirits. In religion, a bigot; but in war, rather faint-hearted, and wanting in perseverance. Yet he could bear hardship with the bravest; and never flinched from his duty as a soldier, when adversity placed him on a level with those around him. He was wonderfully industrious and acute in planning campaigns; but when in the field seemed not to bear in mind with sufficient clearness the importance of his ultimate designs.

He was described as having "a cheerful, smiling countenance," and bearing his years with great, but unpretending dignity.

The name of Aurangzebe is, perhaps, somewhat better known in England than those of his illustrious predecessors, owing to the fact that under him arose the East India Company. He protected our traders, and allowed them to establish their factories at Madras, Bombay, and Calcutta: and their accounts of the splendour of the Oriental court, and the magnificence of the costumes of himself and his officers, reaching this country, caused all persons to revere the name of Aurangzebe as that of one of the noblest princes of the world. With how much truth, the readers of history will discover.

(VIII.)—*Successors of Aurangzebe to the Great Battle of Panipat, and the Extinction of the Mogul Sovereignty,* (1707—1761.)

Bahadur Shah, 1707—1712.—Prince Moazzim, as heir apparent, ascended the throne on his father's death, assuming the title of "*Bahadur Shah.*" At the same time Prince Azim, the second surviving son, had himself declared, but the emperor marched against him and defeated him, and the prince was killed in the battle. Cambaksh also refused to acknowledge Moazzim, and the latter therefore went against him. Cambaksh was defeated and slain while in flight.

Zulfikar Khan, and his father, Assad Khan, were well received at court.

The new emperor directed all his energies to weaken the power of the Mahrattas, which he cleverly and successfully accomplished by fomenting all the internal dissensions amongst the chiefs; finally forcing an unfavourable treaty upon them, when they were too feeble to resist his demands.

He also made favourable treaties with the Rajput states of Oodipore, Marwar, and Jeypore, in the year 1709.

Rise of the Sikhs.—The "Sikhs" were a religious body of deistical Hindus who arose in the north in the time of Akber; that emperor being, as before said, tolerant to all religious movements. Their founder's name was Nanak. Formed into a sect, and directed by their Gooroos, or spiritual chiefs, they remained quietly worshipping God after their own fashion till the Mussulmans persecuted them, and in 1606 put their leader to death. The Sikhs then became possessed with a fanatical hatred for everything Mahomedan; and, forming themselves into a military power under the direction of the celebrated Gooroo Govind, they overran the Punjaub, and by 1711 had become exceedingly turbulent and troublesome.

In that year Bahadur Shah made an expedition against them and drove them to the hills.

Death of Bahadur Shah.—The next year (1712), the emperor died, at the age of 72; and after a great deal of fighting, and many murders, his son Jehander Shah succeeded in securing the throne.

Jehandur Shah, 1712—1713.—Jehandur Shah made Zulfikar Khan his minister; but the choice was not good, for the minister treated his master with supreme contempt; increased by the emperor's foolish conduct in raising slaves to the posts formerly held by nobles.

In 1713, the emperor's nephew, Farokshir, revolted in Bengal, and defeating the Imperial armies near Agra, put both Jehander Shah and Zulfikar Khan to death.

Farokshir, 1713—1719.—Farokshir at once found himself in the difficult circumstances so often attendant on the mode of succession he had adopted, caused by the high-toned pretensions of those who had principally assisted him to attain the throne. In this case there were two principal nobles, Seiad Abdullah and Seiad Hosen, who compelled the emperor by force to elevate them to lofty positions in his court, and he was ever afraid of them.

Quarrels at Court.—Hosen went to the Deckan, and the emperor secretly instigated Daud, Governor of that province, to oppose him. Daud obeyed, and gave open battle to Hosen, but was killed at the moment of victory.

Hosen then went against the Mahrattas, but failed to make any progress and finally made peace with young Rajah Sahoo. Farokshir considered the treaty a disgraceful one, and refused to ratify it.

In 1715 the viceroy of Bengal so persecuted the factories of the English at Calcutta, that the latter sent a mission to the emperor, attended by a clever surgeon, Mr. Hamilton. When the deputation arrived at Delhi, Farokshir was seriously ill, and Mr. Hamilton, seizing the opportunity, effected a complete cure. The emperor, out of gratitude, made a present of thirty-eight villages to the company, and granted them an immunity from tax.

Murder of the Emperor.—Meanwhile great dissensions had arisen between the emperor and Seiad Abdullah. They mutually quarrelled, and plotted, and intrigued; and at last Farokshir and a body of confederates determined to put Abdullah to death. The emperor's irresolution and folly, however, disgusted the conspirators, and they disclosed all to Abdullah, who summoned Hosen from the Deckan to protect him. The Seiad arrived, entered the city, penetrated the mysteries of the seraglio within the palace, and assassinated the emperor with his own hand (1719.)

The rebel nobles, in two months, raised up and deposed two petty princes; and finally fixed upon a prince of the royal blood, by name Mohammed Shah, to succeed.

Mohammed Shah, 1719—1748.—Immediately on Mohammed Shah's accession, several revolts took place. Asof Jah,[1] governor of Malwa, threw off all submission in 1720, and defeated the

[1] Asof Jah's real name was Chin Killich Khan. He was son of a Turki noble, Ghazi-u-din, a favourite officer of Aurangzebe, and soon rose to importance, being made governor of the Deckan, and afterwards of Malwa. He was also called "Nizam-al-Mulkh," and his descendants became "Nizams of the Deckan."

imperial troops, commanded by the Seiads, at Burhampore and Ballapore. The emperor was overjoyed at the discomfiture of the formidable Seiads, and soon afterwards had the hardihood to make Asof Jah vizier. He would have done well had not the emperor found him too active, and taken a dislike to him, when the vizier sent in his resignation (1723) and retired to the Deckan.

Seiad Hosen was murdered by a Calmuck, who, it is believed, acted under orders from the emperor; and Abdullah, attempting to set up a new emperor, was defeated and imprisoned.

At this period the Rajputs wrested Guzerat from the empire.

In 1725 Mohammed Shah instigated Mobariz, governor of Hyderabad, to take active measures against Asof Jah; but the latter defeated the governor, slew him, and sent his head to the emperor at Delhi.

The great disturbances amongst the Mahrattas which ensued drew off the emperor's attention from his refractory subject.

Mahratta Disturbances.—Sahoo, the Rajah, had consolidated his empire by the wisdom of Balaji Wiswanath,[1] his active and clever minister, or "Peshwa." Balaji died in 1720, and was succeeded by Baji Rao,[2] his son, who was exceedingly energetic and ambitious, counselling Sahoo to strike at the Mogul empire itself. Sahoo, never an active prince, committed all power to Baji Rao, who ravaged Malwa, and then invaded Asof Jah at Hyderabad, defeating him signally in 1722.

Baji Rao next ravaged Guzerat, and afterwards settled the country with great wisdom and moderation.

The leaders of the Mahratta armies at this time were the founders of the three great families of the Deckan, namely, Udaji Puar, Malhar Holkar, and Ranaji Sindia.

In 1733 Baji Rajo and Asof Jah made a secret compact to support one another; and by the next year the Mahrattas had captured Malwa and Bundelcund. The emperor, alarmed, conceded the Mahrattas their conquered districts, and gave them a right to levy "chout" on Asof Jah's dominions. This at once broke up the secret alliance, and Asof returned to his allegiance.

[1] This chieftain was the first "Peshwa," a name given to the minister of the Mahratta Rajah. The Peshwas afterwards seized all the real power; while the royal family lived quietly at Sattara, sinking into insignificance, and becoming in time merely "Rajahs of Sattara."

[2] Baji Rao was the greatest of the Peshwas, and the ablest head of the Mahrattas except Sevaji.

In 1737 Baji Rao ravaged the country of the Jumna, and appeared suddenly before Delhi, but retired without attacking. Asof Jah marched against him, was defeated near Bhopal, and forced to cede all the country between the Nerbudda and the Chambal to the Mahrattas.

Rise of Nadir Shah.—A still more formidable opponent now appeared in the north, namely, the great Nadir Shah, who invaded India from Persia. He had been a freebooter who, with a few followers, had joined the exiled Shah of Persia, Tahmasp, when he was driven out by the Khiljies. Nadir assisted Tahmasp to regain his throne, and then, ousting him, seized it for himself. He pushed his arms into Cabul and Candahar, and afterwards began his invasion of India.

Nadir Shah's Invasion of India.—In 1739 Nadir Shah seized Lahore, and defeated Mohammed Shah at Carnal. The emperor submitted and allowed his conqueror to accompany him to Delhi. But the Hindus at Delhi, incensed at this show of weakness, murdered numbers of Persians in the city; and the Persians, in retaliation, committed a wholesale massacre of Hindus.

The rapacity and violence of Nadir Shah were beyond equal, and he returned to Persia in 1740, laden with treasures, and leaving the Mogul empire tottering to its fall.

Immediately on the departure of the Persians the Mahrattas resumed the offensive, but the Peshwa, Baji Rao, died suddenly (1740). His son and successor, Balaji Rao, marched into Malwa in 1743, and renewed his demands on the court of Delhi. The emperor gave him Malwa, which had belonged to Raguji Khan, who had revolted. Balaji beat Raguji, and drove him off, after which he retired to Sattara (1744).

Asof Jah died in 1748; and the next year saw a new sovereign on the throne of Sevaji by the death of the Rajah Sahoo. Balaji placed Ram Rajah,—grandson of Ram Rajah the elder and his wife, Tara Bye,—on the throne, and at once assumed the reins of government.

1st Invasion of Ahmed Khan Durani.—In 1747 Nadir Shah was murdered; and the Afghan tribe of "Abdali," or "Durani" (as it was afterwards called, and by which it is better known), under Ahmed Khan, seized the Punjaub, but was beaten by Mohammed's son Ahmed.

Next year the emperor died (1748) rather suddenly, and was succeeded by his son.

Ahmed Shah, 1748—1754.—Mohammed's son, Ahmed Shah, succeeded in 1748. He soon found it necessary to deal with the "Rohillas," who were Afghans of Oude, and became very formidable; but it was in vain that he tried to subdue them. They penetrated to Allahabad, and the vizier, Sufder Jung, called in the aid of the Mahrattas against them. They were then repelled, and the Mahratta leaders, Sindia and Holkar, were rewarded with jagirs.

2nd Invasion of Ahmed Khan Durani.—In 1753 Ahmed Khan Durani invaded the Punjaub, which was quietly ceded to him; and he then assumed the title of "Shah."

In 1754 Ghazi-u-din, the eldest son of Asof Jah, with whom the emperor had quarrelled, seized his monarch, put out his eyes, and deposed him.

Alamgir the Second, 1754—1759.—Ghazi-u-din at once proclaimed one of the princes of the blood royal emperor, by the name of Alamgir the Second, and made himself minister. He governed execrably, and the people made several attempts to murder him.

Ahmed Shah Durani at Delhi.—In 1756 the vizier foolishly seized, in the most treacherous manner, a son of Ahmed Shah Durani, who, in great indignation, came down and sacked Delhi, retiring in 1757.

Ghazi then called in the Mahrattas, and by their aid retook Delhi.

In 1758 the Mahratta leader, Raghoba, took the Punjaub from Ahmed Shah Durani; and made a conspiracy with the deceitful Ghazi-u-din to reduce the whole of Hindostan under Mahratta rule.

The Mogul Empire extinguished.—In 1759 Alamgir, the last Mogul emperor with any real sovereignty, was murdered by Ghazi-u-din.

The sequel of this was disastrous, and completed the destruction of the Mogul empire; for Sedasheo Bhao, a Mahratta chieftain, then commanding the armies of the Peshwa, made great preparations for the conquest of Delhi, and marched northwards with that object.

He took the capital in 1760.

Immediately they heard of this, the Afghan leaders in Oude, under the orders of Ahmed Shah Durani, crossed the Jumna, though it was in the rains, while Sedasheo Bhao entrenched himself at Panipat; and thus were drawn up, face to face, two gigantic armies of invaders, each bent on the conquest of the capital of India, which was helplessly awaiting the result.

3rd Battle of Panipat, January 6th, 1761.—Both armies remained in entrenched camps, constantly harassing one another, and cutting off their supplies. The Mahrattas suffered severely from starvation and disease, and were in a pitiful state, when, on January 6th, 1761, the chiefs informed Sedasheo that they could wait no longer, and that he must at once give battle, or the army would disperse.

He accordingly marched out. The battle was furious, and was inclining to the side of the Mahrattas, when Ahmed Shah Durani ordered his own centre to charge, and his left to wheel up and attack the enemy's right flank. The movement was decisive. The Mahrattas fled in disorder, with their army almost annihilated. The dead were counted at 200,000 (so it is said), and the wreck of their host retired beyond the Nerbudda.

Ahmed Shah's own force was so shattered in the mighty contest that he retired to the Punjaub without making any profit out of his victory.

Delhi was deserted, because there was no one to govern it; the governments all around were shattered; and the Mahrattas had received a blow from which they never recovered.

And thus, in darkness and desolation, the last dying embers of the once magnificent empire of the Moguls were extinguished!

During the last twenty years the East India Company had been growing in importance and strength, and the armies of the English were in the south fighting battles and fortifying their factories. The year previous to the great battle of Panipat they had driven the French out of the south.

The complete story of their progress has been reserved for another part, as I have thought it best to keep the account of their transactions distinct from that of the Mogul empire, with which they at present came but little in direct contact.

CONTENTS OF PART III.

PART III.

THE ENGLISH IN INDIA TO THE DOWNFALL OF THE MAHRATTAS IN 1823.

(I)—*Early History of the East India Company.*

At the close of the fifteenth century the great adventurer, Vasco de Gama, after having discovered the sea-passage to India, returned to Europe; and excited the envy and astonishment of all persons by his accounts of the wealth, luxury, and magnificence of the Oriental Court, and of the abundance and fertility of the Mogul Empire. His own countrymen were the first to profit by his intrepidity, and Portuguese colonies of merchants were established at Goa, Bombay, and Point de Galle in Ceylon.

About a century later the Dutch followed their example, and obtained a settlement near the present city of Calcutta.

The "London East India Company, 1600."—Five years afterwards, namely in the year 1600, a number of English merchants in the city of London, desirous of emulating the fortunes of the Portuguese and Dutch, carried a petition before Queen Elizabeth praying for permission to constitute themselves an incorporated company for the purpose of prosecuting the trade with the East in silks, cottons, and precious stones. Her Majesty granted them a charter, which was issued December 30th, 1600.

This, then, is the date of the first establishment of the English as traders in India. It was the same year that Akber took Ahmednuggur from Chand Sultana, and five years previous to his death.

The Company was incorporated under the title of "The London East India Company," and was to be managed by "a governor and twenty-four committees."[1]

Their first ships sailed in 1601.

[1] "Committee" was here used in the sense of *member*. The whole body were twenty-five in number.

The Emperor Jehangir granted these merchants a trading port at Surat in 1613, by firman; and two years later, permitted Sir Thomas Roe to come to Delhi on an embassy. This was the first Englishman who had appeared at the imperial court, and the curiosity on both sides was great. He found an unexpected enemy at head-quarters in the person of the heir apparent, Shah Jehan, who tried, happily in vain, to frustrate the succees of the mission.

In 1624 "The Company applied by petition to the King (James I.), for authority to punish their servants abroad by martial as well as by municipal law. It appears not that any difficulty was experienced in obtaining their request, or that any Parliamentary proceeding for transferring unlimited power over the lives and fortunes of the citizens, was deemed even a necessary ceremony."[1] This, therefore, was the first judicial authority given by the Crown to the Company. It extended only over European British subjects.

In 1634 the first factory was established in Bengal by the firman of Shah Jehan, then on the throne; and in 1639 the English were allowed to trade at Madras.[2]

The "Merchant Adventurers," 1659.—Twenty years later, after an enjoyment of fifty years exclusive trade, the Company's monopoly was imperilled by the formation of a new society in England, incorporated under the title of "The Merchant Adventurers." After hot debates in their councils, the old Company thought it better to permit the new comers to be incorporated with them than to run the chance of having their earnings beaten down by competition in the Indian market. This was done in 1661.

Next year our "merry monarch," Charles the Second, was wedded to the daughter of the King of Portugal; and as part of her dower, the fine trading port of Bombay was given over to the English, and became a crown possession. The king gave it to the East India Company in 1668.[3]

[1] Mill's "History of British India," vol. ii. p. 58.

[2] At Madras there is nothing approaching to a harbour, and the only reason for which the site was chosen seems to have been that the merchants found there a fine shelving sandy beach, where the flat-bottomed "Masoolah boats" could easily land bales of goods in spite of the dangerous surf.

[3] In this year the first order for tea (then called and spelt "*tchay*," after the Chinese), was sent from England to Madras.

Soon afterwards, Charles the Second granted to the Company that celebrated charter, the climax of monopoly doctrines, empowering the traders belonging to the Company in India to imprison and send to England any unlicensed person whom they found there trading on his own account! The same charter gave the governors of the principal forts power to administer English law to all the English members of the society there.

In the year 1682 the Court of Directors at home constituted Bengal into a separate presidency,[1] having a governor and council residing at Calcutta. This arrangement did not last long, for six years later, Charnock, the founder of the present capital city of India, was driven out of Bengal by the Moguls, and sailed down the river with the ousted merchants in terrible fear for his life. They returned after two years of exile (in 1690), by permission of Aurangzebe; and Charnock established a permanent settlement in Calcutta, erecting forts and planting garrisons.

A few years previous to their return, James the Second, in England, confirmed a charter drawn up by his predecessor, which appointed courts of equity in the Presidency towns under the guidance of "one learned lawyer, and two substantial merchants."

In 1698, the emperor, Aurangzebe, permitted the Company to purchase the three villages of Calcutta, Chutternutty, and Govindpore, which were then fortified by the English.[2]

The "English East India Company," 1698.—In the same year a new company was formed in England by the charter of 9 & 10 William and Mary, which gave power to any number of persons to combine and open commerce with the East Indies on a loan of two millions, at eight per cent; the subscribers to trade, but their exports not to exceed individually the amount of their separate shares of the loan. This company was called "The English East India Company." It was nearly ruined two years afterwards by a costly and utterly useless embassy which was despatched by its order to the emperor, with Sir William Norris at the head of affairs.

[1] It must be remembered that in those days a "presidency" meant only the few factories and trading marts scattered throughout a province. There was then nothing approaching to the large tracts of subject country now known as Presidencies. The first Governor of Calcutta was Mr. Hedges.

[2] Sir Charles Eyre, then chief agent, named the new fortifications "Fort William," in honour of King William the Third. All public documents are still drawn up under the title of "Fort William, in Bengal."

"The United Company," 1702.—Finally, in the year 1702, the old "London" Company was incorporated with the new one; and so from this year there existed only one company of Anglo-Indians, which assumed the title of "The United Company of merchants trading to the East Indies."

In this same year the Emperor Aurangzebe appointed one Mir Jaffier to be Dewan [1] of Bengal, and Subahdar of Bengal, Behar, and Orissa, under the title of "Moorshed Koolee Khan," by which name he is best known. This man, having conceived a great hatred for the adventurous English, interfered with their trade, and maintained a system of petty persecution so incessant that in 1715 the President sent a mission to the Emperor Farokshir to complain of his conduct. It has been previously narrated how the emperor was at that time very ill—how the English surgeon travelling with the embassy cured him—and how, in gratitude, Farokshir gave the English merchants a noble present of thirty-eight towns, and an immunity from tax (under a "dustuck" or official pass for each bale of goods, saving it from examination by the officials.)

Moorshed Koolee Khan was a very energetic revenue officer, and managed, by unscrupulous systems of extortion and oppression, to create a large surplus out of the revenues of Bengal, which was punctually remitted to Delhi. He divided the province into "*chuklas,*" the chief collector in each being an officer appointed by himself, who farmed the revenue. These officers managed afterwards to constitute their posts hereditary; and then, claiming the title of "*Zemindari Rajahs*" were exceedingly troublesome to the government. Their tenure seemed so secure, yet so completely without foundation, that to the present day it has been found impossible to give them any definite status beyond that granted to them by Lord Cornwallis.

The Subahdar died in 1725, and was succeeded in the Bengal and Orissa appointments by his son-in-law, Shuja-u-din.

Next year, 1726, the "Ostend East India Company," who had

[1] The "Dewan" of a province was an officer of the Mogul Government whose duties were to superintend the collection of revenue and try all civil causes arising within the boundaries of his province. The "Subahdar" was the viceroy of the district; and, as in this case, the two offices were often combined in one person.

[2] The chief civil court in a district was called the "Dewani Adalat;" and the chief criminal court the "Nizamat Adalat," (the "Nizam" being the chief criminal judge.)

been established at a village called Bankibazar, on the Hooghley, by the Emperor of Germany, became so troublesome to the other companies that they united together and drove the interlopers entirely out of Bengal. Three different nations were then left trading on the Hooghley; the English at Calcutta, the French at Chandanagore, and the Dutch at Chinsurah.

This year (1726) George the First established in each Presidency town "Mayor's courts," consisting of a mayor and nine aldermen, to try all civil suits within their jurisdiction. From these there was an appeal to the President in Council: and in cases where the value of the property disputed exceeded one thousand pagodas, to the King in Council. The same charter gave to the Presidency towns courts of "Oyer and terminer," and invested the mayor, aldermen, and councillors with all powers of Justices of the Peace, having authority to hold courts of quarter sessions.

Hence, in the year 1726, all the English common and statute law was extended to India. And all English law now in force in British India bears date back to this year, except in so far as it may have been altered by special regulations.

In the year 1730, the position of the Company at home was very precarious; for a new society, formed on Free-trade principles, earnestly begged a charter from Parliament. At the same time the old company prayed for a renewal of their monopoly charter, as their period of incorporation had expired. And thus there ensued numerous hard fought battles in Parliament between the monopolists, fighting for their lives, and the Free-traders eager for fresh fortunes. Happily for the former, but perhaps unfortunately for the trade of England, the principle of monopoly still held its own, and the charter of the existing company was renewed till 1766.

Ten years later Shuja-u-din, the Subahdar, died, and was succeeded by Aliverdi Khan, the Governor of Behar, who thus reunited the three provinces of Bengal, Behar, and Orissa. He was attacked the next year by the Mahrattas, under the following circumstances.

Baji Rao, the Mahratta Peshwa, had attained great power,[1] having at the head of his armies the three celebrated leaders, Puar, Holkar, and Sindia, and one powerful adventurer named Roghoji Bhonslay. At the time of the Peshwa's death, in 1740,

[1] See pages 69-70.

this adventurer had attained a power and independence so great that the other leaders were united in a private compact to crush him, and he was sent on an expedition to the Carnatic.

The Peshwa left three sons, Balaji Rao, who succeeded him; Roghoonath Rao, afterwards the celebrated "Raghoba;" and another named Shumshere Bahadur, who ruled in Bundelcund. The grants of land which the new Peshwa received brought him into direct opposition to Bhonslay, who thereupon invaded Bengal, but was beaten by the Royal troops.

These hostile occurrences in his own territories forced Aliverdi Khan to assume a powerful defensive against the Mahrattas of either side, and he was reinforced by a body of Imperial troops. Matters came to a crisis, when one Bhaskur, an officer of Balaji Rao, attacked the Subahdar with great success, and pursued him, fighting every foot of ground, to Cutwa. The victor then advanced to the Hooghley, and plundered a factory at Moorshedabad.

Upon this, the English merchants asked for and obtained permission from Aliverdi Khan to surround their territory with an entrenchment, and dug the celebrated "*Mahratta Ditch*," in 1742.

Bhaskur was assassinated by Aliverdi Khan in 1744, and the Mahrattas then retired into the Deckan.

They were bought off by Aliverdi Khan a few years later, and did not again trouble our settlements on the Hooghley.

It is necessary to understand the internal constitution and working of the East India Company, before we pass on to the history of the great revolution they so gallantly effected in India.

(II.)—*Constitution of the Company.*

Courts of Proprietors.—The members of the Company, who had embarked their fortunes as subscribers or shareholders, to the amount of £500 and upwards, were called "Proprietors of the Company's stock."[1] The general meetings of the entire body were therefore called "Courts of Proprietors." They nominally governed themselves and their affairs, by delegating their powers of management to a chairman and body of directors,

[1] Proprietors of £500 stock were permitted to be present, but had no vote in the courts. £1,000 conferred one vote; £3,000, two; £6,000 three; and £10,000 and upwards, four.

whom they chose annually from among their own number. The meetings of the Courts of Proprietors took place four times a year, namely, in the months of December, March, June, and September.

Courts of Directors.—The active agents of the Company's home and Indian government were the Directors. These were twenty-four in number, elected annually; the qualification for office being the possession of above £2,000 of the Company's stock. They could only be dismissed "by the proceedings of two general Courts of Proprietors, at the first of which the grounds for the motion of removal are to be brought forward; and at the second, the question is to be decided by the votes of the proprietors then present."[1] A chairman and deputy-chairman, with salaries of £500 a year, were elected by the Directors annually, to preside over their meetings; each Director receiving £300.

Committees.—The business of the Company was carried on by means of various committees chosen from the body of Directors, the chairman and deputy-chairman being ex-officio members of all.

The Committees were divided under four heads:—

(1.) The Standing Committees.

(2.) The Secret Political Committee; or the Committee of Secresy appointed by Act of Parliament.

(3.) The Secret Commercial Committee.

(4.) The Committee of By-laws.

(1.) *The Standing Committees*—were twelve in number, consisting of the chairman, deputy-chairman, and the nine senior members.

i. *Committee of Correspondence.*—This had by far the most extensive business. All the advices from India of any kind passed through its hands daily. It kept the lists of the Company's servants; and settled all disputes and alleged grievances amongst the civil and military officers in the employ of the Company. The recruiting department, and the naval stations for ships, were also under their control.

ii. *Committee of Law-Suits.*—This committee took cognizance of all legal matters whether at home or abroad.

iii. *Military-Fund Committee.*—This was formed later than

[1] Auber's "Analysis of Constitution of the Company," p. 198.

the period of which we are now treating, namely, in the year 1770, for the purpose of affording relief in the case of officers employed by the Company, or their widows. It was set on foot by Lord Clive, who subscribed largely.

iv. *Treasury Committee.*—For the purpose of dealing with all questions of coin, bonds, and loans.

v. *The Civil College Committee.*—This was also a later institution, regulating all affairs connected with the education of the Company's civil servants.

vi. *Library Committee.*—This again became a necessity only in the later and more prosperous days of the Company.

vii. *Committee of Buying and Warehouses.*—For the management and supervision of all commercial concerns, exports and imports,—arranging orders abroad, and stocking goods sent home,—paying overseers, testers, and other officials,—and in general carrying on the home trade of the Company.

viii. *Committee of Accounts.*—Having an "Accountant's Office," and a "Transfer Office," under its direction, for the purpose of conducting the business of the Company in bills of exchange and the like.

ix. *House Committee.*

x. *Committee of the Military Seminary.*—This was established afterwards for the management of Addiscombe.

xi. *Committee of Shipping.*—The business of which was to purchase ships and stores, fit out trading vessels and pay the wages of the seamen and their officers.

xii. *Committee of Private Trade.*—Which prepared the charter-parties, and regulated the freight of private owners embarked in the Company's ships. It also maintained the by-laws, in connection with this private trade.

There were two more Committees, which were afterwards abolished; one for the management of government troops and stores during time of war, and the other for the prevention of private trade. The duties of the first were ultimately transferred to the Committee of Correspondence. As to the second, its duties were of such a peculiar kind that it is difficult, in the present day, to believe it could ever have existed. Its duties were to carry out all the monopoly principles with which the Company was originally started,—to persecute and imprison all persons trading with India who were not protected by the wing of the Company—and in general to hamper all the commerce of England with the east which interfered with its own chartered rights!

(2). *The Committee of Secresy*, appointed by Act of Parliament, was originated in 1748 on account of the war with France, the first serious political struggle in which the Company's arms were engaged. Its duties were to receive all private despatches, communicate with Parliament, confer with the king's ministers of state, and transact all such duties as were necessary to be carried on in secret, in order to maintain the peace of the country. Its powers were much enlarged at later periods, and it became, as its name imports, a "Secret Political Committee."

(3). *The Secret Commercial Committee* was a growth of much later times, being established in 1815. It consisted of five members, namely, the chairman, deputy-chairman, and one member from each of the Committees of Correspondence, Buying and Warehouses, and Shipping; and its duties were the carrying on of all such commercial transactions as required secresy.

(4). *Committee of By-laws.*—The last was for the framing of all the by-laws of the Company.

The principal exports of the Company to India consisted of bullion, lead, quicksilver, hardware, and cloths.

The imports were calicoes, silk, precious stones, tea, rice, pepper, porcelain, saltpetre, &c.

All sales were conducted by auction at the Company's warehouses.

The ships used for freight were mostly chartered by the Company for each voyage, their own ships being only used for carrying passengers, mails, and despatches.

In India.—For the better government of their possessions in India the Company established three Presidencies, of which the towns of Calcutta, Madras, and Bombay, were the capitals.

Bombay[1] was formerly a Portuguese settlement, ceded to the English crown in 1662, and given by the crown to the Company in 1668.

Madras was founded in 1639, when the English merchants,

[1] Surat was the first English trading settlement on the west coast, a factory being established there in 1612; but most of the merchants removed to Bombay, which possesses a finer harbour, when that port was ceded to the English.

formerly trading at Masulipatam, removed their factories southwards, and built "Fort St. George."

Calcutta was founded by Charnock[1] in 1690, and a fort erected, called, as has been already said, "Fort William."

The government of each Presidency was carried on by a President and Council; the President being sent out by the Company at home,—the Members of Council being civil servants, three in number, appointed by the Board of Directors.

The governor in Bengal was called the "Governor-General," and the other Presidencies were subordinate to him.

The powers of the Governor and Council in each Presidency were large. They had all powers of martial law for the regulation and command of the troops and marine in their service. They were supreme masters over the persons of all the English in the Presidency; and could imprison, and send to England all Englishmen not in their service whom they found in India, and suspected of being unlawfully engaged in trade. They had supreme civil and criminal jurisdiction in their own factories, and over their own servants,[2] and were also the organ of all public correspondence.

The other Company's officials were called respectively "Writers," "Factors," "Junior merchants," and "Senior merchants."

The "Writers" were cadets sent out between the ages of fifteen and twenty-two by interest with the Directors at home. They were placed in the various offices necessary for the conduct of the government, and received a salary merely nominal, at the same time having permission to trade. Under this system even the youngest Writers contrived to amass immense fortunes; and it is said that the Directors complained "that even the junior servants sat down to dinner with a band of music, and rode out in a coach and four."[3]

The Writers, after a period of service, became "Factors," and were entitled to higher pay and enlarged privileges, being considered no longer as cadets, but as members of the Company.

[1] Charnock's name is still given to a portion of the neighbourhood of Calcutta by the natives, whose name for Barrackpore is "Achanuk."

[2] In later times this jurisdiction was much altered. At the period to which we are especially referring, namely the year 1744, all English common and statute law had been extended to India by George the First in 1776, and courts established in the different Presidencies for the due administration of the same.—(See p. 79).

[3] The salary of a writer was £5 a year, with commons, an annual supply of Madeira, and the privilege of private trade.—Marshman, vol. i. p. 220.

The next grade was that of "Junior merchant;" and, finally, "Senior merchant," from which body the Members of Council and the body of Directors at home might be chosen.

The warehouses of the Company were called "factories," which for security were often fortified. In these factories the presiding manager was an English overseer, with his secretary (called, if a native, a "*Banyan*"). If a magistrate, this overseer had his court (or "*cutcherry*"), with an interpreter, and a clerk ("*Mohurrer*"). He had also the control of the accounts, and for this purpose a cash-keeper was necessary. The business of the office was carried on by native paid servants called "*Peons*," and "*Hircarahs.*"

The factories were situated in various districts called "*aurungs*," over each of which was a *Gomashtah*, or principal agent, with his peons.

The defence of the Presidencies was maintained by European soldiers, native regiments of Sepoys, and an armed police.

(III.)—*War with the French in the Carnatic*, (1744—1760.)

1744.—In the year 1744, the great European war between England and France was declared, and the Directors at home trembled for their Indian factories. The French were massed in large numbers at Pondicherry, and the time had arrived when, in India as in England, a deadly struggle between the two nations was to take place. In the north the factories at Calcutta were threatened by the Mahrattas, so that the Madras government could expect no aid from Bengal. Providentially, however, Aliverdi Khan's treacherous assassination of the Mahratta leader, Bhaskur, took place just previous to the declaration of war with France; and the Mahrattas drew off, leaving the English in the north free to help their friends in the south against their enemies.

When war was declared in 1744, the English troops in the Madras Presidency numbered only 600, the French in greater numbers under Labourdonnais being resident at Pondicherry and Isle de France.

Labourdonnais.—Labourdonnais was born in 1699, at St. Malo. He sailed for India at the age of 10; and again returned thither in 1719, 1723, and 1724, as captain of a ship. On the last occasion, pleased with Indian life, he determined to remain at Pondicherry; but being too old to enter the French military service, he applied himself to the study of civil engineering. His force of character and general energy were soon discovered, and he became a distinguished member of society there. In 1733 Labourdonnais returned home; and in 1735 was sent to Isle de France and Bourbon as governor. His term expiring in 1740, he was next year sent out in command of an expedition of nine vessels to damage the trade of the English in India; and on the declaration of war, he sailed to take command of the French in the South.

1746.—In 1746 the French set sail from Pondicherry for Madras with 2,000 trained soldiers: the defenders of Madras numbering some 300 recruits.

Capture of Madras by Labourdonnais.—After a bombardment of five days, namely on September 20th, 1746, Madras was captured by Labourdonnais who, contrary to expectation, behaved with great moderation, refusing to imprison or in any way personally injure the English merchants. This conduct excited the indignation of his rival, Dupleix, Governor of Pondicherry.

Dupleix.—Joseph Francis Dupleix was the son of a French East Indian Director. He was born in 1695, and went to India in 1715. In 1720 he was made a member of the Council of Pondicherry; and in 1730 became Governor of a large French factory at Chandanagore, on the Hooghley. In 1742 he was made Governor of Pondicherry. Dupleix always looked upon Labourdonnais as his irreconcileable rival, and in every way did his best to thwart his designs.

This rivalry ended in the downfall of the French in India; for when the fleet under the command of Labourdonnais was destroyed by a storm, Dupleix refused to send the latter any assistance, and the gallant capturer of Madras was taken prisoner by the English. He was treated with great clemency on account of his gentle and chivalrous behaviour, and was at once liberated on parole.

(This fine officer returned home only to meet with disgrace and ignominy; for, mindful only of the loss of Madras, and regardless of the justice or injustice of their conduct, the authorities seized Labourdonnais and threw him into the Bastille, where he died in 1749.)

State of Parties in the Deckan.—At this time (1746) the

Subahdar of the Deckan, under the Emperor Mohammed Shah, was the celebrated *Nizam-al-Mulkh*,[1] founder of the dynasty of the Nizams, and resident at Hyderabad. The Nabob of the Carnatic was Anwar-u-din, who had been appointed guardian to the hereditary Nabob, a minor, and on the death of the latter in 1740, had succeeded to the Nabobship, by the favour of the Subahdar. Chanda Sahib was Governor of Trichinopoly, and had secured himself in his position by marrying the daughter of Dost Ali, the previous Nabob of the Carnatic. But he was driven out by the Mahrattas who took Trichinopoly in 1741, and, escaping to the French, he took refuge at Pondicherry.

Dupleix at Madras.—While the French were still at Madras at the close of the year 1746, Anwar-u-din attacked that city with 10,000 men, but was beaten back by a body of about 1,000 French, under Dupleix.

The latter afterwards, as it seemed, only for the purpose of violating the treaties made by Labourdonnais, ravaged the town, burnt several factories, and took the principal inhabitants prisoners to Pondicherry.

On December 19th he attacked Fort St. David, twelve miles south of Madras, with a force of 1,700 European soldiers, while the garrison numbered only 200 Englishmen. But during the attack, the Nabob, whose only ambition was to defeat the French, marched against the besiegers, and Dupleix was compelled to retire to Pondicherry.

1747—Next year the French leader succeeded in detaching the Nabob from the English alliance, and in March he again attacked Fort St. David, but retired on the approach of an English fleet under Captain Peyton, who left reinforcements.

In June, Admirals Boscawen and Griffin arrived at Madras with a fleet from England and brought troops, which increased the British force in the South to 4,000. The English at once took the field and besieged Pondicherry; but mistakes in engineering and the advent of the rains prevented them from effecting anything important.

Peace, 1747.—When the news therefore arrived of the Peace of Aix-la-Chapelle, (of which information was received on October 4th,) it found Dupleix apparently master of the situation; although, much against his will, he was forced by the terms of the treaty to restore Madras to the English.

[1] See page 68, and note.

By this time France and England had become considerable military powers in India; and we are not surprised to find a Mahratta prince at Tanjore, Sahuji, fifth in descent from Sevaji's father Shahji whose jagir it was, applying to the English for assistance against his younger brother, Pretab Singh, who had wrested the kingdom from him. He promised to cede Devicottah at the mouth of the Coleroon, which was the stronghold of the rebellion, to the English if they succeeded in taking it. Accordingly Major Lawrence led an expedition thither, in which a young officer named *Clive* distinguished himself by his gallantry. Devicottah fell, and thenceforth became English. But Pretab Singh was too strong for Sahuji, and the latter consented to retire on promise of an annuity of Rs. 50,000.

The Subahdar of the Deckan, Nizam-al-Mulkh, died in 1748, and was succeeded by his son, Nazir Jung. The title being disputed by Muzuffer Jung, the son of a deceased elder brother, a war broke out between the disputants.

War breaks out again, 1749.—Muzuffer Jung at once applied to the French for aid, which was granted; and he promised to make Chanda Sahib Nabob of Arcot, if the latter would assist him to the Subahdari. Chanda Sahib readily consented. Whereupon Nazir Jung called in the aid of Anwar-u-din and the English. Hence the position of parties in 1749 was as follows:—

1749.—	Nazir Jung ("The Nizam,") Anwar-u-din (Nabob of the Carnatic.) The English.	*v.*	Muzuffer Jung. Chanda Sahib. The French.

In the first skirmish Anwar-u-din was killed, and to the consternation of the English, his troops fled to Trichinopoly. But the Nizam's cause was saved by the behaviour of some officers of the French contingent, who mutinied for pay. Their conduct created great confusion, and, after many disputes and much unseemly wrangling, the whole French army marched off home, leaving Dupleix in despair. The Nizam at once advancing, the enemy were defeated with heavy loss, Muzuffer Jung being captured and thrown into prison, while Chanda Sahib desperately fought his way to Pondicherry.

The effect of this victory was destroyed by the unsoldierlike conduct of the Nizam, who, apparently intoxicated by this his first success, went to Arcot, and gave himself up to amusement.

The English indignantly retired to Madras; and thus ended the campaign of 1749.

French successes, 1750.—Mahomed Ali succeeded his father, Anwar-u-din, as Nabob of the Carnatic, and remained all his life the staunch friend of the English, who, by their powerful alliance, had secured him in his office at the outset.[1]

Dupleix victoriously opened the campaign of 1750 by capturing the fortresses of Jinji, Masulipatam, and Trivadi, and defeating Mahomed Ali. He then negotiated secretly with some traitors, Patan Nabobs, in the camp of the Nizam, and they agreed to murder their chief. Seizing an opportunity, when the Nizam was remonstrating with one of their party, they shot him through the heart.

Thus died Nazir Jung, leaving his nephew, Muzuffer Jung, the ally of the French, Subahdar in his own right. Enchanted with this success and revelling in the height of glory to which this event raised him, Dupleix summoned Muzuffer Jung to Pondicherry and with his own hand invested him with the dignities of the great office of Subahdar of the Deckan, whilst he himself wore the gorgeous robes of a Mahomedan of rank.

The new Nizam created Dupleix Nabob of the Carnatic, and made Chanda Sahib Nabob of Arcot.

Thus the French seemed triumphant. But (alas! for the fallacy of human hopes!) while Muzuffur Jung was travelling in state to Hyderabad on January 4th 1751 with a large retinue, the same Patan nabobs who had murdered Nazir Jung set upon Muzuffer and slew him with javelins.

There being no direct descendant of Muzuffer Jung living, the next heirs apparent were the sons of Nazir Jung; and Bussy who commanded the French contingent conferred the vacant office on the youngest, Salabat Jung, who was a prisoner in camp when Muzuffer was murdered. He thus maintained the prestige of the French; and the allies pursued their way to the capital.

Meanwhile Chanda Sahib was attacking his old government of Trichinopoly, whither he had marched from his new seat of office, Arcot. The place was saved by the genius of Captain Clive, who made a counter march to Arcot; upon which Chanda Sahib left Trichinopoly and hurried to the rescue of his capital.

He besieged Clive in Arcot for seven weeks, and finding his efforts apparently hopeless, in spite of all his bombardments and storming-parties, he thought it best to return to Trichinopoly.

[1] He was for this reason often called "the Company's Nabob."

1752.—Clive went thither also, and remained there with Mohammed Ali and Major Lawrence; while Chanda Sahib, defeated at all points, and heart-broken at his losses, wandered about the country with a few followers. His end was tragic; the Rajah of Tanjore, to whom the outcast nabob applied for protection and who owed, as we have seen, a debt of gratitude to the English, paid it by the cold-blooded murder of the helpless fugitive.

The next act in the war was the junction of the French with the Mysoreans and Mahrattas. This was effected by the judicious fomentation of an old grievance. It happened that the English ally, Mohammed Ali, had promised Trichinopoly to the Raja of Mysore, but found himself unable to fulfil his promise since the place was now held by the English. Dupleix skilfully made use of this plea to effect an offensive alliance with Mysore, and, through this country, with the Mahrattas under Morari Rao.

The position, therefore, at this time was as follows:—

<table><tr><td rowspan="3">1753.[1]—</td><td>The French,</td><td rowspan="3">v.</td><td rowspan="3">English,
Mahommed Ali.</td></tr><tr><td>Mysoreans,</td></tr><tr><td>Mahrattas,</td></tr></table>

Siege of Trichinopoly.—The French and their allies marched to Trichinopoly, which was besieged from May, 1753, till October, 1754, but held out successfully under Clive and Lawrence.

Recall of Dupleix.—Dupleix's hour of triumph was now at an end, and he was tottering to his fall. Ever since the year 1751 constant discussions had been taking place in Europe, as to whether Mohammed Ali (the "Company's Nabob," the friend of the English), or Dupleix, the Frenchman, was to be recognised as Nabob of the Carnatic. Dupleix's claim seems the more reasonable of the two, since he had been officially appointed Nabob by the hereditary Subahdar; while Mohammed Ali's claim rested on no official appointment. But the English Government contended that the office could only be transferred from the here-

[1] In 1753 George the Second re-established the "Mayor's Courts," in Madras (which had fallen into disuse after the capture of that city by Labourdonnais in 1746) giving them jurisdiction in all matters between Europeans; and extending their authority to matters between Hindus on the consent of both parties, expressly exempting those who refused to be subject to this tribunal. "This charter is the first instance we find of the reservation of their own laws to the people of India."—(Grady's Hindu Law of Inheritance, Introd. page xliv.)

ditary line by the express firman of the Mogul Emperor, who was then almost powerless [1] and that Mohammed Ali, being the heir, was rightfully Nabob.

The discussion was terminated by the recall of Dupleix in 1754, to which rash act the French government had been led by the outcries of the people, who demanded vengeance for the heavy expenses incurred by that officer. Their conduct signalled the downfall of the French in India.

Peace, 1754.—Dupleix was superseded by M. Godeheu, in 1754; and on December 26th of that year a Treaty of Peace was signed between M. Godeheu and Sanders, the governor of Madras, recognising Mohammed Ali as Nabob of the Carnatic.

Dupleix returned to France, and died in great poverty and misery a few years later.

Bussy and the Nizam.—At this time Bussy, the cleverest of all the French leaders in India, was with Salabat Jung, the new Nizam, at Aurangabad, assisting him in managing the affairs of the Subahdari. The latter was, in 1754, attacked by a large army; for Ghazi-u-din Khan, elder brother of the former Subahdar Nazir Jung headed a large invading force, and was joined by the Mahrattas. Bussy defeated the Mahrattas in the field, and compassed the death of Ghazi-u-din by poison; and out of gratitude for his services the Nizam gave the Northern Circars to the French.

1755.—Soon after this Salabat Jung took the field against the Rajah of Mysore, who had refused to pay the tribute due to him. The movement was ill-judged, since Mysore was at that time allied with France, and the Nizam's conduct had the effect of driving the Mysoreans to ally themselves with the English. (It is said that the Nizam insisted upon this course of conduct against the express wish of Bussy; and it seems very probable that such was the case, for their friendship abated somewhat from this period, and not long afterwards the Nizam ordered Bussy away from court). The expedition was, nevertheless, successful, for the Rajah of Mysore bought off Salabat Jung with large sums of money and presents; and the Nizam, bent on schemes of conquest, then joined with the Mahrattas under the Peshwa Balaji Rao, and defeated Morari Rao, the Mahratta chieftain, who had revolted.

(*Mahratta Affairs*, 1749—1756.—Meanwhile a change had

[1] Ahmed Shah was then emperor. He died in 1754.

taken place at Poonah, for Sahoo the Rajah having died in 1749 leaving no issue, Balaji Rao the Peshwa assumed full powers of government, and elevated the only remaining prince of the blood, Ram Raja, to the bare title, keeping him virtually in prison. At the same time, in order to consolidate his own authority, he sent his bold and refractory son, Raghoba, away from Poonah on the pretext of plundering the dominions of the Gwickwar of Guzerat.)

1756.—When the Nizam ordered Bussy to leave Hyderabad the latter went to Masulipatam, and was greatly distressed to hear soon afterwards that Salabat, declaring himself in favour of the English, had requested their aid to drive the French out of the Subahdari. In order to terrify the Nizam, Bussy immediately assumed the offensive, and entrenched himself in Charmal, near Hyderabad. His object was successfully attained, for Salabat came to terms, and declined the English alliance.

1757.—But the Nizam pined to be relieved from the constant interference of the Frenchman, and again gave permission to Bussy to retire to the Northern Circars This, however, was not for long; for during Bussy's absence, Bassalat Jung and Nizam Ali, elder brothers to the Nizam, brought each an army to attack Hyderabad, and Salabat, taking command of his own force, hastily recalled Bussy. When the latter returned he found matters in great confusion, for four opposing armies were collected round Hyderabad; and, to make matters worse, the Nizam's minister was found to be intriguing with Nizam Ali. Bussy contrived to have this minister slain in an apparently accidental manner during a scuffle, and Nizam Ali fled hurriedly from the scene of action. Bassalat Jung was bought off by the present of the fortress of Doulatabad; and thus once more Bussy averted from his friend an impending disaster.

1758.—Bussy was now arbiter of the fate of the whole of the Deckan; and had not the French government again stepped in to destroy their hopes in India, none can say what the result might have been. But they chose to supersede that fine officer in favour of a brilliant but headstrong soldier of the name of Lally.

Recall of Bussy.—Lally landed at Fort St. David, on May 1st, and at once sent orders to Bussy to march south with all the French under his command. The latter reluctantly obeyed, causing by his conduct the greatest astonishment amongst all the native princes, who could little understand the motives which induced a minister, at the height of his glory and with kingdoms under his control, to give up his whole authority into the hands of an unknown *parvenu*.

Lally.—Lally was an Irish adventurer, who had entered the French army, and had distinguished himself at the battle of Fontenoy. For his conduct in this action he was rewarded by the gift of a regiment; and in 1758, was sent out to take command in India. He was impetuous and headstrong, but his knowledge of the art of war was scanty and superficial.

After his recall of Bussy, Lally captured Fort St. David and Devicottah; and, in order at one blow to drive the English out of the south, determined at once to attack Madras. Feeling the necessity for supplies Lally demanded aid from Pondicherry, but the merchants there, without exception, refused him the smallest pecuniary assistance. He therefore determined to loot Tanjore, which was reported to be very wealthy, and laid close siege to the city. But the Rajah appealed to the English; and a fleet coming up from Madras arrived at Carical, cut off the French supplies, and landed an army who proceeded to draw lines round the parallels of Lally's attack. The siege was therefore raised. The discomfiture of the French was completed by the disobedience of their admiral, who, in direct contradiction to orders, took off the fleet to the Mauritius, and left Lally to his fate.

He was more fortunate in his attack on Arcot, for he captured the town and was joined there by Bussy. The latter strongly counselled Lally to remain at Arcot awhile in order to consolidate the French power, and collect funds for his final descent on the English head-quarters. But Lally wilfully persisted in his own course, and on December 12th, 1758, laid siege to Madras.

Siege of Madras by Lally.—The garrison of that town, commanded by Major Lawrence, held out for two months. On December 14th, the French captured Black Town, and at once drew parallels round the fort. On February 16th, a British fleet appeared in the Roads, and the siege was raised, Lally fleeing in haste and leaving fifty pieces of cannon behind him. Colonel Coote, who was with the fleet, landed at Madras with great ease and, marching out with the garrison, captured Wandewash, utterly defeating Lally who opposed him and driving him in despair to Pondicherry.

1760.—During the remainder of the year, Lally remained at Pondicherry, harassed by his own thoughts, and by the enmitof his countrymen around. He waited for supplies from France, but none came. The troops also were mutinous for pay; and to complete his disasters, at the close of 1759, Coote laid siege to Pondicherry.

Capture of Pondicherry.—On January 14th, 1760, the garrison evacuated the city, and Coote razed the fort to the ground, completely destroying every vestige of French power in India.

Thus were destroyed for ever the hopes of those who longed, for the sake of the advantages derivable from trade or the greatness which accompanies large territorial possessions, to constitute in India a firm French government.

Lally, broken-hearted by his misfortunes, returned to France in despair. His fate was terrible. Immediately on his arrival he was thrown into the Bastille; and being taken from thence and dragged through the streets of Paris on a dungcart, dirt and mud and every kind of filth being showered upon him, he was afterwards beheaded.

(The treatment of their Indian commanders by the French government is one of the blots in the history of that country. Labourdonnais died in prison; Dupleix was consigned to poverty and neglect, and died broken-hearted; while Bussy remained in India for many years, returning only when he felt he was forgotten.)

(IV.)—*Events in Bengal*, 1755—1773.

After the final retirement of the Mahrattas from Bengal in 1751 when they were bought off by Aliverdi Khan, the English settlements at Calcutta were left in peace for some years and the members of the Company remained quietly trading under the protection of the Subahdar of the province.

In 1755, the Bengal government determined to make an alliance with the Peshwa, perceiving at once his increasing power and the weakness of the Mogul Emperor; and this was accordingly done. The tidings of the English successes in the south in the same year, and of the expedition of Clive, who went against a nest of pirates near Bombay and destroyed their stronghold at Severndroog, raised the contentment of the merchants to the highest pitch. But their joy was damped by the anxiety with which they witnessed the close alliance between the French and the Nizam and the hostile attitude of the latter; little dreaming of a worse enemy nearer home.

1756—On April 8th, 1756, Aliverdi Khan died, leaving as Subahdar his grandson, the infamous Suraj-u-dowla. This tyrant's first act was to send a message to Mr. Drake, the governor of Calcutta, ordering him to raze all the British fortifications. The latter resolutely refused to obey this command, fearful of what might follow should he leave the settlement completely defenceless.

The "Black Hole of Calcutta."—Then ensued one of the most horrible tragedies in the history of the world. Suraj-u-dowla marched down on Calcutta with an immense force. The garrison consisted of only 120 English artillerymen, about 50 recruits, and a few Rajputs; the guns being almost useless from age and neglect. There were no supplies in the fort, and the English could expect no help from without. Accordingly Drake gave the order of "*sauve qui peut!*" to the inhabitants; and, himself leading the way to the ships, all fled on board the various vessels, and sailed off down the river on the evening of June 21st. The Nabob seized the outskirts of the town, and that night the garrison, under Mr. Holwell, performed their duties by the light of their burning factories. Next evening, the fort being stormed and carried, the garrison were taken prisoners; and Suraj, promising them their lives, retired to rest giving orders that all the captives should be kept in safety till the morning.

By whose mistake or by whose orders it occurred is not known, but in order to keep them in safety all the prisoners, numbering 146 men, were crushed into a room twenty feet square, and having only one small window. It was a sultry night in one of the sultriest seasons of the year and the horrors that took place could be barely imagined possible had they not been graphically and systematically narrated by Holwell himself. In the morning only twenty-three persons remained alive and their appearance is said to have been more ghastly than the mind can conceive. The unhappy survivors were permitted to sail down the Hooghley, while Suraj-u-dowla retired to Moorshedabad.

Thus were the English expelled from Bengal completely and effectually.

1757.—But at the end of the year, Clive, who had been sent up from Madras with a fleet under Admiral Watson, appeared in the Hooghley, and on January 2nd 1757 recaptured Fort William.

The garrison fled in haste, scarcely a shot being fired, and gave the alarm to the Subahdar who at once marched on Calcutta. He was attacked by Clive whose troops, although they fought with the utmost gallantry, could effect nothing; and night put an end to an indecisive action of many hours.

Next morning Suraj-u-dowla, terrified by the undaunted bravery of these new soldiers in red coats, came to terms and restored to the Company all their old privileges with compensation for the injury already done them.

Clive then marched against and destroyed the French settlement of Chandanagore.

The Subahdar fixed his camp at Plassy, and Clive's astonishment was great when he received secret letters from Mir Jaffier, the commander-in-chief of the Mogul army, offering to desert and come over to the English on any day of a general engagement, if the latter would instal him Subahdar of Bengal, Behar, and Orissa, in the room of Suraj-u-dowla.

Battle of Plassy, June 23rd.—Clive consented to these terms, and on June 13th marched from Chandanagore. He reached Cutwa on the 17th, crossed the river on the 22nd, and on the 23rd engaged the whole Mogul army at Plassy.

The action commenced with the attack of the Nabob on the English lines in the early morning. The English troops sheltered themselves from the enemy's musketry under mud walls, and towards midday Suraj, changing his tactics, took to pounding with heavy guns which soon battered down their slight defences. Clive then ordered a general charge, which was responded to with great ardour as a shower of rain had at once cooled the air and rendered the matchlocks useless. The Moguls fled in terror before the cold steel, and the Nabob himself, panic-stricken, jumped on a camel and fled in haste from the field. Mir Jaffier ceased fighting and came to the British camp, where Clive received him with great distinction.

Mir Jaffier made Subahdar of Bengal.—On June 29th the victorious army re-entered Moorshedabad, and with great state Clive proclaimed Mir Jaffier Subahdar of Bengal, Behar, and Orissa,[1] on condition of his defraying the expenses of the war, and protecting the Company's possessions on the Hooghley. Dulub Ram was made minister of finance, and Ramnarain

[1] This incident is perhaps one of the most remarkable in history. We find a body of merchants ejected from a country, and their property destroyed; and exactly a year afterwards one of their number places a prince on the throne of the country—(and that, too, a country as large as England and Scotland together)—the prince humbly paying all expenses.

governor of Patna. The next day a son of Mir Jaffier discovered Suraj-u-dowla hiding in the disguise of a beggar, and put him to death in cold blood.

Thus were the exertions of Clive crowned with success, whilst a dependent of the English was placed on the throne of the province.

Three revolts which occurred against Mir Jaffier's authority in Behar, Purneah, and Midnapore, were put down without difficulty; and towards the close of the year the arrival of a treasure-ship containing £800,000 from Mir Jaffier for the governor of Calcutta, was the signal for great public rejoicings.

1758.—Next year Clive[1] sent an expedition under Colonel Forde to destroy the French settlements on the coast. This officer was completely successful, defeating the French under Conflans at Vizagapatam, and capturing Masulipatam.

1759.—"*Clive's Jagir.*"—In 1759, Ali Gohur, the "*Shah Zada*," or Prince Imperial, eldest son of the emperor Alamgir II., revolted against his father's authority and was joined by the Subahdar of Oude. He advanced against Patna, which Ramnarain resolutely defended; and when Clive went to the assistance of the latter, the Shah Zada was defeated and put to flight. In reward for this service Mir Jaffier presented Clive with a large jagir, worth £30,000 a year.

Soon after the defeat of Ali Gohur, the English arms were engaged against the Dutch; for a fleet from their settlements in Batavia appeared in the Hooghley, and some troops were landed. Colonel Forde was sent to intercept their advance on Calcutta, and, acting under private orders from Clive,[2] he attacked them by night, and in half an hour drove them to their boats; the result being that the Dutch commander withdrew after promising to pay all expenses.

1760.—On February 25th, 1760, Clive sailed for Europe.

Soon afterwards Mir Jaffier, becoming jealous of the rising

[1] Clive had been made governor of Calcutta immediately after the battle of Plassy, and was now, therefore, civil and military commander of the British in Bengal.

[2] It is said that Clive was quietly seated one evening playing whist, when the news was brought him in a note from Forde, placed in his hands, that the Dutch had landed and were advancing. "I dare not fight them," wrote the Colonel, "without the express orders of Council." Clive asked for a pencil, and wrote on one of the cards, "Dear Forde, fight them immediately; I will send you the Order in Council to-morrow;" and continued his game with a fresh pack. (Marshman's Hist. of India, vol. i. p. 285.)

power of Dulub Ram, the chancellor of the exchequer, caused him to be privately assassinated in a mock mutiny raised for the purpose.

Meanwhile Alamgir the Second had been also murdered by his vizier, Ghazi-u-din; and the Shah Zada, proclaiming himself emperor, marched again on Patna. Ramnarain at once sent to Calcutta for reinforcements, and himself went out bravely against the enemy; but being defeated, he retired to his city, and there held out till a British force under Colonel Calliaud arrived and, on February 20th, defeated the new emperor.

The Mogul immediately, making a clever flank movement, hurried by forced marches to attack Moorshedabad, but on arriving at the river's bank, and finding the English drawn up awaiting his attack, he retired hastily to Patna. Calliaud thereupon despatched Captain Knox to the relief of that city.

Knox's Victory at Patna.—Knox advanced rapidly with a force of 200 Europeans, a battalion of sepoys, and a small squadron of cavalry. He immediately attacked, and having defeated the Moguls, fixed his camp at Patna. While there, tidings arrived that a force of 30,000 men under the Nabob of Purneah were approaching to destroy his little army; and the report was but too true; for one morning (May 20th, 1760) this large force, having with them more than a hundred guns, appeared on the opposite side of the river. But Knox with the utmost daring crossed the river with 700 men and charged straight into the centre of the enemy's lines, in full view of the despairing garrison. A fight of six hours ensued, at the end of which the whole Mogul army was in flight, and Knox, with his gallant and soldierly ally, the Rajput Raja Shitabroy, entered Patna covered with dust and blood and followed by only 300 men, the survivors of that splendid engagement.[1]

Next year the Mogul Empire at Delhi was overthrown by the "Abdalis," or "Duranis," and there ensued the tremendous battle of Panipat between the Mahrattas and Ahmed Khan Abdali, in which the strength of the former was shattered, and the power of the latter so weakened that he retired to Afghanistan.

The "Abdalis" at Delhi, 1757—1761.—Raghoba had taken Delhi from Ahmed Khan in 1757, having been called in by the feeble and ferocious Ghazi-u-din, minister to Alamgir II. The

[1] Marshman justly observes, "It was one of those battles in the early career of the English, which gave prestige to their arms and bewildered the native princes."

Mahrattas returned to the Deckan after having defeated Prince Teimur, son of Ahmed Khan, in the Punjaub. On his return to Poonah, Raghoba quarrelled with Sudaseeb (or Sedasheo) Bhao, cousin to the Peshwa, and was removed from the command of the army, Sedasheo being placed in his position. In 1759, Ahmed Khan again invaded India (a fourth time) and captured Lahore, just at the time when Ghazi-u-din had murdered the emperor, and when Nujib-u-dowla, an Afghan commander, had driven Mulhar Rao Holkar and Dataji Sindia, the Mahratta leaders, across the Ganges. Ahmed Khan's path to Delhi was thus clear, and taking advantage of this opportunity, he arrived before the capital early in 1760. The Bhao at once marched north with an immense army and great pomp; and the two nations met at Panipat on January 7th, 1761, to fight over the prostrate throne of the Empire.

The result is told at length on a previous page.[1] The Mahrattas were crushed, and the Afghans retired with a shattered force to their own country.

State of the Country after Panipat.—The state of the country after this battle was, then, as follows:—

The Mogul Empire was no more; the nominal emperor, Ali Gohur, wandering in Behar.

The Mahrattas had received a death-blow. The Peshwa, Balaji Rao, died of grief, and the power was divided amongst the four great chieftains, the "Gwickwar" in Guzerat, the Raja of Nagpore (Bhonslay), Holkar, and Sindia.

The Nizam at Hyderabad became an independent sovereign; but his power was crippled by losses, and weakened by the protective policy which the French had employed towards him.

The latter power was utterly crushed, and Pondicherry was in the hands of the English.

The Nabob of the Carnatic was dependent solely on the goodwill of the Governor of Madras.

The Nabob of Oude had become independent, and was possessed of large territories and a fine army.

The Rajputs, splendid soldiers though they were, were scattered. There was no union amongst them, and the idea of anything like an united Rajput sovereignty was unheard-of.

The Jauts and the Rohillas were becoming powers of some importance, and were destined afterwards to play a part of considerable prominence in Indian history.

[1] See page 72.

Hyder Ali, with whom the English were soon brought into contact, was acquiring great authority in Mysore.

The English were even now, perhaps, the greatest power in India. They had given away the crowns of two large possessions,—the Subahdari of Bengal, Behar and Orissa, and the Nabobship of the Carnatic: and, very soon after this, their ally Nizam Ali imprisoned his brother the Subahdar of the Deckan and seized his throne, placing the whole of the south of India within the influence of the British.

Vansittart, Governor of Bengal.—Vansittart was appointed Governor of Bengal in the room of Clive; but being a Madras civilian, the Bengalese officers were irritated at the preference shown towards him. The appointment does not seem to have been a good one, for Vansittart was wanting in the firm qualities necessary at this period for the permanent establishment of British supremacy in India.

Deposition of Mir Jaffier.—Vansittart found Mir Jaffier, the Subahdar, indolent and oppressive; his troops revolted for want of pay, and on many occasions he showed open indignation at the humble position he was forced to assume when dealing with the English. Accordingly, when Mir Casim, his son-in-law, pacified the troops by paying them out of his own pocket, and then journeying to Calcutta, promised to live entirely under British protection if the Company would give him the Subahdari of Bengal, Vansittart eagerly consented, and at once proclaimed Mir Jaffier deposed.

Mir Casim then took up his residence at Calcutta; and gratified the President by displaying great energy in his payments of the subsidy, though it amounted to the large sum of £200,000. He also ceded absolutely to the Company one third of his territory, namely, the districts of Midnapore, Chittagong, and Burdwan. But when this was accomplished, irritated at the interference of the President, he commenced increasing and disciplining his army.

Meanwhile Ali Gohur, under the title of the "*Emperor Shah Alum,*" was ravaging Behar, being unable to regain Delhi; and at last, in despair of success, he made an alliance with the English, and being acknowledged by them at Patna, confirmed all the appointments they had made.

1762.—**War with Mir Casim.**—Mir Casim soon began to show his real character, and in 1762 threw off all appearance of quiet submission. He seized the person of Ramnarain and cast him into prison; and employed the utmost cruelty and extortion in collecting his revenues, putting the ryots to the torture, and behaving with great brutality. Searching about to find an open subject of quarrel with the English, he hit upon the Company's transit-duties, and the "*Dustuck*," which, it will be remembered, was granted to them by the Emperor Farokshir.

He seems to have had some justice on his side; and the violent conduct of certain members of the Company, greatly angering the Subahdar, brought on a war and reflected much discredit on the English name. It seems not unreasonable to urge that the emperor's *dustuck* was granted to the Company as a whole, and was not intended to apply to every individual Englishman who came to Calcutta. It ought to have been confined to the public trade of the collective body of merchants; but the very natural rapacity of the private traders showed itself in grasping this boon as their right on every occasion The indignation at Calcutta was therefore great when Mir Casim sent to demand that this unlawful extension of the imperial *dustuck* should be put an end to; and when the Nabob's collectors attempted to carry out his orders and seize goods which had not paid duty, they were openly insulted by the Company's servants.

Vansittart then privately promised Mir Casim that a duty of nine per cent. should be paid. The latter accepted. But the members of council, when they heard of this, voted that the Nabob had no right to impose any duty at all; and without much opposition, passed a formal order of council that his officers should be seized and imprisoned if they attempted to enforce his wishes.

Incensed at this conduct, Mir Casim, in a natural spirit of retaliation for the behaviour of the English, granted a firman to all Mogul traders at the port that they should pass their goods free of duty; and thus placed them on even terms with the rest.

All this led to high feelings, and hot, angry words; and the sparks were fanned into a flame by the intemperate conduct of Mr. Ellis, the head of the English factory at Patna, who openly made preparations for war. Actual hostilities commenced when Messrs Hay and Amyatt, who arrived at Monghir from Calcutta to insist on the Company's claims, were seized by the order of the Subahdar. Hay was held captive as a hostage for the good behaviour of Ellis, while Amyatt was bidden to return to Calcutta with the Nabob's remonstrances in writing.

But Mr. Ellis, apparently bent on fighting, at once seized the city and fort of Patna; and Mir Casim, lashed into fury, gave orders to his officers to seize every Englishman that could be found. Amyatt, on his way to Calcutta, was set upon by a body of Mogul police, and his sword demanded. He fired upon those who stopped his way, and was himself killed in the scuffle that ensued. This was the first blood that was shed, and it at once put an end to all hopes of a quiet adjustment of affairs.

Campaign of 1763.—The Nabob augmented his army and applied for assistance to the emperor and the Nabob of Oude.

The English retaliated by publicly declaring Mir Casim deposed, and Mir Jaffier Subahdar in his place.

The campaign opened on July 19th with a decisive defeat of the Nabob by the English; and again an English victory on the 24th.

The British troops then seized Moorshedabad, and on August 2nd the battle of Gheriah was fought, in which the Nabob was once more signally defeated. In a paroxysm of rage, Mir Casim murdered Ramnarain and all the English prisoners he had taken, including the great Moorshedabad bankers, the Setts. But he paid dearly for his cruelty, for in November the English attacked and carried his camp at Oodwanulla, and the Mogul fled to Patna.

Here he was joined by the Emperor Shah Alum and the Nabob of Oude, with a large force; but the English, successful at all points, carried the city of Patna by assault almost at the first attack.

1764.—Heavy rains confined the English to Patna for a time, during which occurred a rising of Sepoy troops, the cause of dispute being arrears of pay. The native troops in the garrison mutinied, and marched out of the city to join the enemy; but they were attacked and defeated by Major Munro and marched back to Patna, where the ringleaders were blown from the guns. The mutiny was thus quelled, and the Sepoys behaved well in the campaign that followed.

Battle of Buxar.—Meanwhile the Nabob pitched his camp at Buxar, near Patna, and after the September rains Munro marched out towards that station. He reached the enemy's camp on October 22nd, and the next morning attacked and entirely defeated Mir Casim, who was compelled to flee for his life into Oude.

This victory placed the whole valley of the Ganges at the

feet of the English, and made them virtual masters of Hindostan, the emperor himself being under British protection.

Vansittart at once acknowledged Sujah-u-dowla as Nabob of Oude; Mir Jaffier as Nabob of Bengal, Behar, and Orissa; and Shah Alum as emperor, fixing the latter's residence at Allahabad; and he then demanded a subsidy of fifty-three lacs from Mir Jaffier, which was granted.

1765.—Mir Jaffier did not long enjoy his new dignity, for he died next year, and his son, Nujum u-dowla, was appointed successor.

Vansittart's term of office expired in 1765; and Clive, raised to the Peerage, was sent out to take charge of the government of Bengal, Spencer being appointed President in the interim.

Clive's Second Administration, 1765—1767.—On Clive's return to England in 1760 he had been well received by the Court of Directors and the government; but soon found himself subject to much opposition, raised against him by those jealous of his unparalleled success. Irritated by this, Clive unwisely suffered himself to be led into a quarrel with the Directors, who forthwith sent orders to Calcutta to withhold the payment of the rents of his jagir. On the expiration of Vansittart's term of office, however, the Court of Directors. finding no one in whom they could place such implicit confidence as the hero of Plassy, sent Lord Clive to Calcutta, armed with full powers, and having the absolute control of all affairs, civil and military, in Bengal; a hollow truce being patched up between him and the Directors concerning the subject of their previous disputes.

Lord Clive landed at Calcutta on May 3rd, 1765, holding the combined powers of Governor of Bengal, President of Council, and Commander-in-chief.

He found the state of society in Calcutta exceedingly corrupt. Bribery, extravagance, and debauchery reigned supreme in every rank of the service; and, much to his annoyance, Clive learnt on arrival that the members of Council under the leadership of Spencer, had forced the new Subahdar, Nujum-u-dowla, to give presents, amounting in value to nearly twenty lacs of rupees, for their own private use and enjoyment.

The committee of four appointed to assist Clive consisted of General Carnac, Mr. Verelst, Mr. Sumner, and Mr. Sykes; and on June 25th the Governor-General commenced a progress up-country, taking these gentlemen with him.

Grant of Bengal, Behar, and Orissa.—His first act was to relieve Nujum-u-dowla of all management of the affairs of

Bengal, Behar, and Orissa. The Nabob cheerfully relinquished the whole into the hands of the Company in exchange for an annual income of fifty-three lacs, which he spent according to his taste in a life of reckless debauchery.

The Governor then gave the Emperor an annuity of twenty-six lacs of rupees in exchange for the free cession of all territorial rights in the same three districts, securing to him the revenues of Corah and Allahabad. He further requested the emperor to grant absolutely to the Company all powers of the administration of justice in the newly acquired country; which demand was willingly granted.

Grant of the Dewani.—The effect of this was to give over to the English Government the entire "Dewani" of the province, and thus to transfer to them the absolute government over twenty-five millions of people, and an annual revenue of four crores of rupees.[1]

Mutiny of Bengal Officers.—1766.—In this year occurred a

[1] That this grant may be sufficiently understood, and its value appreciated, I append a sketch of what is commonly known as the "*Adalat System*," constituted immediately after the emperor's grant in the year 1765.

The gift of the emperor consisted of the "*Dewani*," and the "*Nizamat*," (see note, p. 78) which thus transferred to the Company the management of all the affairs of the army and police, with full revenue civil and criminal jurisdiction throughout the entire provinces of Bengal, Behar, and Orissa.

Clive's system, founded on that of the Mogul empire, was as follows—

(1.) *Revenue.*—Established at Moorshedabad was a central office which superintended the collection of the revenue, appointed European supervisors with native officials over the various divisions and districts, and kept all the accounts of the entire province. It was not till 1772 that Warren Hastings obtained permission to place all administration in the hands of European officers. The revenue "Supervisors" then became "Collectors," and the central office was removed from Moorshedabad to Calcutta.

(2.) *Criminal Courts*, called "Provincial Courts," were established in each district, and regulated at Calcutta by a central Mofussil "Nizamat Adalat," or supreme criminal court for up-country stations.

(3.) *Civil Courts.*—These were presided over by the "Collectors," or "Supervisors," who thus combined in their own person the respective offices of revenue and civil jurisdiction. They had native officers under their control, and administered Hindu and Mahomedan law.

The "*Phoujdari Adalat*" was a central criminal court in each district, presided over by the judge, assisted by a "Kasi," or "Mufti." It was appointed for the trial of the more heinous crimes.

mutiny amongst the European officers in Bengal. They had been accustomed to receive extra pay called "*Batta*" when employed in the field, and this had been doubled during the recent war, the expense being borne by the Subahdar. In order to compensate for the emptiness of the treasury, due to the large sums given to the native princes, Clive made a general order that on January 1st, 1766, "Double Batta" should cease.

As this was a somewhat large sum, the officers became first discontented, and then mutinous, and conspired simultaneously to send in their resignations. Sir Robert Fletcher the commander-in-chief at once wrote to Clive informing him of this disastrous state of affairs.

At the same time news was brought of the advance of 50,000 Mahrattas against Behar; and the officers in triumph considered that the Government, being unable to dispense with their services, would grant them the Double Batta they longed for. They little knew with whom they had to deal.

Clive accepted every resignation, sent the offenders to be tried by court-martial, and ordered up from Madras all the cadets and officers there to take the command of the Bengal army. The British troops seemed desirous of following the example of their officers, but the Sepoys, behaving with the most exemplary gallantry, by their firm front and faithful adherence to their commanders prevented any outbreak.

The heaviest blow fell on Sir Robert Fletcher, who, whether justly or unjustly is not known, was suspected of conniving in the conspiracy and was peremptorily dismissed the service.

Inland Trade Disputes.—The next trouble was a purely domestic

The "*Sudder Dewani Adalat*," and the "*Sudder Nizamat Adalat*," were the chief civil and criminal courts of the Presidency at Calcutta. The "*Dewani Adalat*" was presided over by the Governor and Members of Council, with native law officers, and was at once a court of original jurisdiction, and of appeal from sentences of the Mofussil courts where the matter in dispute was of a higher value than Rs. 500. The "*Nizamat Adalat*" was under the presidency of a chief officer called a "*Darogha*," with native law officers. Its business was to confirm and revise all sentences of the "*Phoujdari Adalat*" and other criminal courts, when they were for the infliction of capital punishment or fines of more than Rs. 100. It was also a court of criminal appeal.

Besides these courts, there was an authority given to the principal farmers in each pergunnah, to hold courts wherein they should have final judgment in civil matters where the subject in dispute was of less value than Rs.10. And all Collectors and Senior merchants were made Justices of the Peace.

one, arising from the Company's system of inland trade. The Directors had permitted their servants to monopolize the inland trade in salt and areca-nut, and the officers of whatever rank or service eagerly rushed into the speculation, little caring for the condition of the poorer ryots, so that they themselves made some profit out of the transactions. This system produced so much distress and ill-feeling amongst the natives that Clive felt the necessity of putting an end to it; and he accordingly instituted a society for the promotion of inland trade which should give the Company a steady profit, but prevent anarchy and individual speculation at the expense of the natives. The society only existed two years, when it was abolished by the direction of the Board at home, and a regular commission instituted in its place.

Resignation of Lord Clive.—1767.—Lord Clive was attacked with illness in 1767; and much to the regret of all in India, and to the delight of his enemies at home, he was compelled by the advice of his doctors to resign his post and return to England.

His services to England and the East India Company are tersely summed up by Mr. Marshman in the following words:—"When he landed in Calcutta, in 1757, he found the Company's factory a heap of ruins, and their servants in exile. By 1767 he had made the Company the sovereigns of twenty-five millions of people, and masters of a revenue little short of one-half that of England. He had laid the foundation of a great empire, containing an irrepressible element of expansion. He had established the supremacy of Europe in Asia."[1]

Nevertheless, on his return to England he was greatly persecuted by the Directors. His conduct was termed "a mass of unheard-of villanies and corruption;" and after six years of suffering, with a heart half-broken by weariness and disappointment, and a body full of pains and illness, the great conqueror put an end to his existence in November 1774.

Mr. Verelst succeeded him in the government of Bengal, and conducted it quietly and with ability for nearly two years.

1769.—At the end of this period the peace of Hindostan was again seriously troubled by the presence of an immense army of 300,000 Mahrattas, sent northwards by the Peshwa Madhoo Rao for the express purpose of avenging their defeat at Panipat eight years previously.

[1] Marshman's Hist. of India, vol. i. page 315.

This great host marched north without any intimation to the native princes, the emperor, or the English, of their actual purpose; so that the panic was excessive throughout the whole country, none knowing whom was to be first attacked.

The Mahrattas ravaged the whole of Rajpootana, and then, having compelled the Jauts to pay tribute, advanced to Delhi, which city was under the governorship of Zabita Khan, son of Nujib-u-dowla the Rohilla, who had been left there by Ahmed Khan in 1756 and had ruled exceedingly well.

The emperor was at his residence in Allahabad at this time, and the Peshwa, sending an embassy to that city, offered to place Shah Alum in triumph on his ancestral throne if he would place himself entirely under Mahratta protection. The emperor wrote to Verelst asking him for his advice, and the Government of Calcutta most strongly dissuaded him from adopting a course so perilous to the interests of the Company. The bait, however, was too tempting. Shah Alum, dazzled by the prospect of thus easily obtaining the position which had been the dream of his life, accepted the offer of the Peshwa.

1771.—Accordingly, on December 25th, 1771 he was crowned Mogul Emperor at Delhi with great pomp and ceremony by the Peshwa, who invested him with all outward emblems of sovereignty.

1772.—The Mahrattas then overran Rohilcund, reduced the Dooab, and laid waste the whole province. They seized the person of Zabita Khan, threw him into prison, and confiscated his property; and towards the autumn made a treaty with the Rohillas and the Nabob Vizier of Oude, the precise terms of which have never been discovered. All that is known is that the Mahrattas consented to retire on payment of forty lacs of rupees, guaranteed by Sujah-u-dowla, the Vizier, and that the latter afterwards refused this gift.

1773.—In consequence of this refusal the Mahrattas determined to plunder Oude; and the Rohillas, under Hafiz Ruhmut, joined with the Nabob in order to oppose them.

The English were now dragged into the confusion by the unfortunate and headstrong conduct of the Emperor. Wishing at once to get rid of the Mahratta supremacy he attacked their army and was of course thoroughly worsted. As a punishment, the victors forced upon him the cession of the districts of Corah and Allahabad. But since these districts included a portion of the British territory the Bengal Government determined to prevent such an illegal donation from taking place, and they openly announced this intention.

Their territory was thus again in great peril; for although there was a powerful combination in their favour, consisting of the Nabob of Oude, the Emperor. and the Rohillas, yet the force of the enemy was overwhelmingly large; and it is more than probable that the native troops on the side of the English would have been, as was so commonly the case, rendered worse than useless by the panic-fear which the presence of a vast army flushed with victory often inspired in their minds.

But Providence again saved the now rising power of the Company from destruction. The Peshwa at Poonah had planned an expedition in the South; and, completely disregarding his fortunes in Hindostan, he summoned the whole army of the Mahrattas to the Deckan. They accordingly retired, leaving the Company's territories uninjured, and once more the Bengal merchants were at peace.

Progress of Events at Home.—Events at home now demand our attention for a while, as they were of great importance in the history of the Company.

The immense fortunes acquired by numbers of the servants of the Company at this time had excited considerable jealousy in England; while a certain amount of ridicule had been called down on their heads by their ostentatious manner of living, and lavish display of wealth.

The feeling of indignation thus aroused was fostered by many other circumstances; and eventually discussions of a very serious character took place in Parliament. It was declared that the whole constitution of the Company was bad, and that the great fortunes observed had been acquired by wholesale depositions of native princes and by a disgraceful system of oppression and extortion.

The rules described on a previous page, by which a holder of £500 stock possessed one vote in the meetings of the Court of Proprietors, had led to a system of extensive bribery and corruption, which was annually repeated when the time arrived for electing the new Directors.[1] The India House was a constant scene of intrigues and jobbery. To so great an extent was this carried on, that in 1771 Parliament interfered, and after much

[1] It is said that on one occasion Lord Shelburne laid out the immense sum of £100,000, by which he bought two hundred votes, for the sole purpose of obtaining the election of Mr. Sullivan to the Directorate.

discussion appointed a Committee of Three, who were to sail at once for Calcutta, examine into all matters connected with the Company's management, and make such reforms as they should, after due consideration, deem necessary.

Vansittart, Scrafton, and Colonel Forde were appointed Supervisors, and sent out; but the ship never reached land, and was supposed to have foundered in a storm near the Cape. Thus unhappily perished the late Governor, and the gallant soldier, many times saviour of Calcutta!

Soon afterwards a dispute arose between the Company and the Crown as to the actual ownership of the possessions acquired by the former in India, each party claiming them as their own, the former by right of conquest, the latter by the law of the Constitution.

In the midst of this disturbed state of affairs it was discovered that a large deficit had taken place in the Company's revenue,[1] and the Directors begged Parliament for permission to institute a public loan. The excitement which this request caused in England was very great! The confession of temporal bankruptcy gave a deathblow to all the preconceived ideas so rife in England as to the inexhaustible wealth of India; and accordingly, in 1772, a Select Committee was appointed, and the whole system of fraud violence and oppression by which certain individual members had been enriched, was laid bare to the nation.

An impassioned debate ensued in Parliament, in the course of which Lord Clive made his celebrated speech on Indian affairs; and in 1773 the two Houses passed and promulgated a "*Reconstruction Act*," with the following regulations:—

The Reconstruction Act of 1773.—A loan of one million from the public funds was to be granted from the Treasury.—No Member or Proprietor was in any case to have more than four votes in the Courts; and the amount of stock qualifying for one vote was raised from £500 to £1000.—The Governor of Calcutta was to be called "Governor-General," having supreme command over all the Presidencies, and nominated by Parliament every five years.—A "*Supreme Court*" was established at Calcutta, presided over by learned English lawyers, having full civil, criminal, admiralty and ecclesiastical jurisdiction. It was also constituted a Court of Record, of "oyer and terminer," and of

[1] The deficit amounted to a million in India, and a million and a half in England.

Quarter Sessions; and a Chief Justice and five Puisne Judges were appointed to carry out its duties.[1]

By the plan of Warren Hastings, which was partially adopted, the natives were to have their own laws administered to them; and by his 23rd Rule "*Moulavies*," or expounders of the Mahomedan law, and "*Pundits*," or interpreters of Hindu Law, were appointed to attend regularly in each court.[2]

The effect of this Act of Reconstruction upon the state of the Company at home was beneficial; but in India it worked less satisfactorily, owing to the circumstance of its having been drawn up by a Parliamentary Committee, who were all more or less ignorant of the actual state of affairs in that country.

(V.)—*Affairs in Madras and Bombay*, 1761—1773.

1761.—In 1761, Nizam Ali seized and imprisoned his brother, Salabat Jung, the Subahdar of the Deckan, and proclaimed himself Nizam in his place; an event calculated to produce great uneasiness at Madras since the usurper was known to favour the pretensions of France. But no open act took place till two years later, and meanwhile the interests of the residents were directed

[1] The powers of the Supreme Court may be divided into eight classes—

(I.) It tried all actions arising amongst Europeans in Bengal, Behar and Orissa.

(II.) It tried and determined all causes against the Company or the subjects of the Crown, by natives who had property in Bengal, Behar, and Orissa, whether these actions were real, personal, or mixed.

(III.) It was given an equitable jurisdiction similar to that of the Court of Chancery in England.

(IV.) It was a court of "oyer and terminer" over Fort William, Calcutta, and the surrounding factories.

(V.) It was a Court of Probate and Divorce with reference to all British subjects in the presidency.

(VI.) It had a power of appointment of guardians over lunatics and infants.

(VII.) It had civil and criminal jurisdiction in admiralty matters; and lastly—

(VIII.) It had full ecclesiastical jurisdiction.

The only appeal from its decisions lay to the king in council.

[2] In the year 1780, when the Governor-General in council was invested by Parliament with the power of making laws and regulations for the newly-acquired countries, the 23rd rule of Warren Hastings' plan was *nem. con.* made law in India. The 27th section enacted that the "*Koran*" should be the standard of law for Mahomedans; and the "*Vedas*," or "*Dharma Shastras*," for Hindus.

to the affairs of the Carnatic and Tanjore. The occurrences referred to do not reflect great credit on the English officials then at Madras, but they will serve to show what sort of policy was in those days deemed justifiable.

Mahomet Ali had entirely neglected to discipline his army, and believed himself to be perfectly secure in his office with the guaranteed assistance of the English contingent; but in order to provide for the maintenance of this force, the President of Madras demanded a payment of fifty lacs of rupees from the Nabob. Mahomet Ali pleaded inability, but suggested that the combined forces should fleece Tanjore, which was reported to be very rich. The President refused this open attack, but sent a message to the Rajah of Tanjore, that unless he made a large payment of money, his dominions would be ravaged and confiscated. The unhappy Rajah consented; and such was the manner in which the expense of the Carnatic contingent was defrayed!

1763.—In 1763 the "Peace of Paris" acknowledged Mahomet Ali as Nabob of the Carnatic, and declared Salabat Jung to be Subahdar. But those who framed the law little dreamed of what its effect would be. Nizam Ali immediately put his captive brother to death, so as for ever to destroy Salabat's title to the Subahdari, and to secure himself in that office as of right.

Nizam Ali thus became actual Subahdar. His first act was to proclaim hostility to the English, and to refuse to recognise Mahomet Ali as Nabob of the Carnatic.

The danger was obviated by the bold front of one or two regiments of English soldiers, which frightened the Nizam into quietude; whilst a firman was easily obtained from the puppet emperor at Delhi, declaring the Company's ally, Nabob of the Carnatic, independently of the present or any future Subahdar of the Deckan. Thus the Carnatic became a sovereignty for ever removed from the interference of the Subahdar.

1765.—Affair of the Northern Circars.—In the year 1765, on the same day that Clive obtained the grant of the Dewani for the Company, he persuaded the emperor to give up the Northern Circars to the English. (August 12th, 1765.)

The Nizam, however, refused his consent to this arrangement, declaring with much truth that the lands had been given to the French, and, sending a message to this effect to the President of Madras, he threatened to annihilate the British in the South, if any course of action entailing the loss of that district to the French were persisted in.

The President, somewhat startled at this threat, sent Colonel Calliaud to Hyderabad to make a treaty, which was accordingly concluded on November 12th, 1765.

First Treaty with the Nizam.—The terms were that the Northern Circars were to be held by the English as from the *Nizam*, the Company paying him an annual subsidy of eight lacs of rupees, and furnishing a contingent of two battalions of infantry with six guns to defend the district.

It seems clear that this arrangement was founded on a mistaken policy. The Circars were held by direct gift from the *emperor*; and to make this territory the subject of a treaty with the *emperor's officer*, the Subahdar of the Deckan, was a course highly imprudent, being virtually an acknowledgment of the independence of the Nizam, and of the weakness of the Madras Government.

Hyder Ali.—But events of greater importance were about to take place. *Hyder Ali* was now Rajah of Mysore. Though he had hitherto pursued his career without provoking the hostility of the English, a war broke out in 1766 which lasted thirty-three years, and caused terrible loss of life to the soldiers of the Company.

In order to understand the position Hyder Ali occupied at this period, a short sketch of his life is necessary.

Hyder Ali.—Hyder Ali was born in 1702. He was son of Futteh Mahomed, a Mogul officer, who died while in command of a small body of troops in the Punjaub; leaving his son in the somewhat humble position of a "*naik*,"[1] having 200 men under his orders. It happened that at this period the Rajah of Mysore, representative of a family who had reigned for 200 years, consigned all his real power into the hands of his vizier, Nunjeraj; and Hyder Ali, considering any service better than that of the powerless emperor of Delhi, persuaded his soldiers to join the army of Mysore. This was effected in 1750. After five years service, in which he greatly distinguished himself, Hyder was made commander of the fortress of Dindigul, with instructions to raise bodies of troops, and retain them under his orders. The manner in which he accomplished this task was characteristic. He led a marauding life, and

[1] A "*Naik*" in the Mogul army was a rank somewhat analogous to a "*Captain*" in Europe. At the present time a corporal in the native army is called a "Naik."

invited into his fortress all the criminals and freebooters in the country round. These flocked to him in large numbers, so that in 1757, when the Peshwa invaded Mysore, Hyder had a force of 10,000 men under his command with a large stock of guns and ammunition. He soon became a landed proprietor; for on an occasion when the Mysore treasury was exhausted by the heavy payments made to buy off the Mahrattas, and when the royal army mutinied for pay, Hyder, assisting greatly in quelling the disturbances, was presented with a considerable estate in return for his services. He was made commander-in-chief in Mysore in 1759; and receiving presents of more land, became possessed of almost half the Raj in his own right. His power was now so great that Nunjeraj, overawed, retired into private life, while Hyder became responsible minister to the Rajah. A powerful attack being made upon him by one Kundeh Rao, Hyder fled to Nunjeraj, implored him to resume his position, and then, taking command of the army, defeated captured and imprisoned Kundeh Rao.[1] He then compelled Nunjeraj and the Rajah to resign in his favour. Hyder thus became Rajah of Mysore in 1761, and extended his territories by capturing Bednore in 1763 and South Canara in 1764.

In 1765 the Peshwa Madhoo Rao resolving if possible to put a stop to the rising power of Hyder Ali, sent against him an army, which was commanded by Roghoji Bhonslay now Rajah of Berar, and Raghoba brother to the Peshwa. Being twice defeated, Hyder bought off the Mahrattas by a payment of thirty-two lacs of rupees and the cession of all the territories he had acquired beyond the Mysore frontier.

1766.—But next year he again assumed the offensive and captured Calicut and Malabar. The Peshwa then made a grand alliance with the Nizam and the English, who agreed to treat Hyder as a common enemy to the peace of the South of India, and to unite for the purpose of crushing him. Thus commenced the first Mysore War.

First Mysore War, 1767.—The war was commenced by the

[1] It is related that Hyder shut Kundeh Rao in an iron cage like a paroquet, and fed him on crumbs of rice and seeds, in mockery. The unfortunate man soon died under this barbarous treatment.

advance of the Mahrattas, who crossed the Kistna in January, 1767, and plundered the northern districts of Mysore. Hyder diplomatically offered a large payment if they would retire; and the Peshwa, accepting the offer, drew off his troops to Poonah.

The other allies, namely the Nizam, and the English under Colonel Smith, prepared to attack the enemy; but the plans of the English were suddenly upset by the desertion of the Nizam from the confederacy. The latter opened negotiations with the Mysoreans, but, acting with his usual duplicity, he first plotted with Nunjeraj to upset Hyder, and then wrote to Hyder promising to place the late minister in his hands if he would make an alliance. Hyder consented, and Nunjeraj being delivered into his hands was thrown into prison under circumstances of great brutality.

The English thereupon retired, and the Nizam joined Hyder.

The tables were now completely turned; and the united armies of Mysore and Hyderabad attacked Colonel Smith at Changama in September. After a hard struggle, Smith won a decided victory and caused great loss of life amongst the ranks of the enemy. But his force being too weak to effect any important result he wisely continued his retreat to Madras, the army marching in excellent order.

1768.—Soon afterwards the English created a diversion by attacking a place near Hyderabad, which so terrified the Nizam that he retreated northwards in great haste and at once came to terms.

Second treaty with the Nizam, 1768.—A Treaty was accordingly drawn up, the terms of which are perhaps among the most strange of any that have ever received the signature of a British envoy.[1] It is quite clear that that officer was on the present occasion acting under the influence of terror. There were four principal stipulations:—

(1.) The English were to "pay tribute" to the Nizam for the Northern Circars.[2]

(2.) The Guntoor Circar was not to be claimed by the Company till after the death of Bassalat Jung, the Nizam's brother, who now held it.[3]

[1] The peculiar character of the whole of this document might almost be gathered from its preamble, wherein Hyder Ali, then one of the greatest powers in India, was contemptuously styled "*Hyder Naik.*"

[2] But the Northern Circars were held direct from the Emperor. (See page 111).

[3] This clause afterwards involved the company in great difficulties.

(3.) The English were to pay "*chout*" to the Mahrattas.[1]

(4.). In order to pay this, the English guaranteed to conquer the Carnatic Balaghat from Hyder Ali, and pay the money out of the proceeds of the annexation!!

The extraordinary nature of this last clause renders it difficult to believe that it could seriously have formed part of a solemn Treaty intended to be adhered to by both the contracting parties, yet such was the case. The whole affair seems to have been grievously mismanaged.

In the autumn of the same year an expedition was sent from Bombay which was so far successful that the English took Mangalore and Onore and held them a month or two, after which the forts were easily recaptured by the Mysoreans.

But while Hyder was thus occupied on the western coast Colonel Smith marched into Mysore and captured nearly half of his dominions.

The Rajah offered terms, which were, perhaps unwisely, rejected; for the Mysoreans at once marched down on Smith's lines at Bangalore and forced him to raise the siege of that city and retire to Colar.

1769.—Here the English forces remained inactive for many months, during which Hyder Ali ravaged the Carnatic, Trichinopoly, Madura, and Tinnevelly. He accomplished this with such success that before the end of the year he had recovered all the districts previously lost and was able to present a bold front to the enemy, with an army reinforced in numbers and full of energy. Colonel Smith marched into Mysore to meet him; but Hyder by a rapid and clever flank movement evaded that officer, and appeared suddenly and unexpectedly before Madras itself.

Treaty with Hyder Ali, 1769.—The government were panic-stricken, and without attempting a defence humbly promised to grant any terms the Rajah might dictate. Hyder demanded an offensive and defensive Treaty, which was accordingly made; and the Rajah then requested that an order should be sent to Colonel Smith requiring him to remain peaceably in camp without in any way acting on the offensive. This also was acceded to, and the indignant officer was compelled to remain at rest while his enemy marched past him back into Mysore.

1770.—Hyder now believed himself sufficiently strong to defy

[1] "*Chout*," was only paid to the Mahrattas as a kind of black-mail, by those surrounding nations who were unable to defend themselves against the encroachments of those marauders.

the Mahrattas, and he accordingly opposed them openly. But Madhoo Rao brought a large army into the field and, utterly defeating the Mysoreans in the west, forced Hyder to come to terms The Peshwa demanded a crore of rupees as compensation; but the Rajah, considering the amount too great, refused to accede to such an indignity and closed the interview. The Mahrattas therefore again advanced; and Hyder, who was then entangled in the Western Ghauts, fancying that he could fight the enemy better on the plains, retreated inland in order to draw them on. When night came on, however, he found himself entangled in a very difficult pass; and declaring that it was impossible to effect anything till the morning, he caused his tent to be pitched in a convenient spot and invited his principal officers to spend the remainder of the night in drunkenness and dissipation. In the midst of their revelry the camp was attacked by the watchful Mahrattas who had had information conveyed to them by their spies, and terrible scenes of slaughter and confusion ensued. Surprised like the rest, Hyder's eldest son Tippoo Sahib, who commanded the cavalry, galloped in haste to obtain the orders of his father. He found Hyder completely intoxicated and quite incapable of any sensible action. The only attention the Rajah paid to his son's words was to rail at him for daring to disturb the party so unreasonably; and on the latter's remonstrating, Hyder lost all command of himself, used insulting language, and finally struck Tippoo on the shoulder, who, incensed at the insult, swore solemnly not to draw his sword that night. He kept his word, and the Mysorean army were beaten at all points.

A complete rout ensued and Hyder fled in haste to Seringapatam.

He then appealed for help to the English under the Treaty of the previous year. But Sir John Lindsay, who had been sent out by Parliament to control the affairs of Madras, insisted upon making a Treaty with the Mahrattas, and leaving Hyder to his fate.

That prince never forgave or forgot this deliberate breach of faith, and he swore a solemn oath on the Koran (Tippoo Sahib following his example), that he would for ever cherish the direst hatred against the English, and would use every means in his power to crush them out of India.

He succeeded in buying off the Mahrattas with an immediate payment of thirty-six lacs of rupees and a cession of territory promising an annual income of fourteen lacs.

(VI.)—*Warren Hastings' Administration*, 1772—1785.

In 1772, Warren Hastings, for years an eminent Bengal civilian, was appointed to carry on the duties of President at Calcutta.

Warren Hastings.—Warren Hastings was born in 1732, and at the age of 18 was sent to Calcutta in the office of one of the merchants there. His talents early displayed themselves, and in 1757, while at the age of 25, he was appointed representative of the Company at the great Durbar at Moorshedabad, after the battle of Plassy. While at the age of only 28 he became a member of the Calcutta Council (1760), and was nobly distinguished from the rest of the men of his time by his high principle and moral character. In 1763 he returned home, and next year was sent out as second in the Council to Vansittart. In 1772, he was chosen Governor of Bengal to succeed Mr. Verelst, and commenced his duties on April 13th of that year.

His first act was to appoint the Members of Council. They consisted of General Clavering, Colonel Monson, Mr. Barwell, and Mr. Francis.

The new Governor afterwards set himself busily to work to reform the Revenue administration of the country; and for this purpose he transferred the central office from Moorshedabad to Calcutta. At the same time he made some necessary alterations in the arrangements of the Courts of Justice which had been established by Lord Clive in 1765.[1]

The innovations Hastings introduced were for the most part advantageous; though he unfortunately stopped short of the abolition of the system of farming the revenues, which had led to so much distress amongst the ryots, and which was destined to cause considerable trouble to later governors in dealing with the land question of the Bengal Presidency.[2]

1773.—Next year the "*Reconstruction Act*" was passed,[3] and Hastings was constituted first "Governor-General." At the same time the Supreme Court of Calcutta was established by

[1] See notes, pages 104, 109.
[2] See below, pages 138, 153.
[3] See page 109.

13 Geo. III. c. 63; and at the close of the year the judges arrived. Their advent was the signal for the commencement of those troubles which characterized the administration of Warren Hastings, and which ended in his ruin. They were completely ignorant of Hindu customs;[1] and they were apparently imbued with the idea that their functions were those of government, and that, if they pleased, they might issue orders even to the Governor-General himself.

Rohilla War.—In this year a war with the Rohillas broke out, which formed a subject for considerable discussion in England.

Sujah-u-dowla, the Nabob of Oude, announced to the Governor-General that the inhabitants of Rohilcund had refused to pay to him the tribute of forty lacs which they had promised when the Mahrattas retired southwards in 1773, and he offered to yield up the whole of this sum to the English if that nation would assist him to reduce the power of the Rohillas.

Hastings was induced to give his consent owing to the advice of the council, and considering the poverty of the Treasury at this period. But it is difficult to justify his conduct except on the slender grounds of a certain vague policy discernible in the extirpation of a neighbouring people who might at some future time become troublesome.

A Treaty was accordingly made with the Nabob-vizier that, if the war was successful, he should be permitted to purchase the districts of Colar and Allahabad for fifty lacs of rupees[2] The Rohillas were stricken with fear, and Hafiz Ruhmut, their brave chieftain, implored the Vizier to spare his country on condition of the Rohillas defraying whatever expenses Sujah had been put to when defending Rohilcund against the Mahrattas.

But the Vizier demanded the enormous sum of 200 lacs, and the Rohillas to a man declared they would die sooner than submit to such extortion.

[1] Mr. Marshman tells an amusing anecdote illustrative of the ignorance and bigotry of these gentlemen. He says:—"As the judges stepped on shore, one of them observing the bare legs and feet of the natives who crowded to the sight, said to his colleague, 'Our court, brother, certainly was not established before it was needed. I trust we shall not have been six months in the country before these victims of oppression are comfortably provided with shoes and stockings.'"—(Hist. of India, I. 346.)

[2] The government of these districts caused much expense to the Company, and never yielded a surplus. The arrangement thus made was therefore apparently a satisfactory one.

Both sides prepared for war, and on April 23rd 1773 the allied troops marched into Rohilcund and fought the first and only battle of the war, in which the bold Rohillas were almost exterminated, and Hafiz Ruhmut killed. After desolating the country the victors retired to their own territory.

Disorders at Calcutta, 1774—1775.—The council at Calcutta was now divided into various factions, and party feeling began to rise high in the Presidency. The judges and members of council were opposed to Warren Hastings, and a majority was formed against him owing to whose intrigues and misrepresentations the Directors at home commenced a system of hostility to the Governor-General, thwarting him in every endeavour, and misconstruing every action that he undertook.

1775.—One of the earliest symptoms of this ill-feeling was the recall at the commencement of the year 1775 of the Resident whom Hastings had appointed at the court of the Nabob, and the substitution there of a certain Mr. Bristow.

This officer's first act was to demand an immediate payment within fourteen days of all the arrears due from the Vizier to the Company, an act of impolicy so palpable that Hastings warmly denounced it both openly and in private. Still more astonished was he when Mr. Bristow proceeded to order the British troops at once to retire from Rohilcund, a course of action calculated completely to stultify their conquest of the country. Hastings indignantly remonstrated, but the Resident showed him the private orders of the Directors containing definite instructions to himself to adopt this course with the conquered country.

The conduct of the Directors in giving secret instructions to a Resident, instead of permitting the orders to come through the Governor-General direct, implied a wanton insult. The constitution of the Company was violated; and Hastings, now justly incensed, wrote a solemn protest against their behaviour.

The next act of open opposition to the wishes of the Governor-General came from the Council. Sujah-u-dowla, the Nabob-Vizier, died the same year (1775), and his son Asoff-u-dowla succeeding him wrote to Calcutta requesting the support of the Company. But Francis, much against the wishes of Hastings (and Mr. Barwell who always sided with his chief), by means of his majority at the Council meeting compelled the Governor-General to send an order to Asoff-u-dowla to the effect that all relations with Oude were now at an end, and that Asoff's succession must be based on a new Treaty with the Company, ceding Benares absolutely into their hands[1] The Nabob, powerless to effect anything against the English and protesting that the demand was an open violation of justice, was forced to consent, and thus the most sacred city of India fell into the hands of the Company.

Great disturbances ensued mainly owing to the rash conduct of Mr. Bristow.

The Begums of Oude.—When the late vizier died, it was believed that he had amassed large sums of money; and on the zenana being searched after his funeral, rupees to the amount of two millions sterling were found there. This sum the Begums refused to give up to Asoff, declaring that it was bequeathed for their own private use; but the new vizier's treasury being completely empty, he claimed the rupees as public money, basing his demand on the exigencies of the state and the absolute necessity for this fund in order to carry on the government. Mr. Bristow was called in and decided in favour of the Begums, compelling Asoff-u-dowla to return them the whole of the property; the effect of which rash act was that the vizier, being unable to meet the arrears of pay due to his soldiers, narrowly escaped being murdered in the terrible mutiny of the troops which followed and which is said to have cost the lives of 20,000 men!

The disputes at Calcutta now began to assume a more serious aspect. It was truly a "house divided against itself." There was not merely opposition, but even open hostility in the council; and every proposal of the Governor was ridiculed by the majority of three headed by Francis, the most intractable and furious member of council that has perhaps ever sat on that august Board. He seemed to care little for the interests of the public or the state, so that he carried out his plan of opposition to Hastings; and with Clavering and Monson occupied his time in bringing and inviting charges against Hastings and Barwell, condescending even to request the natives to aid in this high and noble crusade. At home the Directors abetted the fractious members and kept ready a complete list of all the charges (however preposterous and unproved) to fling in the face of Hastings on his return.

Nuncomar.—One of the most prominent of these accusations

[1] The chief reason which Hastings urged against this demand was that it was a direct blow at all the religious feelings of the Hindus, to wound which was to alienate them from our rule in the completest manner possible, just at a period when we ought to have striven to gain their affections.

related to the case of Nuncomar, a Brahman, who was accused of the crime of forgery and being on the clearest evidence convicted by the Supreme Court was sentenced to death.

It happened that this Nuncomar had been one of those who accused Hastings of embezzlement, and the members of Council strongly deprecated the execution of the criminal, declaring that Hastings was murdering him in order to prevent the charge being brought forward.[1] The judges were even threatened by Francis if they persisted in ordering the execution; but they haughtily replied that they were the supreme expounders of the law, and would not be dictated to on any pretence whatever.

This was the first instance of the execution of a Brahman, and it caused the greatest horror amongst the entire native population who crowded to witness the profanation with tears in their eyes.

It was afterwards discovered that the entire charge brought by Nuncomar against Hastings was a fabrication, the letter upon which the evidence depended being a forgery.

1776.—The feelings of the persecuted Governor-General had at this time been so worked upon by the constant opposition he experienced, and by the never-ending scenes of strife and hostility which took place, both at home and in India, that he determined to resign: and, happening to mention this intention to his agent at home in a private letter, the latter, unable to keep silence, began to speak openly in London of the Governor's determination.

Before the time arrived however when he proposed to carry out his intention, Hastings obtained a casting vote in the Council by the death of Colonel Monson. He therefore wrote again to his agent announcing his intention of remaining in India.

But the Directors, anxious to get rid of him, seized the pretext afforded them by the first letter (though it was private and unofficial), and declared him to have resigned his appointment.

1777.—Acting on this hasty and ill-judged announcement of the Board of Directors, General Clavering culminated the matter by attempting to assume the insignia of Government as senior Member of Council. He went one day with a body of soldiers to the Council chamber, and read the oaths of office as Governor-General. Hastings at once declared him an usurper, and shut the gates of Fort William against him! The matter was referred

[1] There is not the slightest evidence that Hastings ever promoted or even gave his consent to Nuncomar's prosecution.

to the Judges of the Supreme Court, who decided in favour of Warren Hastings, and Clavering's disappointment was so great that it preyed upon his spirits and caused his death a few months later.

Francis still continued his opposition in the most bitter and open manner, and at last the ill-feeling between him and Hastings broke out into open warfare when Mr. Barwell retired to England. In order not to prevent the latter's resignation, Francis had promised the Governor-General that he would not take any advantage of the majority thus gained in the Council; but as soon as Barwell had sailed, he broke his promise. Hastings openly accused his enemy of deception, and the matter was settled by a duel in which Francis was wounded.

Soon afterwards the latter returned to England, and Warren Hastings was left for a time at rest.

But previously to this the Mahrattas had again become troublesome. Their great families were rising into importance, and the peace of India was again disturbed by open warfare.

Mahratta Affairs, 1772—1775.—Madhoo Rao the Peshwa died in 1772, and was succeeded by his brother Narain Rao whom Raghoba at once caused to be assassinated. In 1773 Raghoba seized the crown and made war on the Nizam, who purchased peace with twenty lacs of rupees. Nana Furnuvese and Saccaram Bappoo, two able statesmen, at once determined to crush the rising power of the bold Raghoba; and they placed on the throne an infant whom they took from the zenana, and who was reputed to be the posthumous child of Madhoo Rao. This child, when only ten days' old, was installed under the title of Madhoo Rao the Second, and the government was assumed by Saccaram Bappoo and Nana Furnuvese.

In 1774 Raghoba took the field against the Regents in company with Morari Rao, and gained a signal victory. But, instead of following this up by marching straight on Poonah, he went off to Burhampore and then to Guzerat, where he begged for the co-operation of his countryman the Gwickwar.

It happened that at this time the kingdom of Guzerat was suffering under domestic troubles. Govind Rao and Futteh Sing, brothers, (sons of Damaji Gwickwar, the son of Pilaji Gwickwar, the first sovereign), were disputing for the possession of the throne. Raghoba's design, accordingly, was to gain the aid and countenance of one of the brothers by assisting him to establish himself as Rajah. He chose to support the claims of

Futteh Sing, and in this undertaking was joined by Holkar and Sindia, the great Mahratta chieftains, with all their forces.

1775.—Next year Nana Furnuvese, by clever intrigue, succeeded in detaching both Holkar and Sindia from this dangerous alliance, promising them large sums of money if they remained neutral. They therefore drew off and left Raghoba and the Gwickwar to act alone.

Raghoba then sent overtures to Bombay to implore the protection of the English; and the Government of that Presidency acting on their own responsibility, and without the knowledge or consent of Warren Hastings, made an arrangement with Raghoba which is known as the Treaty of Surat.

Treaty of Surat, March 6th, 1775.—The Treaty was signed by Raghoba in person at a durbar at Surat, whence it takes its name, the terms being as follows:—

- Raghoba was to cede Salsette and Bassein,[1] for purposes of trade to the English, and to pay an annual subsidy of thirty-seven lacs to the Bombay Government.
- The English were to assist Raghoba to regain the throne of the Peshwa.

This Treaty was at the outset unconstitutional, for the Regulating Act of 1773 expressly provided that the "subordinate Presidencies (namely, those of Fort St. George and Bombay), in the particular cases of concluding Treaties and applying revenues, levying and employing forces, and, in general, in all matters of civil and military administration, are placed under the superintendence of the Government-General of Bengal."[2] Hence the Bombay Government could make no Treaty without the consent of Hastings and the Council. Moreover, the subsidy guaranteed by Raghoba should have been made payable, not to the Bombay Government, but to the Company as a whole.

But the Treaty, once made, might well have been supported; and the conduct of Francis, who forced the Governor-General to disallow the arrangement, embroiled the English in great troubles.

1st Mahratta War, 1775.—Colonel Keating, who commanded a contingent of British troops at Bombay, was then ordered to effect a junction with Raghoba, and co-operate with him during

[1] Salsette is an island, and Bassein an excellent port near Bombay. The territory included was about 150 square miles, and great advantages would have accrued from its possession owing to increased facilities for trading.

[2] "Analysis of the Constitution of the East India Company," by Peter Auber, Secretary to the Court of Directors (published in 1822), p. 376.

the campaign. But he had advanced only as far as the river Mhye when he was attacked by the Regent's army.

Battle of Arras.—A battle was fought at Arras, near Baroda, in which Keating gained a complete victory. The Mahrattas fled to the Nerbudda, leaving their guns in the hands of the English; and immediately afterwards Futteh Siug, marching from Guzerat, effected a junction with Keating. The success was thus complete.

Francis at once employed his power in the Council to undo all that had been done, in opposition to the wishes of Warren Hastings who desired to uphold the Treaty of Surat. The majority was against the Governor-General, and accordingly a circular, expressed in strong terms, was written to the native princes, accusing the Bombay Government of wilful disobedience to orders, disallowing everything that had been done, and declaring the Treaty null and void.

The effect of this conduct was instantly to alienate the Gwickwar and Raghoba without creating any alliance with their opponents, the Regency; to lose thirty-seven lacs of rupees per annum to the Company; and wantonly to disgrace the Bombay Government in the eyes of the native princes.

The Regency at Poonah at once demanded back the districts of Salsette and Bassein, declaring that Raghoba could not *per se* have given away any territory belonging to the Peshwa; and that, at any rate, the Treaty being now null and void, the ceded country belonged to the Mahrattas as before.

But Colonel Upton, acting for the Company, refused to deliver up the ceded districts to Nana Furnuvese, saying that they belonged to Raghoba *as Peshwa*, and, that if they were to be returned, they should be returned to him only. The Regents, highly incensed at this contemptuous denial of their dignity, declared that their young charge Madhoo Rao the Second was alone head of the Mahratta state, and demanded that the Bombay Government should not only give back the districts, but should distinctly refuse to give the pretender, Raghoba, the title or rights of Peshwa.

Accordingly Colonel Upton, on behalf of the Government declared war with the Mahrattas, stating that the Bombay authorities had determined to support Raghoba. Thereupon the Regents offered a Treaty.

If Colonel Upton had seriously reflected he would have remembered that, having lately declared Raghoba to be Peshwa, he could not, with the smallest show of common sense, sign a Treaty with Nana Furnuvese and Saccaram Bappoo as representatives of the Mahratta state. But, acting upon the impulse of the moment, he unhesitatingly accepted.

Treaty of Poorunder, March 1st, 1776.—The Treaty was signed on March the 1st 1776 at Poorunder, and its terms were as follows:—

The British army was to quit the field on the condition of their retaining the island of Salsette, but relinquishing all other territories previously belonging to the Mahrattas. They were to receive twelve lacs a year, and to enjoy the revenues of Broach so long as they interfered not with the Mahratta Government, and acknowledged Madhoo Rao the Second as Peshwa.

Raghoba was to be disallowed; and to receive three lacs a year from the Mahrattas, on condition of his remaining beyond the Godaveri River.

This Treaty was one very advantageous to the Company under the circumstances, and as their Treaty with Raghoba had been broken off by the Supreme Government, it was open to them to maintain the treaty of Poorunder at the expense of that of Surat, one of the two being a necessity.

But the Bombay Government, indignant at the veto placed by the Council upon their first Treaty, determined obstinately to uphold it, and acted in such an imprudent and hasty manner that the whole Mahratta power was at once lashed into fury. They deliberately broke the terms of the Treaty of Poorunder, and, offering Raghoba an asylum at Surat, marched their armies into Broach

The Regency, enraged beyond parallel at this deliberate breach of faith, proclaimed war to the knife; but the Bombay Government treated their menaces with the utmost contempt, and ostentatiously paraded Raghoba as an honoured guest into Bombay itself. Shortly afterwards their triumph was completed by the reception of a despatch from the Court of Directors at home refusing to acknowledge the Treaty of Poorunder and upholding the Treaty of Surat.

1778.—Unexpected discords amongst the Mahrattas themselves now seemed to favour the Company's position at Bombay. For a cousin of Nana Furnuvese, by name Maroba Furnuvese, who had quarrelled with the Nana and induced Saccaram Bappoo to oppose the latter in every way, seized the opportunity to form a party at court, headed by Holkar and himself, and tacitly supported by Saccaram Bappoo, whose object was to support Raghoba's claim to the crown.

This new party of course appealed to the Bombay Government for assistance. The latter at once granted their request, and wrote to Calcutta for advices. Warren Hastings approved of their conduct for two reasons. First, because he felt that, since the Treaty of Surat was now in force, the duty of the Company was to support the title of Raghoba, and it was to their interest to secure him rapidly and safely in his coveted position. Secondly, because he knew that Nana Furnuvese was well disposed to the French, and that it would be advantageous if his power could be overthrown.

Nana Furnuvese at once retired to Poorunder, finding the united strength of Saccaram Bappoo, Maroba Furnuvese, Raghoba, Holkar, and the Bombay Government, somewhat too great for him to compete with single-handed. He then offered a large bribe to Holkar to leave the alliance, which the latter accepted, and thus one of the number was detached; and then, ordering up an army of his supporters in the name of their sovereign, Madhoo Rao, the Nana defeated the forces of Maroba and Saccaram, and pursued their leaders to Poonah. Thither he marched in triumph, threw Saccaram Bappoo into prison, and put Maroba and others to death.

Thus the party of Raghoba at Poonah was extinguished.

But the Bombay Government, annoyed at this unexpected reverse, determined to support Raghoba at all hazards, and at once prepared for war; first making a new treaty with Raghoba, similar to that of Surat.

2nd Campaign, 1779.—An expedition, somewhat hastily planned, was sent under Colonel Egerton to attack the capital of the Mahratta State; and the Government, instead of entrusting the entire command to that officer, committed the grievous mistake of hampering his movements by the presence of civil commissioners, who were directed to march with the army and direct his movements in all but actual warfare. The chief commissioner was General Carnac, who, as superior officer to the colonel in actual command, expected to be obeyed in all matters, and commenced operations by interfering in arrangements over which, as a civilian, he had no control.

When the force arrived near Poonah, the civil commissioners became alarmed, and wished to beat a retreat. But Raghoba protested, and Colonel Egerton refused to give the command to the troops to retire. Their bravery was of no avail,—the commissioners *ordered it;* and for the first time in their history in India the English troops showed the white feather.

The little army was immediately attacked by the Peshwa's cavalry; and the rear-guard, under the command of the gallant Captain Hartley, fought with great spirit while the civil commissioners in the van fled forward with all haste.

During the night the army, encamped at Wurgaom, was shelled by the Mahrattas, and the commissioners, panic-stricken, implored Sindia, who was in command of the Peshwa's troops, to spare their lives and guarantee their safe retreat.

Convention of Wurgaom,[1] *January,* 1779.—The army of Bombay was accordingly permitted to retire without molestation. on condition of their surrendering Raghoba,[2] and giving up every acquisition obtained during the last five years! Such was the miserable end of this most ill-planned and ill-managed expedition.

As soon as the terms of the Convention of Wurgaom were known to the Supreme Government, they were indignantly repudiated, and a new Treaty was proposed. But meanwhile Raghoba had escaped from the clutches of Sindia, and fled to Surat, where he was honourably entertained by Colonel Goddard, the chief in command at that station.

It was a matter of no difficulty for the Company to propose a new Treaty when the only terms bargained for, namely the safe retreat of their army, had been accomplished, and when Raghoba was in their hands; and Nana Furnuvese, feeling this to be the case, refused to treat unless Raghoba were given up. Colonel Goddard ridiculed this notion, and therefore war was again declared.

3rd Campaign, 1779.—Goddard marched at once towards Guzerat, where he was joined by Futteh Sing; and the allies, with Raghoba, advanced to and captured Ahmedabad. Here Sindia and Holkar opposed him at the head of the Mahratta

[1] This is called a "Convention," not a "Treaty," because it was signed, not by an agent of the Supreme Government, but by an agent from Bombay. Nevertheless, it ought perhaps to have received more consideration from head-quarters (however disgraceful it may have been to the English), after the entire terms, so far as they affected one of the contracting parties, were accomplished.

[2] The story goes that Raghoba, knowing from the previous conduct of the Civil Commissioners, that he would be ruthlessly given up to the Mahrattas, refused to submit to such a disgrace, and voluntarily surrendered himself to Sindia, who treated him well.

army, but were beaten, and went into cantonments during the rains, on the Nerbudda river.

4th Campaign, 1780. *Capture of Gwalior.*—At the commencement of the next campaign Hastings ordered a small force to create a diversion from the main attack by operating against Sindia's possessions near Agra, and sent a Major Popham to command the expedition. This officer performed the most brilliant feat of the war by the gallant capture of Gwalior, an almost impregnable fortress on a rock. The Hindus believed that it never could be taken, as it was situated on an almost perpendicular rock of great height. But Popham, determined to take the place, scaled the rock by night with ladders, and attacked the unsuspecting garrison with a few followers. He encountered a feeble resistance, and in the morning the British standard, floating on the battlements, proclaimed the great achievement to the country round. Overjoyed at Popham's success, Hastings declared that this victory had obliterated the evil effects of the "infamous Convention of Wurgaom."

General Carnac was then placed in command of Popham's little army which was reinforced and taken against Sindia. A night attack on the Mahratta camp was successful, and Sindia fled, leaving all his stores behind him.

The Grand Confederacy, 1780.—But these successes only made the Mahrattas more bitter against the English, and towards the close of the year a grand confederation was formed of the Mahrattas and Mysoreans, for the avowed purpose of driving the English out of India; the arrangement being that Holkar, Sindia, and the Peshwa, should attack Bombay, while Hyder Ali marched on Madras, and Madoji Bhonslay, Rajah of Nagpore, assaulted Calcutta.

The campaign was opened by Colonel Hartley, who, under the orders of the Bombay Government, cleared the Concans of Mahrattas. Colonel Goddard at the same time laid siege to Bassein, which he took on December 12th. And on the same day Hartley defeated Nana Furnuvese at Doogaur, though his troops were only 2000 in number, and inferior commissariat arrangements had caused sickness and starvation to a great extent in the army.[1]

1781.—Feeling that the time had arrived when it became

[1] Hartley, on this occasion, held out for two days with this exhausted force, against 20,000 Mahrattas in full health. He was the same officer who, then a captain, fought so bravely in the rear-guard at Wurgaum.

necessary to strike a severe blow, if Colonel Goddard marched straight on Poonah; but being much harassed by Holkar, and his army being exhausted by deprivation, he was compelled to retire.

The confederacy was at the same time weakened by the wavering policy of the Rajah of Nagpore, who treated with the English and sent only a nominal contingent to swell the ranks of the allies; and when Colonel Pearse, proceeding through Orissa to the aid of Madras, asked for assistance from Bhonslay, the request was granted. After this Hastings found no difficulty in detaching him from the grand confederation; and the Rajah sent 2000 horse to assist Colonel Pearse in his undertaking.

1782.—Hastings further succeeded in detaching Sindia as well as Bhonslay before the allies had effected anything in concert.

Treaty of Salbye, May 17th, 1782.—By this Treaty, which was signed at Salbye on May 17th, peace was procured between the English and Mahrattas.

- The English were to restore all territory acquired since the Treaty of Poorunder in 1776.
- Raghoba was to cease all hostilities on condition of receiving three lacs of rupees a year, and permission to choose his own place of residence.
- Hyder Ali was to be required to release all English prisoners within six months, and to relinquish all his conquests. On refusal, he was to be attacked by the Mahrattas.

To this last clause, Nana Furnuvese refused to give his sanction until he heard of the death of Hyder, on December 7th of the same year. At the same time, Hastings made various treaties with the other native princes in order to secure their co-operation and good will.

We must now turn to the progress of affairs in the Madras Presidency where, according to his agreement with the Mahrattas, Hyder Ali was operating with large armies, and, assisted by the French, was causing the utmost anxiety to the Government of Fort St. George.

Progress of Hyder.—After Hyder Ali had bought off the Mahrattas in 1770,[1] he remained at rest till, taking advantage of the confusion that ensued when Narain Rao was murdered by Raghoba in 1772, he subjugated Coorg with much unnecessary cruelty; and by the year

[1] See page 116.

1774 had reconquered all the districts of which he had been dispossessed by the Mahrattas. In 1775 he took Bellary from Bassalat Jung, brother to the Nizam, and in 1776 destroyed Savanore, the Raj of the Mahratta chieftain, Morari Rao. In the same year the Poonah Regency made another ineffectual attempt to crush Hyder's power, on account of the staunch support which he gave to Raghoba; and two years later the kingdom of Mysore was extended to the Kistna River. In 1779, war was declared between England and France, and Hyder, out of his sworn hatred to the Company, declared in favour of the French. (The English, however, captured Pondicherry and Mahé from the French, in spite of his opposition). Hyder joined the Grand Confederacy in 1780, and, according to agreement, prepared to attack Madras.

2nd Mysore War, 1780.—He made great preparations for his expedition; but the President and Council of Madras were hardly aware of the real extent of their danger, imagining that Hyder's intentions were only to terrify the Government into making an advantageous treaty, and not actually to attack them.[1]

They were, therefore, somewhat startled when, on July 20th, Hyder marched through the Changama Pass into the Carnatic, followed by a numerous and well-appointed army, and devastated the country on all sides, behaving with great cruelty. But little could now be done on account of the want of cavalry; and though the President, Sir Thomas Rumbold, at once took all possible steps to check the progress of the Mysoreans, the evil was done, for the smoke of the blazing villages could actually be seen from Madras.

The English army consisted only of 8000 men, which were in three divisions, separated at considerable distances. It was of the utmost importance to effect a junction, and Colonel Baillie, at Guntoor, was ordered to join Sir Hector Munro, the Commander-in-Chief, at once. He obeyed but, being stopped by an impassable swollen stream, was compelled to encamp for six days. After the crossing was accomplished, and while his little force was still in disorder, Tippoo attacked him with a large force of Mahratta cavalry. Baillie with some difficulty beat him off, and proceeded on his march; but Hyder with the whole army, inter-

[1] This false security was fostered by the constant denial on the part of Hastings that Hyder was about to attack the Company.

posed between him and Munro, and, surrounding Baillie's force, annihilated them almost to a man, on September 6th, 1780.

1781.—At the close of the year Hyder captured Arcot, and early in January Sir Eyre Coote, with a well appointed reinforcement, arrived by sea from Calcutta to the relief of the Presidency. In the meantime, Lieutenant Flint's magnificent defence of Wandewash, which is one of the best known incidents of Indian history, took place. He made use of every device which his natural readiness or his acquired experience could suggest, and held out till Sir Eyre Coote, advancing to the rescue, raised the siege.

Coote then attacked Hyder at Porto Novo, near Cuddalore, and gained a signal victory, though his army was far inferior in numbers to that of the Mysoreans.

In July, the Bengal contingent under Colonel Pearse, which, as before narrated, had been assisted by the Rajah of Nagpore on its march through Orissa, arrived at Pulicat and effected a junction with Coote; and the united force met Hyder at the little village of Pollilore. A battle was fought without much result on the same spot where Colonel Baillie and his army had been destroyed the previous year. But a greater success was accomplished somewhat later, for on September 27th, Sir Eyre Coote gained a decided victory at Solinghur. He then went into cantonments at Madras for the rains.

Lord Macartney, President of Madras.—Towards the end of the year Lord Macartney arrived to assume the duties of President of Madras in the room of Sir Thomas Rumbold, who had somewhat suddenly resigned owing to ill-health; and his first act was to order the reduction of the Dutch power in the south, alleging, as his excuse, the danger of an alliance between that nation and the Mysoreans. Accordingly the Dutch fortress of Negapatam was stormed and razed to the ground, and the factories there destroyed. It seems a harsh measure; for hitherto the colonists from the Hague had never been known to cause the Presidency of Madras any anxiety, and it is more than probable that Lord Macartney was acting under secret orders from the Court of Directors, whose only ground of objection to the Dutch in the south was the jealousy of their ever-increasing trade.

The fortunes of the war with Hyder seemed now to favour the English, and another slight success of their arms at Tellicherry contributed to throw the Mysoreans into a state of despondency. So that Hyder felt himself constrained to give up his attempt on the Carnatic, and he determined to attack the Malabar coast instead.

1782.—Early next year a French squadron, sent out to inflict as much damage as possible on the English settlements in India, fell in with an English fleet off Porto Novo, returning from the reduction of the Dutch harbour of Trincomalee, in Ceylon, and an indecisive naval action took place. The French then landed a small force near Pondicherry, which effected a union with Hyder.

In July two other naval engagements took place off Negapatam, both without any result.

A French force, however, landing at Point de Galle, marched to Trincomalee, and re-took the town, destroying the garrison there. The fleet was opposed by several British ships under Admiral Hughes, who fought a fourth engagement near the coast of Ceylon, but without effect; and afterwards, without the smallest apparent reason, sailed off with the fleet to Bombay, leaving the French masters of the seas.

Towards the close of the year Tippoo attacked the English entrenched camp at Palghaut, near Coimbatore; and, failing in his first attempt at storming, he blockaded the camp and remained there till December 7th, when, hearing of the sudden death of his father, he took off all his troops into Mysore.

Death of Hyder.—Hyder Ali died at the age of eighty, on December 6th, 1782, and his minister, the celebrated financier Poorneah, with great prudence concealed the fact of his death from the troops till Tippoo arrived to take command, by this means preserving the army from becoming demoralized.

Accession of Tippoo Sahib.—Tippoo thus became Rajah of Mysore. He succeeded to the command of a splendid army of 100,000 men, and to a countless treasure in money and jewels. He remained, quietly consolidating his power, till March 1st, 1783, when he went off to the western coast to operate against the British possessions about Mangalore.

1783.—At the beginning of June, Bussy, now placed in command of all the French forces east of the Cape of Good Hope, landed at Cuddalore with a French contingent and, to his great astonishment and dismay, found Tippoo gone off to the western coast, and Hyder, whom he expected to join, deceased. He was at once attacked by General Stuart, who had succeeded Sir Eyre Coote, and on June 7th an outpost of Cuddalore was captured by the English, though with heavy loss. (The same day a naval engagement took place off Cuddalore, between Admiral Hughes and Suffrein, the French naval commander. Hughes was worsted, and put back to Madras to refit, while Suffrein landed 2400 marines and sailors to form a brigade attached to Bussy's army).

On the 18th the French made a dashing sortie, but were ably repulsed;[1] and soon afterwards the tidings came to the opposing forces that a peace had been concluded between France and England; upon which General Stuart returned to Madras, and Bussy strengthened his position.

Meanwhile the Bombay Government had sent an expedition, which had captured Bednore, and many other places on the Malabar coast. Tippoo, therefore, marched down, and, after a severe struggle, re-took Bednore, and threw the garrison into prison.

Siege of Mangalore.—He then invested Mangalore, which, under Colonel Campbell, was splendidly defended for nine months by a garrison of 1800 men against an attacking force of 100,000, with 100 guns! The place was only capitulated, when a further defence was impossible.

Colonel Fullarton at the same time led an expedition from Madras into Mysore, captured Palghaut, occupied Coimbatore, and was about to march against Seringapatam itself, when he was recalled by Lord Macartney.

The President considered this a favourable period for opening negociations with Tippoo. But they were conducted with great want of diplomacy; for instead of impressing the Mysoreans with the idea of the greatness and importance of the English nation, Lord Macartney sent his envoys entirely across India to Tippoo's camp as if to supplicate a treaty,—neglecting the advice of his council, who urged him to arrange a meeting half-way. The Mysoreans, delighted with this apparent display of weakness, paraded the envoys through their camp, declaring that Lord Macartney had sent them to "sue for peace."

Treaty of Mangalore.—The first overtures were based upon a cessation of hostilities on either side. But though Lord Macartney accordingly recalled the English troops, Tippoo never ceased ravaging the country round. The conclusion of the matter was that Tippoo, treating the commissioners with great

[1] In this action Sergeant Bernadotte was present, who afterwards became a Marshal of France, and, finally, King of Sweden.

insult and indignity, refused to permit their retirement before they had signed a treaty at his dictation on the basis of mutual restitution of conquests.

Though peace was thus procured, the behaviour of the Madras Government inspired Tippoo with such arrogance that another war soon broke out, which was attended with much bloodshed and loss of life.

Previously to this, however, the English were freed from war for a few years, and the interest of their history during that period centres round the person of Warren Hastings, his sufferings, and his trial. It will be interesting, meanwhile, to examine the events which characterized the administration of three successive Presidents of Madras, Mr. Wynch, Lord Pigott, and Sir Thomas Rumbold, between the years 1771 and 1781.

Mr. Wynch, President of Madras, (1770—1775.)

The behaviour of this President in the matter of the Raj of Tanjore is the principal characteristic of his administration. The occurrences were as follows:—In 1761, Mahomed Ali, the Nabob of the Carnatic, had by force of arms wrested a tribute of fifty lacs of rupees from the Rajah of Tanjore;[1] and in 1771 he again asked and obtained the aid of the English to exact a further payment of 100 lacs. Mr. Wynch sent a regiment to the aid of the Nabob, and Tanjore fell after a fine defence, the Rajah being suffered to remain in possession of his country on condition of paying heavy tribute.

But two years afterwards (1773), the Nabob, coveting the rich land of the Raj, marched down on his own account, without referring to the Madras Government, and plundered Tanjore,—seizing the city, and sending the absurd excuse to Madras that he had committed this depredation in order to crush an enemy who might at some future time become so powerful as to be dangerous to the Company's interests. Mr. Wynch at once acquiesced, and proclaimed that the Raj of Tanjore, having been conquered by Mahomed Ali, was now extinct as an independent sovereignty; and that the country, in the future, should belong to the Nabob of the Carnatic.

The Court of Directors, however, refused to countenance this proceeding, and at once removed Mr. Wynch from his office, sending out in his place the aged Lord Pigott.

Lord Pigott, President of Madras, (1775—1777).

Lord Pigott landed in 1775, and set himself manfully to work to abolish, as far as possible, the corruption and peculation which, to so large an extent, was prevalent throughout the various branches of the public service.

But this energetic conduct had the effect of turning all parties against him, raising up a formidable body of enemies in, and out of, the council.

In 1776, Lord Pigott went in person to Tanjore, and with much state replaced the ousted Rajah on the throne; thus making a most bitter enemy of Mahomed Ali, who immediately stirred up his friends at Madras to organize a determined opposition to every action of the President. Matters were brought to a crisis by the investigation which took place concerning the conduct of a certain Paul Benfield, who brought forward a fraudulent claim to a part of the revenues of Mysore. The demand gave rise to much dispute in the council between the president and the other members; and in consequence of their open violence, Lord Pigott felt himself compelled to use his prerogative, and suspend two members of that body.

The majority of the council then threw off all idea of respect or law, seized Lord Pigott, threw him into prison, and kept him there in close confinement, till from excitement and infirmity he died a few months later.

Sir Thomas Rumbold was at once sent out to take the command of the Presidency.

Sir Thomas Rumbold, President of Madras, (1777—1780.)

Sir Thomas Rumbold landed on February 8th, 1777, and finding his predecessor already dead, at once assumed the duties of his office.

His official career of three years was characterized by little which would particularly distinguish it from others, were it not that some recent discoveries by a very able historian [1] have thrown a

[1] Mr Marshman has, in an appendix to the first volume of his history (to which I here, once for all, take the liberty of referring all readers), given a sketch of his discoveries, the substance of which I have here repeated. The documents, which consisted of private papers in the possession of some members of Sir Thomas Rumbold's family, have been lately printed, and published under the title of "A Vindication of the Character and Administration of Sir Thomas Rumbold."—(Longman's. 1868.)

new light on the transactions which took place. The actions of Sir Thomas Rumbold have, it seems, been much misunderstood. He has been accused of various political crimes, and his conduct has been placed in an exceedingly disadvantageous light by previous writers; but Mr. Marshman has been enabled, by the production of some entirely new documentary evidence, to clear the President's character, and place him before the world in the light of a much ill-used man.

The accusations are for the most part domestic; having reference to Sir Thomas's treatment of the Carnatic Zemindars, the system of bribery carried on at Presidency towns, and his ultimate retirement from office. We will consider them separately.

(I.) It is said that on his arrival, Sir Thomas Rumbold, finding that a commission had been appointed to inquire into the revenues of the Circars which had passed into English hands in 1765, needlessly cancelled that commission in order to injure the individual members; and that he afterwards caused great annoyance and ill-feeling amongst the Zemindars through whom the revenues of the Circars passed to the Madras Treasury, by commanding them to come long distances in person to Madras to answer the charges brought against them;—a command which, as the aristocracy of the country, they felt to be a great indignity.

Mr. Marshman's fresh documentary evidence goes to show that Sir Thomas had sufficient reasons for his conduct. The Zemindars, at so great a distance, had ample opportunities of baffling the investigation of Government; and they were believed to be using this power to such an extent as to render any enquiry on the spot a useless extravagance. He therefore summoned them to head quarters and established a new commission to hear their explanations, and make a report. His conduct was fully approved by the Court of Directors.

(II.) The next accusation is that Viziram, the principal Zemindari Rajah of the Circars, having refused to come to Madras on account of the injury the country would sustain by his absence, was hastily treated as a rebel, turned out of his office without due cause, and his brother, Seetaram (who bribed Sir Thomas heavily for the purpose), placed in his stead.

This is explained by the fact that Seetaram was the rightful heir, being elder brother to Viziram. He had been ejected unlawfully by the present owner; and Sir Thomas, interfering gently and kindly, made up the quarrel, and persuaded Viziram to make his brother Dewan of the Province, since the latter consented to remain satisfied with this position. Bribes, it is true, were offered and accepted, but it was the President's secretary (not the President) who was at fault, and as soon as the affair was discovered Sir Thomas promptly discharged the offender.

(III.) Sir Thomas Rumbold was accused of peculation to an enormous extent; and as a proof of this it was urged that he sent home to England the sum of £45,000 after a six month's residence at Madras.

This sum of money was, it is now shown, the produce of many years of industry when Rumbold was head of a factory in India. It had been accumulating during his absence in Europe, and on his return he sent the whole amount to his agents for security. It is therefore no evidence that he received bribes from anyone.

(IV.) The fourth count in the charge against Rumbold is want of policy. He is declared to have been the immediate cause of the hostility of the Nizam in 1779, owing to his conduct in the case of the Guntoor Circar. Bassalat Jung, brother of the Nizam, had been made Rajah of the Circar; and when Hyder Ali was becoming dangerous to Bassalat on account of his predatory habits, and his proximity to the latter's territory, that prince applied to Madras for aid; promising to rent the Guntoor Circar to the Company in exchange for a forcible assistance in case of attack. The Governor of Madras accepted the gift, though he well knew that the Rajah had not the smallest right to give away lands which he held only as a feudal inferior to the Nizam to whom they really belonged. A British force then took possession. It is alleged that the Nizam, on hearing of this occupation, which he termed a "wanton aggression," declared that the Company had been for a long time seeking a quarrel, and that their conduct now was merely an excuse to bring matters to an open rupture. He accordingly at once ordered off all British subjects from Hyderabad, and joined the "Grand Confederacy."

To lay this animosity of the Nizam, however, to the door of the persecuted Sir Thomas Rumbold, is an unfounded accusation; for it is well known that the Nizam had been for a long time siding with the French, and that though openly expressing the doctrine of tolerance to the Company, he had been for years seeking some opportunity for driving them out of the country; and the immediate cause of his defection in 1779 is said to have been a letter from Warren Hastings to the Rajah of Nagpore, which was intercepted, and found to contain references of a questionable character as to some portion of the Nizam's dominions.[1]

(V.) The last accusation concerns the closing act of his public life in India. The ordinary story goes that, knowing how ill he had discharged his duties, and hearing that orders for his recall had been issued from the Court of Directors, Sir Thomas deserted his post, got on board ship, and sailed for England.

It is discovered, however, that no recall was ever dreamed of at home;—that the Court of Directors had always approved of Rumbold's actions;—and that his sudden resignation was on account of ill-health, and by the strict injunctions of his physicians.

Sir Thomas Rumbold was succeeded by Lord Macartney,[2] who landed towards the close of the year 1781.

End of Warren Hastings' Administration.

Affairs at Calcutta had by this time (1783) grown into great confusion, and the discontent pervading all ranks of society, native as well as European, was great. Hastings was thwarted and harassed in every possible manner; and the members of council were to a man opposed to every wish that the Governor-General expressed, invariably vetoing every attempt that he made to settle the affairs of the country. Hastings himself had by this time become thoroughly soured by his trials, and made enemies, both private and public, by his violent displays of temper.

The judges of the Supreme Court were in their turn especially obnoxious, as they affected to consider themselves "supreme" over all departments of the public service, and even assumed to themselves the attitude of censors over the acts of the Government.

The revenue system was thrown entirely out of order by the conduct of the English law-officers, when dealing with the

[1] This is not an altogether improbable story. It will be remembered that Hastings was at that time using every means, public and private, to detach the Rajah of Nagpore from the grand confederacy; and he may, in a private letter, have made overtures which could not have been made in public.

[2] See page 131.

Zemindars. The Government had passed regulations that the Zemindars, being considered only as collectors of the revenue, were liable to arrest and punishment in case of default; and following this rule with great impetuosity, the European judges, on several occasions, seized the powerful Zemindari Rajahs, threw them into prison, and treated them like common felons, for some slight defalcation.

The credit of the Zemindars thus became impaired, and the ryots often refused to pay their rents into the hands of persons whom they beheld soon after placed amongst the ranks of ordinary criminals. This led to arbitrary persecutions and exactions on the part of the Rajahs, and caused a general want of security throughout the country.

In legal matters the state of affairs was no better; for by the charter of George I. in 1726, and that of George III. in 1773, appointing the Supreme Court, all the common law of England was now in force in India; and being rigorously adhered to by the judges, the natives found themselves, to their astonishment, hanged for crimes they had always considered slight, and fined lightly for offences that the *Shastras* considered worthy of torture and death. This was especially noticeable in the case of Nuncomar, the Brahman, who was hanged for forgery. The prejudices of the Hindus were violently offended in two particulars. No one had been condemned to death for that crime since the days of Menu; and to kill a Brahman was to commit an act considered by their religion the deepest sacrilege of which a man could be guilty.

The troubles in the revenue branch of the service were brought to a climax by what is commonly known as the "*Cossijurah case.*"

The Cossijurah Case.—This arose from the English system of demanding bail from accused persons pending their trial. A revenue cause was being brought in the Supreme Court against the Rajah of Cossijurah, a man of considerable eminence, and one who had always been most punctual and scrupulous in sending in his quota of the revenue to the treasury. Bail was demanded on pain of arrest, and the order was sent to the Rajah on the rough sheet of paper ordinarily used on those occasions. The officers of the court on arriving demanded to see the Rajah, in order to serve the summons on himself; but being refused admittance to the presence, they forced their way into the private apartments, desecrated the sanctuary of the zenana, and actually carried off the family idol as security for his appearance.

Warren Hastings at once interfered, feeling that a period had at last arrived when such an open and disgraceful violation of all the rights due to the higher classes could no longer be permitted. He gave his protection to the Rajah and his family, and issued a general order to the natives that they were not to consider themselves amenable to the Supreme Court in civil matters unless they deliberately bound themselves to abide by its jurisdiction.[1] In retaliation, the judges of the supreme tribunal sent a summons to the Council and the Governor-General for "contempt of court" (!) but the latter peremptorily refused to obey so absurd a demand.

Soon afterwards, Hastings proceeded to remodel the whole of the revenue administration of the country, having gained by this time ample experience of the ill-effects caused by the old system.

New Revenue System.—The principal alterations he made were (1.) to separate the revenue from the civil administration (these having hitherto been combined in one official), calling the former "*Provisional*," and the latter "*District*" courts.

(2.) To create an appeal from both these separate jurisdictions to the "*Sudder Dewani Adalat,*" of which court he made Sir Elijah Massey the Chief Justice.

(3.) He made a code in ninety-five sections which was so admirable that on it has been founded the basis of all subsequent arrangements. It was of great benefit to the country, and goes generally by the name of "*Warren Hastings' Code.*"

Cheyt Sing, 1784.—In 1784 occurred the affair of Cheyt Sing, which constituted one of the principal charges against Hastings at his trial. This man had been made Rajah of Benares by Hastings, under a promise of absolute dependence on the Company, and a regular annual payment. This payment had been for some years getting in arrear, the Rajah in every possible way evading the demand. In 1784, Hastings determined to enrich the Calcutta treasury, which was at that time impoverished —at the same time that he taught the tributary Rajahs a lesson —by inflicting a heavy fine on Cheyt Sing, and enforcing immediate payment of arrears. He therefore demanded five lacs of

[1] See pages 90 (note), 110 (note).

rupees and a contingent of 2000 horse ; and when Cheyt Sing, as usual, attempted to evade compliance with the Governor-General's orders, the latter went in person to Benares to enforce obedience.

He placed Cheyt Sing under arrest, but the Rajah escaped, and so alarmed the English by his openly hostile preparations, that Hastings was fain to escape out of a window one night, and, getting into a small boat, row down the river to Chunar.

Cheyt Sing, then fully alive to the danger of his position, at once raised an army of 20,000 men, and made Bidzeghur his head-quarters. But when Major Popham, who was detached for this service, advanced on Bidzeghur, the Rajah fled, carrying off his wives and treasure. This was a serious blow to Hastings, who remained with the treasury as empty as before, while he had incurred the additional expense of new and futile war brought on by his own rashness. He, however, as far as possible, remedied the evil by placing a nephew of Cheyt Sing on the throne, and demanding a payment of ten lacs of rupees, which the new Rajah promised to remit as soon as his treasury, which was now completely impoverished, should be sufficiently enriched as to be capable of bearing the burden.

Fyzoolla Khan.—A treaty was then concluded with the Nabob vizier of Oude, Asoff-u-dowla, by which the subsidized British force in that country was reduced, and some rights mutually fixed. The third article referred to Fyzoolla Khan. This chief was the nephew of Hafiz Ruhmut, the Rohilla, who had fought so bravely against the Company during the war with that tribe in 1773. He had been bound by treaty, on his succession to the headship of the Rohillas, to provide a contingent of 3000 men to swell the ranks of the Company's army. And Hastings had lately demanded 5000, which Fyzoolla Khan declared himself incapable of furnishing, In this treaty with Oude, therefore, the Governor-General, considering Fyzoolla Khan in the light only of a jagirdar, claimed that his "*jagir*" (namely Rohilcund) should be taken from him by his "feudal" lord, the Nabob of Oude. It was afterwards restored to him on payment of fifteen lacs of rupees.

Departure of Warren Hastings, 1785.—The Governor-General returned to Calcutta ; and soon after, indignant at the unworthy treatment he received on all sides, he resigned his post, and returned to England (1785).

He was well received on his arrival in England. The King, the Court of Directors, and the Ministry, all vied with one another in doing him honour.

But this lasted only a short time. Pitt, then head of the Ministry, was violently opposed to Warren Hastings on several grounds. He disliked the governor's annexation policy;—he felt that during his administration, whether owing to his personal conduct or not, the confidence of the natives of India had been forfeited. Hastings had on more than one occasion openly disobeyed the orders of the Board of Directors at home; and he had been guilty of the crime of raising the salaries of the Company's officers in India, in order to prevent the extortion so commonly practised there by men who looked for fortunes, not to their pay, but to the rupees they could extort from the Hindus.

As soon, therefore, as the excitement of public congratulation had cooled down, it was determined to press matters in Parliament against Hastings; and Burke, being openly challenged by a somewhat hot-headed Anglo-Indian member of Parliament to bring forward any charges he dared against the late Governor-General, threw himself with all his energy into the scheme of impeachment.

Eleven principal charges were first brought against Warren Hastings; and eleven others were subsequently added by the agency of Francis and other opponents. Each of these was brought forward as a separate motion in Parliament, and Hastings then received permission to reply. He appeared at the Bar of the House, and read his defence. But, long before he had arrived at the conclusion, the patience of the members was exhausted by the wearisome prolixity of the document.

His Trial.—The impeachment was then hurried on The motion passed both Houses; and on February 13th, 1788, Warren Hastings appeared before the august tribunal of the two Houses of Parliament in Westminster Hall, as "the prisoner." It was the most pompous spectacle of the "majesty of the law" ever exhibited to English eyes; and the strange character of the scene is graphically described by Macaulay in his well-known essay on the life of this Governor-General.

Burke on this occasion, as prosecutor, made a speech which, in Mr. Marshman's words, was one "of such transcendant power, that Hastings himself was carried away by the torrent of eloquence, and remarked that for half-an-hour he really considered himself the greatest miscreant in England."[1]

[1] "History of India," vol. i. p. 426.

The three principal charges were,—The first Rohilla war;—The conduct of Hastings in the case of Cheyt Sing; and the matters connected with the Begums of Oude, (the wives of Sujah-u-dowla, the late Nabob-vizier).

The first charge was afterwards abandoned, as the war had received the sanction and approval of the Board of Directors. The trial therefore was actually on the last two charges, of which Fox brought forward the first, and Sheridan the second.[1]

The trial dragged on for seven years, at the end of which Hastings was again summoned to kneel before the two Houses of Parliament, and receive his honourable acquittal. The satisfaction at this happy termination was great; but it came too late to afford any relief to the principal sufferer, who was broken in health and almost ruined in fortunes.[2]

He lived for twenty-two years after this at the family place at Daylesford, where he died in 1818, at the age of eighty-six. But before his death he had received from all parties ample assurance that his name, in spite of the calumny that had been poured upon it, was venerated throughout the length and breadth of the land. For being called before the Bar of the House at the age of eighty-one to give evidence on an Indian question, the whole House rose, and, when he retired, remained standing hat in hand greeting him with the loudest applause.[3] Again, the Prince Regent introduced him to the Emperor of Russia as "the most deserving and the worst used man in the empire;" and on many other occasions he had sufficient proof that his country honoured his personal character, and deeply sympathised with his ill fortunes.

(VII.)—*Proceedings in Parliament. The "Indian Bills" of Fox and Pitt, and the "Nabob of Arcot's debts."* (1780—1785.)

The exclusive privileges of the East India Company, which were renewed triennially, expired as usual in March, 1780, and

[1] Sheridan's speech of six hours' duration on this occasion is generally considered as the greatest effort of eloquence ever heard, whether in ancient or modern times. It created such an impression that the Speaker adjourned the debate, declaring that the members were unable, without an interval, to deal calmly with the subject.

[2] The trial cost Hastings £100,000.

[3] It is said that Warren Hastings felt this honour excessively, and was so touched that he burst into tears on reaching the lobby.

were again extended to 1783 by Act of Parliament; with the reservation that the Company were to pay £400,000 to the public funds in part payment of arrears due to the nation by loans from Government.

Some secret committees were appointed by Parliament next year to inquire into certain affairs in India. One took the war with Hyder Ali, and made a strict investigation into its causes, under the chairmanship of Burke; while another examined the petitions sent in by the native Bengalese against the alleged violent acts of the Supreme Council at Calcutta.

Indian affairs were at this time the leading questions in Parliament, on which hot debates took place, and ministers lost and gained their power. On April 9th, 1782, Mr. Dundas, an eminent but somewhat violent member of the Board of Directors, made a speech in Parliament denouncing the conduct of affairs in India, especially alluding to the reckless violation of treaties, and the wholesale plunging into dangerous wars. In May, he moved for the recall of Warren Hastings, which was passed in Parliament; but the Court of Proprietors in a general meeting refused to permit the Directors to send out the order of recall.

Fox's India Bill.—In 1783, the bill known as "Fox's India Bill," was brought forward. The Company had petitioned for another loan,[1] and this second confession of poverty had caused considerable dissatisfaction throughout the country. Fox and Lord North were then at the head of the "Coalition Ministry,"[2] and as it was deemed necessary for the Government to express some decided opinion on Indian affairs, Fox drew up his celebrated India Bill, and presented it to the House.

The arrangement therein proposed was that the Company's charter should be suspended for four years; that during that period the Government of India should be carried on by seven commissioners, parliamentary nominees; and that all matters of trade should be managed by nine assistant commissioners, nomi-

[1] The first loan had been granted by Parliament in 1772.

[2] The ministry of Lord North had fallen in 1782. In April, 1783, Fox and Lord North having formed a new party of the most opposing elements, Tories and Whigs being heterogeneously mixed together, succeeded in overthrowing the feeble administration of Lord Shelburne, and in establishing themselves in office. This peculiar cabinet was known as "The Coalition Ministry." It was looked upon with dislike both by the Crown and the Nation; but the reckless sacrifice of principle which formed the party was the means, also, of creating large majorities; and the ministers held office till abruptly dismissed by the King in January, 1784.

nated by the Court of Proprietors. The Zemindars were to be recognized as hereditary proprietors of the soil;[1] and, lastly, in all matters of War and Treaties, the Government of India were to be subordinate to a Board of Control in England.[2]

The political wisdom of this last measure has been much called in question. Theoretically it might seem advantageous, but on sudden emergencies, the necessity for immediate action would override the constitutional law demanding reference to England.

The bill passed the Lower House, though the Company naturally opposed it with all their energy. The King, however, gave instructions to the Peers to throw out the Bill, and the same evening that it was proposed and negatived in the Upper House, the Coalition Ministry was dismissed.

Pitt was created the new minister, though only of the age of twenty-four. He was friendly to the Company, and in many ways benefited their trade.

Pitt's India Bill.—On August 13th, 1784, he introduced his India Bill, in order to quiet the demands of the country for some ministerial statement on Indian matters.

The principal provisions of his Bill were to appoint a body of six members of the Privy Council to act as a Board of Commissioners for the control of revenue matters; and a Committee of Secrecy, of three Directors, to receive and issue the orders of this Board. The Court of Proprietors was to have no power of government. All war matters and Treaties to be conducted and concluded under the orders of the Board of Commissioners. Annexation policy to be reprobated. And, lastly, every officer under the Government of India to deliver a schedule of his property on his return to England, with a notice of the manner in which it was acquired.

The bill passed in 1784.

Its effect was to remove all power from the Company and transfer it to Parliament, leaving to the Courts of the Company

[1] The status of the Zemindars was one of the great subjects of dispute before Lord Cornwallis for ever settled the question—by securing to them and their families a hereditary ownership in the soil which they had never possessed. It is quite plain that the Zemindars were only farmers of the public revenue under the Mogul Empire. (See below, page 153.)

[2] Notwithstanding the difficulties which it was urged this provision would cause in India, it was embodied in Pitt's bill. Lord Wellesley's general practice was directly opposed to the tenour of the Law. He made his own treaties as he pleased, and trusted in Providence to set him right with the Government afterwards!

only the external pageant of a large establishment. Fox's bill would have destroyed this show with the rest; and Pitt had the sense to perceive that, if he retained this, he would receive more support from the Proprietors. He was not mistaken, and his Bill passed with a triumphant majority.

Henceforth the President of the Board of Commissioners was the real despotic Governor of India. Mr. Dundas was the first who held this office, and performed his duties with great ability for many years.

The Nabob of Arcot's Debts.—The question of the Nabob of Arcot's debts was the first brought before the President of the new Board of Control.

The Nabob of the Carnatic had allowed the affairs of his country to grow into great confusion. Having an empty treasury, a great disinclination for work, and an intense love of extravagance and debauchery, he was in the habit of borrowing large sums from private individuals, whom he repaid by assigning to them the revenues of considerable tracts of land. The lenders soon found this a very advantageous manner of receiving payment for their loans, for it established them at once in the position of large land-owners, and enabled them to amass immense fortunes by oppressing the ryots.

The recklessness of the Nabob and the unscrupulous tyranny of these upstart European zemindars was found to be ruining the whole of the Carnatic, and, in 1785, Dundas and the Board of Commissioners took the matter in hand.

They proposed to appropriate £480,000 annually to the payment of the Nabob's debts, and thus to release the country from the clutches of the money-lenders.[1] The plan was discussed in Parliament at some length, and gave rise to several able speeches, of which the best known is that of Burke. It was ably urged in opposition to Dundas that the plan would secure immense sums to the Benfields, and others who had formed a perfectly unscrupulous crew, and had fraudulently plundered the Carnatic of its lawful revenues. The Ministry was, however, strong enough to bear down all opposition, and the Bill passed both Houses triumphantly.[2]

[1] The Company, with some reason, objected strongly to one of Dundas's arrangements, which was, that all private debts should be paid off before those due to the Company. They declared that for individuals who had ruined the Nabob to be paid before the Company, who had really rendered him valuable assistance, was an act of great injustice.

[2] As an instance of its effect, I may mention that Paul Benfield was, by its agency, secured in possession of £600,000 out of the revenues of the Carnatic.

Dundas divided the debts into three classes, the largest of which was the Consolidated Loan of 1777. It is said that the plan proposed by Warren Hastings would have paid this off for a million and a half, whereas Dundas's scheme occasioned a payment of five millions.

When the last of the old debts was paid off, twenty years later (in 1805), it was found—as might, indeed, have been expected—that Mahomed Ali had contracted meanwhile new debts to the amount of thirty millions! Then a strict scrutiny was set on foot, and after an inquiry which lasted fifty years and cost a million sterling, the affairs of the Nabob were finally settled.

(VIII.)—*Lord Cornwallis's Administration* (1785—1793).—*Third Mysore War—Career of Sindia.—Proceedings in Parliament.*

When Warren Hastings left India in 1785, Sir John Macpherson, the senior Member of Council at Calcutta, became Governor-General *pro tem.* He applied himself with vigour to the reduction of the expenditure, and to reforms in the Financial Department, succeeding so well that by the close of his short administration he had diminished the Government debt by the sum of a million sterling.

1786.—Lord Cornwallis landed as Governor-General early in 1786. He came out possessing the full confidence of his country, who had taken note of his abilities while he commanded a brigade in the American war. Moreover, he was known to be unbiassed, being connected neither with India nor the Company. All parties, therefore, combined to approve of his appointment.[1]

Cornwallis is principally remembered for his admirable Home-administration, and the able manner in which he set to work to reform the various departments of the public service. We will consider these at length on a later page, confining the narrative at present to the story of the war in Mysore, and the foreign policy of the new Governor-General.

"*Affairs of Oude.*"—In 1786 Asoff-u-dowla, the Nabob of Oude, begged that the expenses which the English Government had demanded of him, in order to the maintenance within his

[1] It is said that Lord Macartney had been aiming at the Governor-Generalship, and had actually been nominated; but, having the imprudence to oppose Dundas in Parliament, he was at once shelved.

territories of a British contingent, might be reduced. Cornwallis in a spirit of generosity consented, allowing him to pay fifty lacs instead of seventy-four. This was, however, contrary to the advice of the Resident, who declared that the Nabob was an idle and profligate spendthrift, desiring the extra lacs, not for the benefit of his subjects, but that he might waste them on dancing-girls and hunting expeditions.

The interest now centres round affairs in the south.

Tippoo Sultan, after the disgraceful treaty of Mangalore in 1783, behaved with the utmost arrogance and cruelty, committing depredations on all sides, and openly vowing to drive the English out of India.[1]

In 1786 Nana Furnuvese, in fear of Tippoo, made an alliance with the Nizam and prepared openly for war, discontinuing only when Tippoo offered to pay forty-five lacs to the Mahrattas if they would leave him in peace.

The Guntoor Circar, 1788.—Two years later the Madras Government was involved in a problem of great intricacy, owing to the Treaty with the Nizam of 1768,[2] in which the Guntoor Circar was promised to the Company on the death of Bassalat Jung, then governor of that province. Bassalat died in 1782, and the Madras President claimed the Circar; but the Nizam resolutely held out for six years. Accordingly, in 1788 British troops were marched to the frontier. The Nizam immediately submitted; but, demanding the equal good faith of the English, he requested that they would observe their portion of the same Treaty—namely, to conquer the Carnatic Balaghat from Hyder Ali's family in order to devote the revenues of the country to the payment of "chout" to the Mahrattas! Here indeed was a difficulty. The English had in two successive Treaties acknowledged Hyder and Tippoo as sovereigns of the Carnatic Balaghat!

Cornwallis immediately opened private negotiations with Nizam Ali, and successfully edged the Company out of the dilemma by promising him the aid of the British troops against any power not in alliance with England; and by stating that if at any future

[1] The story of Tippoo Sahib's "Tiger-organ" is well known. It was a little machine which supported on the lid an elaborate representation in gold and jewels of the Indian tiger mangling a figure habited in the dress of an English soldier. The figures moved by mechanism, and the music represented vividly the growls of the beast and the shrieks of the dying Englishman.

[2] See page 114.

time the Carnatic Balaghat became English it should faithfully be given up. The Nizam was wise enough to accept these terms, perceiving the strength of the armies of the Company. But Tippoo Sultan, mortally offended at this double-dealing on the part of the Governor-General respecting a portion of his dominions, seized an opportunity to break out into open warfare with the English.

The Raj of Travancore was the place disputed. The Rajah, who was an ally of the Company, had bought two towns from the Dutch at Cochin and had fortified them with some care. Much to his dismay however, the chief of Cochin, Tippoo's vassal, acting under orders from his superior, declared that the towns belonged to himself. The Rajah appealed to the English, and the chief of Cochin appealed to Tippoo.

The declaration of war between Tippoo and the English which naturally ensued was preceded by the attack of the former on the lines of Travancore, defeated by the energy of the gallant Rajah.

Third Mysore War, 1790.—Cornwallis prepared for the war by making offensive and defensive alliances with Nana Furnuvese and the Nizam; with the avowed object of destroying the power of their common enemy, Tippoo Sultan. This is generally known as the "*Tripartite Treaty of* 1790."

General Medows was appointed to the command of the Madras army; but his movements were hampered by the inability or neglect of Mr. Holland, the president, to provide suitable supplies. The army was consequently unable to move from Trichinopoly till May, when Medows occupied successively Coïmbatore, Dindigul, and Palghaut. This, however, was the last of his successes; for, having unwisely divided his forces, Tippoo attacked, defeated, and almost annihilated one division which was not strong enough to defend itself against him.

Immediately on the declaration of war, Cornwallis despatched a Bengal contingent to co-operate with the army of Madras. It reached the latter Presidency in August, and at once marched to effect a junction, which Tippoo in vain tried to prevent. The armies united on November 17th, and being numbered, were found to amount to 24,000 men.

Colonel Hartley at the same time advanced from Bombay, with his usual success; and on the way defeated a large force of Mysoreans with a loss on his side of only fifty-two men.

1791.—Such was the condition of the contending forces at the close of the year; when Cornwallis, considering the war of sufficient importance to justify such conduct, himself sailed from Calcutta and on arrival took supreme command of the British armies in the south. He found the troops, to his great satisfaction, in a high state of efficiency and good spirits, and confident of success

The Governor-General commenced the campaign by sending a small force as a feint against Seringapatam, while he directed the main attack against Bangalore. The latter city capitulated after a very feeble defence. On receiving the intelligence of this success, the Nizam, who, as usual, had been wavering in his adherence, being anxious to ascertain the probable result before he committed himself to any decided action, sent to the aid of Lord Cornwallis a force of 10,000 horse, which ravaged the north of Mysore, and on April 13th joined the English.

It now only wanted the presence of the Mahrattas in the west, marching against Tippoo from the Malabar coast, to render his position one of extreme difficulty, being attacked on three sides at once.

But the Peshwa had seized the opportunity afforded him by the Treaty to attack Tippoo's realms, not with any reference to the general plan of the allies, but merely for the purpose of reconquering some places which had been lost to the Mysoreans in previous wars. His army sat down before the mud forts of Dharwar, and remained there inactive for many months. Meanwhile the Nizam and Lord Cornwallis marched their united forces from Bangalore at the end of April, and pushed through the heart of Mysore towards Seringapatam to attack Tippoo's head-quarters. On the way they experienced the greatest difficulties and hardships owing to the judicious policy adopted by the Mysoreans in cutting off supplies.

Battle of Arikera.—But the spirits of the soldiers were aroused by their success at Arikera, where a battle was fought, in which Tippoo was completely defeated, and compelled to retire.

This was the only victory of the campaign, however; for immediately afterwards, while even in sight of the capital, and when the enemy were in full flight, Cornwallis had to retire to Madras partly from want of provisions, and partly because his army was exhausted by disease aud starvation, for which there could be no relief saye in a friendly country. His march homewards is one of the most melancholy occurrences in the history of India. The army fell into a very bad state of health; and from the commander-in-chief to the lowest recruit, every man that swelled the ranks was depressed in spirits, and hopeless of any relief. Though harrassed on all sides by bodies of Mysorean cavalry, they at last, however, reached the Changama Pass, and found themselves in safety in British territory.

The Nizam drew off, and successfully laid siege to Gurumconda;[1] while the Mahrattas under Hurri Pant, an able and skilful general, ravaged the west of Mysore with their predatory bands.

1792.—The winter was spent in retrieving as far as possible the losses of the previous campaign by the capture of several isolated but important hill-fortresses about the district of North Arcot, and in making great preparations for the next advance.

Cornwallis took the field in January with an army of 22,000 men, 90 guns, and an immense convoy of provisions and treasure. He was determined to bring matters to a successful issue, and the troops burned with desire to regain their lost prestige. The Nizam and the Mahratta contingent both joined company; and in splendid order the allied armies appeared before the walls of Seringapatam on February 5th. As soon as his camp was pitched, Cornwallis rode out in person to reconnoitre the fortifications, and planned a night attack that same evening. The signal was given at midnight, and the outworks were stormed with the utmost gallantry and enthusiasm, after three hours' hard fighting.

Here the allies remained, battering the fort with heavy siege-guns for several days, till, on February 16th, General Abercrombie came up from Bombay with another contingent; and Tippoo, acting under the advice of his minister, who declared that the fort could not long hold out, sent to Cornwallis to know his requirements.

Terms of Tippoo's Submission.—The Governor-General replied under a flag of truce, and demanded the submission of the Sultan to the following terms:—He was to cede half his territories; to pay three millions sterling for the expenses of the allies; to yield two of his sons into British protection as hostages; and to pay thirty lacs of rupees to the Mahrattas. The Sultan perforce submitted to these rigorous demands, and Cornwallis held a grand Durbar in his camp, at which the two young princes were received with all the honours befitting their rank.

The acquisitions obtained by the allies under this Treaty were

[1] **The Nizam was afterwards discovered to have been all this time holding secret negotiations with the Cabinet at Mysore.**

apportioned by the Governor-General with the strictest fairness. He rigidly adhered to the terms of the Tripartite Treaty made at the commencement of the war with the Peshwa and the Nizam; although these chiefs had been of very little assistance to the Company. One-third, including the Carnatic Balaghat, was given to the Mahrattas, and one-third to the Nizam.

Thus the ill-advised treaty of 1768 was at last fulfilled on all sides, and English honour tardily vindicated.

(The new acquisitions of the Company consisted of Dindigul and Baramahal with the country round, together with some land about Bombay).

Lord Cornwallis was severely censured in the House for this annexation, which was termed a breach of his promise to the nation. But it is evident that the policy was forced upon him by the position of affairs. It was necessary to punish Tippoo with severity, in order to teach him a lesson which might prevent him from again involving the English in war; and the blow dealt to him in wrenching away part of the territories so hardly earned by his father and himself was that which he would naturally feel most acutely. If Cornwallis had been more moderate, Tippoo would have been less humbled. Again, it is evident that the deprivation of territory was the most effective means of weakening the power of the Sultan, and diminishing his opportunities of attacking the English. The Bill was accordingly negatived by a large majority, and Cornwallis was rewarded with the honour of a Marquisate.

1793.—He returned to Calcutta immediately after his signal success in Mysore, and next year sailed for England.

The last event of which he received the tidings was calculated to increase the satisfaction he felt at the results of his administration. He had issued orders for a Madras army to prepare for an attack on Pondicherry; and while on his way home the news reached him that this, the last and most important possession of the French in India, had submitted to Colonel Brathwaite.

We must now review shortly the home policy and administration of Lord Cornwallis.

Cornwallis' Civil Administration.—He commenced his work immediately on landing, by a rigorous enquiry into the many abuses observable in every branch of the service,[1] and by

[1] The instances most observable of the dishonesty and corruption that prevailed throughout the services are the following:—

The sub-treasurer was lending out the public funds at interest. Two generals were receiving increased pay for their services to the Government

correcting them with moderation and judgment. He still further increased the salaries of the public servants, in order, as he said, to give them "the prospect of acquiring moderate fortunes from the savings of their allowances."

Revenue Reforms—Status of the Zemindars.—The matter of the status of the Zemindars also soon claimed his attention, as he found that on all sides the ryots were treated by these hard task-masters with great brutality; and that the collection of revenue in the discontented condition of the country, had become a matter of much difficulty.

Under the Mogul empire in its flourishing days, a "Zemindar" was a *collector of the public revenue.* He was placed over a district, the revenues of which he collected, paying regularly to the Treasury a certain fixed sum, which was considered as the average annual produce of the district devoted to the exigencies of the crown. All that he made over and above this belonged to himself. This system placed the unhappy ryots completely in the hands of the Zemindars, who had uncontrolled power of life and death in their districts; and as the lord was of a different race to the serf, and as his object was to turn to account every available penny, it may be imagined how pitiable was the condition of the labourer. No torture was too brutal, no oppression too cruel, which could force the wretched ryot to pay his exaggerated tax to the minions of the Zemindar.

When the English, in the year 1765, were first placed in a position to deal with these nobles, they found them claiming a position of half-independent hereditary sovereignty, as tributary, but irresponsible "Zemindari Rajahs" This power they had gradually assumed during the decay of the Empire. The *hereditary* nature of their tenure was acquired through the carelessness of the later emperors, who cared not for the mode of tenure, so long as the annual tax was handed in. Their claim to be considered *Rajahs* was caused by their immense acquisitions of money and treasure, obtained at the expense of the humbled and spiritless Hindus, their maintenance of troops, and assumption of

in having raised regiments of sepoys; and Cornwallis, after disbanding the regiments, which were regularly enrolled (the government having no longer any need of them), found that no such regiments had ever existed, and that the enrolled names were entirely fictitious. The collectors of districts acquired immense fortunes by bribes from native litigants; and it is a fact that the Resident at Benares, on a salary of £1200, sent home £4000 annually.

state. The English Government, annoyed by their arrogance, went to the opposite extreme; and, affecting to treat these nobles, now *really* possessed of great power and dignity, as mere subordinate collectors, placed them under legal responsibility, and made them liable to be thrown into prison or deposed from office, on the slightest failure of regular payment. As, at the same time, the condition of the ryots was not raised, the latter became even more humbled and oppressed than before, and the whole revenue system was thrown out of order.

In 1786 the Directors, as a matter of policy, directed that there should be a new engagement entered into with the Zemindars, under the distinct understanding that whatever benefits might be granted should not be considered as obtained of right, but by the favour of the Governor in Council. A commission was accordingly appointed to make inquiries and frame a complete report of the present condition of the Zemindars, with advice to the Government how to act. The Commissioners found their duties difficult of accomplishment, owing to the system of individual extortion and oppression that pervaded every foot of the country. The ryots gave no evidence, because they were in bodily fear of their lords' brutality. The Zemindars themselves, to a man, evaded any inquiries, and the work of the Commissioners was at a dead lock. So that, in 1793, Cornwallis, considering it useless to attempt any further investigation for the reasons above-mentioned, suddenly, and without warning, passed a motion in the Council, which at once assumed the force of law, that the Zemindars were to be henceforth considered as possessing all that they claimed. They were to be for ever considered as hereditary owners of all the soil of the district, paying annually, —not their *quota of the public taxes which they collected for the Government,*—but a sort of *tribute* into the treasury!

Mr. Shore, afterwards Sir John Shore, Cornwallis' successor in office, argued strenuously in the Council against this wholesale destruction of all the previously held opinions of the Hindus; and, finding that the majority of the Council were determined, as it seemed, merely for the sake of relieving themselves from the burden of constant legislation and perpetual disputes concerning the status of the Zemindar, to declare them owners of the soil, urged that there should be decennial settlements. His reasons were clear and logical; namely, that to better the state of the country there was no necessity to make the tenure perpetual; that the same results would be caused by leases for ten years, and that it was of great importance to have some legal hold upon the land-owners, which would be most easily obtained by fresh settlements at fixed periods. But the Council had been so harassed by the long disputes on the subject that they declared for permanency, in order once and for ever to settle the question. And the Board of Commissioners, acting on the same impulse, applauded their resolution, and passed the Bill for the "permanent establishment of the Zemindars of India as hereditary land-owners" in 1793, under the Premiership of Pitt.

The decision was promulgated at Calcutta in March, and caused considerable astonishment to all, and to none more than to the Zemindars themselves, who had never dreamed of such felicity being in store for them.

With regard to the wisdom of the measure, it may be said that, as a political step, the gift was not so unwise as it appears at first sight, for a country which possessed an opulent class of land-owners would generally be in a better condition than one in which the soil was occupied by small farmers. and owned only by the crown. But it was a measure as illegal as it was sudden and unexpected. The English were supposed to be legislating for the Hindus as a race, and as far as possible administering to them their own laws. But the oldest and most honoured doctrine of political status which the Hindus possessed was that all the soil belonged to the king, and that the ryots were tenants holding direct from the crown, and liable only to the government "*schist*," or tax paid to the state. The only wealthy and powerful nobles, (not farming their own land), were officers of the government; and the Zemindars were high officials—collectors of districts. When the soil of Bengal became English it became absolutely the property of the crown, and it was an extraordinary and unheard-of change for the ryots to learn that they were in future to consider themselves, not as tenants of the crown, but of their tax-gatherers!

The government passed at the same time several laws, giving the ryots remedies in the civil court against the Zemindars, and protecting them from increase of rent.[1] These were very desir-

[1] The most noticeable of these measures was a regulation, fixing the rent of the lands for ever. It enacted that a written "pottah," being a document containing the conditions of tenure, and the amount of the sum to be paid annually as rent, should be given to the ryot. This regulation permitted the Zemindar to increase the value of the estate, by the cultivation of fresh lands, and allowed him to increase the rental on fields cultivated

able; but, considering the state of the country, were almost dead-letters. For the ryots were so absolutely at the mercy of their landlords that they seldom dared to raise a finger in self-defence.

Apart, however, from the question of the original justice and wisdom of the measures, the prevalent opinion amongst high authorities is that the system has worked well.[1] But it is a fact that there have been many subsequent legislators in India who would fain have been able to make some alterations in the tenure of the Zemindars, or to have had some occasional hold over individuals at fixed periods, but have been prevented from satisfying their wishes by the bold measures of Cornwallis' government, which made any future alterations for ever impossible.

Civil Courts.—Previous to the Governor-Generalship of Cornwallis the same civil servants had been both judges of the civil court and collectors of the public revenue. Lord Cornwallis, following out the regulations which Warren Hastings introduced, separated their powers. The new system worked beneficially, for it had been a subject of terror to the natives to have to pay their rents to, and plead their civil causes before, the same person. Cornwallis accordingly placed all revenue matters in the hands of the collectors, and all civil legislation in those of district judges appointed for the purpose in each collectorate. Four courts of appeal were established at Calcutta, Dacca, Moorshedabad, and Patna, with a further appeal to the Supreme Court. All fees were at the same time abolished, except those paid to pleaders and witnesses.

Criminal Courts.—For the better conduct of criminal administration Cornwallis established Courts of Circuit, to be presided over by the Judges of the four Appeal Courts above-mentioned. He directed that the Mahomedan law should be the standard of criminal law to both Hindus and Mahomedans. He also appointed high native officials, called "*Daroghas*," who held very much the position of superintendents of police. They could arrest persons on written charges, and send them for trial to the nearest European magistrate. This system proved to be a mistake, as it was soon discovered that these powerful natives used

with the higher-priced kinds of grain. The effect of this enactment was to prevent any undue pressure on the lease-holders, but at the same time to hinder them from largely improving their own position, while to the Zemindars were given ample opportunities of acquiring fortunes.

[1] The revenues of the country have much increased since this date. But there were probably many causes at work besides the permanent settlement.

all their influence to acquire fortunes by bribery from the ryots, and utterly neglected their legal duty.[1]

The Code of 1793.—Cornwallis, at the same time, instituted the framing of a regular Criminal Code, which was accordingly made under his directions; but it was too elaborate for the ordinary administration of justice in India, the Hindus being pro-

[1] As Cornwallis' system is the foundation-stone of the present constitution of the law courts, I think it right to give a sketch of its provisions. There were two great characteristics noticeable. The offices of revenue and justice were absolutely separated; and a regular system of appeals from lower to higher courts was set on foot.

REVENUE.—All causes connected with the revenue were to be tried and determined by the Collectors of Districts, the civil causes being placed under the jurisdiction of the Judges of regular Civil Courts. The old Revenue Court, called the "*Mal Adalat*," was at the same time abolished.

CIVIL.—The lowest grade of civil courts in the district were the "*Courts of Native Commissioners*," which were established in every important town, and were conducted by *Moonsiffs* or native justices, *Salisans* or arbitrators, and *Amins* or referees. They had original jurisdiction in cases of the value of Rs. 50, and under. There was also authority given to the Zillah (or District) Judge to provide "*Registrars*" (covenanted servants), whose duty should be to try all causes not exceeding Rs. 200 in a court attached to the Zillah Court, subject to the restriction that all their decisions must be countersigned by the Zillah Judge himself in order to be final. From both these Courts appeal lay to the *Zillah Court*, or High Court of the District, of which there were twenty-six provided for the Presidency of Bengal. They consisted each of one Judge (a covenanted servant), one "*Pandit*," and one "*Kazi*" or "*Mufti*," for the guidance of the Judge in matters connected with Hindu and Mahomedan law respectively, with native law officers. As a general rule the Judge discharged all the appeals, while the Registrar undertook the original jurisdiction to whatever amount. Appeal from this Court lay to the "*Provincial Court*," of which four were established in the Presidency, at Calcutta, Patna, Moorshedabad, and Dacca respectively. In each of these courts were three European Judges, namely, a Chief Justice and two Puisne Judges, a Registrar, a Kazi, a Pandit, and native officials. In all cases where the amount in dispute was less than Rs. 1000, the decisions of this Court were final. But an appeal lay in all others from this Court to the "*Sudder Dewani Adalat*" at Calcutta, presided over by the Governor-General and Members of Council, which re-assumed thus the position, out of which it had been turned by the "Supreme Court," now done away with. All revenue appeals to a large amount came also before this Court, which in this, as well as in civil suits, had final decision in all cases of a less sum than Rs. 10,000. In cases of a greater amount than this, appeal lay to the Queen in Council.

CRIMINAL.—The lowest Criminal Courts were those of the "*Magistrates' Courts*," held by the various Justices of the Peace in the District. (The Justices of the Peace consisted of the Zillah and City Judges, and Registrars, together with all "*Amins*," or native Judges appointed by the Government).

verbial for their powers of what has been called "legal jugglery." It left open too many opportunities for those delays and technical difficulties which have always hampered the movements of the law when burdened with many formalities.

Lord Cornwallis sailed for England in September, 1793, and was received by all parties at home with much distinction.

Career of Sindia (1784—1794).—By the Treaty of Salbye in 1782, Sindia had been raised to great eminence. He was placed by it in the character of an independent military power, and of importance enough in Southern India to render the English desirous of his co-operation. The effect of this was to create in his mind a strong ambition to place himself in reality in the position which he held nominally.

Accordingly, in 1784, journeying to Delhi, he obtained an interview with the then powerless emperor,[1] and received a patent conferring on him the title of "Executor-General of the Empire," with the command-in-chief of the royal forces and a gift of the provinces of Agra and Delhi.

The successful Mahratta then attacked the Rajputs at the head of the allied forces of his own soldiers and the imperial troops, with the vain hope of destroying their rising power. They were

These had power of sentence up to fifteen days' imprisonment, or fine of Rs. 200; but an offence involving a sentence of a severer nature was sent by them for trial before the Court above. The "*Courts of Circuit*" were the next superior to the Magistrates' Courts. There were four of these established for half-yearly gaol delivery, to go on circuit round the zillahs, each in turn, and a fifth for monthly assizes in the large cities in rotation. Their jurisdiction was original in all cases sent up to them by the Magistrates' Courts for trial, and appellate from the decisions of the same Courts. They could pass sentence of death; but this had to be confirmed by the Sudder Nizamat Adalat. They were presided over by the Judges of the Provincial Courts. The "*Sudder Nizamat Adalat*" was the highest Criminal court, held at Calcutta for all appeals from sentences of the lower courts, and for the confirmation and revision of such sentences as required it. The Governor-General had supreme power of pardon, and of commutation of sentences. The "Sudder Nizamat Adalat" was also a Court of original jurisdiction in the cases of all accused Europeans.

POLICE.—The police arrangements were altered at the same period. In lieu of the old private establishments of the separate Zemindars, a connected Police Service was established, having a "*Darogha*," or chief officer in charge of each district, with a proper suite of Police Peons.

[1] This emperor was "Shah Alum," the once gallant Shah Zada, who had given so much trouble to Clive in 1760, under his real name of Ali Gohur. He was a son of the last real emperor, Alamgir II. (See page 97.)

too strong for him, and after suffering a terrible defeat, the whole of the royal forces, to his great consternation, went over *en masse* to the enemy.

He was now in great straits, and in 1787 suffered still further reverses by the successful attacks made upon him by Ismael Beg, nephew to Mohammed Beg the former Executor-General, whom he had ousted from office. Agra was captured, and the enemy's camp was still further reinforced by the arrival of a strong band of Rohillas under Gholam Khadir, son of Zabita Khan.

Sindia marched out from Delhi and attacked the allies, but was defeated.. The Rohillas then determined to make war on their own account, and marched off from the camp northwards; while Sindia, little dreaming of the real object of this movement, attacked and defeated the small army of Ismael Beg.

Immediately after this victory, Sindia heard, to his dismay, that the Rohillas, having made a rapid movement, had captured the city of Delhi. These wild marauders spent two months in sacking the city with every species of cruelty and violence. Their rapine knew no bounds, and their deeds were at last culminated by the blinding of the emperor whom they had taken captive. This crime was too much even for the forbearance of Ismael Beg, who had been much attached to his former master, and could not countenance the barbarity thus committed on his person. He made overtures to Sindia which were accepted, and the quondam foes marched together on Delhi.

1788.—The city was captured by them early in the year. The emperor, though now blind and suffering intense agonies, was replaced on the throne; and Gholam Khadir, being taken prisoner, was tortured to death with circumstances of great cruelty.

Ismael Beg was content with the present of a large and valuable jagir; while Sindia, now virtually ruler of Delhi, raising a splendid army of Sepoys under European officers—French, English, and some Irish adventurers—occupied his time in establishing large foundries, and casting an innumerable quantity of guns, and gun-carriages, with all the weapons and appliances of war.

Thus, by the year 1791, Sindia was again a great Power having one of the finest armies in India, replete with every contrivance to ensure comfort and success. His first campaign was against the Rajputs, and in this he was completely successful.

1792.—Next year, Sindia found his influence so strong that he proceeded to carry out the ruling passion of his life, which was to render the Mahrattas a power important, not only by their own inherent strength, but by the avowed cousent of the Emperor of Delhi, to whom, though much crushed, the native princes looked with the superstitious reverence due to his title as hereditary Lord of India. Shah Alum, at Sindia's request, gave him a patent conferring on the *Peshwa*[1] the title of "*Vakeel-ul-Mutlak*" (or Regent of the Empire), and on Sindia and his heirs the title of "*Hereditary Deputies.*"

This was to the Mahrattas the triumph of all their long-cherished hopes. It was, as it were, the conferring upon the Peshwa the dignity formerly held by the Mogul Emperor of Delhi; and when with great pomp Sindia invested the Peshwa at Poonah with the insignia of office, the young monarch embraced him in a transport of delight, and placed him on a seat next his own,[2] as the highest dignitary in the state, and equal to the vizier, Nana Furnuvese.

Between Sindia and the Nana there naturally enough grew up a cordial hatred—Sindia was in effect the most powerful noble, and the most dangerous in India; while Nana Furnuvese, the highest in the Mahratta state, was the deepest politician of the age. The plots and counter-plots that soon ensued constitute the great interest of the later history of the Mahrattas.

In 1793, Holkar, the second in power of the Mahratta nobility, quarrelled with Sindia and an open war ensued, in which Holkar was completely defeated; and Sindia left absolute master of the whole of Hindostan.

He died somewhat suddenly in 1794, and his grand-nephew, Dowlat Rao Sindia, succeeded to all his titles and offices.

Parliamentary Proceedings (1786—1793).—It remains to notice some of the more conspicuous acts and charters passed in Parliament during the administration of Lord Cornwallis.

In 1786, a Bill was passed which had great and beneficial effect

[1] This is a significant fact, showing as it does that the ancient title of "*Rajah*" to whom the "*Peshwa*" had been merely a minister, had by this time become extinct; and that the Peshwa was now the real, as well as virtual, head of the Mahratta state.

[2] Sindia behaved with much mock humility on this occasion. He came to the Durbar with an immense retinue, and a vast display of power; and at the entrance to the royal tent, dismounting, he took a pair of embroidered slippers, went humbly on foot into the presence, and there, declaring himself unworthy of any honour, performed the menial office of putting on the Peshwa's slippers. The latter at once bade him rise.

on the subsequent career of the English in India. It provided that, when he deemed fit, the Governor-General might personally legislate without consulting his Council, even though his actions were directly contrary to their advice, Lord Wellesley found this permission to be of great use during his administration. It was promulgated in order to prevent any future recurrence of the difficulties and trials which hampered the action of Warren Hastings.

In 1788 a "*Declaratory Act*" was passed, which arose from a collision between the Board of Directors representing the Company and the Board of Commissioners representing the Crown. The Ministry ordered four new regiments to be enrolled for special service in India; but the Company, anxious to save expense, refused to pay for their embarcation or maintenance. The Board of Commissioners then ordered them to provide the requisite funds; but the Directors declared that they possessed the chief governing power in matters of finance. Pitt referred the question to Parliament, and in the course of his speech declared that the intention of his Cabinet was, at some future date, to transfer the whole of the governing power in India to the hands of the nation. The Company were furious, and a series of debates took place which for violence and turbulence have rarely been equalled in the history of the House.[1] A "Declaratory Act" was at last passed, the effect of which was merely to enforce the Act of 1784, and to give the Board of Commissioners power to direct the conduct of the Company in all matters of State.

In 1793 the privileges of the Company were extended for twenty years by a new charter.

(IX.)—*Sir John Shore's Administration*, (1793—1798.)

Sir John Shore, who was the Senior Member of the Council, succeeded to the chief command, as by rule, on Cornwallis's retirement, and the Board of Commissioners, feeling that they could not make a better appointment, confirmed him in the office of Governor-General for five years.

1793.—At the close of his administration, Lord Cornwallis had expressed a strong wish that a "Guarantee Treaty" should be signed by the three Powers who, in 1790, made the Treaty that is

[1] It is said that on one occasion the debate continued till eight o'clock in the morning, when the Commons adjourned to breakfast!

generally known as the "Tripartite Treaty," namely, the Mahrattas, the Nizam, and the British Government. The terms of that Treaty were an offensive and defensive alliance against their common enemy, Tippoo Sultan; and Cornwallis was desirous of appending a sort of codicil to the effect that if one of the Powers went to war with the Sultan for an illegal object, the others should not be bound by the Treaty. This "Guarantee Treaty" was accordingly drawn up and presented to the Nizam and the Peshwa.

Nana Furnuvese was at this time possessed with a rooted determination to injure the Nizam in some manner in order to curb his power. He therefore persuaded the Peshwa to refuse his signature. The Nizam, on the other hand, was anxious to obtain the firm support of the English in case of an outbreak with the Mahrattas, and he accepted the Guarantee Treaty with much readiness.

1794.—At the commencement of the next year Sir John Shore's weakness was the indirect cause of a war which his ultimate conduct rendered very detrimental to the position of the English in India, permanently injuring them in the eyes of the native princes.

It happened that, as before stated, Mahdaji Sindia had died, and was succeeded by his grand nephew Dowlat Rao Sindia. This youthful chieftain was now the greatest Power in Hindostan, and it was of importance to all his neighbours to obtain his alliance Sir John Shore, however, not only omitted to conciliate him in any way, but seemed anxious to consider his arms as of slight consequence, and the Mahrattas at Poonah at once perceived the advantage thus obtained; for so long as Sindia remained unbound by Treaty to any other Power, his co-operation was secured to them by the ties of blood.

War between the Nizam and the Peshwa.—Accordingly they prepared for war with the Nizam, without even deeming it necessary to fabricate any cause of quarrel against him. It was a war of mere wanton plunder; and. true to their nature, every Mahratta who could bear arms flocked to join their standard. Tippoo at the same time made overtures to the Peshwa, to which the latter, anxious to avoid a war with the English, resolutely lent a deaf ear.

As soon, however, as Tippoo had made public his hostility to the Nizam, the latter claimed British protection under the Tripartite Treaty, and begged that a contingent might be sent to his aid. But Sir John Shore, afraid of the immense army which the Mahrattas were bringing into the field, and anxious not to embroil the Company in a war with a nation so powerful, refused to give any assistance to the Nizam on the ground that the English were not bound by a Treaty which one party, namely, the Mahrattas, had broken. This lame excuse was so plainly resorted to in order to avoid a war between the English and the Mahrattas, that the native princes began to lose faith not only in British honour, but in British strength; while the Nizam, left to his fate, moodily brooded over his misfortunes, and vowed vengeance against the Company.

Deserted by the English, he succeeded in enlisting the good offices of the French, who sent two battalions to his aid; and he further raised a body of 18,000 Sepoys, officered by French adventurers.

In November the Mahrattas, under their leader the young Madhoo Rao, took the field at the head of a splendid army of 130,000 men, with 150 guns,[1] and marched into Central India.

The hostile armies met at Kurdla, and the Nizam suffered a decisive defeat. He thereupon submitted, feeling that his power was too weak to enable him to continue the struggle with any hope of success.

The conditions imposed were that the Nizam should at once pay down three millions sterling; should deliver over lands to the value of £35,000 per annum; and should surrender his ablest Minister as hostage into the hands of the Mahrattas.

The Nizam was highly incensed at the wanton neutrality of the English, and at once dismissed all the British troops in his pay. He then proceeded to raise more French battalions, and placed a French officer named Raymond in command. Finally, he assigned to the French the lucrative province of Kurpa, begging them to take the revenues of that district in payment for a French contingent of some magnitude to be kept at Hyderabad.

Sir John Shore now interfered, saying that as the district of Kurpa was on the borders of the Company's territory, it was unfair of the Nizam to subsidize an inimical force by the gift of that

[1] It will be interesting to compare the comparative bulk of the forces sent to swell the ranks of this fine army. Dowlat Rao sent 25,000 men under General De Boigne; the Rajah of Berar, 15,000; Holkar, 10,000; the Pindarees, 10,000; Govind Rao, the Gwickwar, 5,000; the Mahrattas, under the Peshwa, 65,000; total, 130,000.

particular piece of land; and he demanded that if the Nizam insisted on maintaining a French force, the land assigned should at least be further removed from the English boundary.

The Nizam refused; but soon afterwards a sudden domestic trouble occurred which caused him to reconsider his determination. This was an open rebellion against his sovereignty, set on foot by one of his sons. In bodily fear Nizam Ali recalled the English troops; but the French under Raymond having in the meantime quelled the mutiny, he again dismissed them, and gave his patronage to the soldiers from Pondicherry.

(Matters remained in this state for some years, till Lord Wellesley by bold measures overawed Nizam Ali and compelled him to accept the British alliance.)

Death of Madhoo Rao the Second.—Mahratta affairs now claim our attention for a while. It will be remembered that the present Peshwa was a youth, Madhoo Rao the Second, whom—while an infant of two months old—Nana Furnuvese, the sole surviving Regent, had, in 1774, succeeded in placing on the throne to the exclusion of the bold Raghoba. This boy had now become a man; and as he grew up had yearly shown more and more symptoms of irritation at the virtual imprisonment in which he was kept by his Minister. Chafing inwardly at this restraint, he grew morbid and excited; occasionally bursting into terrible fits of rage, and at other times remaining morose and silent. It was in October of the year 1795 that the young monarch, after a hot and angry argument one day with Nana Furnuvese, became oppressed with the deepest melancholy, and the same evening committed suicide by throwing himself from the window of the palace. His untimely death was a subject of deep regret to all parties in India.

Madhoo Rao was succeeded by his cousin Baji Rao, son of Raghoba, one of the cleverest and most unscrupulous princes of the age. The chain of intrigue that ensued immediately on his accession serves admirably to display the character of the Mahrattas of his day.

Accession of Baji Rao.—His Intrigues.—Nana Furnuvese cordially hated the whole family of Raghoba, and determined if possible to oust the wily politician who succeeded the simple-hearted Madhoo. To effect this he plotted with Baji Rao's younger brother, Chimnaji. But the new Peshwa, hearing of this conspiracy, sent secret messengers to Sindia, the most powerful of his nobles, to ask for his support. It was willingly granted. But it happened that at the same time some servants of

Nana Furnuvese, proceeding to the court of Sindia on the same errand, and hearing of the success of Baji Rao's scheme, returned to the Nana, and informed him of this dash to his hopes.

The minister, never at a loss in diplomacy, felt that at all hazards such a combination as that of Sindia and the Peshwa must be destroyed, and determined himself to support the claims of Baji Rao, in opposition to those of Chimnaji! By this means he would maintain his own power at Poonah by the co-operation of Sindia and the gratitude of the Peshwa. He, however, had not rightly judged the character of young Sindia, who, immediately upon receiving tidings of the duplicity of Furnuvese, determined upon frustrating the latter's designs, and making himself the chief person in the state. He accordingly collected a large army, and, in his turn raising the standard of Chimnaji, advanced on Poonah. Nana Furnuvese and Baji Rao fled together to Poorunder, while Sindia's fine army encamped outside the walls of the capital.

Then were held deep and earnest consultations between Baji Rao and the Nana as to the best course to adopt. They determined, so it is said, to stand by one another to the last; and the same night Baji Rao, leaving Nana Furnuvese to his fate, went off to Sindia's camp to throw himself into the protection of a noble whom he felt to be possessed of greater power than the ex-vizier! The despair of the Nana on receiving intelligence of this treacherous conduct of his friend was considerably softened by the tidings which arrived next morning, to the effect that Sindia had received Baji Rao with great distinction but, keeping both the brothers close prisoners till he should determine which to place on the throne, had afterwards declared for Chimnaji and thrown Baji Rao into prison; for he calculated that the new monarch, mindful of his previous services, would receive him into favour and instal him in the coveted office of vizier.

Chimnaji was thus, though much against his own wishes, raised to the dignity of Peshwa, and crowned with great pomp at the capital, by Sindia himself. The question of the appointment to the office of vizier claimed his first attention; and Sindia yielded to the welcome advice of his own minister, Ballobi Tantia, who recommended him to procure the honour for his Commander-in-Chief, Pureshram Bhao, a proceeding which would be calculated to secure him in the position of the most important personage in the state.

This was accordingly done: and the first act of Pureshram

Bhao was to issue orders for the arrest of their wily enemy, the ex-vizier.

Meanwhile the Nana, in exile, feeling that his own party at Poonah would be inevitably crushed so long as Sindia held the reins of Government, sent out two embassies; one to the imprisoned Baji Rao whom he promised to reinstate; the other to the Nizam to ask for a Treaty. The Treaty of Mhar was accordingly drawn up, by which the Nizam guaranteed to assist Baji Rao with an armed force, on the condition of his receiving back the territories lost to the Mahrattas by the last fatal war. The terms were most advantageous to the Nizam; but the promise was a very dangerous one; since he was brought a second time into collision with the whole Mahratta army, for the purpose of supporting a prisoner at the request of an exile.

As soon as he heard of this Treaty, Ballobi Tantia advised his master that the only prudent course to be adopted was to prevent any action on the part of Baji Rao, by dismissing him as a prisoner, guarded by a strong body of cavalry, to Hindostan, there to be kept in confinement at Gwalior. Sindia willingly gave his consent; and the requisite orders were given. The escort was, however, placed under the command of a deceitful and treacherous officer named Sirji Rao Ghatkay; who, while on the route, was seduced from his allegiance by Baji Rao, and consented to connive at his escape on promise of a heavy bribe. The plot was successfully accomplished, and Baji Rao, now once more a free man, joined Nana Furnuvese at Poorunder; after which, by means of embassies and promises of heavy bribes, never omitting to mention the guaranteed armed support of the whole army of the Nizam, they succeeded in gaining over to their cause the two other great Mahratta chieftains, Bhonslay and Holkar. Finally, by proclaiming loudly the strength of this combination and giving Chimnaji the title of usurper, they collected an army so large that Sindia himself became alarmed.

Conspiracies at Poonah ensued. The case was one of a rightful monarch unjustly ejected, while on the throne was a weak and profligate boy; and a strong party in favour of Baji Rao began to be formed at the capital. Sindia quickly perceived the turn affairs had taken, and when Nana Furnuvese sent messages to him promising him the present of a large jagir if he would join their party, he consented.

His next act was somewhat startling; for he seized and threw into prison *his own minister*, Ballobi Tantia, in order to silence his remonstrances: while Puresham Bhao, to escape the same fate, fled with Chimnaji from Poonah. And thus the cause of Baji Rao triumphed. The throne was vacant; and the whole of the Mahratta State, with the co operation of the Nizam, proclaimed his ascendency.

With great pomp Baji Rao was installed Peshwa on December 4th, 1796, and, seating himself on the throne, caused Nana Furnuvese to station himself on one hand and Sindia on the other. And now the question arose; who was to be the chief man in the state, Sindia or the Nana? Baji Rao's hesitation was but slight. Not a whit did he respect antecedents; not in the smallest degree did he consider himself bound in gratitude to the Nana. He remembered that Sindia had the most powerful and well-appointed force in India, and that Furnuvese was but a courtier. Accordingly, two days after he had assisted to instal his master at Poonah, the Nana, to his horror and dismay, found himself seized roughly, and thrown without warning into the deepest dungeon in the palace by order of his perfidious ally!

Thus Baji Rao was rid of Nana Furnuvese. But his was a character to be little contented with the control of a powerful noble always at his elbow, and he began to consider how he might rid himself of Sindia also. That potentate, in his turn, showed his secret enmity, for he somewhat haughtily demanded the jagir that had been promised him for his co-operation.

The Peshwa determined to profit by the opportunity thus created. He saw that at one stroke he could arouse popular feeling in Poonah against Sindia and his troops, though the means to be employed were barbarous and unscrupulous to an extent rarely equalled in history. Sirji Rao Ghatkay, who had been made commander of the forces, and was a tyrant at once treacherous and cruel, was his worthy instrument. The Peshwa commenced operations by publicly refusing to pay Sindia at once; stating that a monarch must choose his own time for conferring favours. His refusal was couched in gentle and moderate language; and the gossip of Poonah that evening turned on the quiet firmness of the Peshwa, and the indignant countenance of Sindia, when he received this rebuke. But the next day the whole of Sindia's troops were found to be in open rebellion. They rushed into Poonah, and, with the most detestable atrocities, plundered and pillaged the whole city, giving it up to rapine and lawlessness for an entire week. The number of slain was incredible; and the loud voice of the people cried for vengeance on the perpetrator of this horrible outrage.

It had been committed by the private orders of the Peshwa to Sirji Rao Ghatkay; and against the wish of Sindia, who tried in vain to restrain his infuriated and drunken soldiery!

The Peshwa had gained his object. His brother, Amrit Rao, a noble and intelligent young prince, lashed into fury, begged permission to punish Sindia by assassination. Baji Rao consented. But afterwards, remembering that this act would call down on himself the vengeance of the whole army, he contented himself by summoning Sindia to court, and peremptorily commanding him to return to his own country.

Sindia accordingly went north, accompanied by the undeserved curses of all the people of Poonah; and Baji Rao, with the full consent and acclamation of his subjects, remained at last undisputed master of the throne.

Mutiny of Officers in Bengal, 1796.—We must now return to Bengal, where a very serious mutiny of officers took place. It arose from the fact that the officers of the Indian military service were paid less highly than those of the civil service. The former demanded an increase of pay; and on being refused, became insubordinate and at last openly mutinous. They instituted a plan of combined action, and drew up a statement of their grievances. There were four principal demands.

(I.) The number of the Company's regiments was not to be reduced.

(II.) The Company's troops were always to be employed in preference to the royal regiments in India.

(III.) Promotion in the service was to be given according to seniority, and not by purchase.

(IV.) "Double batta"[1] was to be restored.

If these demands were not immediately granted, the officers threatened to usurp the government by force.

Sir John Shore at once collected troops and ordered a fleet from Madras to Calcutta. But happily before the employment of these was rendered necessary, the mutinous spirit was quelled by the courteousness of Sir Robert Abercrombie, who was in command at Cawnpore, and who managed by his civility and good temper to calm the excited feelings of the officers. Concessions were then made, and order was soon completely restored.

The attention of the Government was now called to the affairs of Oude.

[1] The mutiny of officers during the administration of Clive in 1766, had taken place on the "Batta" question. (See page 105).

1797.[1]—*Affairs of Oude.*—The minister of Asoff-u-dowla, the Nabob vizier of Oude, was at this period a certain Tufuzzil Hussein, who had been appointed on the death of the former minister, the able and intelligent Hyder Beg Khan. Asoff-u-dowla, after a life of indolence and debauchery, died, worn out with his excesses, in 1797, and the appointment of his successor rested entirely with the English.

A reputed son, named Vizier Ali, being considered the rightful heir, was accordingly placed on the throne (1797); and though the unanimous voice of the people declared him to be illegitimate, the mistake was not rectified till he had been on the throne some months, when he was hastily deposed, and Asoff's brother, Saadat Ali, installed in his place. The vexation of Vizier Ali may be imagined. He was a man of very violent temper, and commenced a system of rebellion which gave much trouble to the English.

Treaty with Oude.—A treaty was then made between Saadat Ali and the English, guaranteeing a subsidiary alliance. Ten thousand British troops were to garrison Oude. They were to be maintained by an annual payment of seventy-six lacs of rupees, and to have the fortress of Allahabad for their head-quarters. The Nabob at the same time consented to make no treaties without the permission of the Governor-General.

In the month of March of the next year (1798), Sir John Shore returned to England, his term of office having expired. On his arrival he was raised to the peerage by the title of Lord Teignmouth.

[1] In this year the "Mayor's Court" at Madras, which had been established in 1726 by George I., was abolished by act 36 Geo. III. It had been a court for the trial of all offences committed by or against the Europeans in the Presidency. A new court, called the "Recorder's Court," was instituted on the same principle as obtains in the city of London Borough-Quarter-sessions. The Mayor was the nominal, the Recorder, the real Judge. A similar alteration was made at Bombay. The jurisdiction of the court was civil, admiralty, and criminal in all cases concerning Europeans. An alteration was also made in the jurisdiction of the "Provincial courts" which Cornwallis had established in Bengal. (See note, page 157). Their authority was extended from causes of the value of 1000 rs. and under, to those of 5000 rs. and under. In these cases the court had a final jurisdiction. Appeals against decisions involving a greater sum might be made to the "Sudder Dewani Adalat," and ultimately to the Privy Council.

(X.) *Lord Wellesley's Administration* (1798—1805).—*Fall of the House of Hyder.—Annexation of Tanjore, the Carnatic, and Oude.—Fall of Sindia.*

1798.—The Governor-General appointed to succeed Sir John Shore was Lord Mornington, afterwards Marquis Wellesley, during whose administration the English were established as indisputably the greatest military power in India.

State of India.—On his arrival he found matters in a very critical state. Tippoo Sultan had been it was true, humbled, but he was on that account the more revengeful; and while waiting for an opportunity for striking a deadly blow at the English, he was carefully improving his resources. The Nizam, justly offended with the Company for the treacherous policy of Sir John Shore, had dismissed all the English from his service, and subsidized at Hyderabad a French army of 14,000 men, with thirty-six guns, under the generalship of Raymond. Sindia was one of the greatest powers in India; he had possession of the person of the emperor at Delhi, and was acknowledged the principal chieftain in the Mahratta state; and he had an army of 40,000 sepoys, officered by Frenchmen and commanded by De Boigne, with 460 well-mounted guns. To complete the difficulties of the situation, the English officers at Calcutta were mutinous; and the treasury was empty; the accounts showing a deficit.

During his outward voyage Lord Wellesley (for so he may be called in anticipation of his subsequent title) held a long consultation at the Cape of Good Hope with Lord Macartney, concerning Indian affairs; and invited all British residents at the Cape who had been in India,[1] to advise him on the position of parties, and the best mode of dealing with them. He thus landed with something like a defined policy in his mind.[2]

Fourth and Last Mysore War, 1799.—The first information he received at Calcutta was to the effect that Tippoo Sultan had sent publicly to the Mauritius for the aid of a French force to

[1] The Cape was at that time the great place of resort for all Anglo-Indians desirous of change, who did not wish to undertake the long voyage to England.

[2] Wellesley discovered that there could be nothing like a just balance of power amongst parties in India. He had learnt from historical evidence that in that country a power, to have any weight, must be universal ruler, or subservient. "Aut Cæsar aut nihil." He determined that England should be "Cæsar," and he made it so.

assist him in driving the English out of India. This French contingent was granted and landed at Mangalore.

Strength had crushed many Indian princes before, and as diplomacy had been tried with Tippoo and found useless, Lord Wellesley determined that his principal arguments should now be cold steel and round-shot.

He accordingly declared war; and sent orders to Madras that a strong body of troops should at once march on Seringapatam. At the same time he requested the Nizam and the Peshwa to give their assistance, according to the Tripartite Treaty of 1790. Messages were also sent to Sindia, and the Rajah of Nagpore.

The Governor of Madras made answer that he had no money, and that the troops under his orders were not in a fit state to march unsupported into an enemy's country. But he was met by an indignant command that the army should be placed in proper order at once.

The Nizam's troops were at this time entirely officered by Frenchmen, and the Governor-General felt keenly the impolicy of leading them against their countrymen in Tippoo's army. He therefore quickly decided on destroying the French supremacy at Hyderabad. This was effected by obtaining the consent of the Nizam's able minister. Some British regiments were marched to the French cantonments, and by clever manœuvring the Sepoys were disarmed, and rendered incapable of withstanding the bayonets of the English. The regiments were then disbanded, and the French officers paid and dismissed. Thus the English were again established at Hyderabad, and the Nizam consented to aid them against Tippoo by all the means in his power.

The Peshwa also consented to fulfil his share of the treaty, after Wellesley had, in a private letter, promised him the aid of English troops against Sindia, should that potentate ever become troublesome.

Sindia, and the Rajah of Nagpore, both refused any aid or alliance.

A despatch quickly arrived from England giving the consent of the Board of Commissioners to the war; and, all being then in readiness, the Governor-General embarked for Madras.

In reply to Lord Wellesley's communication threatening a declaration of war, Tippoo had written a letter in which it was evident that his object was to gain time till another French force, which it was known he had urgently demanded, should arrive from Europe.

But Wellesley, determined to frustrate his intentions, sent his final orders to Bombay and Hyderabad, and his ultimatum to Tippoo, in January, 1799; and on February 5th, commenced his march into Mysore. His army consisted of 20,000 English, with 100 guns, together with 20,000 Sepoys and native cavalry, General Harris commanding-in-chief.

The Rajah of Mysore at once decided on his plan of action. He determined to destroy the Bombay contingent, under General Stuart and Colonel Hartley, before it could effect a junction with the main army, and with this view he made a vigorous attack upon it; but the Mysoreans were unprepared for the able resistance which they met with, and fled, after hard fighting, having made no impression on their stubborn foes.

The Sultan then turned to oppose the Madras army.

The enemies met at Malavelly, and Tippoo suffered another terrible defeat.[1]

He retired on Seringapatam, wasting the country far and near to prevent the English advance; but General Harris, with ready wit and great ability, threw Tippoo into utter confusion by taking another route. The Rajah's astonishment and rage, when, imagining the enemy behind him, he suddenly found himself confronted by their whole army just when he was approaching his own capital, was beyond parallel!

The rival forces marched on Seringapatam almost together. Each perceived that the time had arrived for a decisive stroke, but Tippoo felt himself too weak to hazard an open battle, and the English were desirous of husbanding their strength for the final blow. There was no fighting on the route, and in silence they approached Seringapatam. The English, however, suffered much from want of provisions, and it was only by constant foraging, and the exertions of a very able commissariat staff that the troops were kept alive, although the march, after the passage of the Cavery, was very short.

At the end of March Tippoo entered his capital, and on April 6 General Harris arrived, and at once placed the city in a state of siege, the lines being completed by the 17th.

Fall of Seringapatam.—Death of Tippoo.—The want of food and stores was most severely felt by the English; and on May 3rd it was discovered that the provisions left would only

[1] It was in this battle that Colonel Wellesley, afterwards the great Duke of Wellington, first drew his sword on Indian soil. He distinguished himself greatly.

suffice for two days, whilst the country round had been exhausted by pillage. It was therefore determined to storm at once, as the breach had by that time been made practicable.

General Baird led the forlorn hope, and though Tippoo was unprepared for this sudden attack, a desperate struggle took place It was one of the most rapid successes on record. Within seven minutes from the first "Hurrah!" order, the British flag was waving on the battlements of the city, and the Mysoreans were driven back in the streets. The fighting was terrible, a hand to hand combat was carried on in every street and lane of the city; while the thunder of the heavy guns was absolutely deafening.

In an hour all was over Major Allen went with a flag of truce to the palace, and forced the officers in charge to open the gates of the city. The troops at once rushed in, and Wellesley rode to the palace to confer with the Sultan.

He was nowhere to be found; and it was not till the evening that his dead body was discovered near the breach, shot through the head, and wounded in many places with sword-cuts and bayonet stabs. He was honourably buried the next day in his father's mausoleum.

Lord Wellesley (created a Marquis, as soon as the news of this splendid victory reached home), might well look back with satisfaction on the events of this his first year of office. He had turned away the French officers at Hyderabad, and reinstated the English: he had annihilated the kingdom of Hyder Ali, and established the supremacy of British arms in the Deckan.

But now came the question, what was to be done with the conquered country, which was completely in the hands of the English. After due consideration, Lord Wellesley determined to deliver it over to the ancient Hindu dynasty of Mysore, whom Tippoo had reduced to poverty and humiliation. A child of five years old was accordingly drawn from obscurity,[1] and replaced on the throne of his forefathers, with the celebrated Poorneah for his minister.[2] With the latter a solemn treaty was made, and the conditions of

[1] The young Rajah lived many years, dying at the age of seventy-four in the year 1868. His adopted son, a child of four years of age, was then placed on his throne.

[2] The appointment of Poorneah was afterwards found to have been an exceedingly wise step. He was the most able finance minister living, and, having been vizier both to Hyder and Tippoo, was well acquainted with the state of the country.

the replacement of the old Mysore family on the throne were distinctly stated.[1]

These conditions were that a military force for the defence of the country should be raised under English discipline and with English officers, and should be maintained by the revenues of Mysore. The Raj was to be considered as a gift from the Government to the young Rajah. There was also an express proviso that in case the mal-administration of the Rajah should endanger the annual subsidy for the payment of the troops, the Company might at any future time take possession of such a portion of the country as they might deem sufficient to provide the requisite annual sum.

The revenues of the country were apportioned amongst the victorious allies as follows:—An annual payment of 777,000 star pagodas[2] was to go the Company, who, out of this sum, awarded an annuity of 240,000[3] to Tippoo's family, and 70,000[4] to the Commander-in-Chief of the Mysore army, he having wisely surrendered, unconditionally, and thus contributed much to the success of the English arms. An annuity of 600,000[5] star pagodas was to be paid to the Nizam, and 230,000[6] to the Peshwa on certain conditions. These conditions, however, the Peshwa refused to accept, and, accordingly, the annuity was withheld, and the land portioned between the Nizam and the Company.

Within a few months it was discovered that the Peshwa and Sindia had made a conspiracy to attack Calcutta, should the expedition against Mysore prove unsuccessful.

A commission was at that time appointed to inquire into the condition of Mysore, and make a report on the best mode of arranging the affairs of the country. It was called the "Mysore Commission," and consisted of five members, all of whom were men of pre-eminent talent.[7]

[1] These conditions have been called in question within the last few years by a party opposed to annexation. They were considered sufficient when they were made, and the intention of the British Government was very plain.

[2] £310 800 per annum. [3] £96,000 per annum.

[4] £28,000 per annum. [5] £240,000 per annum. [6] £92,000.

[7] The members of this commission were Colonel Barry Close, who is called the Prince of Indian diplomatists; Captain Malcolm, afterwards the celebrated Sir John Malcolm, who became Governor of Bombay; Captain Munro, afterwards Sir Thomas Munro, Governor of Madras; Henry Wellesley, who is well known in history as Lord Cowley, Ambassador in Paris; and Colonel Arthur Wellesley, Duke of Wellington. Perhaps the finest assemblage of men of genius that has ever met to settle the affairs of a country.

Against the English assumption of the kingdom of Tippoo, there was only one rebellion of importance, that of Dhoondia Wang, which was suppressed after a few months, the leader being killed.

The Nizam, immediately after the war, requested that he might be allowed to have a larger number of British troops at Hyderabad, and promised to give over certain districts to the Company as payment for their maintenance. The request was granted, and the country, which was thus given to the Company, still goes by the name of the "*Ceded Districts.*"

Annexation of Tanjore, 1799.—After Lord Wellesley's return to Calcutta he found himself called upon to deal with several important questions. The first of these concerned the Raj of Tanjore In 1786 Tuljaji, the Rajah, lineal descendant of Shahji, the father of the famous Sevaji, who founded the Mahratta monarchy, died without issue, leaving a younger brother, Amir Singh, and an adopted son, named Serfaji. The succession to the throne was disputed, and, after reference to the British, who consulted Pundits on the question, it was decided that a Rajah had no power to adopt a son to succeed him while there was a near male relative of his family alive, and able to govern. The Governor of Madras therefore placed Amir Singh on the throne of Tanjore, where he remained till 1798. By the time of Lord Wellesley's arrival it had been sufficiently proved that the government of Amir Singh was pernicious to the country, and the Governor of Madras again began to think seriously of Serfaji. His claims were a second time referred to Pundits, who declared that the decision of the former legal advisers had been entirely opposed to Hindu law; that Tuljaji had a perfect right to adopt a son to succeed him;[1] that the title of Serfaji was therefore good; and that of Amir Singh contrary to law. The Madras Government accordingly deposed Amir Singh, giving him a pension, and placed Serfaji on the throne of Tanjore. A commission was appointed to inquire carefully into the affairs of the country, and, their report being made, Lord Wellesley declared that it would be for the advantage of the Tanjoreans that the English should assume the entire management of the country. This was accordingly done, and Serfaji was pensioned off.[2]

[1] This rule has been adopted in the case of the present succession to the throne of Mysore.

[2] It would seem a very difficult undertaking to justify the conduct of the English in their treatment of this Raj by any arguments, either of law or

Thus, in 1799, expired the independence of Tanjore, 150 years after its foundation, by the father of Sevaji.

Annexation of the Carnatic, 1799.—The next annexation was that of the Carnatic, which was managed with somewhat more show of justice than that of Tanjore.

Mahomed Ali, "the Company's Nabob," died in 1795, after a reign of forty-six years, He was succeeded by his son, Omdat-ul-Omrah, who proved, like his father, a reckless spendthrift, running into hopeless debt in the most cheerful manner, and oppressing the ryots with great rigour, in order to extort from them the largest possible amount of rupees, to be devoted, not to the payment of debts, but to the gratification of his own pleasures and amusements.

When Lord Wellesley entered on the Mysore War he sent to Arcot to demand, according to treaty, a subsidy of three crores of rupees. The Nabob refused to comply, and Lord Wellesley at once informed him that he was rendering himself liable to the loss of his position, since by treaty the English Government had reserved to itself the right of assuming the entire government of the whole, or any part of the country, should the subsidy be endangered. The Governor-General went on to say, that he would consent for ever to abandon this hold on the Carnatic territory, if the Nabob would assign to the Company districts sufficient to yield annually the value of the subsidy.

But Omdat-ul-Omrah was utterly wanting in ability, and without calculating the respective strength of parties, he imagined that this last clause was in reality a display of weakness on the part of the English; that they were without funds for the proper prosecution of the great war; that they would, therefore, in all probability fail; and that he should gain credit with the victorious Tippoo, if he could manage to stand aloof.[1] He accordingly refused either to pay the quota or to cede districts of the value of the subsidy.

In 1799 Omdat-ul-Omrah died, leaving as heir an adopted son. But as this young prince refused to accept any of the conditions which the Governor-General offered as the price of his elevation, Lord Wellesley directed that Omdat's nephew, Azim-ul-Omrah,

[1] The Nabob had bound himself by the treaty of 1792 not to treat with other powers, except under the consent of the Governor-General. But when the state-papers found in Tippoo's palace, after the capture of Seringapatam were examined, it was discovered that both Mahomed Ali and Omdat-ul-Omrah had been holding secret negociations with Mysore.

should be proclaimed Nabob; and Azim consented to the entire annexation of the Carnatic, on promise of an annuity of one-fifth of the revenues for his maintenance.

Annexation of Part of Oude, 1801.[1]—The Nabob vizier of Oude at this time was Saadat Ali, who had been placed on the throne by the English, and was entirely subservient to them. Lord Wellesley, of course, supported his title in opposition to that of Vizier Ali, the illegitimate son of the last Nabob; and in 1799 he became so annoyed at the fierce and turbulent conduct of Vizier Ali that he sent a mission to him, headed by Mr. Cherry, to remonstrate, and bid him desist on pain of imprisonment. Vizier Ali was a man of an uncontrollable temper, which, on this occasion, so far got the better of him that, with his own hand, in open Durbar, he assassinated the envoy, and, in a transport of rage, ordered a general massacre of English. The command was partially obeyed, and several English were killed. Vizier Ali then fled to the Rajput Rajah of Jeypore, who treacherously gave up his guest into the hands of the English.

The following year the Governor-General came to the determination that it was necessary for the defence of Oude to disband the useless troops of the Nabob, and substitute in their place European regiments, or regiments of Sepoys officered by Englishmen. He sent a message to this effect to Saadat Ali, proposing that the funds devoted to the maintenance of the present troops should be diverted to the support of the British regiments. The Nabob felt very keenly that the effect of the measure would be nothing less than to transfer the whole military command in Oude to the Company, and to make him pay for it! He was much distressed at this proceeding, and declaring it to be against his conscience, so completely to barter away the whole independence of the country he had undertaken to govern and protect, he proposed to retire altogether from his office, placing one of his sons on the throne. Lord Wellesley seized upon the offer, as the very thing calculated to simplify his intended annexation of territory, for he could dictate terms to the young monarch as to the conditions of his enthronement. The offer of Saadat Ali

[1] This is one of the most startling annexations that has taken place in India. It was effected in a manner calculated to wound the feelings of the reigning House. The only apology for it is, that Lord Wellesley, fearing the invasion of Zemaun Shah, felt that at all hazards Oude must be well defended, as the frontier state of English territory, and considered the means by which his object was to be obtained of secondary importance.

was therefore accepted, but in the despatch from the Government it was stated, as a condition of his retirement, that the royal treasure should be given up, and the whole country declared to be henceforth English, each succeeding vizier receiving the throne as a gift from the Governor-General.

Saadat Ali's indignation was kindled by this harsh and unjust demand, and he wrote to Calcutta, declaring that he should withdraw his abdication, and should continue his attempts to benefit his country. Lord Wellesley, however, replied, that this was only a trick to gain time: that the vizier had abdicated;[1] that he was now only trifling with the Company; and that he should be compelled to adhere to his former decision, if necessary, by force.

A large body of troops was then ordered to Oude, and the Nabob was informed that he was expected to pay for their maintenance. On his remonstrating the Governor-General contemptuously sent him back his own despatch! The vizier was thus forced to submit, and, having disbanded a large portion of his troops, he, with a very bad grace, devoted the funds that had maintained them to support the British forces.

In November, 1800, Lord Wellesley demanded a fresh disbandment of native troops, and payment for some more English regiments which he then sent to Oude. The Nabob pleaded his poverty, and his inability to suffer an increase of the subsidy.[2] Lord Wellesley angrily retorted that this failure could only be due to his personal extravagance, and bad government[3] that such a scandalous thing as a native chieftain declaring himself unable to maintain troops whenever the Governor-General demanded it was quite unheard-of; and, finally, that the Nabob *must* maintain this fresh contingent.

The vizier, finding that to contend any longer with one so powerful was useless, sent back a despatch, declaring his willingness to cede certain districts for the maintenance of the troops, if

[1] This was certainly untrue, for a mere despatch, stating the intention of a monarch to abdicate at some future time, unless something was done, could not be construed into an actual abdication.

[2] The subsidy had been increased from fifty-five to seventy-six lacs of rupees only two years before.

[3] Lord Wellesley acted on the supposition that Saadat Ali inherited all the faults of his brother and uncle, his predecessors. It is true that the latter did all in their power to ruin the country; but it is believed that Saadat Ali was in reality trying to govern well. This misconception on Lord Wellesley's part was, however, only natural.

the Company would secure to him and his family a regular annuity in exchange.

An arrangement was then made, the vizier freeing himself from the subsidy by ceding for ever the districts of Allahabad, Azimgurh, Goruckpore, and the southern Dooab, with some others, the whole being of the annual value of £1,352,347. The arrangement was of great service to Oude, as a solid defence was guaranteed for the whole country at the expense of the cession of a part; but this advantage could scarcely justify the harsh measures employed to effect it.

A commission, superintended by Henry Wellesley, brother of the Governor-General, and afterwards Lord Cowley, was now appointed to settle the country. It was conducted with great ability, and finished its labours after a year's investigation.

The Embassy to Persia, 1800.—At this time the ruler of Cabul was Zemaun, Son of Teimur Shah, son of Ahmed Khan Abdali, who, in 1757, conquered Delhi from the Mogul emperor. Retiring afterwards from Hindostan, where the treacherous battle of Panipat, in 1761, had shattered his forces, Ahmed Khan had conquered Cabul, and established a Durani dynasty there. His son Teimur succeeded him, and on his death left Zemaun Shah, his son, ruler of Cabul.

This monarch had been planning new invasions of India, and had been corresponding with Tippoo Sultan, begging his aid against the English. The Company were at this time still fearful of his threatened attack, though the power of Tippoo was crushed; and Lord Wellesley had forced the British troops upon Oude expressly to serve as a check to any hostile advance. The alarm of the English was but too well founded, for Zemaun Shah had several times brought armies to the frontier, and retreated through fear of his own country being attacked; and at this time he had collected large bodies of soldiers, received promises of aid from many Hindu Rajahs, and revived the religious fanaticism of the Mohammedans throughout India, by proclaiming himself the champion of Islam.

The French were also, by the direction of Napoleon, making alliances in the East, and were intriguing for the co-operation of Persia. A combination of France, Persia, and Afghanistan was therefore much dreaded at Calcutta; and it was determined to send an embassy to Persia under Captain Malcolm. This mission was immensely costly and completely successful. Malcolm scattered gold and silver around with unsparing hand in order to gain the affections of the populace: and finally, after being received with great distinction, succeeded in obtaining a treaty.

Terms of the Treaty.—It was signed at Teheran by Malcolm and the Shah. The terms were as follows: —

The King of Persia was to discountenance all attacks on India, and if necessary oppose them by force of arms. He was summarily to eject every Frenchman from Persia; and was to give all his patronage of foreign commerce to England.

The English on their part guaranteed to help the King of Persia against Zemaun Shah, should the latter attack him.

The effects of this treaty did not warrant the extravagant praise lavished on it, For it was excessively costly; it gave little commercial benefit to the country, because there was little commerce to establish; and lastly, it tended to show the great fear of the French which obtained to so large an extent at Calcutta. The expedition was, however, completely successful as regards Persia, for the prodigal display of wealth dazzled all eyes, from the Shah to the camel-driver; and secured an alliance the greater because cemented by a hope of gain.

1802.—In 1802, the Governor-General sent in his resignation to the Board of Commissioners; but received a reply begging him earnestly to postpone his departure till 1805. He consented; and as a consequence strengthened in a wonderful manner the English empire in India, for during the remaining period of his administration he crushed all the remaining great Powers of India.

State of India at the Beginning of the Century.—At the beginning of the nineteenth century the political condition of India had undergone a great change. The Mogul empire was completely extinguished, Sindia having possession of Delhi. The strong rule of Hyder and Tippoo had been dashed in pieces by Wellesley. The only other great Power, besides the English, was now that of the Mahrattas, who were divided into five principal parties, more or less on bad terms with one another. These were the Peshwa, nominally the supreme governor, the deceitful and treacherous Baji Rao, reigning at Poonah; Dowlat Rao Sindia, in reality the strongest of the Mahratta families at Gwalior; Jeswant Rao Holkar, at Indore, gaining strength and bearing deadly hatred to Sindia; Raghuji Bhonslay, Rajah of Nagpore, hating nobody in particular, but willing to fight against anybody for a consideration; and Futteh Sing, the Gwickwar of Guzerat, who never joined much in Mahratta politics unless called in to aid in some grand *coup*. There were other smaller states, half independent, but owing feudal submission to the Peshwa, their hereditary sovereign. It was evident to all parties that very soon a grand struggle must occur between the English and the Mahrattas for the empire of India.

Mahratta Disturbances.—In 1800 Nana Furnuvese died in prison; and Baji Rao was thus freed from any further interference on his part.

Sindia remained at Poonah till he was called north by the wanton aggressions of Jeswant Rao Holkar, who, not content with plundering the Peshwa's city of Sagore, had gone, in company with the Rohilla chieftain, Amir Khan, to devastate Malwa, which belonged to Sindia.

The hostile forces met at Ujein. Holkar had 70,000 men under his command, while Sindia's troops were in two divisions; and when, through bad generalship, these forces were separated, Holkar defeated first one division, and then the other, before they could effect a junction. This was the first great defeat that Sindia had experienced.

1801.—He at once sent for aid to Poonah, and Sirja Rao Ghatkay commanding the royal forces, joined him in Malwa. The combined armies then attacked and defeated Holkar on the 14th of October, and advanced on his capital city Indore. This they plundered, while Holkar fled to Candeish, and devastated the surrounding country. Thence he marched to Chandore, and from that city sent a despatch to the Peshwa at Poonah, informing him that Sindia had behaved very cruelly, and that he (Holkar) was about to march with all his forces on Poonah in order to claim the protection of the Peshwa against his enemy.

1802.—But the Peshwa's conscience was uneasy. He had very recently captured Holkar's brother, the warlike young robber chieftain Wittoji, and had put him to death with the most revolting barbarities, being himself present at the scene; when, therefore, Holkar's message arrived, Baji Rao felt that it was nothing more or less than a screen to an open declaration of war. In this difficulty Colonel Close, the British Resident at the Mahratta court, felt himself entitled to offer the aid of the Company's arms against Holkar; but the Peshwa obstinately refused to accept such assistance. He had seen the result of a similar policy in the case of the Nizam, and trembled for his crown.

Sindia quickly marched down and encamped near Poonah to

assist the Peshwa; while Colonel Close quitted the city and encamped on a hill near. On the 25th of October a great battle was fought. Holkar gained a complete victory; and the Peshwa fled to Sungumnere, about fifty miles from Ahmednuggur, and thence to Bassein, which belonged to the Company.

During the two months in which Holkar remained at Poonah, he placed Amrit Rao, brother to the Peshwa, on the throne; while Sindia went northward to await the issue.

The lonely and deserted Peshwa now accepted the offer of Colonel Close, that an alliance should be made between the English and Mahrattas.

Treaty of Bassein, 1802.—A treaty was accordingly drawn up, and signed by Baji Rao and Colonel Close. The terms were,—

The Peshwa to maintain 6000 British infantry, with guns; assigning to the Company for their support certain districts in the Deckan, yielding a revenue of twenty-five lacs of rupees per annum; to keep no Europeans in his service belonging to any nation at war with the English; to refer to the Governor-General as arbitrator all claims against the Nizam and the Gwickwar; and to make no political changes without his concurrence.

Both parties to consider themselves as reciprocally bound in a defensive alliance.

This subsidiary treaty was naturally viewed by all the Mahrattas as an indignity to their name. It would place them in a position no longer independent, but acknowledging the English as a superior power.

1803.—Sindia was not slow to perceive the full extent and danger of these concessions, and he determined to make a great combination of Mahratta princes, in order to deal such a blow upon the English as should stagger them in the midst of their success.

Confederation against the English, 1803.—The confederation consisted of Sindia, Amrit Rao and Bhonslay, Rajah of Nagpore.

Holkar consented to join them, but aftewards failed to carry out his promise, and the Gwickwar wisely determined to remain neutral.

Great Mahratta War.—On April 17th Sindia and Bhonslay met at Nagpore with great pomp, and at once marched on Poonah to join Amrit Rao.

Lord Wellesley at once ordered up troops, and General Wellesley, now for the first time placed in actual command of armies, advanced, by forced marches, on Poonah, with the Mysore army, of about 12,000 men, for the avowed purpose of reinstating Baji Rao on the throne. Holkar retreated to Chandore, and the timid Amrit Rao determined, usurper-like, to burn his capital, rather than let it be taken by the English. Happily, General Wellesley heard of this resolution, and by a dashing march of sixty miles in thirty-two hours saved the city from destruction. Amrit Rao fled to Sindia's camp, and the allies steadily continued their route towards Poonah.

They halted, however, while Wellesley, to whom the Marquis had confided full civil and military powers in matters connected with the campaign, sent to Sindia to demand his intentions. Colonel Collins, the emissary, demanded to know whether Sindia was intending to preserve inviolate the treaty of Bassein or not, and was informed that he should have an answer when Sindia had held a consultation with the Rajah of Berar. This looked so threatening that Collins proceeded to further inquiries, which ended by Sindia's declaration:—"After I have conferred with the Rajah of Berar you shall know whether it is to be peace or war."

The conference was then delayed for two months, Sindia's object evidently being to gain time while he strengthened his resources. General Wellesley at the same time was not idle, and, having completed all his arrangements, he directed Colonel Collins to quit the camp of the allies.

This opened the war.

Wellesley had arranged that General Lake should attack, at Gwalior, Sindia's reserve force, who were commanded by Perron, while two *corps d'armée* should take possession of Sindia's dominions in Broach, and of Holkar's in Cuttack. About 3600 troops were left for the defence of Hyderabad and the ceded districts; and the main army, with Wellesley, numbered 17,000 men.

Ahmednuggur was taken by General Wellesley in August, and the attack on Broach was successfully carried out by Colonel Woodington, while, on the same day, Lake commenced his attack on the fortress of Allyghur.

Capture of Allyghur, September 2nd, 1803.—The capture of this fort was a work of considerable difficulty, but was most gallantly effected by the 76th regiment, who succeeded in blowing down the gates. The place capitulated on September 4th.

Battle of Assye, September 3rd, 1803.—On the 3rd the great battle of Assye was fought by the main army. Wellesley was reconnoitring near Aurungabad, with a flying column of about 4500 men, when he discovered the Mahrattas, some 50,000 strong, posted in a very advantageous position, and apparently awaiting his attack. He at once determined not to disappoint them, and ordered his men to fix bayonets, and advance in line. A tremendous fire poured in upon them, but, such was the indomitable courage with which the English came on, that the Mahrattas, fine soldiers as they were, could not stand it. They broke and fled, and the victory was complete.

British arms were successful at all points. Almost simultaneously with Wellesley's victories, and the successes of Broach and Allyghur, Harcourt took Cuttack, in the Bay of Bengal, and Stephenson reduced the forts of Burhampore and Assirghur, on the Satpura mountains.

Sindia then made a truce with Wellesley, who, joining Stephenson's force from Broach, marched to attack the Rajah of Berar's strong fortress of Gawilghur, for the defence of which Bhonslay at once moved up.

Battle of Argaom, November 28th, 1803.—The opposing armies met at Argaom, near Elichpore, on November 28th. It was evening when Wellesley came upon the enemy. Their front extended five miles, and when the cannonading commenced it was so powerful that three battalions were panic stricken. Wellesley, however, himself managed to recall them to their duty, and the battle began in earnest. It ended in a complete victory, with no great loss, though the enemy suffered severely.

The Rajah fled; Gawilghur was taken; and Colonel Stephenson had commenced his march on Nagpore, when Bhonslay, anxious to save his city, begged for terms.

Treaty of Deogaom, December 18th, 1803.—A treaty was concluded on December 18th, 1803, between the Rajah of Berar and Mountstuart Elphinstone for the Company.

> The English guaranteed to spare the territories of Berar, while the Rajah of Berar promised to cede Cuttack to the Company; to give several districts to the Nizam; to exclude all Frenchmen and Europeans at war with England; and to refer all differences to the Governor-General for arbitration.

Two months previously Delhi had been captured by the English.

Lake's Career—Taking of Delhi.—After his victory of Allyghur, General Lake marched straight on Delhi, in order to complete the humiliation of Sindia, by taking from him the chief city of India, in which an emperor was yet languishing in prison. The English under Lake, and Sindia's troops under French officers, met six miles from Delhi on September 11th. Lake's cavalry being too much exposed to fire, he was withdrawing them to a safer distance, when the enemy, imagining this was a flight, rushed out of their entrenchments to the attack. The British infantry charged, and the result was a panic. The French were completely beaten, and on the same evening the English standard waved on the walls of Delhi.

The blind and aged Shah Alum was rescued from his confinement, and at the age of eighty-three was replaced on the throne of India by General Lake, and received under British protection.

Lake then marched against Agra, which was held by the Rajah of Bhurtpore, and capitulated on October 17th.

Battle of Laswaree.—A considerable body of the enemy from the Deckan and Delhi having collected, General Lake marched out to attack them, and came up with them at Laswaree. A terrible battle was the result in which, after severe loss, a victory was again claimed by the British army. The 76th Regiment, the same who had so gallantly stormed Allyghur, were the main stay of the fight, and the Sepoy regiments fought admirably. The enemy, too, seemed possessed with the very demon of war, and it was not till the decimation of some of the finest regiments in Sindia's service that they at last broke and fled.

This was a final blow to Sindia's hopes, and on December 4th, 1803, he submitted to the hard terms of a treaty dictated by his victorious foes at Anjengaom.

> *Treaty of Anjengaom, December 4th,* 1803.—The terms were that Sindia should cede all his territories north of Jeypore and Joudpore; together with Broach and Ahmednuggur; that he should give up all claims on the Nizam, the Peshwa, the Gwickwar, and the Company; that he should acknowledge the independence of those states recognized by the Company as independent; and in conclusion dismiss all foreigners, and submit in all disputes to the arbitration of the Company.

The Governor-General then proceeded to divide the spoil. He gave Berar to the Nizam, and Ahmednuggur to the Peshwa, reserving Cuttack for the Company.

Finally, in order to strengthen the English position he made treaties with the Rajahs of Bhurtpore, Joudhpore and Jeypore, with the Rana of Gohud, and with Ambaji Inglia, Sindia's general. Gwalior was given to the Rana of Gohud, an arrangement which shortly afterwards involved the English in another disturbance.

Disputes concerning Gwalior, 1805.—At the time when Gwalior was taken by the English, Ambaji Inglia was in command, and the treaty was signed and concluded by him without reference to Sindia. When however Lord Wellesley disposed of Gwalior to the Rana of Gohud as if the city belonged entirely to the English, Sindia interposed saying that the place still belonged to *him*; since the treaty by which it had been transferred to the Company was signed by a subordinate officer acting without orders, and not by himself as a prince.

General Wellesley declared his conviction that Sindia was in the right; but the Marquis, refused to listen to any arguments, and sent a message to Sindia refusing to give back Gwalior, while at the same time he administered a severe rebuke. Sindia, in grievous disappointment, (for the city was the ancient seat of his family) suffered himself to be led away by the rash counsels of Serji Rao Ghatkay, and making secret overtures to Holkar, the Rajah of Bhurtpore, and Amir Khan, mustered an army of 40,000 men, and again took the field against the English.

By this means Holkar and Sindia were once more ranged side by side instead of face to face, and the combination looked serious.

But before Lord Wellesley could effect anything, his term of office expired; and his successors proceeded to undo, as far as possible, all that had been done. (Sir George Barlow gave back Gwalior to Sindia, and made a fresh treaty with him.)

War with Holkar, 1804.—Previously to this, the last Mahratta Power which remained uninjured by the war, namely that of Holkar, had been crushed.

During the progress of the war against Sindia, Holkar, who at first promised to join the confederation, had been amusing himself by plundering Sindia's possessions with an army of 60,000 picked cavalry. His success was, naturally, so universal that in his pride he imagined himself capable, single-handed, of regaining the lost power of the Mahrattas.

He accordingly commenced operations by invading the territory of the Rajah of Jeypore early in 1804, which, as the Rajah was an ally of the English, brought him at once in opposition to the victorious armies of Wellesley and Lake.

No sooner, however, did the English present their front than Holkar retreated from Jeypore across the River Chambal. Whether this retreat was at first intended to secure the object afterwards attained, or whether Holkar seized a convenient moment to inflict a severe blow, cannot be ascertained; but it is certain that he caused the English the only disaster of the campaign, which occurred under the following circumstances:—

Colonel Monson had been sent with a small force in pursuit. His ardour was so great that he allowed himself to advance too far; and when far he found himself in the midst of a hostile country, the pursued enemy turned, and Holkar's cavalry came in crowds to harass his march. Too late he found out his mistake, and determined to retire upon Agra. The retreat was disastrous. The camp and guns had to be deserted, and the troops, harassed and wearied (for Monson, though personally courageous, dared not hazard a regular engagement), fought their way back, through swollen streams and across a flooded country to Agra. On all sides men fell from the fatigue of the journey and the swords of the enemy; and, after fifty days' suffering, the miserable survivors straggled into the city. The guns, baggage, camp equipage, and stores of the division were all lost; and when mustered at Agra, there was found a deficit of nearly five battalions of infantry.

The victorious Holkar at once attacked Delhi, but finding he could make no impression on the city, he left it and ravaged the country round.

Battle of Deeg, November 13th, 1804.—General Lake, burning to avenge the last defeat, followed Holkar with all haste, and came up with his army at Deeg, on November 13th. A battle was fought, where again the fiery 76th distinguished themselves, carrying every thing before them. Holkar was beaten at all points, and fled before Lake to Mattra. The fort of Deeg, which belonged to the Rajah of Bhurtpore, having opened fire upon the British troops during the battle, was with great ease taken by storm, after the victory.

1805.—General Lake then attacked Bhurtpore itself, which held out successfully against the English. The siege was fruitless, but the Rajah, dreading the result, came to terms.

Effects of Wellesley's Administration.—Lord Wellesley's administration was now drawing to a close, for on the 20th of July, 1805, he sailed for England. Holkar had fled, and Lake, having captured Bhurtpore, was planning a new campaign against the Mahratta chief. But Holkar eluded him and joined Sindia, who, enraged at the refusal of Lord Wellesley to give up Gwalior, was now at the head of a new combination of his own forces with those of Holkar, the Raja of Bhurtpore, and the warlike Amir Khan;[1] while Baji Rao was humbly awaiting the issue of the war at Poonah, with a British Resident dictating his every action. At the same time the Nizam was an English ally; Tippoo's family were English prisoners; and the Emperor, Shah Alum, was the sworn friend of those who had restored him to his throne.

Such was the state of India when Lord Wellesley left it.

During his administration he had ejected the French from Hyderabad, and reinstated the English as the military commanders of the country. He had utterly destroyed the dynasty of Hyder Ali, and made Mysore dependent on the Company. He had obtained the ceded districts for the English; had annexed Tanjore; placed the Carnatic under British Government; and assumed sovereignty over half Oude. He had obtained a treaty from Persia, conferring the commerce of the country on England, and banishing other foreigners. He had broken the strength of Sindia, put Holkar to flight, and made the Peshwa as subservient to England as the Nizam. He had taken Cuttack from the Rajah of Berar, and he had made a treaty with that prince, virtually acknowledging the superiority of the British in India. Finally, he had remodelled the administration of justice at Calcutta; and established the College of Fort William there.

Administrative Reforms.—His administration reforms had also been considerable. The Court called the Sudder Dewani Adalat by his orders underwent alterations. It had been established to supersede the "Supreme Court," which had been regulated according to the system of Lord Cornwallis in 1793. The Governor-General and the members of Council presided over it with closed doors; and Wellesley found that there was a great deal of dissatisfaction at this mode of administering justice. He therefore instituted a separate court, open to the public, and over which presided regularly appointed chief justices; the first of whom was the great Oriental scholar Colebrooke.

In the same year (1801) at Madras, instead of the old "Sudder Dewani Adalat," there was established a "Supreme Court" on the principle extant in Calcutta previous to Cornwallis.[3] The

[1] See above, page 181.

[2] For its construction see note page 105.

[3] This court survived till 1862, when it was superseded by the "High court."

Recorder's Courts which George the Third had set on foot on the principle recognised in the city of London, were abolished,[1] and their powers assumed by the new chief justices and puisne judges. The same act also extended vice-admiralty jurisdiction to the chief courts at the Presidency towns of India. These alterations and extensions are interesting, as showing the gradual progress of the Company, and the increase of Europeans in the East.

The Colleges at Calcutta and Haileybury.—Another of Lord Wellesley's important civil reforms was the establishment of a great college at Calcutta, called the "College of Fort William." Its object was two-fold. It was to be a place for the education of the young civilians who came out to India ignorant of the native languages and laws; and a hall for discussions amongst the natives, upon matters of law and religion. Lord Wellesley imagined this would tend much to the spread of knowledge and the advancement of the English rule. The court of directors, however, viewed the project with great dissatisfaction, and confined the agency of the college to the educational department. At the same time they established the College of Haileybury, in England, for the instruction of Writers previous to their departure for India.

The Marquis during his administration became very unpopular amongst the defenders of monopoly, owing to his advanced principles on matters of trade. He wished to extend to private traders, to a far greater extent than before, the permission to carry on their commerce; and it was owing to the opposition which he experienced at home and at Calcutta on this point, that he had resigned his appointment in 1802.

(XI.)—*Lord Cornwallis's Second Administration*, 1805.

Lord Cornwallis arrived at Calcutta on July 20th, and for a second time assumed the insignia of office on August 1st, 1805. His declared principle of policy was that of non-annexation; and, immediately on his arrival, he alarmed the moderate party at Calcutta, by pronouncing it to be his firm intention to give up all lands west of the Jumna, without reference to their political con-

[1] By act 39 & 40 Geo. III. c. 79. The same act gave the new court power to deal with insolvent debtors, a class of delinquents who had hitherto received no particular attention in India.

dition. Lord Lake[1] sent in a powerful remonstrance; but before an answer could be returned, the aged Marquis had written his last despatch, and was lying in state at Ghazipore, on the Ganges. He died on October 5th, of general debility; leaving his successor to cope with the difficult questions now agitating the minds of those in whose hands lay the future of India.

(XII.)—*Sir George Barlow's Administration* (1805—1806.)

The senior member of Council, Sir George Barlow, succeeded provisionally.

His policy was avowedly the same as that of Lord Cornwallis, and he was rigidly faithful to his professions. But however admirable a policy of non-annexation and conciliation might be in time of peace, the position of India at the time we are speaking of seemed to demand something more decisive. Lord Wellesley had reduced all the native states to the verge of despair, and the question which should have ruled the decision of the Governor-General, was, not what Lord Wellesley's policy ought to have been, but what considering the existing state of affairs was necessary for the peace of India and the maintenance of the prosperity of the English in the country. Sir George Barlow, however, seems to have retrograded in forming his opinions; and the result of his policy towards the native princes was that those states which were amicably disposed were rendered timid and fearful, of placing themselves under British protection; while those which were in arms against the Company, but had been well-nigh crushed by the Marquis Wellesley, now received fresh spirit and began a new career of havoc and destruction.

Treaty with Sindia, 1805.—At the close of the year, a treaty was made with Sindia, who, though actually in the field with Holkar against the English, was ready to accept terms. But the conditions offered were such as to give up to him precisely the very lands to gain which he had taken up arms; and thus his feelings of respect for the Company were converted into those of contempt. Gohud and Gwalior were both yielded on condition of the maintenance of the Treaty of Anjengaom; and Sir George added a clause, which unfortunately stultified the most important item in that treaty. It had been Lord Wellesley's object to

[1] He had been raised to the Peerage for his services the previous year, under the title of Baron Lake; and in 1807 was created a viscount.

deprive the native states of the semblance of political importance, by compelling them to refrain from any political action without the consent of the Calcutta government. But Sir George, so far from recognizing the desirability of this step, actually placed the Company in the very position with regard to Sindia in which Lord Wellesley had placed Sindia with regard to the English. For he guaranteed that the British Government would make no treaties with any of Sindia's tributary states in the Rajput territory without the consent of their feudal lord.

Treaty with Holkar, 1806.—Immediately upon Sindia's submission, Holkar left the camp of his ally, and, with his usual ruthless cruelty, commenced ravaging the country near the Sutlej. Lord Lake pursued him, and was supported by Runjeet Singh, the great Trans-Sutlej chieftain. Holkar, was utterly defeated, and forced to flee for his life. He sent to Lake, suing for a treaty, and, his offer of submission being accepted, the terms were drawn up.

Peace was to be granted, on condition of his relinquishing his claims on Rampra, Tonk, Bhoondi, and all places north of the Bhoondi hills.

The treaty was signed in January, 1806, by Lord Lake, and ought to have received the recognition of the Governor-General. But Sir George Barlow, true to his policy, refused to ratify a treaty which conferred Bhoondi on the Company. He declared it to be a wanton annexation, and ordered the English troops to withdraw from beyond the Chambal river; shutting his eyes to the defenceless position of the unhappy Rajah, whose dominions were at once ravaged by Holkar.

The Rajah of Jeypore was in the same manner left a prey to the merciless cruelty of the Mahratta soldiery, though Lord Wellesley, Lord Cornwallis, and Lord Lake, had successively promised him the protection of the English, in return for the unvarying assistance he had always afforded to them.

Upon this, Lord Lake, in great indignation, resigned all civil power into the hands of Sir George Barlow, declaring his intention of never more putting his hand to treaties which were thus negatived immediately afterwards at head-quarters.

Holkar's aggressions were now again becoming serious; for he was convinced that the Company were frightened at his power; and from all sides adherents flocked to his standard.

But a Higher Power interposed to prevent the evils which an unwise policy had created. Holkar, whose temper had always been furious, murdered his brother and his nephew in a fit of passion, and these crimes, coupled with his other excesses, preying upon his mind, destroyed his reason. He lived for some time in a state of insanity and ultimately died at Indore in 1811.

1807.—But four years before that time, Sir George Barlow was superseded by Lord Minto, who came out to India also pledged to the policy of non-intervention.

(XIII.)—*Lord Minto's Administration*, (1806—1813.)

Lord Minto arrived on July 31st, 1807, and at once assumed office; while Sir George Barlow was transferred to the Government of Madras.

Madras.—The Vellore Mutiny.—The new Governor-General found that the first act required of him was to deal with the mutineers of Vellore, in the Madras presidency.

It was in the Fort of that place that the captive sons of Tippoo Sultan had been imprisoned. The garrison consisted of about 1500 Sepoys, with European officers; but the suite and adherents of the unfortunate princes had been allowed to grow so numerous that the Mysoreans far outnumbered the servants of the Company. Perceiving their strength, the vanquished followers of Hyder, by a judicious system of bribery, and by working on the superstitions and the religious feelings of the Sepoys, organized a regular mutiny, which broke out in July, 1806. A murder of the English in the fort took place, and the Mysoreans hoisted Tippoo's standard; but a Dragoon regiment from Arcot[1] came up, overcame the rebels, and put numbers of them to death.

Lord Minto dealt very gently with the mutineers, considering them more in the light of belligerents than in that of rebels.

1808.—It was not till the year 1808 that any further serious political step was deemed necessary, for the broken and harassed Mahratta powers had settled down into an uneasy tranquillity. Sindia was not strong enough to cope single-handed with the English, and he, as well as Holkar, seemed to consider the last treaties made by Sir George Barlow as sufficiently advantageous to answer their present purpose. They, therefore, patiently awaited their opportunities.

[1] The 19th Dragoons under Colonel Gillespie.

The Peshwa and the Rajah of Nagpore were both under British protection, and had accepted the sweeping terms forced on them by the Wellesleys. But from a different quarter of India a new cloud arose.

Runjeet Singh.—Runjeet Singh, a Sikh, was Rajah of all the country west of the Sutlej. He had commenced life as Rajah of Lahore, which district had been given him by the victorious Afghan, Zemaun Shah, whom he had assisted on many occasions, and whom he had promised to aid in his intended incursions into India. Runjeet Singh was thus brought into open opposition to the English, and the minds of several Governors'-General had been troubled by the thought of this hostile chieftain on the frontier.

In 1808 Runjeet Singh, with the intention of adding to his dominions, crossed the Sutlej into the territory of Sirhind, which was under British protection, and attacked the province of the Rajah of Patialah. Lord Minto at once sent Colonel Metcalfe to check this incursion.

Runjeet at first treated the summons which Metcalfe sent him with great contempt, but, on receipt of a peremptory command from Lord Minto, he retired across the Sutlej, and consented to restore the land he had taken south of that river, if the English would promise to refrain from touching Sikh territory on the north bank.

1st Treaty with Runjeet Singh.—Metcalfe consented, and a treaty to this effect was drawn up and signed. The Sikh chieftain faithfully performed his promises.

1809.—The following year there were disturbances nearer home, for the fierce and turbulent Amir Khan, always so dangerous and troublesome to the peace of India, was now the recognised chief of the robber-tribe of the Patans; and, in 1809. he plundered the territories of an English ally, Bhonslay, Rajah of Berar, who appealed to Lord Minto for aid.

His lordship, rather to the astonishment of those who knew the principles he professed, consented to assist him, and somewhat tardily sent a force to Nagpore; but the brave Rajah beat off his enemy without the assistance of the English, and drove him back to Bhopal across the Sutpura mountains.

2nd Embassy to Persia.—The next great event was the celebrated embassy to Persia under Sir Harford Jones, which was so nearly frustrated by its clashing with the simultaneous mission of Colonel Malcolm to the same court.

For some time past there had been at head-quarters, and, amongst all the English in India, a growing fear of the French. The first Napoleon was in the full tide of his glory, and had openly expressed designs hostile to the English possessions in Asia. Under these circumstances it was of the utmost importance to either party to obtain the co-operation of Persia. Lord Wellesley had sent a costly mission for this purpose to the Shah in 1800, which had been so far successful that his friendship was obtained. But, in 1809, the Calcutta cabinet was struck with alarm on hearing that the French, on their part, had opened negociations with Persia, to which the Shah had lent a not unwilling ear, and they at once despatched Sir John Malcolm on an embassy to Teheran.

The same news being carried simultaneously to London, Sir Harford Jones was sent as an ambassador, accredited from the Imperial Government, to Persia. The two embassies arrived simultaneously, and of course quarrelled for precedence, Sir Harford Jones taking his stand on the high ground afforded to him by his position as representative of the King of England, while Sir John Malcolm, burning with the supposed insult offered by Parliament to the Governor-General of India, declared that the matter concerned the Company alone, and that the Home Government was exceeding its powers. Sir Harford said that the question was one which concerned England as a nation, and therefore the Imperial Government ought to deal with it. Sir John held that the matter was merely connected with the Company's trade, and therefore the Governor-General ought to deal with it.

By the good sense of both, however, this difficulty was ultimately surmounted, and a favourable reception was accorded to the English. The envoys were afterwards superseded by Sir Gore Ouseley, who was sent out from England as resident ambassador at Teheran

Embassy to Cabul.—A third mission was at the same time sent by Lord Minto to Cabul, where Shah Soojah, brother and successor of Zemaun Shah, was on the throne. The embassy was entrusted to Mountstuart Elphinstone. It failed, owing to a rebellion, which drove Shah Soojah from his throne and kingdom; while his successor, Mahmud, accepted unhesitatingly the protection of the Russians and French.

Events in Madras.—The attention of the Company was soon drawn off from its chronic state of alarm with regard to France by the disturbed state of the army in Madras.

A regulation had for some time been in force by which commanding officers had the right of providing the tents used by their own regiments. They had been enabled by this means to add considerable sums of money to their annual incomes, and the arrangement was looked upon as a sort of military perquisite. But Sir George Barlow, now Governor of Madras, anxious to do away with this custom, passed a sweeping law by which, not only was the practice forbidden, but the personal feelings of the officers were aroused; for the terms of the law offended their sense of honour as well as their pecuniary interests, and the indignation was great throughout the Presidency.

Colonel Munro, Quartermaster-General, also drew up a report at the dictation of the Governor, in which the custom was denounced as something akin to actual cheating, and General Macdowall, the Commander-in-Chief, put Munro under arrest at the request of his colleagues, for "aspersions on their character as officers and gentlemen." Munro appealed to the Governor, and Sir George hastily ordered the Commander-in-Chief to be deposed from office, suspending, soon afterwards, four officers of high rank. The whole army was thus in a blaze of mutiny, and a protest was drawn up in somewhat angry terms and sent in to the Government.

Sir George showed himself on this occasion in the light of a brave and energetic ruler. He ordered all the officers to sign a pledge in support of the Government on pain of losing their commissions, ordered up large bodies of troops, and called upon the native soldiers to adhere to their allegiance. This conduct brought the officers to their senses, and they submitted with as good a grace as possible.

Expedition against Persian Pirates, 1810.—Lord Minto's attention was next directed to the extirpation of several bodies of pirates and robbers who were injuring the trade of the Company, and various expeditions, all more or less successful, were sent against them.

At the commencement of the year 1810 a horde of pirates in the Persian Gulf, who had frequently damaged the English trade by petty aggressions, attacked and seized a ship called the "Minerva," belonging to the Company. Lord Minto at once ordered up an expedition from Bombay which captured the pirates' head-quarters at Mallia, in Guzerat, and, after being joined by a force sent by the Imaum of Muscat, stormed and burnt their stronghold at Schinas, in Persia, breaking up the confederation and putting the robbers to flight.

Expedition to Macao.—The Governor-General also sent an expedition to destroy the Portuguese settlement of Macao, which was under the protection of the Emperor of China. It was deemed by many an unwise policy, for there was little to gain, and a great deal to lose, by the movement. It ended disastrously, for the Emperor of China at once abolished English trade at Macao, and the regiment which had been landed humbly turned and went back to Bengal, having effected nothing, beyond causing considerable injury to the Company's trade.

Several other expeditions followed, having for their object the prevention of the trade of other nations with India.

Seizure of the Mauritius and Bourbon.—During the French wars the Company's trade had greatly suffered from the aggressions of the enemy in the settlements of the Mauritius and Bourbon, and the islands near those spots; and Lord Minto determined to put an end to this once and for ever. He, therefore, in 1810, sent an expedition with that object, under the command of Colonel Keating.

That officer soon occupied the island of Rodriguez, two hundred miles from the Mauritius, and, making it his basis of operations, commenced operations on a grander scale in May, 1810.

The first attack was against the island of Bourbon. The troops landed, and attacked the city and harbour of St. Paul's. Four batteries were gallantly stormed, in the face of a heavy fire from forts and shipping, and after three hours of fighting the place was won. The enemy's ships were blockaded by the English fleet, and surrendered.

Futher exploits followed against different French stations, in one of which Colonel Willoughby greatly distinguished himself, and in July the organised attack on the island took place. The troops were landed in very rough weather, and with great difficulty, and on the 6th attacked the French lines at the point of the bayonet. The same steady advance which had disorganized the Hindus so frequently was found to have the same effect on this occasion, for battery after battery was captured, and the garrison put to flight; and, in one day, St. Denis, the capital of the island, was taken, and the whole French force driven to surrender.

Colonel Willoughby was left in command, and the arsenal was turned into an English store-house, where preparations were made for an attack on the Mauritius.

In the interval that ensued the English suffered severe losses at sea, for no less than eleven ships were taken by the French.[1]

On October 29th the expedition arrived at the Mauritius, and ten thousand men were landed. After a harassing march a slight action took place, ending favourably to the English, and next day the French commander, feeling himself unable to continue the defence, surrendered the island to the English.

(The Mauritius still belongs to England, but the Isle de Bourbon was restored in 1814).

Expedition to Java, 1811.—In 1811 Lord Minto determined to destroy the Dutch trade in the islands about Java, and accordingly sent a strong force for that purpose. The spice island of Amboyna, in which the terrible massacre by the Dutch had taken place in 1619, was first taken. Owing to the nature of the ground the work was one of great difficulty, but it was manfully accomplished, and in a very short period five smaller islands were also yielded to the English.

Banda Neira was the next object of attack. It was speedily reduced, with the capture of a large number of guns; and the expedition was then directed against Java, with its capital, Batavia.

On August 4th the English arrived in the Bay of Batavia, and landed during the night. The Dutch were concentrated to defend Fort Corselis, and an action took place in the morning, resulting, through the bravery of Colonel Gillespie, of the 19th Dragoons, in the complete reduction of the capital.

After a few days Sir Samuel Auchmuty, who commanded the expedition, had won all the strong places in the island, and the French and Dutch submitted. Sir Stamford Raffles was appointed to the government of the island.

Rise of the Pindarees.—We must now turn to consider the rise of the Pindarees,—a nation of freebooters whom Lord Minto begged in vain of the Home Government for permission to destroy.

The Pindarees were mounted robbers—thieves by profession, who, if they had been treated as Thugs and Dacoits in the early days of their career, and had been sternly

[1] Thornton gives an interesting account of the dashing defence of one of these ships, the "*Néreide*," by Captain Willoughby:—"He fought the ship till every man of her whole crew, consisting of two hundred and eighty, was either killed or wounded."—("History of India," 3rd edition, p. 368).

crushed by the high hand of justice, would very probably never have arisen to the eminence they afterwards attained. They were permitted, however, to continue their depredations, each succeeding Governor-General being puzzled whether to treat them as murderers or as belligerents, and the consequence was, that a few years later Lord Hastings had to put them down at the point of the sword, and at the expense of hundreds of lives.

The Pindarees came into notice under the Peshwa, Baji Rao, and joined in all the fights that took place in later years, ranging themselves under the standard of the chieftain who promised the largest payment for their services. In 1808 two leaders, brothers, named Hiran and Baran, were at the head of the Pindarees. On their death, a Jaut, named Chitoo, took the command, and styled himself Rajah. In return for his assistance Sindia gave this chieftain a small tract of country; and in a similar manner other Pindaree chiefs had become possessed of small jagirs. Two years later Chitoo joined Amir Khan, the great Rohilla freebooter, and, with an army of 60,000 desperate robbers, proceeded to plunder Central India.

Lord Minto might well feel anxious at this powerful aggression; for it was in a similar manner that the Mahrattas had arisen, and become in their day the greatest power in India. He therefore wrote to the government, urging in the strongest manner that it was necessary for the peace of India to crush these adventurers. The Board of Control, however, refused him permission, basing their refusal on the Cornwallis doctrine of non-intervention. This was Lord Minto's last act of foreign policy.

Lord Minto's Home Policy.—The home administration of this Governor-General was mainly directed to the proper carrying out of the Cornwallis system of 1793. It was found to work in some ways favourably, but by no means in all. Lord Cornwallis had imported into India all the cumbersome and complicated formalities of the English law courts; which gave to the natives an impression of dilatoriness and burdensome prolixity; and raised in their minds the same horror of going to law, that is caused to English litigants when they find themselves on the threshold of the Court of Chancery. The Hindoos found ample opportunity of practising their powers of delaying and avoiding the due process of law; and the result of the system was, that the English Judges, fairly beaten by its intricacy, permitted "Sheristadars" (in civil matters), and "Daraghas" (in criminal,) to usurp in their districts far more authority than was advisable.

Ryotwary System in Madras.—It was about this period that the "Ryotwary System," established by Sir Thomas Munro. was first recognized as the basis of the revenue administration of the Madras Presidency, though it was not permanently ordained till the year 1820.

It consisted of an annual settlement made by the revenue officers of the government, early in each year, when the crops were sufficiently far advanced to judge of their abundance and quality; and at the time of which we are speaking, the government tax consisted of one-third of the produce. The cultivator was held responsible for this tax, as assessed and inscribed in the "*Pottah*," or lease granted annually to him. If a failure occurred owing to the accidents of climate, the whole village was ordered to be rateably assessed, to bear the burden of the tax upon the land which failed; but if such a failure occurred in any field by the wilful obstinacy of a ryot who accepted the *pottah*, yet refused to cultivate his land, the collector had power to punish him by fine, or even by corporal chastisement. It is fair, however, to say that the latter punishment was rarely, if ever, resorted to. The collector, having absolute power to withhold or grant the *pottahs*, retained a complete control over the whole district during each year.

Lord Minto sailed for England, in October, 1813, being succeeded by the Marquis of Hastings, then called Earl of Moira.

(XIV.)—*Proceedings in Parliament. Free Trade Discussions.*

By the year, 1813, it was evident to all parties in England, that some serious struggles would soon arise on the question of the Company's monopoly, and their right in the lands they had conquered. For the charter, which had in 1793 been granted for twenty years, expired on the first of March, in the above year; and great changes had of late years taken place in the state of public feeling with regard to free trade.

Various skirmishes took place on different occasions, between the partisans of the Company who argued for monopoly, and the adherents of Lord Castlereagh's government, who for the most part advocated free trade. The pitched battle commenced in

Parliament on March 22nd, when the house resolved itself into a committee to consider the questions in detail.

The chairman of the Board of Directors at the India House, pleading for the Company, urged that the conquered territories belonged as of right to the Company, and not to the crown. He requested a renewal of the charter for a further period of twenty years on the same basis as the previous one; and declared that although monopolies had been to a great extent looked upon unfavourably of late years, yet, that in the case of India it was a necessity, since the government could not be carried on, except under the peculiar constitution of the governing body as it then existed.

The Earl of Buckinghamshire, President of the Board of Commissioners, opposed all these arguments. He contended that the country was conquered by British troops, and belonged to the English as a nation; and that although the Company's trade could be carried throughout the provinces which had been subjugated, yet that the land was crown land, not private. He proposed to establish free trade for all British subjects, doing away with the Company's monopoly for ever; and declared that the existing constitution of the Company was not necessary to the good government of India, but that on the contrary, it might be better managed if taken entirely into the hands of the crown.

On March 23rd, Lord Castlereagh, in committee stated the proposals of the ministry. Their plan was to extend the charter for twenty years; to grant the Company a monopoly in the Chinese trade, but to throw open all Indian trade to the world, on certain conditions and restrictions which would prevent any injury to the Company; leaving to it the command of the army, and the power of appointing its own civil and other servants. After long discussions, this bill, with very slight alterations, was passed at the end of July of the same year.

The Company produced many witnesses before the committee in support of their claims; and amongst others, Warren Hastings, then in his eightieth year. In tribute to his great qualities all the members simultaneously rose to do him honour when he appeared at the Bar of the House to give his evidence, Sir John Malcolm, Sir Thomas Munro, and Sir John Shore (created Lord Teignmouth), were also subpœnaed. Marquis Wellesley and Lord Grenville were amongst the more eminent speakers on this occasion. The latter urged the government to take the whole of India absolutely into its hands, and to establish appointments to the Civil Service by open competition; advice which was not followed till half-a-century later.

In the same year, Christianity was openly introduced into India, by the appointment of a Bishop to the see of Calcutta.

(XV.)—*Lord Hastings' Administration*, 1813—1827. *Ghoorka War—Pindaree War—Fall of the Mahrattas.*

Lord Hastings arrived at Calcutta in October, 1813, and found the country, though apparently tranquil, in reality full of the elements of disturbance. India was in a transition stage.

State of India. Holkar.—Jeswant Rao Holkar had died in the year 1811, and his widow, the celebrated Toolsye Bye, conducted the government. She was a very beautiful, and a very bad woman, and the country fared ill under her direction. Among her many favourites jealousies arose, as might have been expected, and factions were set on foot. One of the favourites, who was also a great pet of the soldiery, having been superseded in his honourable situation, raised an open rebellion, which was with difficulty suppressed. Toolsye Bye very soon after murdered her minister, and installed in his office one Gaupat Rao, who was again superseded in favour of the chief of the robber Patans, Gafur Khan, with whom she lived four years. The Government of Indore was entirely in his power, and as he neglected to take care for the country, the whole population was in a disordered condition.

Sindia.—Sindia, in 1813, was plundering the country far and wide; though his fear of the English government was such that he desisted on the slightest threat of punishment.

Amir Khan.—The Rohilla chief, Amir Khan, was at the head of one of the finest armies in India, consisting of his own bodies of desperate adventurers and of the forces of Holkar, of which he had been made commander-in-chief, after his breach with the Pindarees, in 1811.[1]

The Peshwa—The Peshwa was as usual in a state of nervous excitement, longing to throw off the yoke he had accepted from the English, yet not daring to do so. He had been forced into a position of fresh humility by the energetic conduct of

[1] The combination, so dreaded by Lord Minto, had broken up; Chitoo, the Pindaree, and Amir Khan, the Rohilla, had intended to devastate India with their combined armies, but had quarrelled and separated. (See page 198).

Mountstuart Elphinstone, the Resident at his court, in the case of the favourite Trimbakji Danglia.

This man had been a menial servant, and had risen to be the intimate friend and constant adviser of Baji Rao, assisting him in all his vices, and as far as possible undermining his very few virtues. Disputes having arisen with the Gwickwar concerning the territory of Ahmedabad, the English, according to treaty, were called upon to arbitrate in the case. For this purpose, an able and honest politician, Gangadar Shastri, was sent to Poonah by the Gwickwar, and approved by the President. But Thimbakji Danglia, commenced violent intrigues against this agent on the part of the Peshwa; and when soon after the Shastri was returning to Guzerat, he was cruelly murdered by Danglia's accomplices at Panderpore.

Elphinstone instituted a rigid enquiry, and demanded the surrender of Danglia to justice. But the Peshwa, loth to relinquish his useful favourite, refused any assistance to the President, and sent messages to Sindia, requesting his aid against the English.

Elphinstone, however, at once ordered up troops from Bombay, and the Peshwa, in alarm surrendered the murderer. Danglia was thrown into prison.

Such was the state of India when Lord Hastings assumed office. He found the Treasury almost empty, and yet was immediately called upon to deal with a new and unexpected enemy in the north, the Ghoorkhas.

Rise of the Ghoorkhas.—The "Ghoorkhas" of Nepaul, were a race of Rajputs, who originally issuing from Rajputana, had conquered and settled in the region known as the "Terai," at the base of the Himalayas, in Nepaul. After passing through various changes of government, they were brought, in the middle of the eighteenth century, under the dominion of one chief, who styled himself Rajah of Nepaul. This prince had for a long time been extending the boundary of his kingdom; sometimes coming into contact with Runjeet Singh, sometimes with princes under British protection. Sir George Barlow had remonstrated, and Lord Minto threatened; but it remained for Lord Hastings to make war.

1814.—At the close of the year 1813, the Ghoorkhas had seized a district comprising two hundred villages under British protection in the annexed territories of Oude. At the commencement of 1814, Lord Hastings peremptorily demanded the cession of these villages within twenty-five days. The Ghoorkhas replied by murdering a British magistrate in Bootwal.

Ghoorkha War.—War was at once declared; and Lord Hastings promptly matured his plans for the campaign. General Gillespie, with one division, was to attack the Ghoorkha army, commanded by Armar Singh, on the Sutlej. Another division, under General Wood, was to march on Bootwal; and a third, under General Ochterlony, on Simla. The fourth division, commanded by General Marley, was directed to advance straight on the capital, Khatmander. To meet the expenses of the war, a loan of two millions was obtained from the Nabob Vizier.

General Gillespie's Division.—General Gillespie marched at once to his station, and on October 29th attacked the fort of Kalunga, which was defended by five hundred Ghoorkhas. He had received orders to bombard on all occasions; but Gillespie's reputation had been gained by his many acts of dashing bravery in the Java and other campaigns; and, without reckoning on the quality of the men he was about to oppose, he ordered an immediate assault. It was fatal to himself and to his army. The General was shot through the heart while gallantly leading on the storming party; and, after a loss of seven hundred officers and men, the division retired, completely exhausted, to their camp. General Martindale succeeded to the command; but, going to the opposite extremo from the high-spirited officer who preceded him, he wasted months in a useless blockade, and refrained from ordering an assault till long after the breach was practicable. When the fort was at length captured, success had been rendered almost useless; for its brave defenders had evacuated it, and fled with all their stores on the night previous to the last assault.

General Wood's Division.—General Wood, a timid officer, ruined the success of his division by becoming frightened, and sounding a retreat just as he had gained a decided victory over a force far inferior to his own in size. His pusillanimity was such that he immediately retreated to the British frontier, and remained inactive during the rest of the campaign.

General Marley's Division.—General Marley proved almost inferior to General Wood. His division marched to the frontier and remained there till the beginning of the ensuing year, waiting for a battering-train, in order to attack the capital city, Khatmandu. He then slowly advanced; and having divided his force into two feeble parties, each was attacked and defeated by large bodies of Ghoorkhas. General Marley afterwards alternately advanced and retreated, apparently in complete ignorance of the wisest course to pursue; and his recall was soon ordered from Calcutta. But before his successor had arrived, the General, one morning (February 10th) got on horseback and rode off alone to the frontier, without intimating his intention to anyone,—conduct scarcely to be admired in a general of division.

General Ochterlony's Division.—To General Ochterlony, however, it was given to retrieve the English honour. The successive defeats of the three other divisions had caused considerable excitement throughout India. Hostile preparations were made on all sides; and there is little doubt that had the Simla division been equally unsuccessful, a general rise would have taken place against the power of the English. As it was, the most formidable preparations were made. The Peshwa, the Pindarees, and the Patans coalesced, forming an immense army of unscrupulous robbers and plunderers, in a very efficient state of discipline; and Amir Khan, with his old restless longing for revenge, appeared on the frontier with 25,000 men. But before they had broken out into actual hostilities the successes of the third division, near Simla, calmed their ardour.

General Ochterlony, a clever as well as a brave man, perceived that in wars with such nations as the Ghoorkas the tactics of European strategy would be worse than useless. He therefore wisely determined to fight his enemy as they fought him. He entered the Terai from near Amballa, in the north-west boundary of Rohilcund, and for several months was successful at all points in a variety of engagements and sieges. Amar Singh retired before him to a strong hill-fort, called Malown, on the left bank of the Sutlej river.

Ochterlony bombarded the place for a month, and it fell on May 15th, 1815, the enemy's commander having been killed during the siege.

Meanwhile the city of Almora had been captured by Colonel Gardiner; and as the effect of this success was to cut off all supplies from the Ghoorkhas opposing the general, they wisely came to terms.

1816.—Negociations then took place between the chief of the

Ghoorkhas, who styled himself "Rajah of Nepaul," and the British Government at Calcutta, but they were broken off on account of the hesitation of the enemy, and a fresh campaign commenced.[1]

Sir David Ochterlony effected a very difficult passage through the mountains to Muckwanpore, and repulsed the Ghoorkhas with heavy loss. A few days afterwards a truce was requested for the purpose of fresh negociation; and the general concluded a treaty, binding the Nepaulese to their own territory, and forcing them to cede most of the land they had conquered.[2]

Thus ended the Nepaulese or Ghoorka war. At the outset it was one of the most disastrous in our history, and caused the Governor-General considerable uneasiness; but it has proved of great service to the English, in a manner which, at the time, was little anticipated. The war opened up communications between England and Nepaul; and in consequence of this, numbers of the enemy joined the British army, and were formed into Ghoorkha regiments. In the terrible Sepoy mutiny of 1857, no troops were so faithful to the English as these gallant soldiers.

Disturbances in India, 1815.—At this time, the many reverses of the Company's arms led, as before stated, to much disturbance among the native princes, which was not quelled till Lord Hastings again proved the supremacy of England by the war against the Pindarees.

Meanwhile, in one or two places the natives were emboldened to attack the English. At Hatras, a Jaut Rajah created some trouble, which was not suppressed till a fort had been stormed and razed to the ground. And at Bareilly a serious insurrection occurred; for a British magistrate entering the town was attacked, and had to fly for his life to the Sepoy barracks. The Sepoy regiment was called out, and after a severe fight the Rohilla inhabitants, who numbered some thousands, were worsted; and order was restored.

The Pindarees, 1816—1818.—The attention of the Governor-General was now seriously directed to the state of central India. That part of the country was being ravaged by lawless bodies of freebooters, numbering some 50,000 or 60,000 men; while Amir

[1] Lord Hastings was willing to go very great lengths in order to put a stop to the war. His intentions were, to give up to the Nepaulese the very lands for the defence of which he had taken up arms.

[2] The Nepaulese most rigidly and honourably fulfilled the terms of this treaty.

Khan was threatening the frontier, and all the Mahratta princes had assumed a hostile attitude, and were collecting armies.

Lord Hastings determined first to try the effect of alliances with the princes, considering that he might thus organize so strong a confederation in opposition to Amir Khan and the Pindarees, that peace might be restored through the agency of fear, without rendering a call to arms necessary.

He therefore offered terms to the Rajah of Bhopal, who accepted them unhesitatingly,—and at once opened private negotiations with Amir Khan. The Rajah of Berar refused any closer alliance with the English than that forced upon him by the treaty of Deogaom, in 1803.[1] The Rajah of Jeypore also resolutely refused to treat with the Company.

This hesitation emboldened the Pindarees, and on October 14th, 1815, a large body of horse plundered the dominions of the Nizam and carried off a great quantity of stores and grain. Early in the ensuing February nearly half their number burst upon the Company's own territory in the Guntoor Circar, and ravaged the country in all directions. The people fled, and the Company's servants were in the greatest danger. The Pindarees behaved on these occasions with uniform brutality: and the fear of their name was great upon all the Hindus. Before any regular attack could be made upon them by the Madras army, they had retired, leaving the land which they had plundered a perfect desert.

1816.—Lord Hastings had been for many months holding communications with the Board of Control, over which Mr. Canning now presided, begging permission to attack the Pindarees; but the President urged upon him the necessity of preserving peace, if possible, and suggested a series of alliances instead. Hastings had tried this plan and failed; and early in 1816, on his urgent remonstrance, the long-desired instructions to act as he pleased, came out.

Appa Sahib, at Nagpore.—The Governor-General at once commenced preparations, but intended, if he were enabled to do so, to defer any regular operations till the cool season. Meanwhile Roghoji Bhonslay, Rajah of Berar, died, and his throne was usurped by his cousin, Appa Sahib, who murdered the crown-prince, and in order to obtain the support of the Company, concluded a treaty with them. The terms were, that a subsidiary force of 8000 English soldiers should be garrisoned in Nagpore.

[1] *See* page 184.

The year passed favourably for the Governor-General's intentions, as the Pindarees, apparently satiated with their raid into the Madras presidency, remained quiet. It was known, however, that, proud of their success and of the inaction of the English Government, they were meditating a grand attack in the winter. This took place in November. They commenced operations by making a sudden inroad into the Company's territory; and when the Nagpore force took the field in defence, the enemy baffled the soldiers, by entirely breaking up their army, and presenting no point of attack, they escaped back to their own country in detached bodies, with very little loss.

1817.—Early next year Hastings took the field in person with a grand army of 120,000 men, and proceeded up the country to the subjugation of the Pindarees.[1] It was the largest army that had assembled under the English flag, and far exceeded the actual necessity of the situation; but the Governor-General felt very keenly the necessity of creating an impression on the princes and people of India at this critical period; and the expedition bore accordingly the aspect of a military display, calculated to overawe as much by grandeur as by victory.

Of the great Mahratta powers at this crisis, Sindia had reluctantly promised his aid to the English; the Raj of Holkar was being administered by a woman, and the country was in a state of anarchy; while the Peshwa, bitterly hating the English, was weak and powerless, and, though he knew it not, within a few months of his dethronement.

Lord Hastings employed some time in treating with the native princes, and in subverting the dangerous alliances set on foot to crush the Company.

He was successful at all points. Alliances were made with

[1] In August of this year the cholera broke out with terrible vehemence in India. It was the first outbreak of this disease, which rapidly spread in all directions, appearing originally in the Zillah of Jessore, near Calcutta, and making its way through Asia to Europe. After decimating the Continent, its ravages reached England, and thence spread to America. All the world was panic-stricken with the terrors attendant on the march of this new and fearful epidemic. The army of Hastings was attacked in November, the contagion being brought by the arrival of a new detachment from Calcutta. The army was passing through the low land of Bundelcund, and for weeks the track was strewn with the dead and dying. The men marched in silence, fearful lest each should be the next to be attacked, and mourning over their plague-stricken companions. It was not till they reached a healthier district that the ravages of the disease subsided, and the troops recovered their health and spirits.

the Rajahs of Bhoondi, Jodhpore, Oodipore, Jeypore, and Kotah; while Sindia, who was discovered to be in direct communication with Amir Khan, the Rajah of Berar, and the Rajah of Nepaul, at the same time that he was known to be hotly engaged in exciting the Pindarees, was compelled to sign a treaty, promising to remain neutral.

But the most important event of this period is the downfall of the Mahratta sovereignty, which was immediately owing to the Peshwa's hostile attitude.

Extinction of the Mahratta powers, 1817. The Peshwa.—It will be remembered that Baji Rao had been forced, much against his will, to give up his favourite, Trimbakji Danglia, to justice: and that the latter had been imprisoned. He effected his escape and returned secretly to Poonah, where he was the chief adviser of the Peshwa in the rash attempt against the English which ensued.

Baji Rao began to make great hostile preparations; and when remonstrated with by Mountstuart Elphinstone, he declared that they were planned only with a view to the defence of Poonah against the Pindarees; and that he warmly applauded the intention of the Governor-General to extirpate the robber tribes of Central India. The Resident, however, had ample proof that the Peshwa was stirring up the whole country against the English, and fanning the flame of disorder throughout India. He therefore determined to order up troops from Bombay, to compel the Mahratta to come to his senses. He informed the minister that his master must decide on peace or war within twenty-four hours, and that the only conditions on which the British would suffer him to have peace, were the surrender of Trimbakji Danglia and three of his principal fortresses.

The Peshwa hesitated; but the Bombay troops arrived and he submitted, giving over all the forts to the Company, and promising to apprehend his friend, the murderer.

A treaty was then signed, in which the Peshwa consented never to receive the vakeels of any other power, Mahratta or foreign, at his court, and to remain entirely at the orders of the British Resident. This was in effect an extinction of the Mahratta sovereignty, reducing the court at Poonah to the level of that at Nagpore or Indore. Further articles forced the Peshwa to cede Saugur, Bundelcund, and other places, to the Company. Elphinstone then removed for safety to the British camp, two miles off; and the troops remained stationary there.

After a lapse of a month or two the Peshwa was again found in the act of raising levies of horsemen and troops to act against the English; and on November 5th, having a tolerably large native army encamped close to the British regiments, the Residency at Poonah was attacked and burnt. In the action which followed, the Peshwa's half-disciplined troops were easily beaten, although they considerably outnumbered their conquerors.

Poonah was surrendered on November 17th, and thus fell the sovereignty of the Mahratta State. It began with Sevaji in 1666, and ended with Baji Rao in 1817.

Fall of the Rajah of Nagpore.—At precisely the same period that the Peshwa definitely took up arms against the English, the Rajah of Nagpore acted in a similar manner. He actively engaged in levying troops, and when urged to desist, declared that his only object was to defend himself against the Pindarees. But soon, news came of the treachery and downfall of the Peshwa; and the Resident, Mr. Jenkins, began to feel that Appa Sahib was not to be trusted.

In September he had openly received a Pindaree legate at court with honour; and on November 24th he sent a message to the Resident, that the Peshwa had made him (Appa Sahib) commander-in-chief of the Mahratta forces. The Resident replied, that since the Peshwa was at war with the English, this appointment would involve Nagpore in a war with the Company.

The Rajah's only reply was an attack on the Residency.

Action of the Sitabaldi Hills.—The enemy numbered nearly ten to one; and the English and native infantry, much dispirited, took up a position on some hills close by the city, called the "*Sitabaldi Hills.*" The enemy were successful at all points, and the Company's troops would have been annihilated had not Captain Fitzgerald, with a small body of Bengal cavalry, made a most brilliant charge, and turned the fortune of the day. The Rajah's troops fled, and a complete victory was the result. Nagpore was occupied; and Appa Sahib was deposed after a short interval, in which his inherent treachery became so plain, that any less extreme course would have been useless and weak. He escaped and died as a fugitive at Jodhpore.

(The country was administered by the English till 1826, when a youth who had been nominated obtained his majority, and was placed on the throne under British protection).

Fall of the House of Holkar, 1817.—At Indore matters were also approaching a crisis. Toolsye Bye had made Gafur Khan, the chief of the Patans, her principal adviser and closest friend, and completely neglected the business of government. She was thus harbouring one of the chiefest enemies of the Company; and Sir John Malcolm and Sir Thomas Hislop moved up to demand his dismissal.

The Mahratta troops were placed under proper discipline, and the Ranee prepared for war. But she was not destined even to hear the sound of English guns, for the party at the capital who were hostile to the regency seized her one night, beheaded her, and threw her body into the river. Young Mulhan Rao Holkar was at once proclaimed sovereign, and the army marched nominally under his leadership, though really under that of Gafur Khan.

Battle of Mehidpore.—The English troops crossed the river Sipri, under a terrible fire from the Mahrattas, on December 21st, 1817, and took their guns. The main fight was at Mehidpore, where, after a hard struggle, the English were victors. Mulhar Rao's sister, Buna Bye, was captured and sent to her brother.

A treaty was shortly afterwards made, by which Mulhar Rao Holkar, son of Jeswant Rao, was acknowledged Rajah; but his power was curtailed, and his territory reduced.

Last Campaign against the Pindarees.—We must now return to the Pindarees, who remained hovering about without coming to any decisive action till the close of the year 1817, when matters began to look more serious.

The fall of their friends, the Mahratta princes, caused the three chiefs of the Pindarees,—Karim Khan, Chitoo, and Wasil Mahomed, to feel that the time had really arrived for them to try their powers with the Company's troops.

Lord Hastings, perceiving them concentrating, which was all that he wanted, ordered the various armies of the Presidencies to close around the robber-strongholds in Malwa. He drew a regular cordon round their position, so that none could escape. The leaders of the enemy became panic-stricken at this conduct, and they fled; but their three divisions were attacked, whilst following the example of their commanders. Karim Khan's division was destroyed by General Donkin. General Brown met Chitoo's force and dispersed it; and the third body of Pindarees fled in all directions even without being assailed. Their chief, Wasil Mahomed, committed suicide. Chitoo was found dead in a jungle after the battle; and Karim Khan was permitted to retire, and settle on a small estate, on promise of maintaining peace.

Thus simultaneously fell the sovereignty of the Mahrattas, and the great robber-combination of central India.

India was henceforth English.

Effects of the War.—The effects of this war were immense. When it commenced, the princes of India, almost without exception, were ready to crush the English: at its close, the English had crushed them, and had become universal monarchs.

Sindia was the only chieftain left with an army or the smallest pretence to independence. He was spared the fate which overtook his brethren of the Mahratta State, in consideration of his timely, though reluctant submission, and guaranteed neutrality. But he was left completely dependent on the Company.

Holkar's power was irretrievably broken, and himself a mere puppet in the hands of his Resident.

The Pindarees were entirely dispersed. They found, that to struggle longer was useless; and they disbanded, never again to unite. The Patans, under Amir Khan and Gafur Khan, had been similarly crushed.

The Rajah of Nagpore and the Peshwa were fugitives; the Company managing the entire affairs of the former, while the kingdom of the latter was in a state of anarchy.

Battle of Korigaom, 1818. *The Peshwa* fled from Poonah after his defeat by Elphinstone in a southerly direction, and was joined by Trimbakji Danglia on January 1st, 1818. A severe action was fought between his whole army, consisting of nearly 20,000 men, and a detachment of English, under Captain Staunton. The latter were completely victorious, after a terrible struggle against a host of splendid infantry and cavalry far outnumbering them. But the Sepoys fought admirably, and when some reinforcements came to their aid the Mahrattas broke and fled. General Smith then assumed command and marched on Sattara, which at once surrendered.

Baji Rao fled hopelessly,—now here, now there,—enclosed in a circle of enemies, raging like a caged tiger. He at last surrendered himself to Sir John Malcolm, and was warned that from henceforth he must consider himself dethroned.

The question now was,—what to do with Poonah? It was one of great political interest, for the Rajah of Sattara was the lineal descendant of Sevaji, and actually the head of the Mahratta State, the Peshwa being his responsible minister. The tables had indeed been turned since 1708, when Sahoo, Rajah of Sattara, appointed Balaji Wiswanath to relieve him of the duties of government. Lord Hastings determined now to restore to his original regal splendour the humble descendant of Sevaji; and accordingly the Rajah of Sattara was proclaimed rightful monarch of the Mahrattas, the Peshwa becoming a government pensioner.[1]

Some other important forts were captured, with more or less loss of life, namely,—Talneir, Maligaom, and Assirghur.

And so terminated the war.

The subsequent career of Lord Hastings was marked by few important events, being chiefly memorable for his firm and admirable settlement of the countries he had with so high a hand reduced under British rule.

He encouraged the spread of education amongst the natives, and for this purpose afforded much assistance to schoolmasters, translators, and teachers.

One of the most liberal acts of the marquis was his removal of all restrictions on the liberty of the press in India. It was a bold measure to allow complete freedom of speech in a country but recently conquered, and still anything but favourable to our English rule; but the measure has not been found productive of evil consequences, and has tended much to promote the spread of information and enlightenment amongst the natives, by the multiplication of newspapers.

In 1819 Sir Stamford Raffles, the able administrator of Java, obtained the cession of Singapore from the "*Tumangong*," or Governor of Johore.

Palmer & Co.—In 1820 the Governor-General was called upon to deal with an affair that excited great public interest, both in England and India.

The Nizam had been for several years sinking deeper and deeper into debt. The case was similar to that of the Nabob of Arcot at the close of the previous century. But with regard to the Nizam there were more extenuating circumstances. It was owing to the heavy expense incurred in the maintenance of the Hyderabad contingent, and the scandalous mismanagement of his minister, Chander Lall, that the Nizam was always in want of more money than he possessed. The house of *Messrs. Palmer and Co.*, bankers and agents, supplied all his wants, and eagerly offered him loans to any amount. The Nizam found this system a very convenient one, and for many years drew on these friendly

[1] The execrable *Nana Sahib* was the adopted son of this Baji Rao; and the motive of his rising in 1857 was the hatred he felt for the English, owing to the stoppage, on his adopted father's death, of the payment which, as annuity, had been made to that prince by the Government.

creditors, till the sum he owed them became hopelessly large. The partners of the house thus obtained a very undue influence at Hydrabad; and when the Resident, Mr. Metcalfe, applied to the Governor-General to stop this dangerous state of things, Lord Hastings interfered. He forbad Messrs. Palmer & Co. to make more advances; and directed that the rents of the Northern Circars should be at once capitalized. The funds thus obtained were directed to the payment of the debt. The adventurous house failed soon after, having lost its most advantageous source of income.

The high reputation of the Marquis was unfortunately tarnished by the fact that he had in some way been connected with it. It was said that he had, from motives of friendship for some of the partners, given his sanction to many of their previous proceedings, which were of a very questionable character; and only interfered to stop these practices when the matter had become so public that it could no longer be countenanced by the Governor-General.

Departure of Lord Hastings.—Lord Hastings resigned his post in the end of the year 1822, and on New Year's Day in the following year embarked for England.

He had come to India pledged to a policy of non-annexation, and after five years had made England supreme monarch over the whole of India!

We thus come to an important period of Indian History. India is now English; and the history of the next thirty years is a record of domestic government and distant foreign wars, undisturbed by the aggressions of petty independent sovereigns nearer at home.

CONTENTS OF PART IV.

PART IV.

THE ENGLISH IN INDIA.

FROM 1823 TO THE EXTINCTION OF THE EAST INDIA COMPANY IN 1858.

(I.)—*Lord Amherst's Administration*, 1823—1828. *The First Burmese War.*

AFTER the departure of Lord Hastings in January, 1823, Mr. Adam, the Senior Member of Council, succeeded to the task of governing India, pending the arrival of the next Governor-General at Calcutta.

The choice of the Board of Commissioners fell on Mr. Canning; and that able statesman would have become Governor-General in 1828, had not the death of the Marquis of Londonderry (formerly Lord Castlereagh) created a vacancy in the cabinet. Canning was offered the post of Foreign Secretary, and he accepted it. Lord Amherst was therefore appointed to the Viceroyalty of India, and arrived in Calcutta in August.

He found the country in a very peaceful and satisfactory state, the treasury accounts showing a surplus of ten millions.

First Burmese War.—Lord Amherst was, however, not allowed long to administer the affairs of the government in peace; for early in 1824 a serious war broke out with the Burmese.[1] The haughty and imperious king of that people had for many

[1] The Burmese of Ava were originally mere dependents of the Kingdom of Pegu. But, becoming afterwards free, and being ruled by a talented adventurer named Alompra, who led their armies to invariable success, they conquered Tenasserim from Siam, vanquished the Chinese on many occasions, and, after reducing all Aracan, subjugated their own feudal superiors at Pegu, and became monarchs of the whole peninsula, having their capital city at Ava. In 1822, the Burmese troops, under their "*Maha Bandulah*," or commander-in-chief, conquered and annexed Assam. The King of Burmah styled himself "Lord of the White Elephants. Monarch of the Seas and the Earth."

years past been aiming at a war with England. The victorious career of his nation had blinded him and his nobles to the possibility of defeat; and by the year 1818 the court at Ava had worked itself so firmly into the belief that the soldiers of the English, though they had trampled on the prostrate Hindus, would certainly fall before those invincible warriors, the Burmese, that the king wrote to Calcutta, demanding from the East India Company the cession of Chittagong, and certain other districts, on the ground that they formed part of the territory of Aracan, which appertained to the Burmese Empire. When, however, Lord Hastings returned a courteous answer, to the effect that the king must have been misled by his advisers, and could not have formed a just appreciation of the strength of the English power, his Majesty took no further steps to enforce his claim. In 1823 the frontier of the Burmese territories was extended to the borders of British India, by the king's reduction of Assam; and that monarch, burning with eagerness to attack the English, and blindly following the advice of his headstrong ministers and generals, openly insulted the English by seizing their island of Shahpuri, on the coast of Aracan, and slaughtering the little garrison there.

Lord Amherst at once sent a force to dislodge the Burmese, and wrote as courteously as did his predecessor to the Court at Ava, requesting the king to punish the offenders, for the British Government could not but consider the whole affair to have been a mere piratical raid. This was interpreted by the Burmese into a confession of weakness, and they vigorously prepared for war.

The Burmese commenced open operations in January, 1824, by an invasion of the province of Cachar, which was under British protection; but the English troops sent to oppose their progress successfully defeated them, and drove them to Manipore.

Two expeditions were then despatched from Bengal, one to reduce Assam, the other to capture Rangoon and the seaports of Burmah.

Rangoon was taken without a blow, the garrison fleeing into the interior. Sir Archibald Campbell, commanding the expedition, also took a few neighbouring entrenchments, and, after a more serious but equally successful struggle at Kemmendine, he placed his troops in cantonments at Rangoon, the weather being too hot for campaigning. Provisions, however, failed, and unhappily cholera set in, and the men became dispirited with illness and inaction.

So matters went on till December, when the Maha Bandulah came down with 60,000 men to punish Campbell and his army for their audacity. Unfortunately for them the English were twice victorious, and the Burmese leader retreated up the river to the city of Donabew, followed by the English.

1825.—Donabew was besieged closely, and when in April the Maha Bandulah was killed by a rocket, the garrison gave up all hope, and surrendered it to the English. Campbell at once pushed on and took the city of Pri, or *Prome*, without firing a shot; and here he rested for a while, awaiting the result of the expedition to Aracan.

The force sent to that province, under Colonel Richards, took Rungpore and Silhet, driving the Burmese out of Assam; and in March, 1825, they advanced steadily into Aracan, under the command of General Macbean.

The pass through the hills was vigorously defended; but the troops behaved with great steadiness and bravery, and the enemy was repulsed at all points, the English army debouching into the plains before the capital.

Negotiations were then entered into with the Court at Ava; but the haughty and blinded king would listen to no overtures. In November, therefore, Sir Archibald Campbell commenced his march on the capital, and the enemy fled before him.

In February two decisive actions were fought, ending in the discomfiture of the Burmese; and when, soon after, the main army of the English reached Yandabo, within four days' march of the capital, the Burmese monarch submitted to the conditions imposed.

Treaty with Burmah, 1826.—A treaty was accordingly signed by which the king ceded Assam, Yeh, Tenasserim, and part of Aracan to the Company; promising at the same time to abstain from interference with the province of Cachar. He also agreed to pay a million sterling to the English to defray the expenses of the war; and consented to receive a British resident at his Court.

Thus ended the war. It had proved extremely expensive, costing the Government thirteen millions; and was not popular in England.

Mutinies at Barrackpore, 1824, 1826.—A mutiny of a very serious character had occurred, during the progress of the war, among the Sepoy troops quartered at Barrackpore. Towards the end of October, 1824, the 47th Bengal Native Infantry, then under orders to Rangoon, were found to be in a state of open mutiny, on account of a supposed injustice of the Government. The regiment had been ordered to march down to Calcutta in order to embark for their destination, and the Government had refused to authorize the expenditure of a large sum of money for the hire of cattle to convey their equipments to the place of embarcation. The soldiers were proceeding to acts of violence; and it was not till two regiments of Royal troops and a battery of Horse Artillery had surrounded and opened fire upon them that they laid down their arms, and consented to act as Government required of them.

After the war was ended, another mutiny broke out at the same place (1826); and Lord Amherst, feeling that such symptoms must be at once suppressed, dealt very severely with the ringleaders.

In the same year, Sir David Ochterlony died while holding the office of Resident in Malwa and Rajpootana. The English troops had meanwhile been again called into the field by the condition of the Raj of Bhurtpore.

Bhurtpore.—This kingdom had been founded by the Jauts,[1] during the decay of the Mogul Empire, and was at this time ruled by one *Durjan Sal*, who had seized the kingdom from the rightful heir, the infant Baldeo Singh. The supporters of the young prince applied for aid to the English.

The attitude of Durjan Sal was so hostile to the Company, that Lord Amherst decided to support the claims of Baldeo Singh; and an army under Lord Combermere was accordingly sent to enforce the abdication of the usurper. The Jaut offered battle, deeming that the fort was impregnable. Bhurtpore was indeed amazingly strong; but, after a protracted siege, a breach was at last effected by means of mining: and the storming party was completely successful. The place fell on the 18th of January, 1826. Durjan Sal was sent to Benares as a British pensioner, and Baldeo Singh was installed as Rajah under the protection of the Company.

In 1827 nothing worthy of record took place, beyond the gift of an earldom and the thanks of Parliament to the Governor-General for the successful conduct of the Burmese War.

Lord Amherst returned to England in February, 1828.

[1] The Jauts were the aboriginal inhabitants of the country.

(II.)—*Lord William Bentinck's Administration*, 1828—1835.

Five months later, Lord William Bentinck landed and received the seals of office from Mr. Bailey, who had meanwhile discharged the duties of Governor-General.

The new Governor came out under peculiar circumstances; for the representatives of the Company had previously regarded him as unfit for the post even of Lieutenant-Governor; and had recalled him from his office as Governor of Madras after the Vellore Mutiny of 1806. But the Ministers of the Crown now appointed him to perform the duties of Viceroy, and on July 4th, 1828, he arrived at Calcutta in that capacity.

His administration is principally noticeable for the revenue and magisterial reforms he introduced; his reduction of State expenditure; and the great changes that were then taking place in Anglo-Indian society.

Intervention Policy.—Before considering these, however, it will be well to consider his connection with the native states, and his policy with regard to Runjeet Singh, the great Trans-Sutlej chieftain.

Jodhpore.—The Rajput State of Jodhpore was in a troubled condition at this period. The Rajah, Man Singh, quarrelled with his chieftains, and the latter appealed to the English for aid. But the Governor-General refused to assist them, alleging his adherence to a policy of non-intervention with native states. When, however, the vassals proceeded summarily to depose their lord, and the Rajah urgently begged for aid from Calcutta, it was deemed that something must be done, and accordingly peace was restored by the English Government, and the Rajah replaced on the throne.

Gwalior.—In 1827 Dowlat Rao Sindia, who had for some years meekly submitted in all things to British dictation, died, leaving no issue, and without having adopted a son. The throne being therefore vacant, the Ranee was directed by Lord William Bentinck to adopt a son. She did so, her choice falling on the nearest male relative, Ali Jah Jankaji Sindia, who was accordingly installed. But, five years later, namely in the year 1833, the young monarch, impatient of the constant control of his adoptive mother, excited the soldiery, and commenced actual warfare against her. The Resident interfered,—warned the Maharanee to keep aloof from all government,—and made Sindia actual as well as nominal king.

Jeypore.—In Jeypore the intervention of the English was rendered necessary by the outrages of the Vizier, who poisoned the Rajah with his mother, the Ranee, and attempted to seize the Government. The Resident interfered,—directed the Vizier to retire,—and placed on the throne an infant, the only representative of the royal family who could be found—assuming charge of the country during his minority.

Oude.—The Raj of Oude was, in 1834, found to be in a condition so disgraceful, that the Resident, Mr. Maddock, was compelled to institute strict inquiries into the mal-administration of the Government. He discovered that the public funds were being daily wasted on the frivolous amusements of the King and his Court; and that the former cared in no way for the interests of his subjects, so that he procured funds wherewith to minister to his own personal enjoyments. The Resident, therefore, solemnly warned the King that if he persisted in thus neglecting all the duties he owed to his country, he would incur the severest displeasure of the British Government.

Bhopal.—In 1820 the Rajah of Bhopal dying, left his widow, Secander Begum, to govern the country. She undertook the responsibility, ignoring the fact that the rightful heir, her nephew, was perfectly competent to perform the duties of his office. Accordingly in 1835, when the young Prince appealed to the British Government, Lord William Bentinck interfered and placed him on the throne.[1]

Coorg.—Coorg was annexed by Lord William Bentinck in 1834, the circumstances which led to this step being as follows:—

Vira Rajah, the ruler of the state at this time, had succeeded to the throne in 1820. His character was by nature violent and blood-thirsty, and he commenced his reign by wholesale slaughters of his own relations. His father had been on good terms with the Company, but Vira Rajah on many occasions behaved with the greatest insolence to their representatives; and in 1834 he rashly declared war. An army sent from Madras took his capital in the same year, and the Rajah at once surrendered unconditionally. He was declared to have forfeited his right to the throne,

[1] The present Begum, daughter of this Rajah, succeeded to the Government, and under her rule the State has greatly thrived. The services which she has rendered to the preservation of peace and good government in India have been recognized by the gift of the Grand Cross of the Star of India.

and the Raj was annexed to the Madras Presidency, there being no other royal Prince living who could be created Rajah in his place.

Cachar.—In 1830 the province of Cachar, which had been under British protection during the Burmese war, was annexed to the Company's territories by Lord William, on the death of the Rajah Govind Chandra, there being no successor to the throne.

Mysore.—Lord William's annexation of Mysore is the next event which claims our attention. It will be remembered that, on the fall of Seringapatam, in 1799, Lord Wellesley reinstated on the throne of Mysore an infant of five years old, the only representative of the ancient royal family of the country, who had been deposed by Hyder and Tippoo. He made the celebrated financier, Poorneah, minister and regent, during the Rajah's minority, and this plan had answered exceedingly well; for, by careful management and good government, Poorneah had greatly benefited the country, the annual revenue being increased from twenty-one to twenty-five lacs of rupees, and the Treasury books showing a clear balance of two millions in his favour. In 1811, when the young Rajah obtained his majority, he at once dismissed Poorneah, and himself assumed the entire management of the government. From that period the income of the country steadily decreased. The revenues were wasted to procure for the Rajah all the amusements and dissipation that his mind could invent; and after the complete waste of the entire balance that lay in the Treasury, he ran heavily into debt. To discharge these liabilities he oppressed the ryots with circumstances of much heartlessness and cruelty; and in short was guilty of such execrable mismanagement that, in 1830, half the Raj was in a state of insurrection. A large British force quelled the rising; and thus the matter was brought to a crisis, and Lord William Bentinck called upon to interfere on behalf of the population of Mysore.

He reminded the Rajah, that on many previous occasions he had been solemnly warned by the British Resident, and urged to discontinue his excesses, and attend more to the government of the country; he informed him, that by the conditions of Lord Wellesley's gift of the sovereignty, the government was liable at any time to be taken completely out of his hands, in case he so carelessly conducted it as to endanger the regular payment of the subsidy;—that the period had now arrived when, after full trial, and many warnings, his administration had proved so fatal to the prosperity of Mysore, that he could no longer be considered fit for his position;—and that therefore the Company would take entire possession of his territories, giving him the large annuity of £40,000, with one fifth of the revenues of the country.[1]

This was accordingly done, and Mysore became English.

The Court of Commissioners fully approved of the conduct of Lord William Bentinck in this matter; and refused to permit a policy to which, on the humble solicitations of the repentant Rajah, the Governor-General felt tempted to yield; namely, that he should be allowed to carry on government in some portion of his dominions.

Runjeet Singh.—Lord William's conduct with regard to the trans-Sutlej chieftain, Runjeet Singh, is one of the most note-worthy acts of his administration. It will be remembered, that in 1807 Lord Minto had made a treaty with this prince, in which the latter bound himself to interfere with no State south of the river Sutlej. This treaty he faithfully fulfilled, and had contented himself up to this time with consolidating his kingdom and drilling his splendid armies of Sikh warriors, whom he led victoriously into the field against the territories of Peshawur and Cashmir. In 1827 Lord Amherst, wishing to obtain the cordial support of so powerful a chieftain on the English frontier, sent him a handsome present of English dray horses, with an escort commanded by Lieutenant Burnes. Runjeet Singh received this present with royal honours, and professed the greatest attachment to the English nation; so that, in 1831, Lord William Bentinck, considered that the time had arrived for a still closer union with the Sikhs, and held a magnificent Durbar on the Sutlej, where the warmest promises of mutual friendship were given and received between the chiefs of the English and Sikh nations.

Such were the principal political characteristics of Lord William's administration. But though on the whole it was peaceful and prosperous, yet several domestic troubles caused him much anxiety.

Insurrections.—Insurrections broke out amongst the wild tribes of central India, with which it was found extremely difficult to deal. The most note-worthy were those of the "*Coles*," the "*Dangars*," and the "*Santals*," in the south-west of Bengal, in the territories of Ramgurh, Palamow, and Chota Nagpore; and that of the "*Chooars*," in the country near Bancoorah. These disturbances were all, after a time, successfully quelled, though the operations were on several occasions productive of much slaughter.

A formidable disturbance also took place at Baraset, owing to the

[1] The increase in the revenues of Mysore has made this income an exceedingly valuable one.

religious fanaticism of a body of Mahomedans, headed by one Titoo Mir. Becoming very violent in their conduct towards those around them, they were at last set upon by large troops of indignant Hindus; and in the fights which ensued great slaughter took place. To quiet the country it was found necessary to send a regiment to Baraset, when, after some resistance, the rioters submitted, and order was restored.

Treaty with Sinde, 1832.—A commercial treaty with the Ameers of Sinde was concluded in 1832; and the Sutlej and Indus rivers were then, for the first time, opened for traffic, with the co-operation of Runjeet Singh.

Lord William Bentinck's Civil Administration.—We must now turn to Lord William Bentinck's civil administration.

Retrenchment.—The Governor-General landed in India bent upon retrenchment, finding that the Treasury had been emptied by the heavy expenses of the Burmese war. All went well till he proceeded to touch the pay of officers in the Bengal army; when the "Batta" question nearly created another mutiny. It will be remembered, that in 1765 Lord Clive had found great difficulty in quieting the excited condition of the army, when he reduced this Government grant from "double" to "single-Batta." And now Lord William Bentinck had the hardihood to promulgate a general order, reducing the bonus to "half-Batta." The excitement was great, and even the Commander-in chief was led into signing a remonstrance couched in words of a somewhat turbulent character. But the Government was proof against arguments. The order stood; and the officers were wise enough not to proceed to further steps.

Abolition of the Suttee.—One of Lord William's greatest triumphs was the abolition of the detestable crime of "suttee," or the burning of widows on the funeral pyre of their husbands, which had prevailed all over India up to his date. By him the performance of this rite was declared to be culpable homicide in all the principal actors; and it is strange that though the command aimed a blow at one of the most ancient Hindu customs, it caused but little excitement throughout the empire.

Law and Justice.—Lord William created some wise reforms in the administration of justice, doing away with the old courts of circuit, and substituting in their place courts held by the judges of districts, for monthly gaol-delivery, within their respective jurisdictions. The benefit of this was great, as it saved expense and delay in criminal matters. He gave a new Sudder Court to the north-west provinces, and created a new Board of Revenue at Allahabad. Finally, he permitted all the legal proceedings to be carried on in the vernacular of the district,[1] instead of Persian, which had previously been used, and he threw open several posts of honour to natives.

Settlement of the North-West Provinces.—It fell to the duty of this Governor-General to settle the revenue administration of the north-western provinces, which consisted of territories lately acquired by the Company.[2] After some years of inquiry, and much hesitation between various schemes, his plan was drawn up and made law. The land was to be examined and scheduled by the collectors and village-officials; the assessment fixed by the collector, and the settlement made for thirty years. The framer and controller of this important work was the celebrated Robert Bird.

Abolition of Thuggee.—Thuggee had at this period become a very thriving and lucrative profession. It consisted of indiscriminate murders of travellers and others by ruffians brought up to the trade, and bound to secresy by solemn oaths. The horrid practice grew to such a pitch that Lord William Bentinck determined to wage a general war of extermination against the Thugs; and more than a thousand were executed during his seven years of office. He created a special office for the suppression of this crime, and gave full opportunities of education and improvement to those Thugs who chose to repent, and lead an honest life.

Education.—With regard to education, Lord William's views were liberal and advanced, and he on all occasions gave the greatest assistance to the improvement of educational establishments, and the spread of enlightenment throughout India. In 1835 he founded the Medical College of Calcutta, in order to afford to the natives a more sound instruction in the science of healing than they had hitherto possessed.

Not the least among the many improvements of his administration which have stamped their mark upon the later dealings of England with India, was the establishment of the "Peninsular

[1] The lands ceded by the Nabob of Oude, and the territory conquered from Sindia.

[2] Another beneficial change, made by Lord William Bentinck, was the abolition of the "provincial" courts and those of the Registrar for the trial of civil causes in the presidency; and the substitution in their place of the court presided over by the "zillah and city judge." This was in 1831. In 1838 Lord Auckland authorized a change somewhat similar for the Madras presidency.

and Oriental Company, who opened up steam communication by way of the Red Sea, and brought India two months nearer to England. The Company was established in 1842, and received the cordial support both of the Calcutta and Home Governments.

The seven years' administration of this Governor-General were remarkable for the peace that characterized them, and the progress observable in all branches of society, native and European.

(III.)—*Sir Charles Metcalfe, Provisionary Governor-General, 1835—1836.—Opening of the China Trade.*

On Lord William Bentinck's retirement Sir Charles Metcalfe, then Governor of Agra for the north-western provinces,[1] was placed in his position, to act as Governor-General till Lord William's successor should be sent out from England.

All parties were fully satisfied with the appointment: and at home the Court of Directors urged Parliament to continue Sir Charles as Governor-General; but the ministry preferred to have the power of appointment absolutely in their own hands, and objected strongly to being dictated to by the heads of the Company. They would have done better had they listened to the word of advice from the India House, for the previous career of Sir Charles Metcalfe is sufficient to show that he possessed all the qualities requisite for this important post.

The office was conferred upon Lord Heytesbury, after being refused by Mr. Mountstuart Elphinstone, on the ground of ill-health. But before his lordship had started, the Tory ministry had given place to the Whigs, and Sir John Hobhouse, the new President of the Board, revoked the appointment of Lord Heytesbury, and nominated Lord Auckland Governor-General.

Liberty of the Press, 1835.—The only noticeable act of Sir Charles Metcalfe's administration is the boon he conferred on the public by the liberation of the press. It was a bold measure, and made him exceedingly unpopular at home. But the result has proved its wisdom, for neither the Government nor the residents have ever had cause to regret the freedom of speech conferred on all parties, while the benefits which accrue to the public are immense.

The Court of Directors, however, were beyond measure in-

[1] The north-western provinces were created a separate presidency by the Act of 1833.—(See below).

dignant at this revolutionary policy, and treated Sir Charles with such undisguised rudeness that, on the advent of Lord Auckland, he resigned his post in the Civil Service and retired to England.

The Company thus lost one of the finest officers that has ever set foot in India; and it is not improbable that, had Sir Charles continued Governor-General, the results of the war in Afghanistan would have been more honourable to the Company, and more beneficial to the nation.

Before entering upon Lord Auckland's administration it will be desirable to glance at the position held about this time by the East India Company, and the circumstances connected with the renewal of the charter.

Charter of 1833.—In 1833 the charter of 1813 granted to the Company for twenty years had expired, and, as usual, the debates which ensued were of an exciting nature. It was a time when monopoly and free trade were fighting their last battles, and, as is always the case, the finishing blows were amongst the hardest dealt. Many speeches were made in the House in favour of a complete subversion of the Company's rule, in which it was urged that the country would be in a far more prosperous condition if the powers of Government were placed entirely in the hands of the Crown. Other members pleaded hard for the same powers to be vested exclusively in the Governor-General. But the voice of the country seemed to be opposed to either of these violent changes, and the general plan of administration remained the same.

Opening of the China Trade.—The next point of discussion was the trade of the Company, and especially that with China, which had been reserved by the charter of 1813, to the East India Company, as a kind of set off against the complete freedom given to all trade with India. The debates grew hot upon the question of the removal of all restrictions on trade with China. Long was the struggle, and angry grew the disputants; but in the end free trade principles triumphed, as they had done in the great contest on the Reform Bill of the previous year; and the Court of Directors were obliged to see the last vestige of monopoly swept away before their faces.

Establishment of a Fourth Presidency.—They had also to consent to the abolition of their fleet, and the establishment of a fourth presidency, including the north-west provinces. Another and equally important change was that by which increased powers of interference with the local governments of the several presidencies were given to the Governor-General in council. The local governors were to have no council, and no powers of legislation. The Governor-General was to legislate for all persons, European or native, and for all courts. And a commission was appointed to inquire into the practicability of framing a single code of laws for all India.

On these conditions the charter was extended for twenty years more.

(IV.) *Lord Auckland's Administration,* 1836—1842. *The Afghan War.*

On the 20th of March, 1836, Lord Auckland assumed the reins of government, and at once found himself called upon by the Anglo-Indian public to deal with the difficult questions concerning the north-western frontier of the Company's territory, and the formation of a strong barrier against the dreaded incursions of the Russians. The result was the most disastrous war in which the English have been engaged in the East. It cost thousands of lives and millions of money, and in the end effected absolutely nothing.

As the whole history of the English in India for the next twenty years centres in the north-west frontier, and the states in the neighbourhood, it will be well to understand thoroughly the position of parties in Afghanistan before proceeding to the events of Lord Auckland's administration.

Sketch of the Afghan Dynasties.—It will be remembered that the great Ahmed Shah Durani, who conquered Delhi in 1757, and fought the terrible battle of Panipat, in 1761, against the Mahrattas, was the chief of the Afghan tribe of "Abdali," whose name he changed into that of "Durani." After that disastrous victory, Ahmed retired with his shattered forces to Afghanistan, and there for some years peacefully reigned at Cabul, consolidating his power with much ability and moderation. On his death his son, Teimur Shah, succeeded. Teimur was a prince of little power, and wanting in all the essentials of kingly dignity; so that it is no wonder to find a family of great eminence, the Barukzyes, whose chief Poyndah Khan was the vizier, growing into a party in the state so important as to be absolutely necessary for the maintenance of government. Teimur Shah, however, was fretful at this minister's interference; and accustomed to give full vent to his passion whenever it was roused, without considering what the effect might be, he mortally offended the Barukzyes, who raised an insurrection against him. The Shah seized the opportunity to capture Poyndah Khan, and put him to death. The Barukzyes swore to be avenged on the Suddozyes,[1] and steadily kept their vow.

On Teimur Shah's death his eldest son, Zemaun Shah, came to the throne; and for many years kept the English in India in a state of continual agitation by his restless activity, his proclaimed hatred of the Company, and his constant assemblage of large armies near the frontier for the avowed object of attacking the Company's possessions. His intentions on Hindostan were, however, completely frustrated by the conduct of the Barukzyes and of his own family. Of his younger brothers there were four with whom we are especially brought into contact, Soojah-al-Mulkh, Mahmud, Firuz, and Kaisar.

Poyndah Khan had been succeeded in the headship of the clan Barukzye by his son Futteh Khan, the sole purpose of whose life was to revenge his father's death on the chief of the Suddozyes. He found his opportunity in 1801, when the king was at Peshawur, on his way to Hindostan upon a grand expedition. Having easily won over Mahmud to conspire against his brother, the Shah, Futteh Khan raised the standard of Mahmud and seized Candahar. Zemaun Shah hastily returned, but only to be captured, blinded, and imprisoned. So ended his reign. He lived to an old age, a blind and helpless dependent on the mercy of his family.

Sooja-al-Mulkh, the rightful heir and successor, marched immediately to Cabul to claim his right; but Futteh Khan defeated him, and set up Mahmud as Shah; while, taking advantage of the disturbed state of the country, Firuz seized on the Suddozye dominions at Kerat, and Kaisar on those at Candahar.

Thus matters went on for a few years, till many of the Durani nobles at Cabul, disgusted with Mahmud's folly and Futteh Khan's arrogance, invited back the fugitive Shah Soojah to the capital. He returned, defeated the usurpers, and placed himself on the throne of his fathers. Mahmud submitted and was pardoned; and the Shah, to strengthen his throne by gaining the affections of the people, forgave his erring brothers, and established Firuz and Kaisar in their respective governments of Herat and Candahar. This was in 1808. Futteh Khan in the meanwhile fled, and proceeded to further acts of rebellion.

[1] The name of the royal family was Suddozye.

He first plotted with Kaisar, and induced the young prince to permit his name to be used as a sanction to a new revolt. The conspirators were beaten, and Kaisar was pardoned. The Barukzye then raised the standard of Camran, eldest son to the Ex-Shah Mahmud, and treacherously took Candahar from Kaisar. Again the revolt was quelled and the rebels were forgiven; Shah Soojah being apparently in hope that his moderate and merciful conduct would draw all parties to himself. He little reckoned on the character of the family with whom he had to deal. They had sworn the downfall of the Suddozyes, and their downfall they would have. Finding the cause of Camran hopeless, Futteh Khan deserted him, and once more persuaded Kaisar to head an insurrection. The conspirators seized Peshawur, but were again defeated and again forgiven. This constant and almost culpable mercy lost the kingdom to the Shah's family. The Barukzyes were implacable; and it was evident that the only way to stem the tide of insurrection would be unhesitatingly to employ the national custom of immediate execution.

Shah Soojah's Wanderings.—The mistake of thus sparing Futteh Khan was soon shown. After an unsuccessful attempt in 1807, that chieftain, raising the standard of Mahmud, was victorious at all points, and the Shah, in great distress, fled to Peshawur.

Shah Soojah's wanderings and misfortunes form a romantic incident in Indian history. In his first flight he was taken prisoner, and carried to Cashmir by the governor of that province, and his captor in vain tried to extort from him a gift of the splendid "*Koh-i-noor*" diamond, the only crown jewel he had contrived to save. Soojah fled for refuge to Runjeet Singh, at Lahore, by whom he was at first well received; but his treacherous host soon made him experience the sorrows of a captivity, first honourable, then rigorous and cruel; and, by dint of clever manœuvering, the Shah succeeded in effecting his escape into the British territory of Loodianah, leaving the Koh i-noor in the hands of Runjeet Singh. Here he found one of the few faithful friends of his life, the Rajah Kistawar, who entertained him with regal splendour for a whole year; and used every means in his power to soothe his affliction. But Shah Soojah being ambitious, and not content with the quiet life offered to him, parted from his generous host in order to attack Cashmir; entertainer and entertained being equally full of unfeigned regret at the termination of the king's residence in Hindostan. The expedition after all proved a failure, and Soojah again fled to Loodianah, where he remained some years.

Meanwhile Mahmud was reigning very badly at Cabul, alienating all parties at court by his arrogance, violence, and debauchery; and by the year 1816 all real power was in the hands of the vizier, Futteh Khan, and the Barukzyes. Dost Mahomed, who afterwards became actual monarch of Afghanistan, was a younger brother of Futteh Khan's, and at this time had acquired much power, being incessantly at the side of the vizier. It seems that they jointly formed plans for subverting the reigning house, and raising a dynasty of Barukzyes to the throne; and to this end they desired that all Afghanistan should first be brought under one rule. Accordingly Futteh Khan and Dost Mahomed marched on Herat which was then, as before mentioned, under the governorship of Mahmud's brother, Firuz. With Firuz was living Prince Camran, who seems to have formed an intimate acquaintance with some of the ladies of the harem; for when, with considerable violence, Herat was seized and Firuz compelled to fly, Camran, at the instigation of one of his uncle's favourite wives, swore solemnly to be avenged on Futteh Khan. He therefore went to Cabul, and persuading his half-imbecile father, Shah Mahmud, that this movement on the part of his vizier was equivalent to an insurrection, obtained permission to seize the person of Futteh Khan and bring him to Cabul. This was successfully accomplished, and Mahmud, delighted at the prospect of a speedy release from the interference of his powerful officer, ordered that the Khan should be put to death in his presence. The horrible sentence was carried out with the most atrocious barbarity; joint being slowly cut from joint, and limb from limb, till the sufferer died from loss of blood and the agonies which he endured—both Shah and Crown-Prince watching with greedy satisfaction the dying throes of their unhappy victim.

This act signalled the end of the dynasty of the Suddozyes. Dost Mahomed, in fury at his brother's death, came up with a large army, and, supported by all the Burukzyes, captured Cabul, driving Mahmud and Camran into exile. The worthy pair fled to Firuz at Herat, and remained there till the death of Firuz, some years later,—the Barukzyes meanwhile seizing the kingdom of Afghanistan.

Futteh Khan had besides Dost Mahomed, several brothers, who now seized on different portions of the kingdom; one, Mahomed, becoming Sultan of Peshawur; another, Azim Khan, the eldest, marching up to claim Cabul, as head of the family, from Dost Mahomed; while Pur Dil Khan, Kohan Dil Khan, and Shere Ali Khan seized on Candahar and the country of the Khiljies.

Dost Mahomed consented to give up Cabul to Azim Khan, as chief of the clan, himself submissively retiring to Ghazni. But this was not for long. All the brothers began to quarrel for the supremacy; and had not Dost Mahomed been a man of great energy of character and wonderful ability, the House of the Barukzyes might have tottered to its fall.

Azim Khan set up a puppet sovereign, Prince Ayub, a representative of the ancient dynasty of the Suddozyes, as nominal Shah at Cabul; but Dost Mahomed also set up another representative, named Sultan Ali. Ayub succeeded in murdering Sultan Ali; and soon after, when the two Barukyze brothers were, apparently in a most friendly manner, making an expedition against the Sikhs, Azim Khan heard that Dost Mahomed had leagued against him with Runjeet Singh; and in terror he fled to Jellalabad, where in 1823 he died. Runjeet Singh gave Peshawur to Dost Mahomed, and thus that chieftain became actual head of the whole state of Afghanistan. The Candahar Barukzyes, however, seized the moment of confusion to take possession of Cabul; and it was not till 1826 that Dost Mahomed became finally master of the capital, by driving out the other claimants.

For many years Dost Mahomed remained at Cabul, reigning well, and with much moderation; his policy being to exalt the Barukzyes, and, as far as possible, crush the Durani tribes, who might support the ancient dynasty of Ahmed Shah. In 1834, Shah Soojah, raising an army in Sinde, again made an attempt to regain his kingdom, and obtained the co-operation of several of the Barukzyes, who were jealous of their brothers' sudden rise to power. He failed however in gaining the support which he hoped for from Lord William Bentinck; and the assistance volunteered by Runjeet Singh was offered at so high a price, that Soojah refused it. He marched into Afghanistan, and invested Candahar; but the city held out bravely, and when Dost Mahomed came up in the rear with a fine fresh army from Cabul, Shah Soojah fought one feeble battle, and then again fled to India.

Runjeet Singh seized this opportunity to take Peshawur from Afghanistan, and to annex it to his own dominions. In retaliation Dost Mahomed proclaimed a religious war against the Sikhs, and gathering together an immense army, marched into the Punjaub. The expedition was entirely frustrated by a certain

General Harlan, an American in the pay of Runjeet Singh, who, entering the Afghan camp as ambassador, cleverly succeeded in creating so much disaffection there, that half the army broke up, and marched back again by different routes. The expedition was therefore abandoned, and the Dost returned to Cabul.

In 1837 Runjeet Singh seized Cashmir and Multan; and in the expedition against him, although it was unsuccessful, Akber Khan, Dost Mahomed's brave son, first distinguished himself.

The same year ensued the great siege of Herat, which lasted ten months. It was undertaken by Mohammed Shah, King of Persia,[1] at the instigation of his Russian ambassador,[2] and against the will of the English; and had reference to some tribute which the Shah demanded, but which was refused by Camran, now styled "Shah of Herat." The siege was unsuccessful, and the Persians finally withdrew in September, 1838; nominally, at the request of the English,—really, because they could make but little impression on the stubborn Afghan's garrison.[3]

We thus come to consider the position of the various foreign powers as regarded the fate of the Suddozyes and the condition of Afghanistan. Amongst others that of the English.

Russophobia.—There had been for many years a gradually increasing fear of Russian aggression amongst the English in India. It was felt that Russia was gaining ground in Persia with

[1] Aga Mohammed and his son Futteh Ali, successively Shahs of Persia, had raised that kingdom from a state of anarchy to a position of considerable eminence. Futteh Ali had two sons, Abbas Mirza, the "Shah Zada," and Mohammed. The former, a brave but ambitious prince, bent on the conquest of Afghanistan, had prevailed on the aged Shah, his father, to sanction an expedition to Herat in 1834; but the Shah died in that year, and Abbas Mirza having previously been killed, Mohammed (as mentioned above) came to the throne, threw himself warmly into the arms of Russia, and undertook the siege of Herat with much vigour.

[2] Count Nesselrode, then head of the Cabinet at St. Petersburgh, on being remonstrated with by Lord Durham, solemnly declared that if such was the case, his ambassador at Teheran, Count Simonich, was acting in direct opposition to orders. In favour of this statement, letters have been produced; but it is difficult to believe that the ambassador at Teheran would have urged such a step, had he known it to be against the wishes of his government, and contrary to his written instructions. We are therefore, in spite of Count Nesselrode's denial, led to think that he did so under orders from his sovereign.

[3] It was in this siege that Eldred Pottinger so greatly distinguished himself. Though only a young lieutenant, he gained the hearts of the Afghans in Herat by his prowess and unflagging energy; and by sustaining their drooping courage he saved their city.

immense strides, both diplomatically and commercially; and it was imagined that the aim of the Czar was to extend his dominions, by combining with the native princes to drive the Company from the shores of India. All eyes were therefore anxiously turned towards the three great powers beyond our frontier; first, Runjeet Singh and the Sikhs; secondly, the Duranis and the Barukzyes in Afghanistan; thirdly, the Shah of Persia. Nor must we forget to mention the Ameers of Sinde, with whom it was thought advisable to negotiate.

In 1836 the British minister at the Court of Persia wrote to the Governor-General concerning the intended Persian expedition to Herat; warning him that it was in reality a war of conquest, undertaken at the instigation of Russia, in order to advance the Persian frontier to Herat, which was considered the key to a position in Afghanistan. He therefore urged the Government to oppose this. Since by treaty the English were prevented from interfering between Persia and the Afghans, Lord Auckland considered that a sufficient opposition to this step could be effected by entering into warm and affectionate treaties of commerce with the Court at Cabul, in order to gain the support of the Shah against Persia and Russia.

Burnes's Mission.—Accordingly in 1837 a mission was sent under Captain Alexander Burnes, to obtain a commercial treaty and place England on closer relations with Afghanistan. That officer found Russian influence greatly at work on his arrival at Cabul; the Candahar chiefs had begged Russia for aid against Runjeet Singh, and Dost Mahomed seemed inclined to follow their example. During Burnes's residence at Cabul, the Candahar Barukzyes actually made a treaty with Persia under Russian dictation; and Mr. Macneile, the English ambassador at Teheran, was treated with open indignity. The mission proved ultimately a complete failure, Dost Mahomed demanding that whichever party he treated with should procure for him Peshawur from Runjeet Singh. The Russian ambassador promised this. Captain Burnes was unable to do so. Therefore Dost Mahomed declared for Persia, and Burnes left the country.

The Tripartite Treaty, June 26th, 1838.—Thus was all attempt to defend the frontier by treaty with the chiefs in power in Afghanistan frustrated. And the question for Lord Auckland to decide was,—how was the frontier to be defended? or was it to be abandoned? If it was to be defended, the English must replace Shah Soojah on the throne, and make with him a firm treaty.

offensive and defensive, against the nations to the west; thus gaining a powerful friend, commanding the whole line of frontier. Lord Auckland determined to take this step; and accordingly a tripartite treaty was entered into between Runjeet Singh, Shah Soojah, and the British Government. The terms were, that the Peshawur, and the States on the Indus, should be absolutely renounced by the Shah in favour of Runjeet Singh; and that between the Afghans and Sikhs relations should be entered into, guaranteeing mutual support and courtesy. The Shah was to relinquish all claims on Sinde, on condition of a payment, to be fixed by the Governor-General; to leave Herat untouched, and in possession of his nephew, Camran; and to prevent all other foreigners from invading either British or Sikh territory. Such was the Tripartite Treaty of Lahore, signed June 26th, 1838.

And then commenced the Afghan War, undertaken for the purpose of placing the English ally, Shah Soojah, on the throne of Afghanistan.

On October 1st, 1838, Lord Auckland made the famous "Simla Proclamation," stating the position which the Government had determined to take; their intentions; and the reasons that had influenced their decision. And the remainder of the cool season was spent in making preparations for the expedition.

Opposition in Parliament.—At home, much opposition was made by influential members of Parliament to the measures of Lord Auckland. It was urged, that the Persians, if left to themselves, would have been forced to retire from Herat, from sheer inability to carry the place; that the expedition from Bombay, which had seized the island of Carrack, in the Persian Gulf, in order to overawe Persia, was needless, since that State had of itself discovered its inability to operate successfully against the Afghans; and finally, that since the weakness of Persia was thus proved, it was absurd for England to embroil herself in an uncertain war in order to guard a frontier, which a little patience would show to be sufficiently protected already. This, however, did not alter Lord Auckland's determination; and the British armies commenced their march towards the Punjaub.

Negotiations with Sinde.—Previously to this, however, a council of war had been held, and the movements of the troops determined on. The main army was to join with Runjeet Singh's force at Ferozepore, while the Bombay contingent sailed to the mouth of the Indus. The three divisions were to meet at Shikarpore, in Sinde, and march together to Afghanistan. To this end, it was necessary to secure the co-operation of the Ameers of Sinde. These "Ameers" were Beloochees, chiefs of the tribe *Talpura*, who had conquered the country from the Afghans in 1786. The victors had portioned the country amongst themselves, and established a constitutional government on the feudal system. Captain Burnes had treated with them when he was on his way to the court of Runjeet Singh with his troop of dray horses, in 1831; and the same year a formal treaty had been drawn up with them by Lord William Bentinck, by which they consented to open up the trade of the Indus for British merchants. In 1835 Runjeet Singh, coveting some provinces on the frontier, had commenced a war against the Ameers; but the Company interfered, and he desisted. In 1838 the Tripartite Treaty had guaranteed to the rulers of Sinde the peaceable possession of their provinces, on condition of a payment fixed by the English Government to be made to Shah Soojah. And now, early in 1839, the passage for the English troops was to be rendered safe by the co-operation of the Ameers. Pottinger was sent to demand of them a large payment, nominally in favour of Shah Soojah, to whom, in his character of Shah of Afghanistan, the feudal Ameers owed tribute. They pleaded, that the Shah when in exile had given them a release from this, in consideration of a certain immediate payment made to him in 1833. Pottinger replied, that the British Government demanded the funds, and would have them, even though every Ameer in Sinde should have to be displaced first. They accordingly yielded with a very bad grace, and the sum was paid.

March of the Army.—The Bengal army reached the Sutlej in November, and with great rejoicings the force of Runjeet Singh joined them there. On December 10th, 1838, under the command of Sir Willoughby Cotton (Sir Henry Fane, the commander-in-chief, having resigned in indignation at the whole proceeding), the united armies marched from Ferozpore, *en route* for the rendezvous at Shikarpore, in Sinde.

They crossed the Indus in fine array and brilliant weather, and in high spirits marched southwards. On January 14th they reached the Sinde territory, and heard that Sir John Keane had safely arrived at Tattah, after his voyage from Bombay with the troops from that Presidency.

Operations in Sinde, 1839.—The Ameer of Hydrabad having proved somewhat fractious, it was determined that the Bengal contingent should march down so as to overawe the Ameers by a show of strength, and, if necessary, by actual force. Sir Alexander

Burnes, therefore, demanded of the Ameers the cession of the fort of Bakar, on the Indus, as a depot for the British troops. The request was reluctantly granted, and possession was taken on January 29th. The army then pushed on down the left, or eastern bank, for Hydrabad. The Bombay contingent at the same time marched up the right, or western bank, and halted opposite that city.

Kurrachee was at the same time taken by a British ship with some reserve forces on board, and converted into an English fort.

On perceiving the strength of the British army the Ameers wisely submitted in everything to the Company; and, somewhat disappointed, the main army turned their backs on Hydrabad and marched towards Shikarpore. They arrived at the end of February; and, without waiting for Sir John Keane and Shah Soojah, who had joined that general in Sinde, Sir Willoughby Cotton pushed on for the Bolan Pass.

March through the Bolan Pass.—On their way, the army had to cross a parched desert of 146 miles in extent, and suffered severely, the baggage animals dying by scores; so that when, on March 10th, the column reached Dadur, at the mouth of the Pass, Cotton rested a few days to recruit the force, and examined the country before him. He found that Mehrab Khan, of Khelat, had thrown every difficulty in the way of an onward march: no supplies were to be obtained. And it was plain, that from henceforth every step of the advance would have to be made through a hostile and exceedingly dangerous country.

The Bolan Pass was traversed from end to end in six days, without the smallest opposition, and Cotton halted the army at Quettah to await the arrival of Sir John Keane; meanwhile effecting a favourable Treaty with Mehrab Khan, to strengthen the British position. In April, Sir John Keane with his staff joined Sir Willoughby, and thus the whole expedition was massed at Quettah, with Shah Soojah in the camp. The three divisions, now united, at once pushed on for their destination; though the soldiers were on quarter rations, and all parties were suffering from privation and sickness.

Taking of Candahar.—The allies soon reached Candahar, which submitted without a struggle; and early in May, 1839, Soojah was crowned Shah of Afghanistan with much pomp.

Ghazni and Cabul.—At the end of June the army marched on Ghazni. The fort was considered impregnable; but the gates were blown down by some engineers under the direction of

Captain Thompson, and in one morning the city was carried and the garrison put to flight. Dost Mahomed was at this time at Cabul, and, in fear for his life, after hearing the news of the fall of Ghazni, he fled towards Hindu Cush, while the English marched on the capital. They reached Cabul without a blow being struck, and on August 7th Shah Soojah was installed in the palace of his fathers at the Bala Hissar.

Soojah's son, Prince Teimur, and a fresh Sikh contingent, who came through the Khyber Pass, joined the main army at Cabul soon afterwards.

Death of Runjeet Singh.—Meanwhile, full of years and full of honours, Runjeet Singh, "the Lion of Lahore," died on June 27th. He left the Sikh kingdom to his eldest son, Kurruk Singh, and bequeathed the "Koh-i-noor" to the temple of Juggernauth.

Rest at Cabul, 1839, 1840, 1841.—The object of the expedition had thus been successfully accomplished. The Afghan capital cities had been easily taken, and Soojah had been crowned. But the question now arose as to the destiny of the British armies. It was a point of great difficulty; for to retire would be to bring the Afghans in force against Soojah, and thus to undo all that had been done, whilst it had never been contemplated to effect a permanent occupation of the country. It was, therefore, determined that for the present at least a large British force should remain at Cabul; and accordingly for two years the English and Sikhs rested tranquilly at the capital city, congratulating themselves on their victory, and awaiting their orders to return home. They little thought of the terrible fate in store for them. Indeed the security was considered to be so great that Sir William Macnaghten, the political agent, brought up his wife and daughter from Hindostan, with other ladies closely related to the officers in the army, in order that they might enjoy with their husbands and relatives the pleasant fresh climate of Afghanistan.

The Bombay force retired southwards to Sinde, taking Khelat on October 15th, and demolishing the town. They put Mehrab Khan to death, and ravaged the country in return for that chief's treachery in violating the treaty made with him.

1840.—Early in 1840 Shah Soojah requested that the immensely strong Bala Hissar at Cabul should be given up to him for the reception of his harem, and that the troops should be removed into cantonments. Yielding to a false sense of security, Sir William Macnaghten and Sir Willoughby Cotton consented to this step, though it converted the strongest fort in the country into a Zenana.

And now commenced at the capital a series of revolts, totally unexpected, against the sovereignty of Shah Soojah, damaging the British position, and causing considerable loss of life. These disturbances lasted throughout the year, and caused some anxiety; but the hopes of the English were raised to a high pitch by the submission of their chief enemy in November.

Surrender of Dost Mahomed, 1840.—Dost Mahomed had fled into Bokhara, where he was but ill received, and, leaving that country, he advanced again towards his own dominions. He was joined by large numbers of Uzbeks and Afghans, but the army was defeated by Brigadier Dennie, and put to flight. In November, 1840, he reappeared, close to the capital, followed only by a small body of horsemen, and of his own free will submitted to the English. Sir William Macnaghten promised him every kindness, and, being sent to Calcutta, the Dost was received with the greatest distinction, and treated as his bravery and chivalric character demanded.

State of the Country, 1841.—During the remainder of the year, and during the spring and summer of 1841, it was found necessary to resort to very stringent measures in order to quell the hostile attitude of the whole population of Afghanistan. At Candahar serious insurrections took place, which were put down with a high hand; and the people of Herat openly declared against the British. All this augured ill for the future. Throughout the country the people were roused to indignation against the usurping foreigners, and many officers of distinction amongst the English foretold terrible disasters.

In October, 1841, a most serious revolt took place amongst the Khilji tribes of the great Khyber Pass, which caused much loss of life amongst the troops returning to Hindostan through that defile. It was with difficulty suppressed.

Murder of Burnes, 1841.—But a far more terrible affair drew the attention of all parties to Cabul itself. In that city a secret conspiracy was organized, and, on November 2nd, the house of Sir Alexander Burnes was attacked by a crowd of insurgents, and he himself was foully murdered, with many other officers, before any aid could arrive. Several regiments were sent to quell the insurrection, but by some mistake they were blocked in the narrow streets of the city, and for several days the frantic mob were left to work their will unopposed. A fort used for commissariat stores was attacked, and General Elphinstone (the commander-in-chief in Afghanistan in the place of Sir Willoughby Cotton), afforded so ineffective a support to the efforts of the little garrison that the officer in charge was compelled to evacuate the place.

Sir William Macnaghten then sent urgent messages to General Sale, who was at that time near the Khyber Pass, and to General Nott at Candahar, to come at once to the relief of the garrison at Cabul. But the snow lay thick on the ground, and any communication was rendered hopeless.

Thus were the head-quarters of the expedition blocked up at Cabul for the winter months amidst a population thirsting for revenge, and encouraged by their late success. The troops were in two divisions, one at the Bala Hissar, under the able Brigadier Shelton; another in cantonments, under the commander-in-chief, General Elphinstone. Sir William Macnaghten summoned Shelton into cantonments, hoping thus to get some firm and definite policy carried out; but the two military commanders failed to agree on the main points, and nothing was done.

Disasters.—In November the Afghans commenced a regular attack, and seized some hills near. Ineffectual attempts were made to dislodge them, and on the 23rd a general action was fought, in which the English, overpowered by the crowd of Afghans who streamed out of the city, were completely beaten, and returned in despair to cantonments. The General determined on a complete abandonment of Afghanistan, and a retreat to the frontier. But Sir William Macnaghten insisted first on an attempt at negociation. It utterly failed; and when a few days later Akber Khan, the fiery and unscrupulous son of Dost Mahomed arrived, further resistance was felt to be hopeless. On December 11th the provisions gave out, and as, with one voice, the inhabitants of the country round refused to provide them, Macnaghten was compelled to consent to a Treaty with the insurgents.

Treaty of December, 1841, at Cabul.—The terms were, that the whole of the British and Sikh troops should quit the country; that Dost Mahomed should be released, and Shah Soojah permitted to reside crownless, either in Afghanistan or India, as he pleased, unmolested, while the Afghans guaranteed to assist the safe retreat of the British army by all means in their power,—by money, protection, and provisions.

The Retreat.—In accordance with this Treaty, and relying on the faith of the Afghans, the 15,000 British troops commenced their miserable retreat to the frontier, while the enemy, so far from assisting them, according to the terms of the Treaty, took every opportunity of despoiling the soldiers, and seizing their stores.

Murder of Macnaghten, December 23rd, 1841.—But before the troops had started from the city they were destined to hear of a last tragedy, which should still more serve to crush their hopes, by depriving them of the great leader whom they so implicitly trusted and so deeply reverenced. The treacherous and bloodthirsty Akber Khan sent in a draught of a fresh Treaty to Sir William Hay Macnaghten, and requested a private audience. The request was granted; and to all the remonstrances of his companions Sir William replied, that he would dare anything, if by doing so he could secure better terms for the army. He met Akber by appointment in a retired spot—met him confidingly and openly. The prince gave a sign, and the envoy's escort was surrounded. Akber advanced to Sir William, stood in front of him an instant, and then seized him by the right hand. Macnaghten tried to step back a pace, but Akber's grasp was firm, and the Englishman unarmed; and, coolly drawing a pistol from beneath his shirt, the black-hearted prince deliberately shot his noble enemy through the heart.

1842.—Major Pottinger at once stepped into Macnaghten's place, and in vain tried to urge some decided course on the despairing generals. He made a final Treaty securing a safe retreat for his army, and then abandoned Cabul. But Akber Khan had sworn the annihilation of the British, and in spite of all Treaties he kept his vow.

The Massacre.—Almost before the troops had cleared the cantonments the enemy were upon them back and front. The snow was thick on the ground, and the cold intense; so that the sufferings of the soldiers were terrible. After three days' march the head of the column entered a pass in the mountains; and Akber Khan, appearing with a troop of horse, demanded the surrender of all the ladies and children (including Lady Macnaghten and Lady Sale), with several officers, as hostages for the safe retreat of the force. These were all given up, and thus saved from the horrible deaths that awaited their compatriots. For in the defiles the natives poured a rain of bullets from the heights above, and hundreds fell before the end of the pass was cleared, where only five or six hundred half-starved and wounded men remained to continue their retreat. But still the fury of the Afghans was unappeased. They slaughtered the soldiers like sheep during their straggling march to the frontier; and on the

13th of January the sentries on the walls of Jellalabad descried a solitary traveller, in a tattered English uniform, mounted on a miserable pony—horse and man being desperately wounded—forcing his way through the snow to the city gates. This was Dr. Brydon, the sole survivor of the army of fifteen thousand British troops who started from Cabul three weeks before. He was dying of starvation!

It may be easily imagined what were the feelings of the Governor-General at this terrible disaster; the most fearful reverse that had ever befallen the English arms in the East. Lord Auckland was almost prostrated by the difficulty of the position, and the shame and reproach which he felt sure awaited him in England. He, however, determined to do his best for the remaining few months of his administration; and at once ordered the advance of a fresh brigade for the purpose of relieving the brigade of General Sale, which was in Jellalabad, harassed by the Afghans.

Lord Ellenborough succeeded Lord Auckland early in the year.

(V).—*Lord Ellenborough's Administration*, 1842—1844. *Close of the Afghan War. Wars in Sinde and Gwalior.*

Lord Ellenborough came out pledged to a peace policy; but during the two years he was in office the sword was never sheathed.

The first news that greeted him on his landing was that the brigade under General Wild, which Lord Auckland had sent to the relief of Jellalabad, had been disastrously beaten in the Khyber Pass; and that the Sikh army were refusing to co-operate any longer with the English, even threatening their own commanding officers if they ordered an advance. The Sepoys, too, in Wild's brigade, were in a state of panic.

Shere Singh at Lahore.—Meanwhile the crown of the Punjaub had fallen into the hands of Shere Singh, one of the sons of "*The Lion of Lahore.*" On the death of the latter in 1839, Kurruk Singh, his eldest son, had succeeded to the throne. He made one Cheyt Singh his vizier; but this appointment was very distasteful to the ex-minister Dian Singh, who accordingly murdered Cheyt Singh, and deposed Kurruk, declaring in favour of Nao Nehal, his son. In 1840 Kurruk Singh died in prison, and Nao Nehal was accidentally killed. Dian therefore sent for Shere Singh, a brave and energetic prince, in character much like his father, and placed him on the throne. Shere Singh seemed disposed to give all the aid in his power to the English Government, and expressed great regret at the refusal of his troops to enter the Khyber Pass with General Wild.

"The Army of Retribution," 1842.—A fresh brigade under General Pollock was at once sent to the assistance of General Wild, with directions that the united forces should penetrate the Khyber, and joining Sale at Jellalabad, there await orders

Advance of Pollock's Brigade.—On April 5th, 1842, General Pollock ordered two columns to scale the heights on each side of the Pass, and clear the way for the advance of the main body. This was accordingly done; and the Khyberees, defeated on their own ground, fled towards the Afghan end of the defile. The army marched through the pass unopposed, and reached Jellalabad in ten days, where they learned that Akber Khan had in person laid siege to the city, but had been beaten off in a gallant sortie of the garrison, and had retired none knew whither.

Meanwhile General Nott, at Candahar, had, in January, ably concentrated his small force, and defeated the Afghans on more than one occasion. He had been afterwards besieged in the city and had defended the position with great ability. But Ghazni was surrendered to the enemy; and General England, commanding a convoy from Quettah which was intended to join Nott's force, had been repulsed and forced to retreat.

Lord Ellenborough ordered General Pollock to remain at Jellalabad till October, when he was to retire from Afghanistan altogether; and orders were sent to General Nott to evacuate Candahar, and retire to the Indus after destroying the city. But this policy of retreat caused such a fury of indignation throughout India, that the Governor-General, in July, gave permission to the officers in Afghanistan to advance on Cabul and seize the capital again, for the purpose of retrieving national honour as far as possible, and punishing the Afghans for their treacherous conduct.

Death of Shah Soojah.—At Cabul, Akber Khan had installed himself Shah of Afghanistan; the unfortunate Shah Soojah having, as might have been expected, been barbarously murdered immediately on the retirement of the English. Akber Khan's first act was to take under his authority the English ladies, officers, and other prisoners, and send them to a fort at Tegeen. Here General Elphinstone died. The captives were treated with great consideration, and the captivity was made as light as possible for them by their guardians.

Second Seizure of Cabul.—In August, the two armies of

Candahar and Jellalabad marched in opposite directions on the capital. The force under Pollock gave the Khiljies some decisive beatings; and in September the two divisions joined at Tegeen, and advanced together. Akber Khan was defeated, and on the 15th of the month the capital was again in the hands of the English.

On the route General Nott passed through Ghazni, and brought away from thence, by request of Lord Ellenborough, the sandal wood gates of Somnath, eight centuries old, which Mahmud of Ghazni had taken from the Temple in Sinde, in the year 1024. They had been placed at the entrance to his tomb, and were much venerated by the inhabitants.

The Prisoners recovered.—On the advance of General Pollock from Jellalabad, the English prisoners at Cabul had been sent to Bamian, in Hindu Cush, and left in charge of Sala Mohammed. That officer, on hearing of the defeat of Akber, entered into negotiations with Pottinger, and offered to release the whole party and accompany them to Cabul, on promise of protection and a large monetary recompense. This was readily granted; and on September 20th the prisoners found themselves restored to their loved fellow-countrymen, after their long and wearisome confinement. The joy at Cabul knew no bounds.

Return of the Army.—In October, after destroying most of the fortifications at the capital, the whole British force started for the frontier. Without experiencing any further opposition, they marched steadily through the Khyber Pass into the Peshawur territories; entered once more the English territory, and were nobly entertained by the Sikh Commander-in-Chief at Ferozepore.

Lord Ellenborough was now able to report the conclusion of the war; and in the despatch which he sent to England, he strongly urged that England should for the future, remain content with the territories east of the river Indus.

War in Sinde, 1843.—The attitude of the Ameers of Sinde had, during the whole of the Afghan War been so hostile to the English, that it was determined to punish them; and at the close of the same year (1842) that witnessed the termination of the war, Sir Charles Napier took command of an army, formed partly of the regiments from Candahar, and partly of fresh troops purposely brought from Bengal and Bombay. The depot was at Sukkur, on the Indus, and after a few ineffectual attempts at negotiation, by Colonel Outram, the political agent at Hydrabad, matters were brought to a climax by a desperate attack of Beloochee cavalry on the residence of the Colonel. With difficulty escaping, Colonel Outram joined the camp of Sir Charles Napier, who had steadily advanced, and was then at Halla, about sixty miles north of Hydrabad.

Battle of Meeanee, Feb. 17, 1843.—On February 17th the Ameers took up a position at Meeanee, near Hydrabad, with 22,000 men, and awaited the approach of Sir Charles, who was marching on the capital with about 3,000 troops. The battle that ensued was of a very deadly nature. The Beloochees fought with desperate energy, and for nearly three hours a hand-to-hand combat was maintained along the banks of the river. A gallant charge of British cavalry on the enemy's flank decided the day; and being followed up by a steady advance of the infantry with fixed bayonets, the enemy gave way and fled in disorder, six of the Ameers surrendering themselves prisoners Hydrabad was immediately occupied and plundered, and the English garrisoned the city.

In March, the garrison was reinforced by some regiments of the native army from Bengal; and the troops under Sir Charles Napier then amounted to somewhat over 6,000 men. On the 24th of the month, another action, took place near the capital, against Shere Mahomed, Ameer of Meerpore. The English troops were again victorious; Meerpore being at once seized and sacked.

A strong fort in the desert named Omerkote was next taken, the garrison evacuating the town without striking a blow; and the subjugation of Sinde was completed in June, on the defeat of Shere Mahomed by Colonel Jacob of the Sinde horse.

Sinde has since this time been a British province; useful as regards the preservation of peace on the frontier, but financially unprofitable, as it costs the government a considerable sum annually to retain it.

Gwalior, 1843.—The attention of Lord Ellenborough had at this time been considerably drawn towards the Mahratta state of Gwalior, the possession of the Maharajah, Sindia; and by the month of December, the English troops were in the district fighting with their ancient enemies. The breach of amity arose in the following manner:—

Dowlat Rao Sindia, who in 1817 made a favourable treaty with Lord Hastings, died ten years later without issue; and was succeeded by one of the family, the only heir that could be found, named Mugat Rao, who ascended the musnud under the title of "Ali Jah Jankaji Sindia." He died childless in 1843, his widow being a young girl of only thirteen years of age, named Tara Bye.

The Maharanee at once adopted a successor, a child of eight years of age, named Bhagerat Rao, who was proclaimed under the title of "Ali Jah Jyaji Sindia." The question of a regency was then considered.

The two claimants were a maternal uncle of Jankaji Sindia, usually called the "*Mama Sahib;*"[1] and the steward of the household, Wala, who was a distant relation of the deceased Maharajah, and was known as the *Dada Khasji.*[2] The Mama Sahib was appointed by Lord Ellenborough, through the Resident; though much against the wish of Tara Bye, who favoured the pretensions of the Dada.

The consequence of this was that two parties were formed at Court; and, after great confusion and some bloodshed, the Dada was appointed Regent by the Maharanee, and the Mama dismissed. But Lord Ellenborough at once wrote, to inform the Maharanee that this could not be permitted by the English Government, since they had for good reasons preferred to appoint the Mama. He directed the Resident to leave Gwalior; and the Dada, hot-headed and rash, prepared his troops to oppose the armies of the Company.

War in Gwalior, 1843.—Lord Ellenborough ordered Sir Hugh Gough to take command of the Gwalior expedition, and at once to cross the Chambul river into the territories of Sindia. No sooner had this been done than the Ranee and the Dada proffered their submission. But their army, consisting of 60,000 men, with 200 guns, who had been for a long time in a state of semi-mutiny, refused to countenance this weakness, and marched out to drive the English back across the Chambul.

Battle of Maharajpore, Dec. 1843.—On the morning of December 29th Sir Hugh Gough, with Lady Gough, the Governor-General, and other non-combatants, was riding forward to the village of Maharajapore, having no idea that the Mahratta army had even taken the field, when on a sudden the line of march was

[1] "*Mama,*" "maternal uncle." "*Sahib,*" "Lord."

[2] "*Dada*" means either a "paternal grandfather" or an "elder brother." But it is believed that this "Dada" did not stand in either of these relationships to the deceased Maharajah. "*Khasji*" is "steward of the household."—(Thornton's "Gazetteer," head "Gwalior," note.)

attacked by 14,000 picked soldiers of the enemy, with many batteries of admirably-served artillery. A terrible fight ensued; the Mahrattas fought with the utmost gallantry; and in the ranks of the English army all was confusion. Sir Hugh having no guns at command, was forced to hurl his regiments against the enemies' batteries, whence the artillerymen were driven at the point of the bayonet. The loss was very large, but the enemy were at last defeated, and put to flight.

Two days afterwards the Maharanee and the young Sindia came into camp, and humbly submitted. The State of Gwalior was retained to Sindia, but the Ranee was pensioned off; the Mahratta army was reduced to 6000 men, and the British subsidized force increased to 10,000 men.

Sindia was to succeed to the throne on the attainment of his majority; and meanwhile a council was appointed to manage the affairs of the kingdom.

Soon after this Lord Ellenborough was recalled by the Court of Directors, who professed annoyance at his warlike progress. They urged that his lordship had never allowed the Company a moment's peace since he landed at Calcutta; and they accordingly revoked his appointment. Sir Henry Hardinge was sent out to supersede him.

(VI.)—*Lord Hardinge's Administration*, 1844—1848. *First Sikh War.*

Sir Henry Hardinge arrived in June 1844, and at once proceeded to take energetic steps to arrest the ambitious projects of the Sikhs in the Punjaub, who were now meditating a concentrated attack on English territory.

Politics in the Punjaub, 1844.—It will be remembered that the sovereignty of the Punjaub was in 1842 vested in Shere Singh, one of the numerous sons of Runjeet Singh, and that Dian Singh was appointed his vizier. In the course of the same year Shere Singh contrived to quarrel with his Minister on the ground of his policy towards the Company (for Dian was a most cordial opponent of everything British); and the treacherous vizier conspired against the life of his master. The crime was successfully accomplished, Shere Singh being shot through the head after a review, by one Ajeet Singh. But the accomplice proceeded to further crimes than the Minister had intended; for when the two conspirators met, Ajeet stabbed Dian himself to the heart, and concluded the day's work by slaughtering the Maharajah's eldest son, Prince Pretab Singh. The murderers were punished next day by the brothers of the dead vizier, Soochat and Heera Singh, who surrounded the city with troops, and, seizing the rebels, put them one and all to death.

Heera Singh then proclaimed Dhuleep Singh, the only remaining son of Shere Singh, Maharajah, making himself vizier.

Thus commenced the reign of the last Maharajah of Lahore. He was a boy of ten years old, and gifted with great talents.

The most difficult question with Heera Singh was how to deal with the Sikh or "Khalsa" army, for the troops were so numerous, so fiery, and so independent, that in reality they formed the dominant power in the State. Heera tried in vain to curtail their number, or curb their power; and in so doing excited the indignation of all the officers, who soon raised a conspiracy, and, following the prevailing fashion of the day, murdered Heera in cold blood.

Lall Singh, a Brahmin, and a favourite of the Ranee, obtained the office of vizier by her favour, and attempted to pacify the troops by sending them on an expedition against Gholab Singh, the Rajput Rajah of Jummoo, a district lying between Lahore and Cashmir; but the soldiers mutinied for pay and marched to Lahore. Some considerable advances were made to them, and they were then sent against Moolraj, Dewan of Mooltan, who submitted, and paid tribute.

Soon it was found that nothing could restrain the ardour of the troops but an expedition into English territory; and in the spring of 1845 hostile preparations at Lahore were of so marked a character, that Sir Henry Hardinge quietly concentrated a force of nearly 50,000 men on the east bank of the Sutlej. The Lahore Government perceiving a collision to be inevitable, determined to make the expedition, if possible, a successful one, and used all their influence to excite the soldiers.

1st Sikh War, 1845, 1846.—At the end of November 60,000 well-trained and fiery Sikhs crossed the Sutlej, and encamped on English territory near Ferozepore.

Battle of Moodkee, Dec. 18th, 1845.—The Governor-General and Sir Hugh Gough, who were at Amballah, at once marched to oppose them; and in the afternoon of the 18th of December the armies met at Moodkee, a village about twenty miles from Ferozepore. The Sepoy troops were far inferior to those of the Khalsa army, and several regiments gave way; but the European soldiers and the cavalry retrieved the disgrace of this retreat, and Lall Singh fled from the field at nightfall, followed by the whole army. Darkness stopped the pursuit.

Battle of Ferozeshur, Dec. 21*st*, 1845.—A second serious battle took place three days later at Ferozeshur, whither the English had marched after the victory of Moodkee. The Sikhs were assembled in great force to protect their camp; and their strong position was defended by heavy siege guns. Sir Hugh Gough divided his army into three parts, himself commanding the right wing, the Governor-General being in the centre, and Sir John Littler on the left. The battle commenced in the afternoon, and was one of the most disastrous on record. Sir John Littler advanced first, and, according to orders, charged the batteries, in order to carry them at the point of the bayonet. Sir Hugh Gough seemed to forget, that in dealing with the Sikhs he had an opponent differing greatly from the easily frightened Hindus of the south: and his cold-steel strategy invariably resulted in terrible loss of life. On this occasion the European troops were compelled to retire, overwhelmed with the tremendous fire poured in upon them by the enemy. Sir Harry Smith, who was on the right with the Commander-in-chief, led his division gallantly into the enemy's camp, and occupied the village; but was driven out, and forced to retire. The centre also attacked most bravely, but were repulsed with terrible loss of life. The most extraordinary display of valour was exhibited by the 3rd Dragoons, who charged a battery (crossing the ditch over a bridge formed of the bodies of their companions and horses, shot down from the ramparts), spiked the guns, and then dashed into the Khalsa camp, which they traversed from end to end. Night fell on a scene of horror; and next day the Governor-General, wisely disregarding the policy of retreat suggested by many officers, renewed the attack. The Sikhs were disheartened by their heavy losses, and were plainly unprepared for such an unusual event as a renewal of a battle on the morning after a defeat.[1] The opposition was therefore slight; and without much difficulty the enemy's position was carried, and the camp destroyed. An hour after sunrise found the Sikhs in full retreat, and the English victoriously resting on their arms; for they were too exhausted for pursuit.

[1] Amongst most oriental nations a defeat means a panic and general flight.

The loss on the side of the English was very great, and numbers of officers celebrated for their bravery, and distinguished by their previous exploits, were buried side by side on the field of Ferozeshur.

Battle of Aliwal, January 28th, 1846.—It was determined at once to crush the Sikhs by attacking Lahore, but some delay was occasioned by the necessity for providing heavy guns, which had to be brought up from a considerable distance. Lord Gough ordered up several batteries from Delhi, which were reported to be on the route in the middle of December. An attack on the convoy was expected, and Sir Harry Smith, in order to prevent this disaster, was directed to attack the enemy, who were encamped at Aliwal, a small village near Loodianah. He was completely successful, and, after a stubborn resistance, drove the Sikhs into the river.

Battle of Sobraon, February 10th, 1846.—The victory of Aliwal prevented any attack on the convoy from Delhi, which arrived safely at the camp a few days later. Meanwhile the Sikhs had raised some very strong fortifications, which they garrisoned with nearly 40,000 men, and prepared to defend to the last gasp. On the morning of February 10th the English army marched out to attack this position, and another victory was won with great loss of life. The battle commenced with heavy artillery fire on both sides, and about nine o'clock the infantry advanced, under Brigadier Stacey, supported by field batteries of the royal artillery. One after another the lines were carried; and by tens and twenties the gallant troops fell under the murderous fire of the Sikhs. But they pushed on steadily, and the interior of the intrenchments was the scene of terrible carnage. For nearly an hour a hand-to-hand fight was carried on at every point, and the deafening roar of the guns, mingled with explosions of the enemy's magazines, and the incessant musketry fire, proclaimed this one of the hottest actions in which the English troops had ever been engaged. Still the Sikhs would not give in. They devoted themselves to death, and a small body who attempted to cross the river were decimated by the well-directed fire of the English horse-artillery on the bank. By-and-bye the fire slackened from the Khalsa army, and their defeat was completed by several cavalry charges upon the exhausted masses of their troops who were gathered on the river-bank preparing to cross, By eleven o'clock the battle was over, and the power of Runjeet Singh irretrievably broken. Never was an army so completely shattered.

Occupation of the Punjaub.—The Governor-General issued a despatch immediately, declaring it to be his intention to occupy the Punjaub, and not to leave it till full satisfaction had been taken for the outrage on the English; and a strong government capable of restraining the Khalsa troops, and well-disposed to the Company had been established. Accordingly the army crossed the Sutlej, and, without opposition, occupied the strong fort of Kussoor. Here the young Rajah, and a body of influential chiefs, headed by Gholab Singh, waited on Sir Henry Hardinge to hear the terms on which their submission would be accepted.

The demands were: that the country between the rivers Beeas and Sutlej should be ceded to the Company; that a million and a-half sterling should be paid as indemnity; and that Lahore should be for the present garrisoned by English troops. These terms were agreed to, and on February 20th the army entered the capital in triumph.

It was then found that the Sikh Treasury was unable to pay the sum required as indemnity, and Sir Henry proclaimed Cashmir annexed to cover the expenses. But Gholab Singh offered himself to purchase Cashmir of the Company for a million, and the offer was accepted. By this means the Governor-General paid the expenses of the war, and established in the province a firm government, well-disposed to England.[1]

Sir Henry Hardinge then caused the troops of the Khalsa army to be paid off and disbanded, and retired to Calcutta, after having recognised the independence of Dhuleep Singh, and held a grand parade at Lahore as a proof of the greatness of the Company's power.

Major Henry Lawrence was left at Lahore with an English garrison, by request of the chiefs, to settle the affairs of the Punjaub; and the main army, carrying with them the captured guns, retired into Loodianah.

The Governor-General and the Commander-in-Chief were both raised to the peerage for these services, and all persons engaged received the thanks of Parliament.

[1] Gholab Singh was a Rajput, and was known to be at heart a great hater of the power of Runjeet Singh. It was much to the interest of England to have the northern frontier of the Sikh kingdom occupied by a family hostile to the latter, and therefore on good terms with the English.

The remainder of Lord Hardinge's administration was undisturbed by war; and in the Punjaub Henry Lawrence was busily engaged in his vain attempt to quiet the country. The Governor-General resigned the seals into the hand of his successor, Lord Dalhousie, in January, 1848, and sailed for England in March.

(VII.)—*Lord Dalhousie's Administration*, 1848—1856. *Second Sikh War. Second Burmese War.*

Lord Hardinge retired from office with the conviction that his successor would have nothing to do but remain at Calcutta and attend to the home administration of India; but the result proved that he was considerably mistaken.

The Sikhs were not yet sufficiently crushed to be harmless; and in Multan events occurred which brought on another war, scarcely less disastrous than the previous one.

1848.—Multan was a dependency of Lahore, and was at this time governed by the celebrated Moolraj, who succeeded his father, Sawan, in 1844. In April, 1848, he was deposed from office by the Maharajah, Dhuleep Singh; and Sirdar Khan Singh was sent to assume the reins of government. Mr. Vaus Agnew, a civilian, and Lieutenant Anderson, accompanied the new Governor to Multan, and entered the fortress on April 19th. On the 20th Moolraj formally handed over the keys of the city, and the same evening both officers were attacked and wounded by the adherents of the ex-governor. They shut themselves into the fort for safety; but after three days the garrison opened the gates, and the Sikhs, rushing in, murdered both Anderson and Vaus Agnew.

At once Lord Dalhousie ordered up troops, and perceiving that the whole of the Punjaubees in Lahore and other cities were inflamed against the English, and ready to revolt at a moment's notice, he prepared to declare war a second time, should such a step be necessary.

Sir Herbert Edwards at Multan, 1848.—But before any large army was called into action a young officer, Lieutenant Edwards, had greatly distinguished himself at Multan, with a few raw levies. He was stationed near that city with a regiment of Sikhs, who began to desert when they heard of the rising amongst their brethren. Finding himself in danger, he sent to the Rajah of Bhawalpore for aid, which was willingly granted; and on May 20th, he joined Colonel Cortland at Dhera Ghazi Khan, on the Indus. Colonel Cortland's force of 4000 had been attacked on the 18th, by a body of cavalry, under the orders of Moolraj, whom they had thoroughly chastised. Since then they had been joined by two bodies of Beloochees: so that the two officers, with 7000 men under their command, determined to make a bold stroke, and attack Multan. They advanced with rapidity, and in high spirits, and after one or two slight skirmishes, and a serious engagement at Sudusain on July 1st, in which Moolraj was signally defeated, and driven to shut himself up in Multan, they found themselves investing his fortress. Edwards sent at once to the frontier for European troops and siege-guns, and prepared to hold the position till the reinforcements arrived.

In the meantime Shere Singh came from Lahore with a large body of troops, ostensibly for the purpose of aiding the British, but in reality with the intention of hindering them by all means in his power. Day after day this contingent grew more and more mutinous, and Edwards was greatly alarmed at the prospect before him; but though he remained before Multan for two months there was no open attack, and in September he was joined by a large force of Europeans, under General Whish. The garrison were summoned to surrender, but refused, and the same day Shere Singh went over to the enemy.

2nd Sikh War, 1848.—The whole of the Punjaub was now in a state of revolt. The intrigues of the Maharanee, and the determined rebellions of several minor chieftains, had inflamed the excitable soldiers of the Khalsa to so great an extent that the Governor-General perceived there was no course left open to him, but to assemble a large army, and invade the Punjaub a second time. The Lahore Cabinet at the same time made preparations for war, and secured the alliance of Dost Mahomed, the chief of the Afghans, by promising him the gift of Peshawur.

The army was ordered to assemble at Ferozepore; and in October Lord Dalhousie joined them at that place, and at once prepared to cross the Sutlej.

Sir George Lawrence, brother to Sir Henry, was Resident at Peshawur at this period, and for a considerable time contrived with great tact to stave off a rising; but the endeavours of the Sikh chieftains were indefatigable, and on October 24th the Residency was attacked, and taken, and the English were kept close prisoners.

Lord Gough crossed the Sutlej at the end of October, and joined General Wheler at Jallemder, experiencing no opposition in the country between the rivers Sutlej and Beeas. The Sikhs were massed in the Dooab, between the Ravee and Chenaub rivers, and there it was determined to attack them. On the morning of November 22nd the main army of the English found themselves at Ramnuggur, with a large force of the enemy under Shere Singh, drawn up on both sides of the river to oppose him.

Battle of Ramnuggur—Lord Gough without hesitation attacked and drove back the Sikh infantry. But several batteries from the other side of the river effecting great havoc amongst his troops, he ordered them to retire. This movement drew over a large mass of the enemy from the opposite bank; and they were charged by the 14th Dragoons and 5th Native Cavalry with success. But Colonel Havelock and Brigadier Cureton unfortunately went too far into the bed of the river, which was at this time lying deep with fine white sand. Their horses sunk in this soil, and the cavalry, being surrounded by innumerable masses of the enemy, were cut to pieces while in this helpless condition; Havelock and Cureton both paying for their rashness with their lives. The enemy then retired across the river.

Lord Gough wisely determined not to hazard his fine army by attempting to cross the river in the face of the Sikh batteries, and marched north, to effect a passage at a more favourable spot. This was successfully accomplished on December 2nd. The army then moved down to attack the enemy's left flank. Sir Joseph Thackwell, in command of the advanced column, was attacked at the village of Sadulapore by the whole force of the enemy, who had unexpectedly marched to meet him. He suffered severe losses, but nobly maintained his ground till nightfall, when Shere Singh retreated with his force towards the Jhelum River.

There the Sikh army entrenched themselves strongly, while for six weeks the English remained inactive.

Battle of Chillianwalla, January 14th, 1849.—On January 12th, Lord Gough advanced towards the village of Chillianwalla, where the Sikhs were known to be in great force; and on the morning of the 14th he perceived from a slight eminence that they were strongly massed in the middle of a dense jungle in the plain. He gave the order for a general attack, against the wishes of many of his officers, who perceived the danger of the situation. The action did not commence till the afternoon, for the line of march had to be formed into a line of battle. Cannonading continued during the day, and at three o'clock, with only two or three hours' daylight before them, the British troops rushed bravely into action. The 24th Europeans, who belonged to the 2nd Division, advanced too rapidly through the thick jungle, and suddenly found themselves face to face with a large body of the enemy, unsupported. A murderous fire was opened upon them, and the regiment was cut to pieces. The Brigadier, the Colonel of the 24th, twenty-three officers, and nearly five hundred men, were killed or wounded, and the regiment was driven back with the loss of their colours. The reserve was ordered up to retrieve the loss, but missed their way in the jungle; and it was left to General Campbell's brigade to save the infantry of the 2nd Division from annihilation, They then beat back the enemy, and put them to flight. The 1st Division was successful at all points. But the cavalry, who, considering the nature of the ground, ought (according to the opinion of many high authorities) never to have been brought into action at all, were left in the jungle, exposed to a heavy fire of artillery, and unable to operate. They were attacked by bodies of desperate Sikhs, and the 14th Dragoons, with two native cavalry regiments, turned their backs, and fled in haste from the field. The enemy captured several guns; but were ultimately driven back by a gallant charge of the 5th Native Cavalry. Night now put an end to this disastrous conflict, and, with a loss of 2300 men, the English army lay down to rest at Chillianwalla, thoroughly worn out and completely dispirited. (Three regiments had lost their colours). The enemy retired, and took up a fresh position.

Capture of Multan, January 22nd, 1849.—Meanwhile the operations against Multan had been crowned with success. A Bombay contingent had joined General Whish and Lieutenant Edwards in November, and for a whole month the siege was pushed on with vigour. Several sorties were ably repulsed, and the fire of the besiegers is described as terrific. Moolraj defended himself with the most obstinate bravery. On the 30th of December a magazine containing 400,000 pounds of gunpowder was blown up, and at last the fire of the English became insupportable. Moolraj therefore submitted (January 22), and was allowed to march out. The army of the English, thus set free, advanced to join Lord Gough, whilst Edwards remained at Multan with a British garrison.

The capture of Multan was announced to Lord Gough's army on January 26th, and a few days later Shere Singh offered to treat. But the Governor-General refused to consent.

Shere Singh's Flank March.—This was followed by a very clever flank march on the part of the Sikhs. Shere Singh left his camp on February 12th, and succeeded in completely turning the flank of the English before he was discovered. His object was to rush down on Lahore while the whole British army was in the north. Lord Gough at once started after him, and overtook him at the village of Goojrat, near the Chenaub, where General Whish joined the Commander-in-Chief, having effected a rapid march with the contingent from Multan.

Battle of Goojrat, February 20th, 1849—The British army, 24,000 strong, marched, in battle order, straight on the enemy's encampment on the morning of February 20th. Elaborate precautions had been taken to bring the fight to a successful issue; and the engineers, under the command of Brigadier Cheape, had been indefatigable in making preparations; while Lord Gough, following the earnest advice of his officers, determined, on this occasion, to allow his artillery to break the ranks of the Sikhs, before he ordered a charge of infantry to capture the enemy's guns. The Sikh batteries opened upon the English troops while they were yet far off. The infantry were halted, and the field-batteries ordered to the front at a gallop, so that a terrible artillery fire ensued between the opposing lines. This continued for more than two hours, at the end of which the Sikhs slackened their fire, overcome by the storm that poured in upon them; and Lord Gough ordered a general advance. Two villages were assailed, and carried, though desperately defended by the Sikhs; and then the whole line of the enemy fell back. Some terrible charges of cavalry completed their discomfiture. The Siks fled panic-stricken, and a comparatively bloodless battle placed the Punjaub at the feet of the English.

Shere Singh and his generals gave themselves up to despair, and on March 12th submitted, with 16,000 of the finest men in the Khalsa army, to General Sir Walter Gilbert, who had been sent in pursuit. The conduct of the Sikhs was as fine in defeat as in battle. They proved themselves real soldiers, chivalric, and high-spirited; and, on this occasion, behaved with characteristic dignity, tears rolling down their cheeks as they threw their arms on the pile formed of the swords, shields, and match-locks of their comrades.

Annexation of the Punjaub.—Lahore was immediately occupied, and the decision of the Governor-General was soon known. It was a severe sentence. The kingdom of Runjeet Singh was declared to be at an end; the Punjaub was to be annexed to England; the young Maharajah Dhuleep Singh was to place himself under British protection; and the army of the Khalsa was to be disbanded. The "Koh-i-noor" diamond was at the same time delivered up to deck the crown of the Queen of England.[1] The private landed possessions of the leaders of the Sikhs were declared confiscated and their owners were told to consider themselves prisoners within a radius of four miles from their respective places of residence. Moolraj was tried by court-martial for his rebellion, and the murder of the English officers at Multan, and sentenced to imprisonment for life.

Its Settlement.—The troops then left the Punjaub; a commission, headed by Sir Henry Lawrence, being appointed to settle the new province, with the assistance of Sir Henry's brother, Sir John Lawrence (afterwards Governor-General), Mr. Mansell, and Mr. (now Sir Robert) Montgomery. They performed their duties with the most exemplary zeal, and the success they achieved testified to the wisdom of their appointment. The Khalsa soldiers were first disarmed, and then formed into regiments of police for the maintenance of order. A small irregular Sikh army was organized at the same time, and officered by Europeans on the Sepoy principle. Roads were made, schools established, and rural pursuits

[1] The history of the "Koh-i-noor" is very romantic. It originally decorated the crown of the King of Malwa, the celebrated Rajah Bhoja, who reigned in the year 1070. In 1231 the Mahomedans, under Shams-u-din Altamsh, King of Delhi, conquered Malwa, and Altamsh transferred the glittering gem to his own turban. With the kings of Delhi it remained till, in 1526, the Mogul, Baber, established there the great empire, which lasted two hundred years, and was extinguished by the battle of Panipat, in 1761. The jewel passed into the possession of Akber, Aurangzebe, and all their successors. In 1757 Ahmed Shah Durani conquered and sacked Delhi, carrying off the Koh-i-noor to Afghanistan, to glitter in the head-dress of the Shahs of Cabul. Shah Soojah thus came into possession of the diamond, and when he fled to Cashmere, in 1808, he took it with him. Submitting afterwards to Runjeet Singh, that monarch stripped the unfortunate exile of all he possessed, and, amongst other treasures, forced him to sell the Koh-i-noor. So now it formed one of the crown-jewels of the "Lion of Lahore," and, in 1849, was in the possession of his young son, the Maharajah, Dhuleep Singh. In that year the Punjaub was annexed to England, and the Koh-i-noor transferred to the possession of the Queen.

encouraged, till, in an incredibly short period, the wild and bloodthirsty followers of Runjeet Singh had become peaceable, hard-working, and contented villagers. The amount of good done by the wise and sound administration of the Lawrences and their fellow-workers can never be fully estimated; for it is only by comparing the kingdom of Lahore as it was, with the Punjaub as it is, that the change effected by them can be at all understood.

In May of the same year Sir Charles Napier arrived to supersede Lord Gough, and by a policy of retrenchment he contrived so to offend the Sepoys that several trivial mutinies broke out. Their excuse was the much-vexed "Batta" question; and, although the insubordinate spirit was soon quelled, the annoyance remained; and there can be little doubt that the gentle treatment the Sepoys received on these occasions tended to foster rather than allay the flame of discontent, which seven years later burst forth so furiously throughout India. The effect of this movement did not end here, for Sir Charles and the Governor-General openly disagreed, and a dispute ensued, which terminated in the resignation of Sir Charles's appointment.

Annexation of Sattara, 1848.—During the war in the Punjaub an event had occurred in the south which demanded the attention of Lord Dalhousie. The Rajah of Sattara, representative of the house of Sevaji, who had been placed on the throne by the free gift of Lord Hastings in 1818, died, leaving no son to succeed him; but on his death-bed, the day before he breathed his last, he adopted a son according to the Hindu custom, and declared him his heir. Lord Dalhousie, after perusing several able minutes, decided in favour of annexing the Raj, and in this view he was upheld by the Court of Directors. The Raj of Sattara was accordingly declared to be at an end, and the territory was absorbed in the Bombay Presidency. Thus was swept from the face of the earth the last vestige of the royalty of Sevaji.

The three years of peace which followed the war in the Punjaub were ably employed by Lord Dalhousie in quieting the feelings of the natives, settling disputes, and putting down outbreaks amongst the hill-tribes.

In these actions he was ably seconded by various officers; and Colonel Campbell amongst the Khonds, Sir Colin Campbell amongst the Afreedis of Kohat, Mr. Strange with the Moplahs of Colatoor, and Colonel Outram at Baroda, in Guzerat, sufficiently proved to the natives that the British Government was determined to resent opposition, to correct abuses, and to put down with a high hand the many barbarous customs which at that time held so great a sway in various parts of India. A general war was declared against dacoity, thuggee, infanticide, human sacrifices, suttee, and the like; and the attention of all servants of the Company was directed to the maintenance of a firm, sound, and benevolent administration of justice to the natives.

2nd Burmese War, 1852.—In 1852 the second Burmese war broke out. Ever since the Treaty of Yandabo, in 1826, the Burmans had been restlessly active in thwarting English trade by every means in their power; and, in 1851, they proceeded to a further act of more open outrage, by besieging the Residency at Ava. The Resident left the capital, and retired to Rangoon, where the Burmese governor of the province was actively engaged in fomenting disturbances. At last several English merchants at Rangoon were seized and exposed to public ridicule in the stocks, and the Resident remonstrating was treated with such indignity that he retired on board one of the men-of-war in the river, commanded by Commodore Lambert, who was in charge of the station. In the course of the next few days numerous outrages were committed, and Commodore Lambert warned all the merchants to leave the town, and embark on board the English shipping. He then proceeded down the river, with several merchant ships and two gun-boats. On the way the convoy was fired upon by one of the Burman forts, and the Commodore replied by bombarding, storming, and razing the fort to the ground. He then proceeded with his charge to Calcutta, and, after apologies and compensation had been demanded by the Company, and refused on the part of the Burmese, Lord Dalhousie declared war.

With the utmost celerity a fleet was collected and despatched to Rangoon to blockade the river, while troops were put in readiness for the expedition, in Calcutta and Madras. The commissariat and medical arrangements were carefully studied: and on April 2nd the transports arrived at the mouth of the Rangoon River.

The Campaign, 1852—Martaban was attacked and taken in an hour by a regiment from Bengal; and the commander-in-chief of the expedition then ordered an advance to Rangoon. The troops landed at that town on April 12th, and at once attacked the great Pagoda, which was resolutely defended. The heat of the weather was so great, and the fire of the enemy sustained so rapidly and with such effect, that the first day passed without any progress. On the next day the town was bombarded heavily, and the governor fled into the interior of the country in fear for his life. On the 14th, at daybreak, the Pagoda was again attacked, and gallantly taken after a fine defence and great loss of life on both sides. To the surprise of General Godwin the townspeople at once became most friendly—offered their services for all kinds of labour required to place the English troops in comfort on land—and overwhelmed the army with presents of provisions and stores. It was evident that the mass of the people,—Peguers,—were well-disposed to the Company, and anxious to secure their aid against the tyrannical rule of their conquerors, the Burmese. After resting a month at Rangoon, the port of Bassein in Burmah was seized by Commodore Lambert, and a fleet proceeded up the Irawaddy river as far as Prome, which was abandoned by the garrison, and occupied by the English on October 9th. A month later Major Hill, who had been besieged in Pegu, was relieved by a contingent sent for the purpose; and the campaign closed with the successful expedition under Sir John Cheape against the Burmese leader Myahtoon. Sir John started from Prome on February 18th, 1853, and moved down to Donabew, where his little army was attacked with cholera and dysentery, which considerably thinned its ranks. On March the 17th he again advanced, captured a strong breastwork which had been thrown up by the enemy, and then marched on through a country every inch of which had been rendered difficult for troops, till in the afternoon a pitched battle ensued, ending in the flight of the Burmese. Next day the fight was resumed. The enemy fought with great courage and determination, but were eventually worsted after a heavy loss on the part of the English. Myahtoon fled, and his band dispersed in all directions, nor did they again annoy the invading Europeans. Sir John marched his little army back to Donabew; and thus ended the second Burmese War.

Negotiations were opened at Prome; but the Burmese envoys threw every opposition in the way of a final settlement; and the British commissioners, Sir John Cheape, Commodore Lambert, and Captain Phayre, abruptly closed the conference, and dismissed the envoys to Ava.

Annexation of Pegu.—Lord Dalhousie had then to deal with the conquered country. He was strongly disinclined to a policy of annexation, but felt such to be on this occasion the only course left open to him, on account of the friendliness of the Peguers to England, and the hostility and treacherous nature of the ruling

Burmese. On December 20th, accordingly, a proclamation was issued declaring Pegu to be henceforth a portion of the British dominions; and it was hailed with delight by the inhabitants of that province.[1]

Annexation of Berar, 1853.—On December 11th, 1853, the Rajah of Nagpore, who had been raised to the throne by Lord Auckland in 1840, as successor to the perfidious Appa Sahib, died, leaving no issue, and without having adopted a son according to the Hindu custom. The territory of Berar was thus left entirely to the disposal of the Company; and Lord Dalhousie, after much deliberation, decided on annexing it to England. This was accordingly done, greatly to the benefit both of the natives and the Company; the Ranees and dependents of the ruling house being pensioned off.

Annexation of Jhansi, 1854.—In November, 1854, another province, though of much smaller dimensions, fell into the possession of the Company. The Rajah of Jhansi, in Bundelcund (originally a tributary of the Peshwa, but acknowledged independent Rajah in 1832), died, leaving an adopted son as successor to his honours; but Lord Dalhousie, acting on the recorded opinion of Sir Charles Metcalfe when Governor of Agra, decided to prevent any succession by adoption in this province; and therefore took the Raj entirely into the government of the English. Three years later the Ranee, who owing to her deposition had acquired an intense hatred for the English, became the most prominent leader in the Sepoy mutiny.

Annexation of the Carnatic, 1853.—At the same period the Governor-General was called upon by Lord Harris, Governor of Madras, to decide on the future policy to be adopted with regard to the Carnatic. In 1801 the Nabob of that province had consented to retire absolutely from government, on condition of receiving annually a guarantee income of one-fifth of the revenues of his country. This was acceded to; and when the Nabob died in 1819, his son was placed on the throne and reigned six years. On the decease of this prince his infant son was proclaimed Nabob, and held the rank till 1853, when he died childless, and his uncle, Azim Jah, claimed the title. Lord Harris, however, recommended that the title and dignity should be dropped, considering that it was pernicious to make the title

[1] This occupation has been fraught with blessings for the Peguers, and has materially increased the revenues of the English. Pegu is now one of the most peaceable and friendly districts of our Eastern Empire.

perpetual without the sovereignty, and that the present was a fitting opportunity for putting an end to such an empty mockery. Lord Dalhousie and the Court of Directors fully concurred. A liberal pension was given to Azim Jah, who was allowed to take precedence of all the other nobles in the Madras Presidency, and permitted to keep a guard of cavalry. (He has been lately gratified by having the title "Prince of Arcot" conferred upon him by the Queen, and he resides quietly in his palace at Madras, the Carnatic being ruled entirely by the servants of the English Government.)

Nana Sahib, 1854.—We now come to the first mention of Dundu Punt, otherwise known as the "*Nana Sahib.*" He was adopted son to the Peshwa Baji Rao; and in 1853, when that monarch died, having enjoyed a pension from the English of nearly £100,000 a-year, Dundu Punt claimed that he should succeed to this princely income. His request was refused, on the ground that the ex-Peshwa had held merely a life-interest in this annuity, and that it had never been contemplated that the rupees should be paid to any one after his death. The Nana was compelled to submit, but he revenged himself by fearful atrocities when the Sepoy mutiny broke out in 1857.

The Santhal Mutiny, 1855.—All these events were, however, merely political, and afforded little interest to the bulk of Europeans in India. It was not till the rainy season of 1855 that some excitement was aroused in Calcutta by the news of a lawless outbreak of the Santhals in the Rajmahal Hills in Bengal. The Santhals were a half savage tribe (wholly savage not many years since, but tamed and pacified by the exertions of the celebrated Cleveland), who had now broken out anew, infuriated by the false tales spread amongst them by their fakirs, and had burst over the plains committing depredations and massacres on all sides. They numbered many thousands, and had pushed as far as Raneegunj and Moorshedabad before they received a check. Troops were then sent against them; and by dint of constant guerilla warfare for seven months they were at last hemmed in, the ringleaders captured and executed, and the rest dispersed. Martial law was proclaimed in the disturbed districts; and, finally, by February, 1856, the country was at rest.

Mysore, 1856.—Early in the same year (1856) a humble request from the Rajah of Mysore was presented to the Governor-General. It was a submissive appeal, praying that Lord Dalhousie would permit the government of the country to be restored to the Rajah on promise of amendment of his evil ways and good-conduct for the future. Lord Dalhousie, after due deliberation, decided to refuse this petition, on the ground,—first, that the original tenure was merely personal; secondly that the subsidy had been endangered; thirdly that the Rajah had had opportunity of amendment previously to his deposition, but had neglected to change his mode of government, though solemnly warned of what the result would be if he persisted; and, finally, that there was no security that the country would be properly governed, except by being placed under the orders of the Governor-General in council.

Annexation of Oude, 1856.—Lord Dalhousie's last important act was the annexation of Oude. It was forced upon the Government by precisely the same system of mal-administration and oppression which had characterized the downfall of the states of Mysore and the Carnatic. The Nabob vizier or "king," as he was now called, had plundered and harassed the people on all sides; he had been frequently warned by the Resident, but had refrained from any attempt at amendment, and matters had grown to such a pass that a commission was now appointed to make a progress through the territories of Oude, and examine the actual condition of the country. This was accordingly accomplished, and the result was the exposure of a system of government so radically bad that the Governor-General felt the deposition of the king and the establishment of English supervision throughout the country to be the only course which offered the slightest benefits to the populace at large. The arrangement was accordingly made, and in 1856 the decision of Lord Dalhousie, fully supported by the Court of Directors, transferred the ownership of the territories of Oude from the king to the East India Company.

Lord Dalhousie's Farewell Minute.—Within a month from this date Lord Dalhousie had left his post in India to his successor, Lord Canning, recording in a most able farewell minute the principal acts of his administration. He is justly celebrated for the clearness, conciseness, and ability of his written opinions on various subjects, and this his last statement was no exception to the general rule. It gave a graphic sketch of the condition of India, stating that there was apparently every prospect of peace for some years to come. It reviewed his policy with regard to the native states, and rapidly glanced at the improvements effected in the establishment of canals, railways, and the electric telegraph. It showed that he had increased the revenues of the country by four millions, exclusive of the annexation of

Oude; that the tonnage of the ships which traded at Calcutta had nearly doubled; and that although there was a deficiency in the public accounts, it was due to the heavy expenditure granted for public works. It noticed, as a significant fact, that the Maharajah, Dhuleep Singh, of the Punjaub, had embraced Christianity, and that the Queen of England had stood sponsor by proxy at the baptism of the infant princess of the deposed house of Coorg. And thus summed up, with a pardonable pride, the incalculable benefits that the great Marquis had conferred upon India in all ways, diplomatic and social.

Lord Dalhousie lived only four years after his retirement, being at the period of his return to England, completely broken in health.

(VIII.)—*Lord Canning's Administration*, 1856—1858. *War with Persia. The Sepoy Mutiny.*

Lord Canning assumed his office on February 29th, 1856, and found India, as Lord Dalhousie had stated, in profound peace. He, therefore, set to work to advance administrative reforms and educational improvements, in which he effected much beneficial alteration.

The principal judicial change proposed by Lord Canning was the promulgation of a regular "Penal Code," which should be applicable alike to Hindus, Mahomedans, and Europeans in British India, and should be made so clear that all might know the punishment for crimes committed. This was not, however, completed till the year 1861.

Cholera.—In August, 1856, a terrible outbreak of cholera took place. The disease ravaged Central India, and is said to have caused fifteen thousand deaths in Agra alone.

Persian War, 1856.—Three months later war broke out with Persia. That nation had for years been in the habit of treating the representatives of England with growing contempt. In 1855 this conduct had become so marked that the British Commissioner at Teheran was compelled to leave the city. And at the commencement of the year 1856 the Persian Government had committed a wanton outrage, by the seizure of Herat from the Afghan Ezah Khan. Accordingly Lord Canning declared war on November 1st, and by the 13th several ships had sailed from Bombay to attack Muscat.

Capture of Bushair.—Early in December the troops landed

twelve miles south of Bushair, in the Persian Gulf, and an action ensued between the British and the enemy, who had marched down to prevent a landing. The Persians were protected by a strong fort, guarded by earthworks, and it was not until after heavy losses that the final embankments were at last carried. The army then marched on Bushair, and the fleet also advanced thither, and commenced bombarding the town. A breach was easily effected, and the infantry were preparing for a general rush, when the flag on the fort was lowered, and the town surrendered.

Treaty with Dost Mahomed, 1857.—Meanwhile negociations had been opened between Sir John Lawrence, who had succeeded his brother Henry as Chief Commissioner of the Punjaub, and Dost Mahomed the Ameer of Cabul. Early in 1857 a complete reconciliation was effected, and mutual promises of alliance and good-will were exchanged, which, to the honour of both parties, were rigidly kept.

Battle of Khooshab, 1857.—Sir James Outram joined the army at Bushair as Commander-in-Chief of the expedition on January 27th, and at the beginning of February led out a column to attack the Persian camp. On the 7th the Persians, about 8000 strong, offered battle near Khooshab. The engagement ended in their complete discomfiture; and on the 8th the column returned to their head-quarters.

Peace Proclaimed.—The capture of Mohamreh in April was followed by a Treaty of Peace, guaranteeing that Persian troops should be for ever withdrawn from Herat and Afghanistan, and that the English Commissioner should be treated with all distinction at Teheran. And thus ended the war.

Commencement of the great Mutiny, 1857.—Events of far greater importance were now about to take place in India. For many years the Sepoy army had been in a highly disorganized state. Constant mutinies had broken out, and had been suppressed with more or less difficulty. The men were bound together by strong ties of fellowship, and it was known that in the ranks of the native army there were no less than 40,000 soldiers from Oude, who thus added the ties of caste and nationality to the chain of routine by which they were bound together. The whole body of Sepoys were actuated, as it were, by one common pulse, and any action of their superiors that offended one regiment was felt as a grievance alike by all the rest. The officers were powerless, and the laxity of real discipline in the native regiments at the period is a well-known fact. The men went through their routine work steadily, but any change was looked upon by them with the greatest jealousy. Open acts of mutiny were frequent; and the downright refusal of the Bengal army to cross the sea for the attack of Rangoon, necessitating the substitution of Sikh regiments, was the last symptom of this spirit which displayed itself before the great mutiny of 1857. Such a condition of affairs was well calculated to excite fears in the minds of those placed at the head of the Government.

One of Lord Canning's earliest general orders was excessively distasteful to the Bengal army. The Sepoys of Madras and Bombay had been accustomed by regulation to enlist for general service all over the world; but those of Bengal had enlisted only for service in India. Lord Canning ordered that "general service enlistment" should become the rule in Bengal as well as in the south; and this innovation considerably fanned the flame of discontent. The "fakirs" went about spreading all kinds of false and malicious statements, to the effect that the English were attempting to abolish caste; and every order was construed by them into some part of a general scheme of tyranny.

The greased Cartridges.—At the beginning of 1857 the fakirs industriously circulated rumours that the cartridges lately issued had been greased with the fat of pigs and cows, expressly for the purpose of causing every Sepoy to break his caste. The sullen fury created by this false idea broke out into open acts of violence at Barrackpore and Raneegunj where the men of the 34th Native Infantry set their bungalows on fire, and committed other depredations.

On February 26th the 19th Native Infantry broke out into mutiny at Burhampore, and were only quelled by the presence of European troops and artillery. The regiment was then marched down to Barrackpore, disarmed, and disbanded, in the presence of four native regiments, one of them being the fractious 34th.

A fortnight later the 34th were in a state of insurrection, and several men of the regiment were hanged in the barrack square for an attempt to murder one of their officers.

In March and April the Sepoys at Amballa and Meerut, though fearful of committing open violence, displayed their resentment by constantly and secretly setting the barracks on fire. And throughout the districts of Oude and the north-west, the fakirs went about inflaming the people against the English.

Nana Sahib.—Nana Sahib, Rajah of Bithoor, was the mainspring of the rebellion. His hatred against the Company for their refusal to give him the ex-Peshwa's retiring pension was displaying itself in a deep-rooted conspiracy to drive the English from India He plotted with the Russians, with Persia, with the princes of Delhi, and the ex-king of Oude; and took advantage of the greased-cartridge disturbance to obtain the assistance of the Sepoys against their masters.

Rising at Lucknow.—At Lucknow on April the 24th an open mutiny broke out amongst the 48th Bengalese, the 3rd Native Cavalry, and the 7th Oude Irregulars; which was quelled by the energy of Sir Henry Lawrence, who brought up the European troops. The natives fled, but were pursued by the cavalry; and numbers of them brought back prisoners into cantonments.

Rising at Meerut.—But it was at Meerut that the first great storm of rebellion occurred. The 11th and 20th Native Infantry attacked the Europeans, shot their officers, and after firing the town, and slaying every English lady and child they could find, went off to Delhi.

At Delhi.—During the night some of the mutineers galloped into Delhi, and immediately every Sepoy in the great city was in arms and commencing the work of destruction. The commissioner, the chaplain, the officers were one and all murdered; and the whole of the 54th, 74th, and 38th Native Infantry vied with one another in works of cruelty and violence. The magazine was defended with desperate energy by nine English officers, and blown up only when resistance was hopeless, two of their number perishing in the explosion. The remainder of the Europeans in the city fled to the jungles, where most of them perished by the hands of the excited natives, or the terrible heat of the weather. Some arrived safely at Meerut, now deserted of troops. But the ancient capital of India was left in the hands of a drunken and lawless soldiery.

At Ferozepore.—At Ferozepore the 45th and 57th Native Infantry attempted to seize the fort, but were charged by the 61st Europeans and driven off. They then plundered the town and set it on fire; and during the night all was confusion. But the next day the cavalry turned out and drove the mutineers into the jungles.

Lahore.—The news of the terrible condition of affairs at Meerut and Delhi had no sooner reached the ears of the commanding officers at Lahore than they determined immediately to disarm the native troops at the station. A general parade was ordered; the Sepoys, consisting of the 8th Cavalry, and the 16th, 26th, and 49th Native Infantry, were cleverly, and quietly surrounded by English troops; and then halted, while General Corbett ordered them to lay down their arms. The men obeyed sullenly on perceiving that the artillery and infantry surrounding them were ready to open fire at a moment's notice.

Peshawur, Noushera, and Merdan.—On the 20th of May the regiments at Peshawur, the 64th, 55th, and 39th Native Infantry were disarmed in the same manner as those at Lahore, and put under close guard; while the remainder of the availing Europeans and faithful Sikhs marched off to relieve the beleaguered stations of Noushera and Merdan. Before they arrived, the native troops there had disbanded and fled with their arms into the country. They were, however, thoroughly punished for their misdeeds; for Colonel Nicholson chased them with his cavalry, and killed not a few; while the remainder were cut up by the faithful Punjabees, or seized and sold into slavery by the wild tribes of the hills.

Amballa.—The large station of Amballa was saved by the promptitude and bravery of the officers; and at the end of May was garrisoned by several European regiments, assembled from the stations near. At this point was collected the nucleus of an army under the command of General Anson, destined to combined action against the mutineers.

Simla.—The hill-station of Simla was at this time crowded with European families resident there for the hot season; and there was great fear lest the station should be attacked. Happily, however, no rising took place, and soon the interest of every one was directed to the march of Anson's column on Delhi. On the 25th of May the little army was clear of Amballa, and marching eagerly for the capital.

Anson died of cholera on the 27th, and his place was taken by Sir Henry Barnard, who on June 7th was joined by a body of European troops from Meerut under General Wilson. Some fighting had taken place on the route, as the Sepoys had massed in considerable numbers at this time, and were preparing for some combined action.

More Risings.—The flame of rebellion had now spread through the whole of Hindostan, and in twenty different places at once the Sepoys mutinied and murdered all the English they could lay hands on. Agra, Barreilly, and Moradabad were amongst the principal scenes of destruction and horror.

The universal fury against everything Hindu which at this time took possession of the English mind was agreeably softened by the chivalrous fidelity of some of the princes. Sindia was loyal, though his troopers joined the enemy; and the Rajah of Patialah sent a large body of soldiers to aid the English.

At Mynpoorie.—At Mynpoorie a young lieutenant, by name De Kantzow, saved the treasury and the fort by his almost unexampled gallantry.

At Cawnpore.—At Cawnpore affairs looked very threatening; for the town was garrisoned by three Sepoy regiments, and three regiments of native cavalry, with only one battery of European artillery. Sir Hugh Wheeler, who was in command, sent for aid to Lucknow and Calcutta, and obtained a slight reinforcement. But about fifteen miles off was Nana Sahib, Rajah of Bithoor, who now for the first time took open command of his soldiers; and, being joined by the mutinous regiments from Cawnpore, laid siege to the fort and barracks, whither all the English, men, women, and children, had fled for refuge. On June 6th commenced the siege. It lasted for twenty-one days, during which the helpless garrison suffered untold horrors of death by fire, by shot, by starvation, and the heat of the sun. The place was defended desperately; and on several successive days the enemy's attempts at storming were nobly frustrated by the energy of despair which characterized the fighting of the English. The ladies behaved with unexampled courage. But all was of no avail. The position became more and more hopeless, and when, on the 26th, the Nana offered a safe retreat for all the Europeans if Cawnpore was delivered up, Sir Hugh Wheeler felt compelled to accept the terms. The place was evacuated on the 27th, and some four hundred of the survivors were allowed to embark in boats and proceed down the river. But no sooner had they started, than the fiendish lord of Bithoor opened fire upon the boats from several guns, and from either side a terrible hail of musketry was poured in upon the helpless fugitives. One boat only escaped, but it was attacked lower down, and of the whole garrison only four men survived to tell the tale of horror. Another boat which had stuck fast on a sandbank, and was filled with ladies and children, was seized, and the whole party were marched into Cawnpore, where they were shut up close prisoners. To these were added, a fortnight later, several more European prisoners from Futtehgurh, who had been dragged thence by the rebellious and exultant Sepoys.

But meanwhile the English troops had massed, and were advancing in various directions against the rebels.

Preparations at Calcutta.—At the seat of Government the

confusion and panic was great. None seemed at first to know what to do, or how to deal with this new enemy. But Lord Canning, when he had once thoroughly ascertained the extent of the evil, set himself energetically to work. Troops were immediately ordered up from Madras, Bombay and Ceylon. The Madras reinforcement, under Neill, landed on May 23rd, and the Bombay contingent proceeded up the Indus towards Lahore. On June 17th Sir Patrick Grant (appointed to succeed General Anson as Commander-in-Chief in Bengal), and General Havelock, the Adjutant-General, arrived at Calcutta, and without delay started up country to direct the movements of the troops.

The Mutiny at Lucknow.—Meanwhile the whole of Oude had risen, and at Lucknow Sir Henry Lawrence was staving off from day to day, by energetic and timely conduct, a general attack, which had already been commenced by murders and incendiary fires, and which every day seemed imminent. At Fyzabad, Sitapore, and Sultanpore the officers were shot down, or driven with their wives and children into the jungles, to struggle, starving and half-dead with fatigue, into Lucknow or Dinapore.

At Allahabad.—In Allahabad the month of June had opened quietly; but on the 6th, the same day that witnessed the commencement of the siege at Cawnpore, the Sepoys mutinied in the town, butchered their officers, with their wives and children, and attempted to seize the fort. But Colonel Simpson defended the place gallantly for four days, and on the fifth Colonel Neill came up with the Madras Fusileers from Calcutta to his relief.

Progress of Neill.—The last-named officer had marched from Calcutta, and occupied Benares, where he arrived in time to defeat the 37th Native Infantry in the earliest stage of their mutiny, and to save the mint and the whole town from destruction. The Sepoys fled, and left the station in peace, while Neill marched on to Allahabad, to the relief of Colonel Simpson and the garrison. He at once occupied the fort, turned out all the Sikhs, and garrisoned the place entirely with Europeans. Here he established his basis of operations, and troops flowed in from all sides to swell the army destined for the relief of Cawnpore.

Advance of Havelock, July.—On June 30th General Havelock took the command, and marched off towards Cawnpore, at the head of a force numbering some thousands of Europeans. On the morning of July 12th, Havelock was at Futtehpore, where he first met the enemy, several thousand strong. A rapid and furious fire was kept up on both sides, but not a man was struck in the English ranks. The enemy were finally repulsed with some loss; and, with the addition of twelve captured guns, the column continued its march. Some more actions took place, in one of which the brave Major Renand lost his life; and on the 16th the army was on the outskirts of Cawnpore.

Battle of Cawnpore, July 16th.—Massacre of Cawnpore.—The enemy were here massed in considerable numbers; but by a clever and rapid movement Havelock turned their flank, and, after two hours hard fighting, sent them flying from the field. Day was too far advanced to think of entering the citadel till the next morning; but that night Nana Sahib, seizing all his prisoners—officers, ladies, and children—butchered them in cold blood, hacked their bodies to pieces, and threw them into a well. He then blew up the magazine and abandoned the town. The next day the English troops entered the place, and the horrors that revealed themselves are almost without parallel in history. No wonder that the gallant Highlanders and their companions swore solemnly to be revenged on the treacherous demons who had worked this fearful outrage!

Seizure of Bithoor.—Havelock determined to punish the miscreant who had ordered this massacre, before he pushed on to Lucknow. He marched to Bithoor, took the place without opposition, destroyed the palace, blew up the fort, and then returned to Cawnpore, where Colonel Neill was left to garrison and hold the station while the General advanced to the relief of Lucknow.

To the progress of events in that city we must now turn for a while.

Defence of Lucknow.—Death of Sir Henry Lawrence, July 4.—In spite of all the efforts of Sir Henry Lawrence, the mutiny at Lucknow began to spread more and more, until the whole city, with the exception of the Residency, was in the hands of the mutineers, and on June 30th it was deemed necessary to lead out the whole strength of the garrison against a body of rebels reported to be in the neighbourhood. Unfortunately no accurate reports had been received as to their number, and in the action which ensued some eight miles beyond the walls of Lucknow, the Europeans were driven back by a force vastly superior to their own, and compelled again to take shelter within the walls of the Residency. The enemy advanced in great numbers, and laid close siege to the place while Sir Henry Lawrence made preparations for a blockade of several weeks. He was killed by the explosion of a shell which mortally wounded him on July 2nd, and caused his death two days later. The garrison then fought under the command of Colonel Inglis. For three months did this noble band hold out against a force vastly superior to their own, and in the midst of hardships inconceivable. Day by day a galling fire swept in upon them, and all night long the storm of battle raged around them. Each man worked incessantly, now at mining operations, now at artillery duty, now at attending to the sick and wounded, and burying the dead, till their energy seemed almost superhuman. The women, too, laboured without ceasing, and by their cheerfulness and courage aided the soldiers beyond measure in their daily toils and sufferings. Several times the position was saved by a general rush of the garrison out of the works against the enemy's mining parties: and many times the gallant conduct of individuals in blowing up houses outside the intrenchments, wherein the enemy's soldiers had effected a lodgement, caused signal service to the brave defenders.

The Relief.—By the end of August something like despair of assistance had taken possession of their minds, when they were again reanimated by the tidings brought in by a spy, that Havelock would be with them in three weeks. On September the 5th a terrible assault was nobly repulsed, and the enemy returned to their lines. On the 23rd the exhausted garrison heard to their joy the sounds of distant firing,—it was Havelock storming the Alumbagh. Two days later his Highlanders were inside the Lucknow intrenchments, and the Residency was saved.

Havelock's March on Lucknow. — Havelock had, as before stated, left Colonel Neill in Cawnpore, and marched towards Lucknow on July the 25th. Crossing the Ganges into Oude, he fought the enemy at Oonao; and then, his troops being decimated by sickness, fell back on Mangalwar to await reinforcements. He was now only thirty-eight miles from Lucknow, but two months elapsed before he reached that city. An advance was ordered on August the 4th, but again the swamps of Oonao caused Havelock to retire to Mangalwar. A third time on the 11th the same events were repeated. By this time the troops were so exhausted and sick, that the General thought fit to recross the Ganges and fall back on Cawnpore. This was accordingly done after some severe fighting on the right bank of the river. At Cawnpore they rested for nearly a month, and the army was swelled by the arrival of Sir James Outram with a large body of troops, and by the reinforcements of many detached regiments collecting at this sttation from various mutinous districts. On September the 19th the whole force moved out and crossed the Ganges with Havelock, Outram, and Neill at their head. On the 20th they were at Mangalwar; on the 21st at the little Sye river; and on the 23rd they stormed the Alumbagh, the summer palace of the kings of Oude, about eight miles from Lucknow. The 24th was devoted to rest; and on September the 25th the final rush was made. The first advance was easy, but the last two miles lay through streets where every house was crowded with armed natives, and where stockades had at several places been erected. In spite of the galling fire which poured in upon them from every side, the gallant fellows pushed on, and after a loss of 500 men, reached the Residency gates, and scrambled in great confusion through the portals of the place they had come to save. It is said that the surprise of the relieving army was great, when they found that every man of the garrison kept at his post, instead of rushing down to the gates to welcome their deliverers. Among the slain was the noble General Neill; while Outram had received a severe wound in the arm. The whole united force were compelled to remain in the Residency, closely blockaded for two months more.

Siege of Delhi.—We must now turn to the progress of events at Delhi, where was the mainspring of the rebellion. Round the person of the aged emperor or "Padshah" the mutineers assembled, and it was evident that at Delhi itself would be decided the fate of the rebellion. Sir Henry Barnard had started from Amballa on May the 25th, and on June the 7th was joined near Delhi by a body of troops from Meerut. On the 8th he stormed the hill of the flag-staff tower before Delhi and entrenched himself there. The city was very strong, and the circumference of the walled defences measured seven miles, while the Sepoys outnumbered by thousands the little band of besiegers. Barnard, therefore, remained in his intrenchments, waiting for the opportunity of striking a decisive blow, or for the arrival of fresh troops from Calcutta. Day after day attacks were made on his position, and frustrated by the efforts of his soldiers. On the 19th General Hope Grant with the cavalry defeated a large body of troops who had crept round to the rear of the hill; and on the 23rd the rebels, reinforced by four mutinous regiments from Jallindur, made a desperate attack on the ridge, and were successfully repulsed. By the 3rd of July, the British force numbered nearly 7000 men of all arms, while the Delhi garrison received fresh reinforcements of six regiments from Rohilcund. On the 4th Sir Henry Barnard died of cholera, and Generals Reed and Chamberlain assumed the command. On July the 9th, on the 14th, and on the 23rd severe onslaughts of the enemy were repulsed, while all day a heavy fire was kept up between the city and the ridge of the flag-staff tower. General Wilson then took the command, and on August the 14th was joined by 2000 troops under the brave General Nicholson, who had put down the mutinies that had arisen at Jhelum, Amritsir, and Sealkote in the Punjaub, and now marched to join Wilson at Delhi.

The siege train which had been ordered to Delhi, was soon reported to be on its way to the assistance of the besiegers; and immediately a large body of rebels started off from the city to intercept the convoy, while Nicholson left the hill with 2000 men to bring it in safely. The opposing forces met at Najufghur, and the Sepoys were repulsed with considerable loss. The siege train arrived in camp early in September, and on the 7th of that month the real siege began. Batteries were erected at various points, and the Henry guns commenced pounding the old walls of the city, much to the discomfiture of the aged king, who offered in vain to treat. On the evening of the 13th the Cashmir and water bastions were reported fit for storming, and the army prepared for a grand assault. Early on the 14th the storming parties were ready, the word was given, and the men advanced at the double. The breaches were easily carried, but the work of blowing in the Cashmir gate to admit of the free passage of troops, was one of far greater danger. A little body of sixteen engineers, officers and others, advanced with a bugler. Four only survived, but the task was successfully accomplished, and the whole column swept into the city.

The attack on the right failed, and in the main attack the British loss was severe; Nicholson amongst others was killed in the moment of victory.

Taking of Delhi.—The city was finally captured on August 19th. No quarter was given, and terrible was the slaughter of the rebels by the avenging comrades of those who had been murdered at Cawnpore and shot down at Lucknow. Thus, after six days of actual fighting, was Delhi won.

Treatment of the King and Princes.—Hodson, at the head of his celebrated body of horse, had been in the thick of the fight; and now pushed on into the palace and seized the king and his queen,

Zeenat Mahal. Placing these under a strong guard, he went in search of the princes; and finding them, shot them dead with his own hand. The king and queen were then thrown into prison to await the decision of Lord Canning; and the city was garrisoned and quieted.

Reinforcements from Home.—Meanwhile, reinforcements from home were arriving in rapid succession; and regiments of volunteers were being raised; while Peel's naval brigade, and Probyn's and Fane's horse were about to enter the scene of action. Sir Colin Campbell took command at Calcutta in August, and prepared to carry out war on a greater scale than heretofore in point of numbers.

Immediately after the fall of Delhi, Colonel Greathed had set out from that place for Agra, and near the latter city he met and defeated a strong body of mutineers from Holkar's capital, Indore. He arrived in Agra on October 10th, and thence pushed on for Cawnpore, which he reached on the 26th. Meanwhile at Azimghur, at Chattra, near Hazaribagh, at Cajwa, and in the country round Delhi, the mutineers had been defeated by bodies of troops under the command of Captain Boileau, Major English, Peel, and Showers; and thus the rebellion was weakened by constant reverses.

Sir Colin Campbell's Campaign, 1857.—Sir Colin Campbell left Calcutta in October; and on November 12th, having joined company with Sir Hope Grant, arrived at the Alumbagh with a large force to relieve the garrison of Lucknow. The next day he attacked and, after hard fighting, took the palace of "Dil-Khooshah," and the "Martiniére College." On the 19th he had seized the strongly defended "Sikender Bagh," and was at the Residency. How welcome was his arrival to the worn-out garrison need hardly be told. Depressed with starvation, sickness, and exhaustion, the heroic survivors of that terrible siege hastened, with shouts of triumph and tears of joy, to welcome the brave comrades who had fought so hard to relieve them; and the noble garrison, glad indeed at length to come and go as they listed, found themselves encamped before the city in the shady groves of the Dil-Khooshah park on November 23rd. Their joy was, however, marred by the loss of their great leader, Sir Henry Havelock, who only lived long enough to see the place relieved for which he had so stoutly fought; and died in the camp at Dil-Khooshah, on the 24th of the month.

On the 25th Sir Colin retired on Cawnpore, carrying with him the rescued defenders of Lucknow. At Cawnpore he had left General Windham in charge, and that officer was beaten back from the city by a desperate onset of thousands of mutineers from Gwalior and other places; so that when Sir Colin arrived he found the city again in the hands of the rebels. He at once crossed the Ganges, and sending the survivors of Lucknow in safety down to Calcutta, prepared to cope with the enemy energetically.

2nd Battle of Cawnpore, Dec. 5th, 1857.—On December 6th he commenced operations by engaging the whole force of the rebels about Cawnpore. The enemy had taken up a position on the other side of some canals, and several bridges had to be crossed at various points before anything like a close engagement could take place This was accomplished in the face of a heavy fire, and the mutineers, defeated at all points, fled hastily, leaving the city deserted. They were pursued and severely cut up by Sir Hope Grant and the cavalry.

A few days later the rebels suffered some more reverses by the brilliant actions of Pattiali and Mynpoorie, where Colonel Seaton and the celebrated Major Hodson distinguished themselves; and in many other places the British arms were signally triumphant.

The King of Delhi sent to Rangoon, 1858.—The year 1858 thus opened on brighter prospects, and it was evident that the strength of the mutiny was crushed; many of the ringleaders had been captured and put to death, and on January 25th the King of Delhi was tried before a military commission for his treacherous conduct. Hodson and others sat on the Bench, and the representative of the Mogul Dynasty, which since the year 1526 had ruled at Delhi, was arraigned for treason and murder in his own capital city, and like a common felon sentenced to death! This punishment was commuted into transportation for life; and at the close of the year the aged king was conveyed to Rangoon, with a small retinue of attendants, and forbidden on pain of the forfeiture of his life to return to India.

Sir Colin Campbell's Campaign of 1858.—On January 2nd Sir Colin Campbell took possession of Furruckabad and Futtehghur, and then established himself at Cawnpore, whither he ordered up all available troops, stores, and guns from every quarter, in preparation for the final struggle. The rebels were massed about Lucknow, where the veteran Sir James Outram was in command, nobly keeping the mutineers at bay, and sustaining all attacks with unvarying success.

Many other successes took place in various quarters before all was ready for the general advance. At Huldwanie, in Rohilcund, Major Ramsay defeated a large body of rebels. Outram beat back a desperate onset of the Oude mutineers at Lucknow on January 12th; while six days previously a body of Nepaulese, or Ghoorkhas, under Jung Bahadur, had marched down to assist the English, and had taken Goruckpore, in Oude. General Franks, marching towards Cawnpore, gained a victory on the 24th over large bodies of insurgents, and a day or two later was joined by the Ghoorkhas. On the 29th Sir Hugh Rose stormed the hill-fortress of Ratghur, and relieved the garrison of Saugur, which had been besieged for some months. Some days previously a mutiny at Nagpore had been checked by the prompt action of the Deputy-Commissioner, Mr. Ellis, of the Madras Civil Service. On February 11th, Sir Hugh Rose, pushing on from Saugur, captured the strong fortress of Garrakotah. On the 21st Outram was again attacked, and again successfully beat back his assailants. On the 23rd Sir Hope Grant took by storm the town of Meeangunj; and the same day General Franks fought a fierce battle at Sultanpore, on the Goomti River, against a body of the enemy 25,000 strong. By dint of a clever flank movement, and hard fighting, in which his army were greatly assisted by the noble band of Ghoorkhas, he succeeded in gaining a complete victory and routing the enemy at all points. He then pushed on for Lucknow. Meanwhile the list of successes was swelled by the destruction of some forts near Fyzabad by the naval brigade under Captain Sotheby; and the storming of Berozepore by the Ghoorkhas.

Such were the principal doings which preceded the march of Sir Colin Campbell from Cawnpore. They served to dishearten the mutineers, and to raise to the most ardent pitch the spirits of the inactive troops at the rendezvous; who were longing to be led against the rebels; and to whom no day seemed brighter than that on which the order for the advance was given.

The Advance on Lucknow.—This was at the end of February. The army consisted of four divisions of infantry under Outram (who joined from Lucknow), Lugard, Walpole, and Franks (newly arrived); two brigades of cavalry under Sir Hope Grant; and one of engineers under Wilson. On

March 2nd, after a slight skirmish, this fine array of veteran soldiers encamped in the park of the Dil-Khooshah palace before Lucknow, and entrenched themselves securely. The enemy consisted of some eighty thousand rebels.

The last Struggle at Lucknow. March.—Sir James Outram crossed the Goomtie on the 6th, and marched in a northerly direction, in order to batter the enemy's works on that side. On the 9th the contest actually commenced. Sir James opened a heavy artillery fire on the city, and on the outlying works of the Martiniére College, which the rebels had strongly fortified; while he stormed another strong entrenchment known as the Chakkar Kothie. In all attempts he was successful, and night closed upon a general scene of congratulation. Next day the bombardment continued heavily on both sides; and on the 11th the Sikandar-Bagh, and the Begum-Kothie, the palace of the Queen of Oude, were stormed. The success at the latter place was marred by the death of Major Hodson, who was shot inside the works during the melée. On the two days following Outram and Campbell were both hotly engaged; the Imambarra and the Kaiserbagh were stormed, and by the evening of the 14th all the important posts were in the hands of the English. The taking of all these palaces was followed by extraordinary scenes of plunder and destruction on the part of the British soldiers. The greatest treasures of oriental art were stored up here in profusion, and were "looted" with reckless prodigality. On the 15th the last stronghold of the enemy was seized, and Lucknow was in the hands once more of the victorious English, the mutineers leaving all their stores behind them, and fleeing with the greatest haste in all directions. The fighting was not, however, over till the 21st; for during the intermediate days several works of strength outside the city, in which bodies of the enemy had taken refuge, had to be destroyed. The last gun was fired on March 23rd; and, for the first time since June of the year previous, the city was relieved from the sound of firing. ×

Capture of Bareilly. April, May.—This success was followed by the capture of Bareilly, whither the routed mutineers had betaken themselves. They were headed by Prince Firuz, Shah of Delhi; Nana Sahib of Bithoor; the Moolvie of Fyzabad; and Hazrat Mahal, Begum of Oude. Campbell marched from Lucknow, and with Walpole's division advanced against Bareilly. Shahjehanpore was taken with little difficulty on April 25th. On May 2nd, when near the city, the line of march was desr rately attacked, but the rebels were beaten back after some loss: and on the 6th the siege-guns of the division opened on Bareilly, while General Jones, who had come up by appointment after having seized Moradabad, appeared before the walls on the opposite side. The Nana and his followers hastily fled, and without striking a blow Bareilly was taken.

Meanwhile Shahjehanpore had been closely invested by the enemy after Sir Colin Campbell's departure, and General Jones was despatched to its relief, when the rebels broke up their camp and dispersed.

Lugard's division, marching from Lucknow, was attacked and suffered severely by the violent onslaughts of a body of mutineers under Koer Singh; but at the same time Sir Hope Grant defeated the Begum; and the Moolvie of Fyzabad being killed soon after, the Queen fled to the Gogra river, and prepared again to rally her forces.

Thus by the middle of June the mutineers were defeated at all points; but though incapable of joint action, they were broken up into separate bands of marauders, who gave great trouble to the divided forces of the English by their numbers and pertinacity. The centres of action being, of course, the standards of the Begum, the Prince of Delhi, and the Nana.

Sir Hugh Rose in Central India, 1858.—The finishing stroke was dealt to the rebellion by the splendid campaign of Sir Hugh Rose in Central India during the months of May and June.

Jhansi taken, April.—That officer, after his seizure of Ratghur in January, and Saugur and Garrakoteh in February (1858), marched on Jhansi, where the Ranee had taken her stand. He found the enemy's position very strong, but by means of his heavy guns succeeded in making the place practicable for storming by the end of March. Before the final assault took place, a severe action was fought with Tantia Topee, cousin of the Nana, who had advanced from Calpee to the relief of Jhansi on April 1st. It ended in his total defeat; and three days later the city was in the hands of the English.

There still remained two great rebel strongholds, Calpee and Gwalior, which Sir Hugh Rose soon marched to destroy.

Calpee taken. May.—At Calpee, Tantia Topee and the Ranee of Jhansi, who had escaped, awaited the approach of the English. On the 7th of May, Sir Hugh, advancing towards that city, met a large body of the enemy at the town of Kooneh, and signally defeated them, and on the 16th found himself within a few miles of Calpee. Two days sufficed him closely to invest the rebels' entrenchments, and on the 22nd the mutineers made a desperate sortie. They were thoroughly worsted, and fled in the utmost disorder, leaving the brave but exhausted army of Sir Hugh Rose, free to occupy their city. Thus Calpee fell on the 23rd May.

Here Sir Hugh rested his soldiers for a few days, for they were completely worn out by their incessant exertions in the heat of a peculiarly oppressive Indian summer. He was, however, called again into active service by the progress of events at Gwalior.

Gwalior taken. June.—It has been previously stated that Sindia, the young Maharajah of Gwalior, had behaved with the utmost gallantry and fidelity to the English in these trying times; but that his troops were to a man rebellious. On the 2nd day of June he was driven out of Gwalior, after hard fighting, by the mutineers from Calpee, and forced to flee for his life to Agra. Sir Hugh, accordingly, marched at once to attack this last refuge of the now disheartened rebels. Commanded by the Ranee of Jhansi and Tantia Topee, they gave battle at the Lashkar Hill before Gwalior, on June 19th; and the Ranee being killed, the whole army dispersed after much slaughter. The city accordingly fell into English hands, and thus the last severe blow in the great mutiny was struck.

The rebels were disorganized, and the whole country was covered with strong bodies of victorious English troops; who now had léisure to rest for awhile from their almost unparallelled exertions.

During this period of repose the East India Company had ceased to exist, and the government of the country was assumed absolutely by the crown of England. This will be presently noticed. It will be well first to describe the final events of the rising.

Final Struggle. November.—Sir Colin Campbell, Sir Hope Grant, and General Walpole were engaged during the fiercely hot months of July, August, and September in hunting down the more prominent rebels, and taking all forts whose possession was disputed. The Begum made some final stands, and then fled with the Nana across the Rapti river, and into the territories of Jung Bahadur, of Nepaul. That chief, however, gave permission to the English to pursue the rebels into his country; and thus the last bands of desperadoes were dispersed, the Nana and the Begum taking refuge amongst the hills, whilst their followers laid down their arms.

Fate of the Leaders, 1859.—Early next year Tantia Topee's

hiding place was discovered, and the rebel leader tried and executed. The Nana died, as it is supposed, in Nepaul. The Khan of Bareilly was seized and shot, and Mammoo Khan, of Lucknow, condemned to life-long imprisonment. Others were transported or imprisoned for various terms; while the bulk of the rebels, their regiments being disbanded, laid down the sword, and humbly assumed the garb of the ryot. The Begum of Oude lived neglected at Khatmandu, in Nepaul.

Confiscation of the Soil of Oude. 1859.—The most sweeping punishment fell on guilty Oude; for Lord Canning declared all the soil of that country to be henceforth vested exclusively in the Indian Government, offering at the same time reasonable advantages to those natives who should aid in restoring order. Sir Robert Montgomery was made Chief Commissioner, in the room of Sir James Outram; and at once proceeded with great ability to commence his task.

Such were the final events that characterized the sway of the East India Company. It remains to notice the manner of its abolition.

(IX.)—*The East India Company abolished*, 1858.

It will be remembered that on many occasions, when circumstances of serious importance had arisen to cause discussions in Parliament on Indian questions, there had been a strong feeling that the conquests of the East India Company would be better governed, if the management of affairs was vested entirely in the Crown and the Parliament. So long ago as 1784, Pitt, then Prime Minister, had declared his conviction that such a course would be fraught with advantage to both English and Hindus. It may be well imagined, therefore, that the terrible events of 1857 and 1858 had aroused strong feeling in England against the rule of the Company.

Lord Palmerston's India Bill.—Accordingly, when in December, 1857, Lord Palmerston announced that a Bill to work the desired change was in progress of preparation, the satisfaction that pervaded the public mind was great. In February next year the Board of Directors submitted a solemn protest to Parliament. It was worded in a calm and dignified spirit, and laid their case clearly before the world. But the voice of the people was against them. The Bill was read and discussed, and the first reading carried after a debate of three nights.

Mr. Disraeli's India Bill.—The Liberal Government of Lord Palmerston was however on February the 19th superseded by a Conservative Cabinet; and it fell to Mr. Disraeli to frame a new Bill, which provided that the Government of India should be vested in a council of eighteen members.[1]

Lord Stanley's India Bill.—This Bill, like its predecessor, was not destined to be carried through, and Lord Stanley framed another Bill on the same basis, but with several desirable alterations. He vested the government in a Secretary of State, and a council of fifteen (appointed partly by the Directors, partly by the Crown)[2] which should have absolute control of all Indian affairs; and he also made several fresh changes in the internal management of the Company.

The Company ceases to exist. August 2, 1858.—The Bill, so amended, passed triumphantly through all the phases of the three readings, discussions, and committees in the two Houses; and on August the 2nd, 1858, received the royal sanction and became law.

Thenceforth the East India Company ceased to exist; and the empire of the Moguls became a portion of the empire of England.

[1] By Mr. Disraeli's Bill the eighteen members of council were to be appointed in the following manner:—Nine of them were to be representatives of the nine principal Indian services, civil and military; four were to be chosen from amongst the body of retired officers of either service; and five were to be elected from the principal Anglo-Indian merchants.

[2] The arrangement was that the first Board should be formed of eight members elected by the Company; and eight by the Crown; the latter, inclusive of the Secretary of State, who was to preside, and have a casting vote. Afterwards, on each successive vacancy, the Crown and the Company were alternately to appoint a member of the council.

APPENDIX I.

GENEALOGICAL TABLES

OF THE

PRINCIPAL DYNASTIES AND FAMILIES OF INDIA.

(i.) Genealogical Table

OF THE

HOUSE OF MAHMUD AT GHAZNI (999—1152).

Sebektegin.
An ennobled slave.—Succeeded Alptegin as Governor of Ghazni.—Died in 997 A.D.

1. Sultan Mahmud.
The great invader of India.—Proclaimed himself independent Sultan of Ghazni in 999 A.D.—Died in 1030.

2. S. Mohammed.
(1030.)
Blinded and thrown into prison by his brother Masaud, after one month's reign.

3. S. Masaud I.
(1030—1041.)
A brave and energetic monarch.—After his defeat by the Seljuks he was deposed.—His nephew, Ahmed, murdered him in 1041.

7. S. Abul Raschid.
(1051—1052.)
Murdered very soon after his accession by a rebel chief, Togral.—With him ended the immediate line of Mahmud.—(No issue).

4. S. Ahmed.
(1041.)
Murdered with all his family immediately on accession, by his cousin Modud, in revenge for Masaud's death.—(No issue).

5. S. Modud.
(1041—1050.)
Murdered Ahmed, and became Sultan.—Lost most of the Indian possessions, but annexed Ghor.—Died in 1053.—(No issue).

6. S. Abul Hassan.
(1050—1051.)
Owned nothing but Ghazni itself.—Deposed by his uncle, Abul Raschid.—(No issue).

(Sebektegin.)

8. S. Farokshad.
(1052—1058.)
Found in prison on Abul Raschid's death.—Being connected with the house of Sebektegin, he was placed on the throne.—Reigned quietly.—Died naturally.

9. S. Ibrahim.
(1058—1089.)
Reigned very peacefully.—Date of death uncertain.—Supposed to be 1089.

10. S. Masaud II.
(1089—1114.)
Did nothing of any great importance.—Died naturally.

11. S. Arslan.
(1114—1118.)
Imprisoned his brothers.—Behram escaped, and aided by the Seljuks, returned and deposed Arslan.—(No issue).

12. S. Behram.
(1118—1152.)
After a quiet reign was driven out by a Ghorian Prince, whom he defeated and murdered.—The Ghorians came, drove off Behram, and utterly destroyed Ghazni.—The royal family fled to Lahore.—Behram died on the journey.

13. S. Khusru I.
(1152—1163.)
Reigned at Lahore, and died naturally.

14. S. Khusru II.
(1163—1182.)
At Lahore—with him ended the Ghaznevite dynasty.

(ii.) Genealogical Table

OF THE

HOUSE OF GHOR, RULING AT GHAZNI (1152—1206).

Seif-u-din.
Murdered by Sultan Behram of Ghazni.—His death avenged by his brother.

1. Ala-u-din.
(1152—1156.)
Seized Ghazni from Sultan Behram to avenge the death of his brother.—Established himself independent King of Ghazni in 1152.—Died, 1156.

3. Gheias-u-din.
(1157—1202.)
Lived a very quiet life at Ghazni, his brother doing all the active work of conquest. —Died naturally in 1202.

4. Shahab-u-din.
(1202—1206.)
Made commander of the armies of Gheias in 1157. —Conquered Khorassan.—Destroyed the last of the House of Ghazni at Lahore in 1176.—Took Sinde in 1181.—Delhi and Ajmir in 1193.—Canouj and Benares in 1194.—Came to throne in 1202.—Murdered while on expedition to Kharism in 1206.—(No issue).

2. Seif-u-din.
(1156—1157.)
Having murdered an offending chief, the deceased man's brother slew the king, 1157.—(No issue).

5. Mahmud.
(1206.)
The kingdom was at once seized by a slave, Eldoz, against whom Mahmud was powerless to cope.—All the dominions of Shahab went to pieces.

(iii.) Genealogical Table

OF THE

SLAVE KINGS OF DELHI (1206—1288).

1. Kutb-u-din.
(1206—1210.)
He was an ennobled slave, and commander of the armies of Ghazni.—On the dissolution of that kingdom, declared himself independent King of Delhi.

2. Aram.
(1210.)
Immediately deposed by Shams-u-din Altamsh, in 1211.

A SISTER,
Married
3. Shams-u-din Altamsh.
(1211—1236.)
Reigned well.—First irruption of the Tartar Moguls under the Great Chengiz Khan, 1217.—Annexed Sinde and Multan.—Reduced Behar, and Malwa.—King of all Hindostan, 1232.—Died 1236.

4. Rukn-u-din.
(1236.)
Quite powerless.—Dethroned by his sister, Sultana Rezia.

5. Sultana Rezia.
(1236—1239.)
A clever princess.—She married Altunia of Batinda, who had taken her prisoner.—Assassinated by her nobles, 1239.

6. Moizz-u-din Behram.
(1239—1241.)
Murdered soon after his accession, in consequence of his despotism.

7. Ala-u-din Masaud.
(1241—1246.)
Licentious and powerless, murdered in 1246.

8. Nasir-u-din Mahmud.
(1246—1266.)
A very able prince.—He had for his minister the ambitious Gheias-u-din Bulbun, who after his death seized the throne.

9. Gheias-u-din Bulbun.
(1266—1286.)
Succeeded to the throne on the death of his patron.—During his absence from Delhi, in 1279, his throne was seized.—He returned and slew the rebels.—Died of a broken heart, in 1286, in consequence of the death of his son.

Mohammed.
Killed during a battle in his father's lifetime. — His death broke his father's heart.

Kei Khusru.
Murdered by Kei Kobad's minister, Nizam-u-din.—(No issue.)

Bakarra Khan.
Acquiesced in his son's accession to the throne of Gheias.

10. Kei Kobad.
(1286—1288.)
Gave himself up to intemperance of all kinds. — Alienated all his friends. — Murdered his minister, Nizam-u-din.—Dethroned by the family of the Khiljies, who seized the crown, and put him to death.

(iv.) Genealogical Table

OF THE

HOUSE OF TOGHLAK, AT DELHI (1321—1414.)

1. Gheias-u-din Toghlak.
(1321—1325.)
Son of a slave of Gheias-u-din Bulbun.—Killed accidentally by the fall of a building, in 1325.

2. Mohammed Khan.
(1325—1351.)
His real name was Juna Khan.—He destroyed Delhi by his wild and absurd conduct.—Lost all the possessions that the Khiljies had acquired.—Died of fever in 1357.—(No issue).

3. Firuz Toghlak.
(1351—1388.)
Recognized the independence of Bengal and the Deckan.—Died at an advanced age in 1388.

6. Nazir u-din.
(1390—1394.)
He had at first been nominated successor of Firuz Toghlak, and assumed government; but was driven out by his nephews.—In 1390 he brought an army and regained his power.—Died 1394.

5. Abubekr.
(1389—1390.)
His uncle, Nazir-u-din, took Delhi, and made him prisoner.

4. Gheias-u-din.
(1388—1389.)
Deposed by his cousins in favour of his brother.

7. Humayun.
Succeeded his father; but reigned for only 45 days, when he died without issue.

8. Mahmud.
(1394—1414.)
The whole country in disturbance at his accession.—Malwa, Guzerat, and Candeish proclaimed themselves free.—The Tartars, under the great *Tamerlane* came down and sacked Delhi.—Mahmud fled, and Tamerlane left a Seiad, Khizr Khan, to govern Delhi, 1414.

(v.) Genealogical Table

OF THE

"SEIAD" RULERS OF DELHI (1414—1450).

---

1. Khizr Khan.
(1414—1421.)

Placed on the throne of Delhi by Tamerlane, for whom he affected to govern.—Died 1421.

|

2. Mobarik.
(1421—1436.)

Reigned quietly and well.—Murdered by his vizier in 1436.

|

3. Mohammed.
(1436—1444.)

The King of Malwa invaded Delhi.—Mohammed called in Behlol Lodi, Governor of the Punjaub, and beat him off.—Died 1444.

|

4. Ala-u-din.
(1444—1450.)

Removed his capital to Budayun.—Behlol Lodi immediately seized Delhi.

(vi.) Genealogical Table

OF THE

HOUSE OF LODI, AT DELHI (1450—1526).

---

1. Behlol Lodi.
(1450—1488.)

Seized Delhi on its evacuation by Ala-u-din.—Defeated and annexed the Kingdom of the Rajah of Jounpore.—He much enlarged the Kingdom of Delhi.—Died, 1488.

|

2. Secunder Lodi.
(1488—1506.)

Reigned well.—Annexed Behar.—Died 1506.

|

3. Ibrahim Lodi.
(1506—1526.)

A great tyrant.—The Governor of the Punjaub, in fear for his life, called in the aid of the Moguls.—They came, headed by the great *Baber*, and conquered Delhi and the whole of Northern India.—First battle of Panipat, 1526. Ibrahim killed.

(vii.) Genealogical Table

OF THE

FAMILY OF TAMERLANE, OR TEIMUR,

Reigned in India from 1526—1759.

Chengiz Khan.

Born 1164.—Died 1227.—He was the great Mogul leader.—Began life as head of a small tribe; ended Emperor of all Asia.

(*By the : Female Line.*)

Tamerlane.

Born 1336.—Died 1405.—He succeeded his father as Prince of Kech; then seized the Khanate of Djaggathai.—Led armies to Persia, and conquered afresh all Asia.—Invaded India in 1398, and left Mogul governors at Delhi.

THE ELDEST SON. Died in his father's lifetime.

- **Pir Mohammed.** Seized the greatest share of Tamerlane's possessions, including Samarcand, where he reigned.—He was turned out by Shah Rokh, his uncle.

Miranshah. Died during Tamerlane's life.

- **Mirza Mohammed.**

SEVERAL SONS, Who died before Tamerlane.—He left 35 grandsons.

Shah Rokh. Youngest and only surviving son.—Seized Samarcand from Pir Mahommed.—Died 1446.

- **Ulugh Beg.** Seized Samarcand on his father's death, and held it three years.—He was murdered by his son.

Abusaid Mirza.

Attempted to take Samarcand in Ulugh Beg's lifetime but failed.—Succeeded on the latter's death.—Turned out by Abdal Latif.—He fled to Bokhara.—Then seized Bokhara and Samarcand.—Conquered Khorassan, 1459.—Killed at Irak, 1468.—Kingdom divided amongst sons.

Abdal Latif.

Murdered his father, but was himself assassinated in a mutiny of his army.

Ahmed Mirza.

Reigned in the head-quarters of Samarcaud and Bokhara.

Mohammed Mirza.

Reigned in Hissar, Kundez, and Badakshan.

Ulugh Beg Mirza.

Succeeded to Cabul and Ghazni.

Omer Sheik Mirza.

Seized the Kingdom of Ferghana.—Married a sister of Mahmud Khan, a Mogul prince, and direct descendant of Chengiz Khan, by the male line.—Died by a fall, 1493.

1. Baber.

(1526—1530).

Of the blood of Chengiz Khan by both father and mother.—Born 1481.—Succeeded to Kingdom of Ferghana.—Died, with an immense empire, in 1530.—Took Delhi.

2. Humayun.

(1530—1543. 1555—1556.)

Reigned twice, once from 1530—1543; secondly from 1555—1556; in the interlude being driven out by Shir Khan, whose family reigned till Humayun drove them out in turn.—Died naturally, 1556.

Camran.

Made Governor of Cabul on Baber's death; and declared himself independent.—Ousted by Humayun in 1545, but regained the kingdom in 1546.—Driven out 1547. Surrendered 1548, and was forgiven.—Rebelled again, 1549. — Again expelled 1550.—Blinded, 1553.

Hindal.

Made Governor of Sambal.

Mirza Askeri.

Governor of Mewat.—seized Candahar.—In 1544 refused to receive Humayun in Candahar.—Humiliated and forgiven by his brother in 1545.

(Family of Tamerlane or Teimur—Continued.)

3. Akber.
(1556—1605.)
Reigned at Delhi from 1556 till 1605.—Reduced Agra, Ajmir, Gwalior, Malwa, the Rajput States, Guzerat, Bengal, Behar, Orissa, and Cabul. Then Cashmir, Sinde, Candahar, Berar, Candeish, and Ahmednuggur.—Died Emperor of Hindostan, Cabul, and half the Deckan in 1605.

Hakim.
Seized Cabul in 1566, and ruled there for many years.—He invaded the Punjaub in 1582, was beaten, but pardoned by Akber, and returned to Cabul as governor for the emperor.

Sons of Akber:

4. Jehangir.
(1605—1627.)
His real name was Selim. He had a very violent temper.—Conquered Mewar, Oodipore, and other places.—Died in 1627. —He gave Surat to the English.

Morad.
Died in his father's lifetime.

Danial.
Died in his father's lifetime.

Sons of Jehangir:

Khusru.
Was very rebellious, and at his father's accession rose in open revolt.—He was defeated and imprisoned.—Died in confinement, 1621.

Parviz.
Declared by his father incompetent to govern.

5. Shah Jehan.
(1627—1658.)
Reduced Ahmednuggur, Balkh, and Golconda. —Deposed in 1658, by his son, Aurangzebe.

Sons of Shah Jehan:

Dara Sheko.
He commanded his father's armies against the rebellion of the three other sons, but was imprisoned by them in 1658; escaped from prison, and fought against Aurangzebe, by whom he was murdered.

Shuja.
Defeated by Dara Sheko, and fled.—He went to Aracan, and was never more heard of.

6. Aurangzebe.
(1658—1707.)
Deposed his father and murdered Dara Sheko, Soliman, and Morad.—Shah Jehan died in 1666.—The Mahrattas rose, and their leader, Sevaji, was recognized as Rajah in 1667. —By the close of the reign the whole of the Deckan with the Rajput States were lost to Delhi; the former by Mahratta conquests, the latter by revolt.—Died 1707.

Morad.
Acted at first in conjunction with Aurungzebe, but was afterwards thrown into prison and murdered by him.

Soliman.
Murdered in prison by Aurangzebe.—No issue.

Mohammed Sultan.
Revolted against his father, 1660.—Thrown into prison, where he died.—No issue.

Bahadur Shah.
(1707—1712.)
Real name Moazzim.—Always treated favourably by his father, whom he succeeded.—He made treaties with the Rajputs, and Mahrattas.—Died 1712.

Azim.
Employed in many expeditions.—Revolted against Bahadur Shah.—Defeated and slain, 1707.—No issue.

Cambaksh.
Employed in some military duties by Aurangzebe.—(He was the favourite son.)—Killed in a battle against Bahadur Shah in 1708.—No issue.

Akber.
Plotted with Durga Das, the Chief of the Rajputs; and being beaten, fled to the Mahrattas.—No issue.

8. Jehandur Shah.
(1712—1713.)
Real name Moizz-u-din.—Murdered by Farokshir in 1713.—No issue.

Azim-u-Shan.

10. Farokshir.
(1713—1719.)
Great trouble with the Sikhs and Mahrattas.—Murdered, in 1719, by one of his ministers.—No issue.

11. Mohammed Shah.
(1719—1748)
A prince of the royal blood, raised to the throne after Farokshir's death (there being no other royal prince living).—Lost Guzerat, Malwa, and Bundelcund.—Invasion of Persians, under Nadir Shah, who seized Delhi, but retired, 1740.—Died 1748.

(Family of Tamerlane or Teimur—Continued.)

12. Ahmed Shah.
(1748—1754.)

The whole of India in arms.—The Rohillas, Duranis, and Mahrattas.—Deposed, and blinded, 1754.—No issue.

13. Alamgir II.
(1754—1759)

Raised to the throne.—Made Ghazi-u-din minister.—Delhi sacked by Ahmed Shah Durani, 1757.—The Mahrattas called in to aid.—Murdered 1759.

14. Shah Alum.
(1759—1806.)

As crown prince or "*Shah Zada,*" gave some trouble to the Company.—Succeeded his father in the bare title.—his real name was Ali Gohur.—The great battle of Panipat, in 1761, between Ahmed Shah Durani, and the Mahrattas, destroyed the last vestige of the Empire.—Shah Alum lived quietly at Allahabad, under British protection.—In 1771 was imprisoned by Sindia; and afterwards blinded by Gholam Khadir.—Replaced on the throne by Lord Lake, in 1803.—Died 1806.

Akber.
(1806—1837.)

Called himself by the title of "*Padshah*" (no longer "*Emperor*"). —Died 1837.

Mohammed Bahadur.
(1837.)

"*Padshah of Delhi.*"—Pensioned by the English, and made to leave Delhi by Lord Dalhousie, in 1849. Acquiesced in the great mutiny of 1857, and was taken prisoner. Several of his grandsons were shot by Hodson. He was tried by court-martial, and being sentenced to transportation, was sent to Rangoon. So ended the House of Teimur.

(viii.) Genealogical Table

OF THE

DYNASTY OF THE "NIZAM," OR SUBAHDAR OF THE DECKAN.

---

1. Nizam-al-Mulkh.
(1713—1748.)

His real name was Chin Killich Khan.—He rose to distinction under Aurangzebe; and, under the name of "Asof Jah," was vizier to Mahommed Shah.—He was recognized Subahdar of the Deckan in 1713, and became independent on the downfall of the Mogul Dynasty.—Died 1748.

Ghazi-u-din Khan.

Was not heard of till 1754, when he brought an army to wrest the Subahdari from Salabat Jung, by whom he was poisoned.

2. Nazir Jung.
(1748—1750.)

Allied himself with the English, and fought against his nephew, Muzaffer Jung; who claimed the Subahdari, and joined the French.—He was shot by a Patan, in 1750.

(Dynasty of the "Nizam," or Subahdar of the Deckan—Continued.)

3. Muzaffer Jung.
(1750—1751.)

Fought for the Subahdari with Nazir Jung.—Acknowledged Nizam by all parties on the latter's death.—Killed by some Patans on his way to Hyderabad, 1751.

Bassalat Jung.

In 1757 brought an army against Salabat Jung, and was defeated.—Nizam Ali obtained the Subahdari in 1761, and gave Bassalat the Circars to buy him off. —He died in 1782.

5. Nizam Ali.
(1761—1803.)

In 1757 brought an army against Salabat Jung, and was defeated.—Deposed Salabat in 1761, and put him to death, 1763.—He was generally an ally of the English, and aided them in crushing the Mahrattas and Mysoreans; but his alliance was of the most treacherous description.—He died in 1803.

4. Salabat Jung.
(1751—1761.)

Succeeded Muzaffer Jung, and was an ally of the French, being assisted much by Bussy.—He was deposed in 1761, by Nizam Ali, and imprisoned. — The Peace of Amiens, in 1763, declared him to be the "Nizam," whereupon Nizam Ali promptly put him to death.

6. Secunder Shah.
(1803—1829.)

On the death of his father, he was placed on the throne by Lord Wellesley.—Ruled feebly; and died 1829.

7. Fur Kundeh Ali.
(1829—1857.)

Ruled under the direction of an English resident at Hyderabad; but very badly.—The English deprived him of Berar in 1853, to secure the regular payment of the subsidy.

8. Futteh Jung.
(1857—1869.)

Succeeded just when the Sepoy mutiny broke out, during which he was faithful to the English.—Made Sir Salar Jung his minister.—Died in January, 1869.

9. AN INFANT.
(1869.)

Sir Salar Jung, a very able financier, administers the government under the direction of an English Resident.

(ix.) Genealogical Table
OF THE "NABOBS OF THE CARNATIC."

1. Zulfikar Khan.
Made Nabob by Aurangzebe, subject to the Subahdar of the Deckan.

2. Daud Khan.
Was appointed successor, and governed till 1710, when he was made Commander-in-Chief at Delhi.

3. Sadutullah.
(1710—1732.)
Bahadur Shah, the successor of Aurangzebe, made him Nabob.

Bakir Ali.
Was made Governor of Vellore by his father, in 1732, and remained contented with this office.—No issue.

3. Dost Ali.
(1732—1737.)
Succeeded his father.—Killed in a battle against Roghoji Bhonslay, in 1737.—His daughter married Chanda Sahib.

4. Sufder Ali.
(1737—1740.)
A minor.—Nizam-al-Mulkh made one Anwar-u-din his guardian.—But Sufder was soon assassinated, and Anwar-u-din was nominated Nabob.—No issue.

5. Anwar-u-din.
(1740—1749.)
Appointed by Nizam-al-Mulkh.—He always sided with the English against the French.—His capital was Arcot, and his family are sometimes called "Nabobs of Arcot," though the real title was "Nabob of the Carnatic."—He was killed in 1749, in a battle against Chanda Sahib.

6. Mohammed Ali.
(1749—1795.)
Known as "The Company's Nabob;" the English having placed him in office.—He was always dependent on the English, and was a great spendthrift.—His were "The Nabob of Arcot's debts."

7. Omdat-ul-Omrah.
(1795—1801.)
He was as great a spendthrift as his father, and not so true to the English.—Died 1801.—No issue.

~~~~~~~~

8. Azim-ul-Omrah.
(1801—1819.)
Placed in office by Lord Wellesley, on his promising to give up all real power to the Company.

9. ~~~~~~~~
(1819—1825.)

10. ~~~~~~~~
(1825—1853.)
Died without issue.

11. Azim Jah.
(1853.)
The present Nabob of the Carnatic.—Created "*Prince of Arcot*" by the Queen, in 1868.
~~~~~~~~

(x.) Genealogical Table

OF THE

MAHRATTA DYNASTY, AND THE "PESHWAS."

Maloji Bosla.
An officer of Malik Amber, of Ahmednuggur, had a son.

Shahji.
Married Jadu Rao, daughter of a Mogul officer of rank.—They had issue,

1. Sevaji.
(1666—1680.)
He began ravaging the country in 1660.—In 1664 became possessed of large tracts of land by the death of his father.—Recognized as Rajah in 1666, by Aurangzebe.—By 1673 he was Monarch of all the Concans.—Died 1680.

2. Sambaji.
(1680—1689.)
He lost most of the possessions he received from his father.—Offended Aurangzebe, by whom he was seized and murdered in 1689.

3. Rajah Ram I.
(Regent, 1689—1700.)
Held all the power, though the nominal Rajah was Sahoo. —He re-organised the Mahratta predatory bands, and ravaged the Deckan.—Died 1700.—On his death his son seized Sattara for himself.

4. Sahoo.
(1700—1749.)

When Aurangzebe murdered Sambaji in 1689, he seized Sahoo, and kept him prisoner till Rajah Ram's death, when he was liberated.—Sahoo ejected his cousin Sambaji from Sattara, and seized it for himself in 1708.—He appointed a "*Peshwa*" to govern for him, and led an idle life.—The Peshwas became afterwards the real sovereigns.—He died 1749, and Rajah Ram the Second was acknowledged.—(No issue).

Sambaji.
(In Colapore, 1708—1741.)

He was turned out of Sattara by Sahoo, and established himself in Colapore, by the help of his clever mother, Tara Bye.

5. Rajah Ram II.
(1749.)

Acknowledged by the Peshwa Balaji Rao, on Sahoo's death.—He had no power, all the government being carried on by the Peshwas.—He was kept always in confinement.

"THE PESHWAS."

1. Balaji Wiswanath.
(1708—1720.)

Appointed by Sahoo to govern.—His head-quarters were at Sattara.

2. Baji Rao.
(1720—1740.)

He was appointed to succeed his father, and soon usurped all the real power.—The great leaders, Puar, Holkar, and Sindia, rose under him.—He overran Malwa, and Bundelcund; and levied "*chout*" on all the country round.—Died 1740.

3. Balaji Rao.
(1740—1761.)

Made peace with Aliverdi Khan, Subahdar of Bengal, in 1751; allied with the French in 1756.—Died of grief after the battle of Panipat, in 1761.

6. Rogoonath Rao, or **"Raghoba."**
(1773).

A very dashing soldier.—Ravaged the territories of the emperor in 1755, and captured Delhi.—Defeated Nizam Ali in 1765.—Assassinated Narain Rao and became Peshwa in 1773.—Nana Furnuvese succeeded in ousting him in favour of Madhoo Rao II.—Negotiated with the English, and was pensioned by them.

Shumshere Bahadur.
(Remained in Bundelcund.)

Mahratta Dynasty and the " Peshwas "—Continued.

4. Madhoo Rao I.
(1761—1772.)

Established at Poonah, on the death of his father, by the aid of Raghoba.—Died of consumption in 1772.

7. Madhoo Rao II.
(1773—1793.)

(A posthumous son of Madhoo Rao I., set up by Nana Furnuvese, who aimed at the power).—Kept in retirement all his life.—At the age of 20 he threw himself, in a fit of passion, from the palace window, and was killed.

5. Narain Rao.
(1772—3.)

Seized the throne on his brother's death, but was at once murdered by Raghoba, who became Peshwa, and remained so till 1773.

8. Baji Rao.
(1793—1817.)

Succeeded Madhoo Rao II., in 1793.—Nana Furnuvese was his minister, Sindia having great power.—He was uniformly deceitful and cowardly, professing friendship for the English, but steadily plotting against them.—Driven out of Poonah by Holkar, in 1802, and made a treaty with Lord Wellesley, who reinstated him.—In 1817, Elphinstone forced him to sign a treaty, giving up for ever the Sovereignty of the Mahrattas to the English.

(Adopted.)
Dundu Punt.

(The "*Nana Sahib,*" who headed the terrible mutiny, against the English in 1857.)—His reason for revolt was that the Governor-General, Lord Dalhousie, refused to continue to him the pension granted to his adoptive father in 1817, when the latter died.

Chimnaji.

Amrit Rao.

[The Mahratta Dynasty was extinguished by the treaty of Baji Rao with the English, in 1817.]

(xi.) Genealogical Table

OF THE

HOUSE OF SINDIA AT GWALIOR.

Ranaji Sindia.

Entered the service of the Peshwa, Balaji Wiswanath, as a menial.—Rose by his talents to high office.—Received a jagir in Malwa.—He was a *Sudra* of the cultivator caste.—Died 1750.

1. Mahdaji Sindia.

(1750—1794).

The dissensions at Poonah on the death of the Peshwa, in 1761, enabled Mahdaji to usurp all the territory about Gwalior, which was his capital.—The British took Gwalior in 1780, but gave it back.—Recognised as a sovereign by the treaty of Salbye, in 1782.—Became possessor of Agra and Delhi, and kept watch over the Emperor Shah Alum, in 1788.—Collected immense armies.—Died 1794.—No issue.

Dataji Sindia

Assisted his brother, to whom he was always quietly subservient.

2. Dowlat Rao Sindia.

(1794—1827.)

Grand-nephew to Mahdaji. — Succeeded him in 1794.—Aided in placing Baji Rao on the throne of the Peshwas.—Invaded the Nizam's territories in 1803.—Fought against the British with the rest of the Mahrattas, and was crushed by the defeats of Assye and Argaom.—Utterly overthrown by Lake's victory of Laswaree.—Made treaty of Anjengaom with the Company, ceding large territories. — Aided Lord Hastings, in 1817, against the Pindarees.—Died, without male issue, in 1827.

3. Ali Jah Jankaji Sindia.

(1827—1843.)

Real name Mugat Rao, (the nearest heir that could be found on Dowlat Rao's death in 1827.)—Died childless in 1843. — Married a young girl, whom he left, a widow of 12 years old.—No issue.

Succeeded by his widow, Tara Bye, the Maha Ranee, who ruled through ministers.—The soldiers mutinied.—The British came to the rescue.—The country in a very bad state.—Lord Ellenborough determined to interfere.—A hard fight took place.—The Mahrattas were defeated, and Gwalior captured, 1844.—Treaty made.—The country placed under British protection.

(Adopted.)

4. Ali Jah Jyaji Sindia.

(The present Maharajah).—Succeeded on attaining his majority in 1853.—Has ruled very well under the protection and supervision of the English Government.—His unflinching loyalty to the English during the mutiny was of the greatest value to them.

(xii.) Genealogical Table

OF THE

FAMILY OF HOLKAR AT INDORE.

---

1. Mulhar Rao Holkar.

Came into eminence under the Peshwa Balaji Wiswanath, about 1730. He was the son of a cowherd, and raised himself to the dignity of a prince. He died, 1767.

A SON married **2. Aylah Bye.**
Died 1762. (1767—1795.)

She took command of her husband's territories, placed a relation, Tokaji, at the head of the army, and ruled well. —Died 1795.

A SON.
Died 1766.

A DAUGHTER.

3. Tokaji Holkar.

(1795—1797.)

A distant relation of Mulhar Rao Holkar.—Made commander-in-chief by Aylah Bye; and succeeded at her death.—He died 1797.

Kashi Rao Holkar.

A weak and deformed Prince.—Fought for his throne against Jeswant Rao; but was murdered by him.—No issue.

Mulhar Rao Holkar.

Seized the chief power on his father's death, but was assassinated by Kashi Rao.

Kundi Rao.

Assassinated by Jeswant Rao Holkar.—No issue.

4. Jeswant Rao Holkar.

(1797—1811).

Illegitimate.—Began a predatory career, and became very strong.—Murdered Kashi Rao and Kundi Rao, and became head of the family.—Defeated Sindia in the Battle of Poonah, 1802.—Fought against the English, under Lake, with whom he made a treaty, 1805.—Died insane, 1811.—Married

Wittoji Holkar.

Like his brother Jeswant, began to lead a predatory life, but was captured, and put to death with the most cruel tortures by the Peshwa.—No issue.

5. Toolsi Bye.

Who reigned after his death.—Factions were raised against her, and she was murdered in 1817.

6. Mulhar Rao Holkar.

(1811—1833.)

Made a treaty with England.—Died 1833.—No issue.

7. Hurri Rao Holkar.

(1833—1840.)

A distant relative, elected to succeed Mulhar Rao.—Ruled very badly.

Adopted.

Kamdi Rao Holkar.

(1840—1844.)

Succeeded.—Quite subservient to English.—Died 1844.—No issue.

On the death of Kamdi Rao Holkar, in 1844, there being no near relative, the Governor-General chose a distant connection, a boy named *Malkaji Holkar*, whom he caused to be educated. On his attaining his majority, in 1852, he assumed the reins of Government. The arrangement has answered admirably. He is still on the throne, and the country is prosperqus.

(xiii.) Genealogical Table

OF THE

HOUSE OF BHONSLAY AT NAGPORE.

Parsoji Bhonslay.

Rose to distinction under the Mahratta Rajah, Sahoo, who allowed him to farm the revenues of Berar.

1. Roghoji Bhonslay.

Succeeded his cousin as farmer of the revenues of Berar.—Invaded Bengal, and was permitted by the Peshwa Balaji Wiswanath to levy "*chout*" in Bengal and Behar.—He died 1755.—He assumed the title of "Rajah."

2. Janaji Bhonslay.

(1755—1772.)

Ruled well and with a firm hand.—Died 1772, leaving no issue.—He adopted his nephew, Roghoji, making his Ranee and his brother, Sabaji, regents.

Madaji Bhonslay.

Was disappointed at being excluded from all control on Janaji's death; and, after many quarrels with his brother, killed him in an open fight, and assumed the regency.—Died 1788.

Sabaji Bhonslay.

Made regent for his nephew, Roghoji.—Quarrelled with Madaji, and was killed by him.

3. Roghoji Bhonslay.

(1772—1816.)

Came into actual power on his father's death, in 1788.—Joined Sindia in the war against the English, in 1803.—Surrendered Cuttack when defeated in 1804.

A son, incapable of governing, and cruelly strangled by Appa Sahib who seized the throne.—No issue.

4. Appa Sahib.

(1816—1826.)

Murdered the crown prince, and seized the throne.—Attacked the English, 1817.—Defeated.—Pardoned.—Again he was about to attack them, when he was discovered and thrown into prison.—He escaped, and fled, but was never again heard of till he died at Jodhpore in 1840.

When Appa Sahib fled, the Governor-General directed that the only remaining relation, by the mother's side, to Roghoji Bhonslay should be installed. He was formally nominated "Rajah" in 1826, and remained governing, under British protection, till 1853, when he died. The Government then assumed authority.

(xiv.) Genealogical Table
OF THE
HOUSE OF THE "GWICKWAR" OF GUZERAT.

Pilaji Gwickwar.

Nephew to Danaji Gwickwar, whom he succeeded as second in command of the Mahratta armies.—Made himself chief of large territories in Guzerat.—The Peshwa, in 1721, made him commander-in-chief of the armies.—Died, 1732.

1. Damaji Gwickwar.
(1732—1768.)

Considerably extended his father's lands.—Threw off his allegiance to the Peshwa.

3. Govind Rao.
(1792—1800.)

Supplanted by his brother Siyaji, who was recognised by the Peshwa.—Succeeded on his death in 1792.—Was unsuccesful in his struggle for the throne, owing to the support which Raghoba and the other Mahrattas gave to Futteh Singh.—His minister was Rawaji.—No issue.

2. Siyaji.
(1768—1792.)

Was recognised by the Peshwa, though a weak and irresolute prince.—His brother Futteh Singh was made regent.—Died naturally, 1792.—No issue.

Futteh Singh.

Recognised by the Peshwa as regent for Siyaji.—(He bribed the Peshwa heavily for this purpose.)—Was the actual ruler of Guzerat till 1792, being supported by Raghoba, the Mahrattas, and the English.

4. Anand Rao.
(1800—1819.)

His minister was the same Rawaji whom his uncle had employed.—Mulhar Rao, a relative of Govind Rao's wife, made a rebellion, which was suppressed by the aid of the English.—
—Baroda was seized by his Arab mercenaries, and himself thrown into prison.—Rescued.
—Made a subsidiary alliance with England.
—Died, 1819.

Kanaji.

Usurped the government, but was ejected by Rawaji.—He was always troublesome, and at last was taken to Bombay as a state prisoner.—No issue.

Siyaji.
(1819.)

Ran much into debt, and part of his territory was annexed by Bombay to secure payment of the subsidy.—In 1838 strong remonstrances were made by the Resident, whose demands were complied with by the Gwickwar.
—He abolished "suttee," and raised the "Guzerat Irregular Horse" for the Company's service.

(xv.) Genealogical Table

OF THE

HOUSE OF SHAHJI AT TANJORE (1649—1799).

Maloji Bosla.

An officer of Malik Amber of Ahmednuggur.—Founder of the Mahratta dynasty of Poonah.

1. Shahji.

Married Jadu Rao, daughter of a Mogul officer of rank.—Obtained the land of Tanjore as a jagir.

Sevaji.

The first sovereign of the Mahrattas.

2. Vencaji.

Obtained possession of the country on his father's death, in 1678.—The decay of the Mogul Empire made Tanjore an independent Raj.

3. ~~~~~~~~

4. ~~~~~~~~

Sahuji.

Turned out by his brother, Pretab Singh, on the ground of imbecility.—He applied in 1749 to the English for aid, which was granted.—The Fort of Devicottah, on the Coleroon, was stormed, and given to the Company.—Pretab Singh bought off Sahuji with an annuity of Rs. 50,000.

5. Pretab Singh.

Wrested the kingdom from his brother, and ruled it with a firm hand.—Died, 1767.

6. Tuljaji.

Succeeded his father in 1767.—In 1769 was attacked by the Nabob of the Carnatic on the ground of some imaginary tribute due.—The English aided the Nabob.—Tanjore was taken, and the Rajah expelled.—In 1776 reinstated by Lord Pigott.—Died, 1786.

7. Amir Singh.

Disputed the right of Serfaji to succeed, in 1786; and was placed on the throne.—He governed ill, and the English deposed him in 1798.

(Adopted Son.)

8. Serfaji.

Amir Singh disputed the crown, and obtained it; but reigning badly was deposed, and Serfaji placed on the throne in 1798.—In 1799 he gave up the country to the English, receiving in return a regular annuity.—Thus ended the independence of the Raj.

(xvi.) Genealogical Table
OF THE NABOB-VIZIERS OF OUDE.

Saadat Ali Khan.
"Nabob of Oude."

A Persian adventurer of ancient family who came to India, and attained high office under the emperors, being made Nabob of Oude.—One of his daughters married

Sufder Jung.
"Nabob of Oude."

Who succeeded him in the Nabobship of Oude, and, in 1747, was made vizier to the emperor Mahommed Shah (then on the throne).—He died, 1756, and his son succeeded.

1. Suja-u-dowlah.
("*Nabob-Vizier*," 1756—1775.)

Succeeded in making himself actually independent about the year 1760, and declared himself so after the battle of Panipat, in 1761.—Fought against the English and was defeated at Buxar.—Shah Alum made him vizier.—The title was thenceforth "*Nabob-Vizier*."—Received Corah and Allahabad, in 1773, from the English.—Died, 1775.

2. Asoff-u-dowla.
("*Nabob-Vizier*," 1775—1797.)

Completely dependent on the English for protection, Mr. Bristow being Resident. — His treasury being empty, he seized the money in the seraglio of the Begums.—The affair was taken up by Warren Hastings, and formed part of the charge against the latter.—He made several subsidiary treaties with the Company.

(Reputed Son.)
Vizier Ali.

Tried to gain the throne, but was ousted by the Company, and Saadat Ali installed.

3. Saadat Ali.
("*Nabob-Vizier*," 1797—1814.)

Asoff-u-dowla died without issue, and a reputed son, Vizier Ali, tried to gain the throne. —The English upheld Saadat's claim, and in 1798 raised the subsidy to 76 lacs.—He ceded large districts in 1801 to the Company.

4. Ghazir-u-din Hyder.
("*King of Oude*," 1814—1827.)

The Company gave him the Terai. — He proclaimed himself, formally, independent King of Oude in 1819, with the consent of Lord Hastings. — Assisted in the Burmese War.

6. Mohammed Ali Shah.
("*King of Oude*," 1837—1842.)

Succeeded his nephew. —Made a treaty with the English ceding new districts, promising to rule well, and confessing his dependence.—Ruled very badly.

5. Nazir-u-din Hyder.
"*King of Oude*," 1827—1837.

Entirely dependent on the English. — He reigned well. — Died without issue, 1837.

Abunzaffer Maslah-u-din, or **Wajid Ali.**
("*King of Oude*," 1842—1856.)

Made a few reforms under the direction of the English, but reigned always ill.—Oude was annexed by the English Government in 1856.

(xvii.) Genealogical Table

OF THE

"DURANI" DYNASTY OF AFGHANISTAN.

---

1. Ahmed Shah Durani.

Of the "Suddozye" family.—Head of the "Abdali" tribe, whose name he changed to "Durani."—Rose under Nadir Shah.—In 1757 conquered Delhi.—Fought the great Battle of Panipat with the Mahrattas, and retired to Afghanistan, 1761.

|

2. Teimur Shah.

Weak and cruel.—He was mainly supported by the "Barukzye" family, whose chief, Poyndah Khan, he assassinated.

|

3. Zemaun Shah.

Kept the English in consent anxiety by his hostile attitude. — In 1801, Futteh Khan, son of Poyndah Khan, and head of the "Barukzyes," rebelled, and proclaimed Mahmud Shah.—The rebels were successful, and Zemaun was captured, blinded, and deposed.

Hyder.

Fled from Cabul on the deposition of his father in 1801.

4. Soojah-al Mulkh.

He obtained the throne in 1801, and kept it till 1808, when Mahmud Shah and Futteh Khan drove him out. — He fled to Runjeet Singh, and then to the English. —Made several vain attempts to regain his throne. — In 1839, his cause was taken up by Lord Auckland, in order to oust Dost Mahommed, who had shewn much favour to the Persians.—The Afghan War terminated so far successfully, that in 1842 he was placed on the throne; but he was murdered soon afterwards.

Teimur.

A spirited prince, of great assistance in the Afghan War.—Ousted by the Barukzyes.

5. Mahmud Shah.

Blinded and deposed Zemaun Shah in 1801.—He wrested the throne from Soojah, in 1808, and ruled till 1818; when the Barukzyes seized the throne, out of revenge for the murder of Futteh Khan, their leader, by Mahmud and Kamran —The Shah fled to Herat, and died there.

Kamran.

Made some unsuccessful attempts to gain the throne from Soojah, and then took up his residence with Firuz, at Herat.—Barbarously murdered Futteh Khan, in 1818. —Made Herat almost independent; and sustained a long siege by the Persians in 1840.

Jehangir.

Governor of Cabul during his grandfather's sovereignty.

Firuz.

Captured Herat when Soojah was driven out in 1808. — Was succeeded there by Prince Kamran.

Kaisar.

Seized the Government of Candahar when Soojah was driven out, and reigned there till the place was seized by the Barukzye brothers.

Sultan Ali.

Set up by the Barukzye, Dost Mahommed, in 1818, but immediately murdered by Ayub.

6 Ayub.

Set up by the Barukzye, Azim Khan. — Being deposed he fled to Lahore.

(xviii.) Genealogical Table

OF THE

HOUSE OF THE BARUKZYES IN AFGHANISTAN.

Poyndeh Khan.

The able minister, and chief supporter of Teimur Shah—head of the "Barukzye" family.—Murdered by his monarch.

Futteh Khan. Avenged the death of his father by deposing Soojah-al-Mulkh, and setting up Shah Mahmud.—He was murdered by the latter and Prince Kamran; and his family revenged his death by seizing the throne, 1818.

Azim Khan. Governor of Cashmir under the Durani Mahmud.—On the downfall of the Suddozyes, took Cabul as head of the Barukzye family.—Proclaimed Ayub, son of Teimur Shah, his sovereign.—Fled to Jellalabad out of fear of Dost Mahommed, and died there, 1823.

Dost Mahommed. Rose by his talents to be Futteh Khan's right-hand man.—Deposed Mahmud to avenge the death of Futteh Khan.—Proclaimed Sultan Ali Shah, but the latter was murdered by Shah Ayub.—Became chief of the Barukzyes, in 1823, by Azim Khan's flight.—Took Cabul from his brothers, 1826.—Ruled with a high hand till 1840.—Defeated Shah Soojah.—Made alliance with Persia.—Driven out of Cabul by the English in 1842; submitted, and was sent to Calcutta.—Freed, 1843, and restored.—Conquered Attock; which he lost by the English conquest of the Punjaub, in 1848.—In 1856, concluded a treaty with England against Persia.—Reigned under the title of "*Ameer of Cabul.*"

Pur Dil Khan. Seized Candahar on the downfall of the Suddozyes.—Afterwards seized Cabul, in conjunction with Kohen Dil Khan, and Shere Dil Khan.—Driven out by Dost Mahommed.

Kohan Dil Khan. Acted generally in conjunction with Pur Dil Khan, at Candahar.

Shere Dil Khan. Acted generally in conjunction with Pur Dil Khan, at Candahar.

Akbar Khan.

A fine soldier, but cruel and reckless.—Assassinated Sir William Macnaughten at Cabul in 1841.—Died in 1846, from poison.

Afzul Khan.

Was prevented from succeeding Dost Mahommed by Shere Ali, who threw him into prison.—Delivered by his son Abdul Rahman after the battle of Shekabad, and made Amir.—He died soon after.

Shere Ali.

Seized the throne on Dost Mahommed's death, throwing Afzul into prison.—Fled on the latter's release from prison by Abdul Rahman.—Assisted by his son, Yakul Khan, Shere Ali defeated Abdul Rahman, and again seized the throne.—He has been recognised as Amir of Cabul (1869).

Shuruf Khan.

Azim Khan.

On Afzul Khan's death, the latter's son, Abdul Rahman, took up the cause of Azim Khan, and the two were together at Cabul when Shere Ali and Yakul Khan returned and defeated them.—He is now a fugitive (1869).

Ishak Khan.

Fled to Turkestan.—Assembled an army for his father in 1869, but desisted on Lord Mayo's recognition of Shere Ali.

Abdul Rahman.

Fought for his father against Shere Ali, whom he defeated at Shekabad.—Placed his father on the throne, and, on the latter's death, set up Azim Khan in opposition to Shere Ali.—Defeated by Shere Ali, and fled.—His cause is for the present hopeless (1869).

Mohammed Ali Khan.

A fine soldier.—He lost his life at Candahar.

Ibrahim Khan.

A weak prince; surrendered the Bala Hissar at Cabul to Abdul Rahman, without attempting a defence.

Yakul Khan.

A dashing and clever officer.—Commander-in-chief of the armies of Shere Ali.—Defeated Abdul Rahman, and secured the throne for the present amir, Shere Ali (1869).

APPENDIX II.

GEOGRAPHICAL INDEX TO THE PLACES MENTIONED IN THE TEXT.

(N.B.—For any further information required, consult Thornton's "Gazetteer of India.")

Abbreviations:—*Pres.* for Presidency. N. W. P. for North Western Provinces. L. P. for Lower Provinces of Bengal.

(The names within brackets show the method of spelling adopted by Mr. Thornton, where a difference exists.)]

A.

AFGHANISTAN.—The central portion of the country lying between Persia and the river Indus.

AGRA.—Capital city of the district of the same name, N. W. P.; lat. 27° 10′, lon. 78° 5′.[1]

AHMEDABAD.—Chief city of the district of the same name, Bombay Pres.; lat. 23° 0′, lon. 72° 36′.

AHMEDNUGGUR.—Chief city of the district of the same name, Bombay Pres.; lat. 27° 44′, lon. 78° 38′.

AJMIR.—Chief town of the district of the same name, N. W. P.; lat. 26° 39,′ lon. 74° 43′. [*Ajmere.*]

AKHSI.—A fortified town in the ancient kingdom of Ferghana (q. v.)

ALIWAL.—On the Sutlej river; lat. 30° 57′, lon. 75° 36′.

[1] Throughout this Index the latitude is always north and the longitude east, unless specially distinguished.

ALLAHABAD.—Chief city of the district of the same name, N. W. P.; lat. 25° 26,′ lon. 81° 53′.

ALLIGHUR.—Chief town of the district of the same name, N. W. P.; lat. 27° 56′, lon. 78° 8′. [*Allygurh.*]

ALMORA.—Chief town of the district of Kumaon, N. W. P.; lat. 29° 35′, lon. 79° 42′.

ALOR.—An ancient city in Sinde, now in ruins; lat. 27° 40′, lon. 69° 2′.

AMBALLA.—Chief town of the district of the same name, Bengal Pres.; lat. 30° 24′, lon. 76° 49′. [*Umballa.*]

AMBOYNA.—An island in the Eastern Archipelago; lat. (south) 3° 35′ lon. 128°.

AMRITSUR.—A town in the Punjaub; lat. 31° 40′, lon. 74° 45′.

ANDRA.—An ancient kingdom in the Deckan, having for its capital city Warangal (q. v.) [*Amritsir.*]

ANHALWARA.—An ancient city in Guzerat, once the capital of that kingdom, now called Pattan; lat. 23° 46′, lon. 72° 3′.

ANJENGAOM.—In the dominions of the Nizam; lat. 21° 40,′ lon. 77° 51′. [*Anjengaum.*]

ARACAN.—Chief city of the province of the same name, east of the Bay of Bengal; lat. 20° 42′, lon. 93° 24′. [*Arracan.*]

ARCOT.—Gives its name to a district of the Madras Pres; lat. 12° 54′, lon. 79° 24′.

ARGAOM.—In the Nizam's dominions; lat. 21° 2′, lon. 77° 2′. [*Argaum.*]

ARIKERA.—In Mysore; lat. 12° 0′, lon. 77° 49′.

ASHCANDRA.—An ancient city in Sinde, on the river Indus (site unknown.)

ASSAM.—A province on the north-east frontier of Bengal.

ASSIRGHUR.—A hill-fort, north-east of the Bombay Pres.; lat. 21° 6′, lon. 76° 26′. [*Asseergurh.*]

ASSYE.—In the dominions of the Nizam; lat. 20° 18′, lon 75° 55′. [*Assaye.*]

ASTRACHAN.—A district of Russia, on the north-west shore of the Caspian Sea.

ATTOCK.—Lat. 33° 54′, lon. 72° 20′.

AURANGABAD.—In the dominions of the Nizam; lat. 19° 51′, lon. 75° 21′. [*Aurungabad.*]

AVA.—Capital city of the Burmese Empire; lat. 21° 52′, lon. 96° 1′.

AZIMGHUR.—Chief town of the district of the same name; lat. 26° 0′, lon. 83° 14′.

B.

Badakshan.—A tract of Central Asia, on the western frontier of the Chinese Empire, bounded by Bokara, Pamer, Kunduz, and Little Thibet.

Bagdad.—On the River Tigris; lat. 44° 25′, lon. 33° 45′.

Baglana.—A fortress on the frontier of Guzerat, towards Ujein.

Bakar.—On the River Indus, in Sinde; lat. 27° 39′, lon. 68° 56′. [*Bukkur.*]

Balaghat.—A tract of land in the Madras Pres., comprising the present districts of Cuddapah, Kurnoul, and Bellary.

Ballapore.—In the dominions of the Nizam; lat. 17° 18′, lon. 78° 33′. [*Balapore.*]

Bamian.—In Hindu Cush; lat. 34° 50′, lon. 67° 45′.

Bancoorah.—Chief town of the district of the same name, Bengal Pres.; lat. 23° 14′, lon. 87° 6′.

Banda Neira.—The principal of the Molucca spice islands; about lat. (south) 4° 20′, lon. 130° 0′.

Bangalore.—In Mysore; lat. 12° 58′, lon. 77° 38′.

Bankibazar.—A village on the Hooghley, near Calcutta, opposite Chandanagore.

Baraset.—Near Calcutta; lat. 22° 43′, lon. 88° 23′.

Bareilly.—Chief town of the district of the same name, N. W. P.; lat. 28° 23′, lon. 79° 28′.

Baroch.—(*See* Broach.)

Baroda.—Capital city of the state of Guzerat; lat. 22° 16′, lon 73° 14′.

Barrackpore.—Near Calcutta; lat. 22° 46′, lon. 88° 26′.

Bassein.—An island belonging to the North Concan, Bombay Pres.; the chief town is in lat. 19° 20′, lon. 72° 52′.

Batavia.—Capital city of the island of Java; lat. (south) 6° 3′, lon. 106° 50′.

Batinda.—A town in the Sikh State of Patialah; lat. 30° 10′, lon. 75° 0′.

Beder.—Anciently the capital of one of the Bahmani kingdoms of the Deckan; lat. 17° 58′, lon. 77° 36′.

Benares.—On the Ganges; lat. 25° 17′, lon. 83° 4′, N. W. P.

Bednore.—In Mysore; lat. 13° 50′, lon. 75° 6′.

Bellary.—The chief town of the district of the same name, Madras Pres.; lat. 15° 8′, lon. 76° 59′.

BELOOCHISTAN.—The southern portion of the country lying between Persia and the River Indus.

BERAR.—A province lying south of the Sutpura mountains; its chief town is Elichpore (q. v.)

BEROZEPORE.—A small fort near Fyzabad (q. v.), N. W. P.

BHATIA.—A tract between Bhawulpore and Bikanir, formerly inhabited by the Rajput tribe of the Bhatties, whence the name, N. W. P. [*Bhuttiana, Bhutneer.*]

BHAWULPORE.—A native state south of the Punjaub; lat. 29° 24′, lon. 71° 47′.

BHOONDI.—A Rajput State, site of the capital city; lat. 25° 26′, lon. 75° 43′. [*Boondee.*]

BHOPAL.—A native state in Malwa, site of the capital city; lat. 23° 14′, lon. 77° 33′.

BHURTPORE.—On the Jumna, chief town of the Jaut State of the same name; lat. 27° 12′, lon. 77° 33′.

BIANA.—In the territory of Bhurtpore; lat. 26° 57′, lon. 77° 20′.

BIDZEGHUR.—N. W. P.; lat. 24° 34′, lon. 83° 9′. [*Bidjey Gurh.*]

BIJAPORE.—One of the ancient Bahmani kingdoms; the capital city is now in ruins; lat. 16° 50′, lon. 75° 48′. [*Beejapore.*]

BIKANIR.—A Rajput State, bounded by Bhatia, Hurrianah, Jodhpore, and Jesulmir. [*Beekaneer.*]

BITHOOR.—On the Ganges; lat. 26° 37′, lon. 80° 20′.

BOKHARA.—Capital city of the territory of the same name in Central Asia: lat. 39° 45′, lon. 64° 30′.

BOLAN PASS.—In Beloochistan, on the route between Shikarpore, in Sinde, and Candahar in Afghanistan; lat. 29° 56′, lon. 67° 6′.

BOOTWAL.—On the frontier of Nepaul; lat. 27° 37′, lon. 83° 34′. [*Betaul.*]

BOSRAH, (Bussorah, or Basra).—On the Tigris River, at the head of the Persian Gulf; lat. 30° 36′, lon. 47° 40′.

BRAHMANABAD.—An ancient city of Sinde, near Tattah, a few ruins alone remain.

BROACH.—Chief town of the district of the same name, Bombay Pres.; lat. 21° 42′, lon. 73° 2′.

BUDAYUN.—In Rohilcund, a town and district of the same name; lat. 28° 2′, lon. 79° 11′. [*Budaon.*]

BUNDELCUND.—A tract of country bounded by Gwalior, the River Jumna, Rewah, and Saugur.

BURDWAN.—Chief town of the district of the same name, Bengal Pres.; lat. 23° 12′, lon. 87° 56′.

BURHAMPORE.—Bengal L. P.; lat. 24° 5′, lon. 88° 17′.

BUSHAIR.—In Persia: lat. 28° 40′, lon. 51° 18′.

BUXAR.—On the Ganges; lat. 25° 32′, lon. 84° 3′.

C.

CABUL.—The chief city and country of Afghanistan; lat. 34° 28′. lon. 68° 50′.

CACHAR.—A province of the Bengal Pres.; bounded by Assam, Tipperah, Manipore, and Silhet.

CAGGAR.—River in Sirhind, rising about lat. 30° 52′, lon. 77° 7′, in Patialah, N. W. P. [*Guggur.*]

CAJWA.—In the N. W. P.; lat. 25° 12′, lon. 82° 46′. [*Kuchuhwa.*]

CALIAN.—Anciently the chief city of the Concans, Bombay Pres.; lat. 19° 14′, lon. 73° 12′. [*Callianee.*]

CALICUT.—In Malabar, Madras Pres.; lat. 11° 5′, lon. 75° 50′.

CALINGA.—Ancient name for a tract of country along the east coast of India, south of Orissa.

CALINJAR.—Hill fort in Bundelcund; lat. 25° 0′, lon. 80° 32′. [*Kalleenjur.*]

CALPEE.—A town near Gwalior; lat. 26° 7′, lon. 79° 48′.

CANARA.—A district in the Madras Pres., divided into North and South Canara; bounded by Goa, Mysore, Coorg, and the Indian Ocean.

CANDAHAR.—A large city in Afghanistan; lat. 37° 30′, lon. 66° 50′.

CANDEISH.—Territory in Bombay Pres., formerly an independent kingdom, comprising the country between Burhampore and Nassik.

CANOUJ.—One of the wealthiest of the ancient Hindu kingdoms. Capital city of the same name; lat. 27° 3′, lon. 79° 59′. [*Kunnoj.*]

CARICAL.—French settlement in Tanjore, Madras Pres.; lat. 10° 53′, lon. 79° 53′. [*Karical.*]

CARNATA.—One of the ancient divisions of Southern India; probably including the countries where the Tamil language is spoken. (See page 8 of this work, note.)

CARNAL.—Near Lahore, N. W. P.; lat. 29° 41′, lon. 77° 3′. [*Kurnal.*]

CASHMIR.—The dominions of Gholab Singh, north of the Punjaub; the chief city being Sirinagar (q. v.) [*Cashmere.*]

CAWNPORE.—N. W. P., chief city of the district of the same name; lat. 26° 29′, lon. 80° 25′.

CHAMPANIR.—A hill-fort in Guzerat; lat. 22° 30′, lon. 73° 30′. [*Champaneer.*]

CHANDA.—On the river Warda, on the north-east boundary of the Nizam's dominions; lat. 19° 57′, lon. 79° 23′. [*Chandah.*]

CHANDANAGORE.—A town on the Hooghley, close to Calcutta.

CHANDORE.—In the district of Ahmednuggur, Bombay Pres.; lat. 20° 20′, lon. 74° 14′.

CHANGAMA.—In South Arcot, Madras Pres.; lat. 12° 19′ lon. 78° 51′. Near the town is a pass over the Ghauts.

CHARMAL.—Near Hyderabad; lat. 17° 20′, lon. 78° 29′.

CHATTRA.—Near Ramghur, Bengal Pres.; lat. 23° 39′, lon. 85° 36′. [*Chattur.*]

CHERA.—An ancient Deckan kingdom, including Travancore-Coimbatore, and part of Malabar.

CHILLIANWALLAH.—A village in the Punjaub, near the river Jhelum; lat. 32° 40′, lon. 73° 39′.

CHINSURAH.—A town on the Hooghley, near Calcutta.

CHITORE.—In the territory of Oodipore, Mewar; lat. 24° 52′, lon. 74° 41′. [*Chittor.*]

CHITTAGONG.—A province of the Bengal Pres., bounded by Aracan, the Bay of Bengal, and the Yumadoon mountains; the capital city Islamabad or Chittagong, is in lat. 22° 20′, lon. 91° 54′.

CHOLA.—An ancient kingdom of the Deckan, having for its capital Congeveram (q. v.)

CHOTA NAGPORE.—Near Ramghur, Bengal Pres.; lat. 23°, lon. 84°.

CHUNAR.—A fortified town on the Ganges; lat. 25° 5′, lon. 83° 0′.

CHUTTERNUTTY.—A small village on the Hooghley, near Calcutta.

CICACOLE.—In Ganjam, Madras Pres.; lat. 18° 18′, lon. 83° 58′. [*Chicacole.*]

CIRCARS (The).—A tract of country in Madras Pres., along the eastern coast of India, including the districts of Guntoor, Masulipatam, Rajahmundri, Vizagapatam, and Ganjam.

COCHIN.—A native state in Madras Pres., western coast; lat. 9° 58′, lon. 76° 18′.

COIMBATORE.—A town and district in Madras Pres.; lat. 11° 0′, lon. 77° 1′.

Colapore.—Chief town of the district of the same name Bombay Pres.; lat. 16° 42′, lon. 74° 18′. [*Kolapoor.*]

Colar.—In Mysore; lat. 13° 8′, lon. 78° 10′.

Colatoor.—In the district of Tinnevelly, Madras Pres.; lat. 9° 1′, lon. 78° 15′. [*Kollatoor.*]

Comorin (Cape).—The southernmost point of India, in the native state of Travancore; lat. 8° 5′, lon. 77° 37′.

Concans (The).—A tract of land in Bombay Pres., between the Indian Ocean and the Ghauts, along the coast, bounded by Goa and Damaum.

Congeveram.—In the district of Chingleput, Madras Pres.; lat. 12° 50,′ lon. 79° 46′. [*Conjeveram.*]

Coorg.—A district formerly independent, now absorbed in Madras Pres., bounded by Mysore, Malabar, and Canara.

Corah.—Near Futtehpore, N. W. P.; lat. 25° 48′, lon. 80° 35′. [*Korah.*]

Coromandel Coast.—Name given to the eastern coast of India, as far north as Masulipatam—southwards to Point Calimere.

Cuddalore.—In South Arcot, Madras Pres.; lat. 11° 43′, lon. 79° 50′.

Cuddapah.—A town and district in Madras Pres.; lat. 14° 28′, lon. 78° 52′.

Culbarga.—In the Nizam's dominions; lat. 17° 19′, lon. 76° 51′. [*Koolburga.*]

Cuttack.—Province in Bengal Pres.; site of the chief town; lat. 20° 28′, lon. 85° 55′.

Cutwa.—Near Burdwan, Bengal Pres.; lat. 23° 38′, lon. 88° 10′.

D.

Dacca.—A town and district in the Presidency of Bengal; lat. 23° 43′, lon 90° 25′.

Dadur.—In Beloochistan: lat. 29° 30′, lon. 66° 40′.

David (Fort. St.).—A fort ten miles south of Pondicherry, belonging to the French.

Deckan (The).—The name given to the whole of the south of India within the Ghauts and south of the Vindhya mountains. Its proper boundaries are the Kistna and Nerbudda rivers.

Deeg.—In the territory of Bhurtpore; lat. 27° 29′, lon. 77° 23′.

Delhi.—Lat. 28° 39′, lon. 77° 18′.

DEOGIRI.—See Doulatabad, of which it was the ancient name.

DEVICOTTAH.—At the mouth of the river Coleroon; lat. 11° 22′, lon. 79° 52′. [*Devikotta.*]

DEWAL.—An ancient sea-port town in Sinde, supposed to have been somewhere near Kurrachee.

DHARWAR.—A town and collectorate in the Bombay Pres.; lat. 15° 28′, lon. 75° 4′.

DHERA GHAZIE KHAN.—A city on the Indus; lat. 30° 4′, lon. 70° 54′. [*Dera Ghazee Khan.*]

DINDIGUL.—In the district of Madura, Madras Pres.; lat. 10° 22′, lon. 78° 3′.

DIZAK.—In Central Asia, near Samarcand; lat. 40° 29′, lon. 67° 40′.

DJAGGATHAI.—One of the four Khanates into which the empire of Chengiz Khan was divided after his death.

DONABEW.—In Pegu, on the river Irawaddi; lat. 17° 10′, lon. 95° 27′.

DOOAB.—The name given to the tract of country between a river and its tributary. The principal Dooab is that between the rivers Jumna and Ganges.

DOOGAUR.—In the territory of Bhoondi, Rajputana; lat. 25° 40′, lon. 75° 52′. [*Doogaree.*]

DOULATABAD.—In the territory of the Nizam; lat. 19° 57′, lon. 75° 18′. [*Dowlutabad.*]

E.

ELICHPORE.—In the territory of the Nizam; lat. 21° 10′, lon. 77° 36′. [*Ellichpoor.*]

F.

FERGHANA.—In Kokan Tartary (Central Asia), on the river Sir or Jaxartes.

FEROZEPORE.—On the Sutlej river, in Sirhind; lat. 30° 55′, lon. 75° 35′. [*Ferozpore.*]

FEROZESHAH.—Near the Sutlej river; lat. 30° 52′, lon. 74° 50′.

FURRUCKABAD.—A town and district, N. W. P.; lat. 27° 24′, lon. 79° 40′.

FUTTEHGHUR.—Military station three miles from Furruckabad, N. W. P.; lat. 27° 22′, lon. 79° 41′. [*Futtygurh.*]

Futtehpore.—Chief town of the district of the same name; N. W. P., lat. 25° 57′, lon. 80° 54′.

Fyzabad.—In Oude; lat. 26° 47′, lon. 82° 10′.

G.

Galle (Point de).—South of Ceylon; lat. 6° 4′, lon. 80° 9′.

Garrakotah.—Near Saugur; lat. 23° 47′, lon. 79° 12′. [*Garakota.*]

Gawilghur.—In the territory of the Nizam; lat. 21° 20′, lon. 77° 23′.

Ghazipore.—On the River Ganges, chief town of the district of the same name; lat. 25° 32′, lon. 83° 39′. [*Ghazeepore.*]

Ghazni.—In Afghanistan, south of Cabul; lat. 33° 36′, lon. 73° 19′.

Gheriah.—In the Southern Concan, Bombay Pres.; lat. 16° 32′ lon. 73° 22′.

Ghor.—A large tract in Afghanistan, between Cabul and Bokhara.

Goa.—Capital of the Portuguese settlement on the western coast; lat. 15° 30′, lon. 74° 0′.

Godavery River.—A large river of the Deckan, rising in lat. 19° 58′, lon. 73° 30,, and falling into the Bay of Bengal, forming a large Delta at its mouth.

Gogra River.—A tributary of the Ganges, into which it falls in lat. 25° 46′, lon. 84° 40′. [*Ghogra.*].

Gohud.—In Sindia's territory of Gwalior; lat. 26° 25′, lon. 78° 26′.

Golconda.—In the territory of the Nizam; lat. 17° 22′. lon. 78° 29′.

Goojrat.—In the Punjaub; lat. 32° 35′, lon. 74° 8′. [*Gujerat.*]

Goomti River.—Rising in lat. 28° 35′, lon. 80° 10′—falling into the Ganges, lat. 25° 29′, lon. 83° 15′.

Goruckpore.—Chief town of the district of the same name, N. W. P.; lat. 26°. 42′, lon 83° 23′.

Govindpore.—In the Punjaub; lat 31° 44′, lon. 75° 33′. [*Govindpoor.*]

Guntoor.—Chief town of the district of the same name, Madras Pres.; lat. 16° 30′, lon. 80° 30′.

Guntoor Circar.—One of the five Circars (q, v.).

GURUMCONDA.—In the district of Cuddapah, Madras Pres.; lat. 13° 46′, lon 78° 38′. [*Goorum Conda*].

GUZERAT.—Province of the Gwickwar; capital city, Baroda, (q. v.)

GWALIOR.—Chief town of Sindia's territory of the same name; lat. 26° 13′, lon. 78° 15′.

H.

HALLA.—A town in Sinde; lat. 25° 39′, lon. 68° 24′.

HASTINAPURAM.—An ancient royal city north of Delhi, now only a small village; lat. 29° 10′, lon. 78° 3′. [*Hustinassore.*]

HATRAS.—Near Allighur, N. W. P.; lat. 27° 36′, lon. 78° 9′.

HAZARIBAGH.—Chief town of the district of the same name; lat. 24° 0′, lon. 85° 24′. [*Hazareebagh.*]

HERAT.—A large city in Afghanistan, on the confines of Persia; lat. 34° 55′, lon. 68° 5′.

HINDU CUSH.—A mountainous district forming the northern boundary of Afghanistan.

HINDUSTAN.—The name given to the portion of the continent of India north of the Vindhya mountains; bounded by the Punjaub, the Himalayas, and the Bay of Bengal.

HOOGHLEY.—A river in Bengal, formed by the junction of two branches of the Ganges, joining in lat. 23° 25′, lon. 88° 22′, and flowing into the bay of Bengal. Calcutta is situated on this river.

HULDWANIE.—A village in the district of Kumaon, N. W. P.; lat. 29° 17′, lon. 79° 25′.

HYDASPES RIVER.—Also called the Jhelum, (q. v.)

HYDERABAD.—Capital city of the Nizam, in the Deckan; lat. 17° 22′, lon. 78° 32′.

HYDRABAD.—In Sinde. Formerly the capital city, but now of less importance; lat. 25° 22′, lon. 68° 28′.

I.

INDORE.—Capital city of the Mahratta state of Holkar; lat. 22° 42′, lon. 75° 50′.

Indus River.—The great river which divides India from Afghanistan, Cabul, and Beloochistan, flowing into the Indian Ocean.

Irak.—A large tract on each side of the mountains of Lorestan. That to the north is called Persian Irak. That to the south, Arabian Irak.

Iran.—One of the four great divisions of the Empire of Chengiz Khan after his death.

Irawaddi River.—The great river of Burmah; rising about lat. 28° 5′, lon. 97° 58′, and falling into the Bay of Bengal in lat. 15° 50′, lon. 94° 26.

J.

Jallendur.—In the Punjaub; lat. 31° 21′, lon. 75° 31′. [*Julindur.*]

Jellalabad.—Near Shahjehanpore, N. W. P.; lat. 27° 46, lon. 79° 50′. [*Jelalabad*].

Jessore.—Near Calcutta, Bengal Pres,; lat. 23° 10′, lon. 89° 10′.

Jesulmir.—Chief town of the Rajput state of the same name; lat. 26° 56′, lon. 70° 58′. [*Jessulmere.*]

Jeypore.—Chief town of the Rajput state of the same name; lat. 26° 56′, lon 75° 55′. [*Jeypoor.*]

Jhansi.—Chief town of the native state of the same name; lat. 25° 58′, lon. 78° 38′.

Jhelum River.—The most western of the rivers of the Punjaub; rising in Cashmir, in lat 34° 8′, lon. 75° 48′, and falling into the Chenaub in lat. 31° 10′, lon. 72° 9′.

Jinji.—In South Arcot, Madras Pres.; lat. 12° 16′, lon. 79° 27′. [*Gingee.*]

Jodhpore (or Marwar).—The most extensive of the Rajput states. The capital city of the same name lies in lat. 26° 19′. lon. 73° 8′. [*Joudpore.*]

Johore.—A principality in the Malayan straits to which the island of Singapore appertained.

Jounpore.—Chief town of the district of the same name, N. W. P.; lat. 25° 44′, lon, 82° 44′.

Juggernauth.—In the district of Cuttack, Bengal Pres.; lat. 19° 49′, lon. 85° 53′. [*Juggurnauth.*]

JUMMOO.—In the north of the Punjaub; lat. 23° 44′, lon. 74° 54′. [*Jamoo.*]

JUMNA RIVER.—Rises in lat. 31° 0′, lon. 78° 32′, and joins the Ganges at Allahabad.

JUN.—A small territory in Sinde, S.E. of Hydrabad, now extinct.

K.

KALUNGA (or Nalapani).—In Nepaul; lat. 30° 20′, lon. 78° 8′. [*Kalunga.*]

KAPTCHAK.—One of the four divisions of the empire of Changiz Khan after his death.

KARAK.—An island in the Persian Gulf; lat. 29° 20′, lon. 50° 30′.

KAZAN.—In European Russia; lat. 55° 40′, lon. 49 26′.

KECH.—Near Samarcand (Central Asia); lat. 40° 48′, lon. 67° 15′.

KEMMENDINE.—In Pegu, four miles from Rangoon; lat. 16° 44′, lon. 96° 16′.

KERALA.—Ancient kingdom of the Deckan, including Malabar and Canara.

KHARISM (also called Khiva).—A large tract south of the Sea of Aral (Central Asia), having its capital city, Urgenj, in lat. 42° 15′, lon. 60° 14′, not far from the mouth of the Oxus.

KHATMANDU.—Chief city in Nepaul; lat. 27° 42′, lon. 85° 18′. [*Khatmandoo.*]

KHELAT (or Khelat-i-Ghilji).—In Afghanistan, lat. 32° 40′, lon. 67° 25′.

KHELAT.—Between Sinde and Afghanistan; lat. 29° 0′, lon. 65° 50′.

KOONEH.—Between Calpee and Gwalior; lat. 25° 59′, lon. 79° 13′.

KHOOSHAB.—In Persia, between Bushair and Burasjoon; lat. 28° 44′, lon. 57°, 20′.

KHORASSAN.—In Persia, a large tract of country between Herat and Teheran.

KHYBER PASS.—The principal pass between Afghanistan and Hindustan; lat. 33° 58′, lon. 71° 30′.

KISTNA RIVER (or Krishna).—A river of the Deckan, rising in lat. 18° 1′, lon. 73° 41′; falling into the Bay of Bengal in lat. 15° 45′, lon. 80° 53′.

KOHAT.—About 40 miles S. of Peshawur; lat. 33° 32′, lon. 71° 27′.

KORIGAOM.—A village near Poonah, Bombay Pres; lat. 18° 39′, lon. 74° 8′. [*Corygaum.*]

KOTAH.—Chief town of the Rajput state of the same name; lat. 25° 10′, lon. 75° 52′.

KURDLA.—Near Ahmednuggur, Bombay Pres.; lat. 18° 40′, lon. 75° 34′. [*Kurdlah.*]

KURNOUL.—In Madras Pres., chief town of the district of the same name; lat. 15° 50′, lon. 78° 5′. [*Kurnool.*]

KURRACHEE.—The principal seaport of Sinde; lat. 24° 51′, lon. 67° 2′.

KUSSOOR.—In the Punjaub; lat. 31° 9′, lon. 74° 27′.

L.

LAGHMAN.—A valley in the mountains of Afghanistan, between Ghazni and the Khyber Pass.

LAHORE—in the Punjaub; lat. 31° 36′, lon. 74° 21′.

LASHKAR HILLS (The).—Close to Gwalior, (q. v.)

LASWAREE.—A village 128 miles S. of Delhi; lat. 27° 33′, lon. 76° 59′. [*Laswari.*]

LOODIANAH.—Chief town of the district of the same name, in the Cis-Sutlej territories; lat. 30° 55′, lon. 75° 54′. [*Loodiana.*]

LUCKNOW.—Capital city of the Kingdom of Oude; lat. 20° 52′, lon. 81° 0′.

M.

MACAO.—At the mouth of the Pe-kiang River, near Canton, China; lat. 22° 10′, lon. 113° 30′.

MADURA.—Chief town of the district of the same name; lat. 9° 55′, lon 78° 10′.

MAGADA.—An ancient kingdom of Hindostan, of which no trace now remains.

MAHARAJPORE.—In Gwalior, or the possessions of Sindia; lat. 26° 29′, lon. 78° 5′. [*Maharajpoor.*]

MAHAWAN.—In the district of Mattra; lat. 27° 25, lon. 77° 49′. [*Muhabun.*]

MAHE.—A French settlement in Malabar; lat. 11° 42′, lon. 75° 36′.

MALABAR.—District of Madras Pres., from which the south-western coast of India derives its name of "The Malabar Coast." The principal towns are Mangalore, Telicherry, Calicut, Cochin, and Trivandrum.

MALAVELLY.—In Mysore; lat. 12° 23′, lon. 77° 7′.

MALIGAOM.—In Candeish, Bombay Pres.; lat. 20° 32′, lon. 74° 30′. [*Mulligawm*]

MALLIA.—In the Peninsular of Kattywar, Guzerat; lat. 23° 4′, lon. 70° 46′.

MALOWN.—In Nepaul; lat 31° 12′, lon. 76° 52′.

MALWA.—A tract in Central India, one of the ancient kingdoms of Hindostan, bounded by the Aravalli and Vindhya mountains by Bundelcund, and the valley of the Ganges.

MANDCHOWRI.—A large division of Asia, in the north of the Chinese Empire.

MANDU.—In Malwa, now in ruins; lat. 22° 20′, lon. 72° 27′. [*Mandoo.*]

MANGALORE.—In South Canara, Madras Pres.; lat. 12° 52′, lon. 74° 54°.

MANGALWAR.—Near Cawnpore, N. W. P.; lat. 26° 33; lon. 80° 28′.

MANIPORE.—A native state adjoining the dominions of Burmah. The chief town of the same name is in lat. 24° 49′, lon. 94° 1′. [*Muneepoor*].

MARTABAN.—In Pegu; lat. 16° 3′, lon. 97° 40′.

MARWAR.—(See Jodhpore.)

MASULIPATAM.—At the mouth of the River Kistna; lat. 16° 10′, lon. 81° 13′. Also the name of a district, Madras Pres.

MATTRA.—One of the ancient Hindu kingdoms. The chief town of the same name is in lat. 27° 30′, lon. 77° 45′. [*Muttra.*]

MECCA.—In Arabia Felix; lat. 21° 45′, lon. 40° 0′.

MEDINA.—In Arabia Felix; lat 25° 4′, lon. 39° 45′.

MEEANGUNJ.—A town in Oude; lat. 26° 48′, lon. 80° 33′. [*Meeahgunj.*]

MEEANEE.—In Kattywar, Guzerat; lat. 21° 50′, lon. 69° 31′.

MEERPORE.—In Sinde; lat. 24° 41′, lon. 68° 20′. [*Meerpore*].

MEERUT.—Chief town of the district of the same name, N. W. P.; lat. 28° 59′, lon. 77° 45′.

MEHIDPORE.—Near Indore, in the possessions of Holkar; lat. 23° 30′, lon. 75° 40′. [*Mehedpoor.*]

MERDAN.—Near Peshawur, north of the Punjaub; lat. 34° 22′, lon. 78° 48′.

MERV.—In Central Asia; lat. 43° 3′, lon. 62° 10′.

MEWAR.—A tract S.E. of the Aravalli Mountains, one of the ancient Rajput sovereignties, the principal town being Oodipore (q. v.) [*Meywar.*]

MEWAT.—A district of Guzerat.

MHAR.—Bombay Pres.; lat. 18° 6′, lon. 73° 30′.

MIDNAPORE.—Chief town of the district of the same name, N. W. P.; lat. 22° 24′, lon. 87° 33′.

MOHAMREH.—Persia. At the junction of the Karoon River with the Shatt-el-Arab mouth of the Euphrates; lat. 30° 41′, lon. 48° 35′.

MONGHIR.—Chief town of the district of the same name, Bengal Pres.; lat. 25° 19′, lon. 86° 30′. [*Monghyr*].

MONGOLIA.—The name given to the north-west territories and frontier of the Chinese Empire.

MOODKEE.—(Cis-Sutlej States); lat. 30° 48′, lon. 74° 55′.

MOORSHEDABAD.—Chief town of the district of the same name, Bengal Pres.: lat. 24° 12′, lon. 88° 17′.

MORADABAD.—Chief town of the district of the same name in Rohilcund, N. W. P.; lat 28° 49′, lon. 78° 50′.

MUCKWANPORE.—In Nepaul; lat. 27° 22′, lon. 85° 11′.

MULTAN.—A city of the Punjaub; lat 30° 12′, lon. 71° 30′.

MUNJ.—Near Etawah, N. W. P.; lat. 26° 55′, lon. 79° 13′. [*Munjh.*]

MUSCAT.—In Oman, Eastern Arabia; lat. 23° 30′, lon. 58° 42′.

MYNPOORIE.—Chief town of the district of the same name, N. W. P.; lat. 27° 14′, lon. 79° 4′.

MYSORE.—Native state of the Deckan. The city of the same name is in lat. 12° 18′, lon. 76° 42′.

N.

NAGARCOT.—An ancient temple N.W. of Lahore, on a spur of the Himalayas.

NAGORE.—In Tanjore, Madras Pres.; lat. 10° 49′, lon. 79° 54′.

NAGPORE.—Chief city of Berar, the territory of the Bhonslay family: lat. 21° 10′, lon. 79° 10′.

NAJUFGHUR.—A town near Delhi; lat. 28° 36′, lon. 77° 2′, [*Najafgarh.*]

NEGAPATAM.—In Tanjore, Madras Pres.; lat. 10° 46′, lon. 79° 54′.

NEPAUL.—A kingdom of Northern India, bounded by the Himalayas, Sikim, Purneah, Goruckpore, and Kumaon.

NERBUDDA RIVER.—A large river rising near Ramghur, in lat. 22° 39′, lon. 81° 49′; falling into the Gulf of Cambay, in lat. 21° 35′, lon. 72° 35′.

NOUSHERA.—In the Punjaub; lat. 34° 8′, lon. 73° 8′.

O.

OMERKOTE.—In Sinde; lat. 25° 22′, lon. 69° 47′. [*Omercote.*]

ONORE.—In North Canara, Madras Pres.; lat. 14° 17′, lon. 74° 30′. [*Honahwar.*]

OODIPORE.—Chief city of the Rajput state of Newar; lat. 24° 37′, lon. 73° 49′. [*Oodeypore*].

OODWANULLA.—In Bhawulpore, Bengal Pres.; lat. 24° 58′, lon. 87° 53′. [*Oondwa Nullah*].

OONAO.—In Oude, near Cawnpore; lat. 26° 33′, lon. 80° 33. [*Unao.*]

ORISSA.—An extensive tract, comprising Cuttack and Midnapore, bounded by Palamow, Ramgurh, Midnapore, Berar, the ceded districts of the Nerbudda, and the Bay of Bengal. (See *Cuttack.*)

OUDE.—A native state in the north, bounded by Nepaul, Goruckpore, Jounpore, the Dooab, and Shahjehanpore; its capital city is Lucknow. (q. v.)

OXUS RIVER.—The great river of Central Asia, rising in lat. 35° 40′, lon. 71° 36′; falling into the sea of Aral in lat. 43° 15′, lon. 58° 56′.

P.

PALAMOW.—Chief town of the district of the same name, Bengal Pres.; lat. 23° 50′, lon. 84° 1′.

PALGHAUT.—In Malabar, Madras Pres.; lat. 10° 45′, lon. 76° 43′.

PANCHALA.—Ancient kingdom of Hindostan, supposed to have comprised part of Oude and the lower Dooab.

PANDERPORE.—between Poonah and Sattara, Bombay Pres.; lat. 17° 40′, lon. 75° 24. [*Punderpoor.*]

PANDYA.—An ancient kingdom of the Deckan, having its capital at Madura (q. v.). It included Madura and Tinnevelly.

PANIPAT.—Chief town of the district of the same name, near Delhi, N. W. P.; lat. 29° 23′, lon. 77° 2′. [*Paneeput.*]

PATIALAH.—A native state in Sirhind, in the Cis-Sutlej states. Its chief town, of the same name, being in lat. 30° 20′, lon. 76° 25′. [*Putteeala.*]

PATNA.—A large city on the Ganges, Bengal Pres.; lat. 25° 35′, lon. 85° 15′.

PATTIALI.—Near Futtehghur; lat. 27° 41′, lon. 79° 4′. [*Putteealee.*]

PEGU.—In Burmah; a province on the Irawaddi River. The city of Pegu is in lat. 17° 40′, lon 96° 17′.

PESHAWUR.—A large city in the extreme north-west, near the Khyber Pass; lat. 34° 0′, lon. 71° 38′.

PLASSY.—On the Hooghley, near Calcutta; lat. 23° 46′, lon. 88° 15′.

PLITHANA.—Mentioned by the Greek author of Periplus as being a sea-port town of importance. Supposed by Elphinstone to be the ancient city of Paitan, on the Godavery River.

POLLILORE.—A village 40 miles north of Madras, near Pulicat; lat. 13° 45′, lon. 80° 20′.

PONDICHERRY.—French settlement south of Madras; lat. 11° 56′. lon. 79° 54′.

POONAH.—Capital city of the Mahratta state; lat. 18° 31′, lon. 73° 53′. [*Poona.*]

POORUNDER.—Near Poonah; lat. 18° 16′, lon. 74° 2′. [*Poorundhur.*]

PORTO NOVO.—In South Arcot, Madras Pres.; lat. 11° 31′, lon. 79° 49′.

PROME (or Pri).—A city in Pegu; lat. 18° 47′, lon. 95° 3′.

PULICAT.—In the district of Chingleput, Madras Pres.; lat. 13° 25′, lon. 80° 22′.

PUNJAUB.—The name given to the tract of country in the north-west, including the countries between the Indus and Sutlej Rivers, bounded on the north by Cashmir.

PURNEAH.—Chief town of the district of the same name, Bengal Pres.; lat. 25° 46′, lon. 87° 30′.

Q.

QUEDAH.—A native state on the Malay Peninsula; the chief town of the same name is in lat. 6° 0′, lon. 100° 30′.

QUETTAH.—A town in Sewestan, in the south of Afghanistan; lat 30° 41′, lon. 66° 46′.

R.

RAISIN.—In Malwa, near Bhopal; lat. 23° 22′, lon. 77° 56′. [*Raiseen.*]

RAJAHMUNDRY.—On the delta of the Godavery River; lat. 17° 0′, lon. 81° 50′.

RAJMAHAL.—A town in Bengal, on the hills; lat. 25° 1′, lon. 87° 50′.

RAMGHUR.—A district in the N. W. P., taking its name from a town in lat. 22° 49′, lon. 81° 1′. [*Ramgurh.*]

RAMNUGGUR.—In the Punjaub, on the Chenaub River; lat. 32° 20′, lon. 73° 50′. [*Ramneghur.*]

RAMPURA.—In Rajputana; lat. 25° 58′, lon. 76° 14′. [*Rampoora.*]

RANEEGUNJ.—Near Bancoora, Bengal Pres., lat. 23° 35′, lon. 87° 10′. [*Raneegunge.*]

RANGOON.—A town in Pegu, on the Irawaddi River; lat. 16° 46′, lon. 96° 17′.

RATGHUR.—In Saugur, N. W. P.; lat. 23° 47′, lon. 78° 29′.

RAVEE, (River)—One of the five rivers of the Punjaub, rising in lat. 32° 26′, lon. 77° 0′, falling into the Chenaub in lat. 30° 36′, lon. 71° 50′.

RINTAMBORE.—A little fortress in the Rajput State of Jeypore; lat. 25° 56′, lon. 76° 26′. [*Rintimbore.*]

ROHILCUND.—A tract of country formerly the state of the Rohillas; including Moradabad, Bareilly, Budayun, and Shahjehanpore.

ROHTAS.—A fort in the Punjaub, on the River Jhelum; lat. 32° 59′, lon. 73° 38′.

RUNGPORE.—Chief town of the district of the same name, Bengal Pres.; lat. 25° 40′, lon. 89° 16′.

S.

Sadulapore.—In the Punjaub, near Rungpore; lat. 25° 22′, lon. 89° 29′. [*Sadoolapoor.*]

Sagore.—In the territory of Indore; lat. 22° 30′, lon 75° 40′. [*Sagor.*]

Salbye.—In Gwalior; lat. 25° 50′, lon. 78° 16′.

Salsette.—An island near Bombay, about twenty miles north of that city.

Samaghar.—Twenty miles from Agra, N. W. P.; lat. 27° 15′, lon. 78° 7′.

Samarcand.—In Central Asia; lat. 39° 45′, lon. 66° 46.′

Sambal.—In Cashmir; lat. 34° 11′, lon. 74° 47′. [*Sambul.*]

Sangamneir.—Near Ahmednuggur, Bombay Pres.; lat. 19° 35′, lon. 74° 14′. [*Sungumneir.*]

Satpura Mountains.—The range dividing the valley of the Taptee from that of the Nerbudda. [*Satpoora.*]

Sattara.—A city fifty miles from Poonah, Bombay Pres.; lat. 17° 45′, lon. 74° 4′.

Saugur.—Chief town of the district of the same name; lat. 23° 50′, lon. 78° 49′. [*Saugor.*]

Savanore.—Near Dharwar, Bombay Pres.; lat. 14° 55′, lon. 75° 19′. [*Savanoor.*]

Schinas.—A small seaport in the Persian Gulf.

Sealkote.—In Punjaub, on the Chenaub River; lat. 32° 29′, lat. 74° 33′.

Sehwan.—In Sinde; lat. 26° 24′, lon. 67° 55′.

Selimghur.—A fort on the Ganges, opposite Delhi; lat. 28° 40′, lon. 77° 19′.

Seringapatam.—Capital city of the territory of Mysore; lat. 12° 25′, lon. 76° 45′.

Sersooty River.—In Sirhind, rising in lat. 30° 30′, lon. 77° 29′, falling into the Caggar River in lat. 29° 52′, lon. 76° 10′. [*Soorsutty.*]

Severndroog.—*See* Suwandroog.

Shahjehanpore.—A large town in the N. W. P.; lat. 27° 52′, lon. 79° 58′.

Shahpuri.—An island off the coast of Aracan; lat. 20° 41′, lon. 92° 20′.

Siam.—A kingdom to the north of the Malay Peninsula, bounded by Pegu, Malay, Lao, and Cambodia; the capital city of the same name is in lat. 12° 14', lon. 100° 44'

SIKRI.—A town in the N. W. P.; lat. 28° 17', lon. 77° 21'.

SILHET.—A province of Bengal, bounded by Cachar and Tipperah; the chief town of the same name is in lat. 24° 54', lon. 91° 50'.

SIMLA.—On the Himalayas; lat 31° 6', lon. 77° 14'.

SINDE.—A tract of country about the southern portion of the River Indus, having for its capital city Hydrabad (q. v.)

SINGAPORE.—In the Straits of Malacca, at the southern extremity of the Malay Peninsula: lat. 1° 16', lon 103° 53'.

SIPRI RIVER.—A river of Malwa, rising in the Vindhya Mountains, lat. 22° 37', lon. 76° 12'; and falling into the Chumbul in lat. 23° 54', lon. 75° 29'. [*Seepra.*]

SIRHIND.—A division of the north of India south of the Punjaub; the town of the same name is in lat. 30° 38', lon. 76° 29'.

SIRINAGAR.—Capital city of Cashmir; lat. 34° 5', lon 74° 57'.

SISTAN.—An extensive district in the south-western frontier of Afghanistan, bordering on the dominions of Persia.

SITABALDI HILLS.—Some hills on the outskirts of the town of Nagpore; lat. 21° 10', lon 79° 9'.

SITAPORE.—In Oude, 50 miles from Lucknow; lat. 27° 35', lon. 80° 44.' [*Setapoor.*]

SOBRAON.—A village on the left bank of the Sutlej River; lat. 31° 8', lon. 74° 54'.

SOLIMAN MOUNTAINS.—A lofty range, forming the western boundary of British India, running due north and south, from lat. 33° 50' to lat. 29°. [*Suliman.*]

SOLINGHUR.—In North Arcot, Madras Pres.; lat. 13° 4', lon 79° 29'. [*Sholanghur.*]

SOMNATH.—An ancient town in Sinde, in the province of Kattywar; lat. 20° 55', lon. 70° 23'. [*Somnath Pattan.*]

SUDUSAIN.—Near Multan; lat. 30° 12', lon. 71° 26'.

SUKKUR.—In Sinde, on the Indus; lat. 27° 40', lon. 68° 54'.

SULTANPORE.—In Oude, on the River Goomti; lat. 26° 16', lon. 82° 8'. [*Sultanpoor.*]

SURAT.—At the mouth of the River Tapti; lat. 21° 10', lon. 72° 52'.

SUTLEJ (RIVER.)—The most easterly of the rivers of the Punjaub, rising in lat. 30° 8', lon. 81° 58', and falling into the River Beeas in lat. 31° 11', lon. 75° 4'.

SUWANDROOG (or Severndroog.)—A fort on an island near Bombay; lat. 17° 50′, lon. 73° 8′. [*Soowurndroog.*]

SYE (RIVER.)—In Oude, rising in lat. 27° 10′, lon. 80° 32′, and falling into the Goomti below Jounpore. [*Saee.*]

T.

TAGARA.—An ancient seaport town, mentioned by the Greek author of "Periplus;" probably on the Godavery River.

TALNEIR.—In Candeish, 60 miles north-east of Maligaom; lat. 21° 15′, lon. 75° 6′. [*Thalneir*]

TANESAR.—In Sirhind, 23 miles from Carnal; lat. 29° 58′, lon. 76° 54′. [*Thunnesir.*]

TANJORE.—A native state (recently annexed) in the Madras Pres., its chief town being lat. 10° 47′, lon. 79° 12′.

TATTAH.—In Sinde, on the Indus; lat. 24° 44′, lon. 68° 0′. [*Tatta.*]

TEHERAN.—The capital city of Persia; lat. 36° 0′, lon. 51° 40′.

TELLICHERRY.—On the Malabar coast, Madras Pres.; lat. 11° 45′, lon. 75° 33′.

TENASSERIM.—A province on the eastern shore of the Bay of Bengal, between lat. 10° 48′ and lat. 18° 25′.

TERAI.—The name given to the strip of forest-country lying at the base of the Himalaya mountains.

TEZEEN.—In Afghanistan, near Jellalabad; lat. 27° 33′, lon. 79° 31′.

TINNEVELLY.—In Madras Pres.; lat. 8° 44′, lon. 77° 45′.

TONK.—In Rajputana, a small native state; lat. 26° 10′, lon. 75° 56′.

TRAVANCORE.—A native state in the south of India; the town of Travancore is in lat. 8° 14′, lon. 77° 19′.

TRICHINOPOLY.—In the Madras Pres.; lat. 10° 50′, lon. 78° 46′.

TRINCOMALEE.—In Ceylon, a Dutch settlement; lat. 8° 33′, lon. 81° 30′.

U.

UJEIN.—In Gwalior, one of the sacred cities of India, and anciently an independent kingdom; lat. 23° 10′, lon. 75° 47′. [*Oojein.*]

V.

VELLORE.—In North Arcot, Madras Pres.; lat. 12° 55′, lon. 79° 11′.

VIZAGAPATAM.—Chief town of the district of the same name, Madras Pres.; lat. 17° 41′, lon. 83° 21′.

W.

WANDEWASH.—In North Arcot, Madras Pres.; lat. 12° 30′, lon. 79° 40′. [*Vandivash.*]

WARANGAL.—In the dominions of the Nizam; the ancient capital of Telingana; lat. 17° 58′, lon. 79° 40′. [*Warungul.*]

WARDA RIVER.—In the district of Saugur; rising in lat. 21° 44′, lon, 78° 25′, falling into the Wein Gunga river in lat. 19° 37′, lon. 79° 51′. [*Wurda.*]

WURGAOM.—In the Nizam's dominions; lat. 18° 49′, lon. 75° 50′.

Y.

YADAVA.—An ancient kingdom of the Deckan; site unknown, probably in East Telingana.

YANDABO.—A town of Burmah, on the Irawaddi River, 63 miles from Ava; lat. 21° 38′, lon. 95° 4′. [*Yandaboo.*]

YEH.—A province of Tenasserim, the chief town of the same name being in lat. 15° 15′, lon. 98° 4′.

Z.

ZENDECAN (or Dandunaken).—Near Merv, Central Asia; lat. 37° 0′, lon. 63° 40′.